The Final Battle

CW00922840

In many ways the German soldiers who marched back from the Western Front at the end of the First World War held the key to the future of the newly created republic that replaced the Kaiser's collapsed monarchy. To the radical Left, the orderly columns of front-line troops appeared to be the forces of the counter-revolution, while to the conservative elements of society they seemed to be the Fatherland's salvation. However, in their efforts to get home as soon as possible, most soldiers were indifferent to the political struggles within the Reich, while the remnant that remained under arms proved powerless to defend the republic from its enemies. This book considers why these soldiers' response to the revolution was so different from that of the rest of the army, and the implications this would have for the course of the German Revolution and, ultimately, for the fate of the Weimar Republic itself.

Scott Stephenson is Associate Professor of Military History at the Department of Military History, US Army Command and General Staff College.

Studies in the Social and Cultural History of Modern Warfare

General Editor
Jay Winter, *Yale University*

Advisory Editors
Omer Bartov, *Brown University*
Carol Gluck, *Columbia University*
David M. Kennedy, *Stanford University*
Paul Kennedy, *Yale University*
Antoine Prost, *Université de Paris-Sorbonne*
Emmanuel Sivan, *Hebrew University of Jerusalem*
Robert Wohl, *University of California, Los Angeles*

In recent years the field of modern history has been enriched by the exploration of two parallel histories. These are the social and cultural history of armed conflict, and the impact of military events on social and cultural history.

Studies in the Social and Cultural History of Modern Warfare presents the fruits of this growing area of research, reflecting both the colonization of military history by cultural historians and the reciprocal interest of military historians in social and cultural history, to the benefit of both. The series offers the latest scholarship in European and non-European events from the 1850s to the present day.

For a list of titles in the series, please see end of book.

The Final Battle

*Soldiers of the Western Front and
the German Revolution of 1918*

Scott Stephenson

CAMBRIDGE
UNIVERSITY PRESS

CAMBRIDGE UNIVERSITY PRESS
Cambridge, New York, Melbourne, Madrid, Cape Town,
Singapore, São Paulo, Delhi, Mexico City

Cambridge University Press
The Edinburgh Building, Cambridge CB2 8RU, UK

Published in the United States of America by Cambridge University Press, New York

www.cambridge.org
Information on this title: www.cambridge.org/9781107632363

First published 2009
First paperback edition 2013

A catalogue record for this publication is available from the British Library

Library of Congress Cataloguing in Publication Data
Stephenson, Scott.
  The final battle : soldiers of the western front and the German revolution
  of 1918 / Scott Stephenson.
    p. cm. – (Studies in the social and cultural history of modern warfare)
  Includes bibliographical references and index.
  ISBN 978-0-521-51946-5 (hardback)
  1. Germany–History–Revolution, 1918. 2. Soldiers–Germany–Political
  activity. 3. Germany. Heer–History–World War, 1914–1918. 4. World War,
  1914–1918–Europe, Western. I. Title. II. Series.
  DD248.S74 2009
  943.08′49–dc22
  2009018068

ISBN 978-1-107-63236-3 Paperback

For Rose

Contents

Illustrations

Maps

Preface

Ninety years on, the Great War still casts a long shadow. Certainly no single event has done more to shape both the last century and the century we have just begun. One imagines, then, that the upcoming 100-year anniversary should serve to remind us of the war's enormous impact on modern history. It should also remind us of the terrible costs of the war and the unbearable demands the war made on the soldiers who suffered and bled in the trenches of the Western Front. As one of my teachers once observed, if war is privation and suffering, then the Western Front was "war distilled." Privation and suffering was certainly the experience of the million and a half soldiers who held the German lines in late 1918. This book examines the experience of those men in the final, terrible weeks of the war and the first weeks of the uncertain peace that followed.

I teach the history of war to men and women who have experienced war first-hand. Almost all of my students at the US Army's Command and General Staff College have recently returned from deployments to Iraq and Afghanistan. Teaching them – or trying to teach them – military history can be exhilarating and exasperating. Exhilarating, because the experience of combat has given them insights my students rarely had before. These majors understand what Clausewitz meant when the famous military philosopher described the environment of war as one saturated by fear, friction, fog, and fatigue; I need no historical vignettes to illustrate these ideas. Exasperating, because my students are often very cynical, very tired, and frequently doubt that the past has much to offer them. My heart goes out to them but they are a tough audience. They remind me of why I find the story of the German soldiers on the Western Front at the end of the First World War so compelling. The fatigue and cynicism of my students serves as a point of reference for the way I have approached the experience of the *Frontschweine,* the war-weary "front hogs" in the German trenches of 1918.

My own experience has been important as well. I was commissioned as a second lieutenant of Armor in 1976 – the year after Saigon had fallen to the Communists – when the US Army was struggling to regain its moral focus, its sense of purpose, and its standing in American society. During that tumultuous time, the army was shaken by racial tensions, rampant drug use, and break-down in fundamental discipline. My peers and I discovered that, to survive in such an environment, an officer must become a student of soldier behavior and motivation, a sort of amateur psychologist. At the same time, I discovered that a modern army was a complex social system, a mélange of communities, tribes, and mafias. Thus, serving in a tank battalion on a tiny American caserne in Germany, I found that the values, experience, and attitudes on soldiering among my men were dramatically different from the "rear echelon" maintenance unit on the other side of the installation. It was these two insights – the need to understand soldiers and the divisions within an army – that shaped my approach to the historical problem posed in this study: why did German soldiers on the Western Front respond so passively to the German Revolution of 1918 when they stood to gain more from the revolution's success than any other group in German society?

Fortunately for me, my approach was shaped by some very fine scholars as well. I owe an enormous debt of gratitude to my graduate adviser at Syracuse University, Dr. Fred Marquardt, and my first advisor at the University of Kansas, Dr. Carl Strikwerda. Beyond that, I owe a very special thanks to the current Director of the Department of Military History at the US Army Command and General Staff College, Dr. Jim Willbanks, who pushed me to take the research sabbatical that made this book possible.

The research for this project was supported by people who went beyond the scope of their duties as librarians, archivists, and friends to make my work possible. They include Ed Burgess and his staff at the Combined Arms Research Library (CARL) at Ft. Leavenworth. Among these, I offer heart-felt thanks to Ms. Sharon Strein, who supported my seemingly insatiable requests for inter-library loan support, and her predecessor in the ILL office, a truly special lady, Ms. Dorothy Rogers. The people at CARL have earned their worldwide reputation for gracious support of soldiers and scholars alike. I offer my sincerest appreciation to the archival staffs at the *Bundesarchiv-Militärarchiv* at Freiburg, the *Bundesarchiv-Reich* at Berlin-Lichterfelde, the US National Archives at College Park, Maryland, and the Military History Institute at Carlisle Barrack. In particular, I must highlight the assistance of Dr. Mitch Yockelsen at College Park, who supported the efforts of a rookie researcher with both patience and the insight of a genuine subject-matter expert.

In the last two years, as I began writing in earnest, my efforts brought me into contact with a number of scholars who blessed me with insights and collegial support. I thank Dr. Dennis Showalter for his encouragement and advice on an early draft of Chapter 5. I am grateful to Dr. Alex Watson of Cambridge University, who, via e-mail, offered me the critical insights of someone who has made the German soldier of the First World War his own area of scholarly interest. Dr. Jon House sacrificed many hours in reviewing my drafts and attempting to untangle my most egregious lapses in style and proofreading. I owe an enormous debt of gratitude to Dr. Jim Corum, who offered invaluable advice on navigating the German archives. I owe a similar debt to Dr. Gerhard Weinberg. Years ago, he headed the effort to catalogue the National Archive's holdings of German documents from the First World War. He made me aware of the holdings and pointed me to sources that ultimately proved invaluable.

One man, above all, made this book possible: Dr. Ted Wilson of the University of Kansas. Over the years, his guidance has opened the way for countless naïve officers to navigate the unfamiliar perils of academia. I am blessed to be one of them. As my advisor, he offered good humor, steady counsel, and a willingness to listen to my tales of woe. A number of times, I despaired of finishing this project, and each of these times, Ted intervened with a gentle nudge and a sage word of encouragement. He truly epitomizes what Germans mean by the word *Doktorvater.*

I am extraordinarily grateful to Michael Watson and Helen Waterhouse of Cambridge University Press for their encouragement and advice and especially for their patience with a rookie author.

Finally, no list of benefactors would be complete with mentioning my family. Along with love and guidance, my parents encouraged my enduring passion for history. My amazing wife Rose typed the original seminar paper I wrote on this topic. At the time, I was serving on the ROTC cadre at Syracuse University and trying to earn a Master's degree in history. During that same assignment, my daughters, Jennifer and Elena, were born in snowstorms common to that part of the country. It is a measure of how long this project has taken that, as this book was submitted to the editor, one of those daughters is finishing a Master's program and the other is a semester away from an undergraduate degree. My three ladies have endured my physical absences on research trips and my even more frequent mental absences when my mind was wandering down the trench systems of the Western Front or the wintry boulevards of Berlin in late 1918. I thank God for their love and loyalty.

I conclude by emphasizing that any remaining errors are mine and appear in spite of the best efforts of the many wonderful people who helped me along the way. By the same token, if this work has any merit, let it be to the glory of Him who makes all things possible and all things new.

Abbreviations and glossary

BA-B	*Bundesarchiv-Bild* (German picture archive in Koblenz)
BA-MA	*Bundesarchiv-Militärarchiv* (German military archive in Freiburg)
BA-R	*Bundesarchiv-Reich* (German political archive in Berlin-Lichterfelde)
BT	*Berliner Tageblatt*
Drückebergerei	front-line slang for shirking
Etappe	support organization behind the front
Feldheer	Field Army
Frontschweine	"front hogs" (front-line soldiers' self-deprecating nickname)
GKSD	*Garde Kavallerie-Schützen Division* (Guards Cavalry Rifle Division)
Jäger	light infantry
Landsturm	third-line units of older, unfit, or untrained men
Landwehr	second-line units of older men
MSPD	*Mehrheitssozialdemokratische* Partei Deutschlands (Majority-[Moderate]-Social Democratic Party)
Nachlass	personal papers
NARA	National Archives and Records Administration (US archive collection in Alexandria, VA)
OHL	*Oberste Heeresleitung* (Supreme Army Headquarters)
RdV	Rat der Volksbeauftragten (the Council of People's Deputies: the six-man "cabinet" of the provisional government that led Germany from November 1918 to January 1919)
UDZ	*Die Ursachen des deutschen Zusammenbruchs im Jahre 1918* (Reichstag investigation into the "Origins of the German Collapse in 1918," published in multiple volumes)

USPD	*Unabhängige Sozialdemokratische Partei Deutschlands* Independent Social Democratic Party
VMD	*Volksmarinedivision* (People's Naval Division)
VZR	*Vollzugsrat* (Executive Council of the Berlin Workers' and Soldiers' Council)
VZ	*Vossische Zeitung*

1 Introduction: the divided army

> Had we returned home in 1916, out of the suffering and strength of
> our experience we might have unleashed a storm. Now if we go back
> we will be weary, broken, burnt out, rootless, and without hope. We
> will not be able to find our way any more.
>
> Erich Maria Remarque, *All Quiet on the Western Front*[1]

The German empire's defeat in the First World War was comprehensive. By late 1918, Germany military and civilian leaders had cause to wonder which would give way first, the enfeebled institutions of the Second Reich or the front held by its beleaguered army on the Western Front. The question was decided in late October, when naval mutinies at Wilhelmshaven spread to other naval bases and, in turn, launched a revolutionary tidal wave that swept irresistibly across a nation exhausted by war. The day after the sailors' uprising, Erich Ludendorff's replacement as First Quartermaster General, General Wilhelm Groener, told the imperial cabinet that the army's powers of resistance on the Western Front were nearly spent.[2] When the armistice came a week later, it found the German forces in France and Belgium, the *Westheer*, exhausted, depleted, and staggering under the blows of the Allied armies. If defeat meant a complete breakdown of an army's organization, one might argue that the German Army in the field still remained undefeated. Yet, such a standard for judging military outcomes is relatively useless. The resistance offered by the *Westheer* in late 1918 might ameliorate the final terms forced on Germany, but it had no hope of

---

[1] The quotation is a reflection on the last year of the war by Remarque's main character, Paul Baumer, in Erich Maria Remarque, *All Quiet on the Western Front*, trans. A.W. Wheen (New York: Fawcett Press, 1984; first published 1928), 253–4.

[2] "Only for a brief period can that resistance last which the Army will be able to lend against the assault of our outside enemies in view of their tremendously superior numbers and the threat from the direction of Austria-Hungary." Document No. 514: Extract Concerning Session of the Secretaries of State on November 5, 1918, Ralph Lutz, ed., *Fall of the German Empire, 1914–1918* (Stanford University Press, 1932), vol. II, 500–7.

wresting the initiative from the Allies and reversing the inevitable outcome of the war. Had the German Army held out in 1919, the odds
faced by the decimated divisions holding the German front were only
going to get worse. A series of political and diplomatic events – the declaration of the republic in Berlin, the Kaiser's abdication and flight to
Holland, and, finally, the armistice agreement signed at Compiègne
on 11 November 1918 – may very well have spared the *Westheer* from a
humiliating battlefield collapse.

Foch, Haig, and the other Allied military leaders had been surprised
by the German request for armistice at the beginning of October.
Dogged German resistance along the front had led them to believe that
the war would drag into 1919. They feared the Germans would use
an armistice to regroup and prepare for further resistance, and they
remained wary after the guns had fallen silent on November 11. A few
weeks after the fighting had ended, Major General C.D. Rhodes, an
American officer working with the International Armistice Commission
in Spa, Belgium, offered additional reasons to doubt the totality of the
Allied victory. In an urgent report to General Pershing, he wrote:

Observation of German troops passing through this city convinces me that a
large portion of the German Army is in extremely fine physical and moral condition to resume active military operations east of the Rhine. It would appear
that the *reports* of disorder and demoralization among German troops have
applied only to second-line troops which were sent to the rear early in the
present withdrawal. The first-line troops who have come under my observation have been well-disciplined, orderly and apparently still full of fight. Their
transportation has been covered with evergreens and German flags and their
retreat has been given the aspect of a triumphal return to Germany.[3]

If this American observer discerned a clear contrast between "second-
line" German troops who had left the scene and the combat formations marching through Spa later, a German general on the staff of the
Crown Prince's army group recorded the same distinction. During the
early days of the German revolution, Lieutenant General Hermann
von Kuhl, an army group chief of staff, was gratified to find that
front-line units had remained under the control of their officers but
was appalled at the anarchy that prevailed in the army's rear areas.
There, he observed, troops plundered supply trains, released prisoners, and sold their weapons to Belgian civilians. The garrisons of the
supply installations and replacement depots seemed to lose all trace

---

[3] Historical Division, Department of the Army, *The Armistice Agreement and Related
Documents of the United States Army in the World War, 1917–1919* (Washington, DC:
Center of Military History, 1948), vol. X, 148.

of discipline. He observed in disgust, "Trucks filled with booty hurried toward the homeland."[4]

The American and German generals drew similar conclusions. The German Revolution of November 1918 had apparently provoked dramatically different responses from the troops in France and Belgium and those elsewhere. The troops at the front remained under the control of their officers, while the troops in the rear overthrew their chain of command and replaced its authority with their own soldiers' councils. However, the contrast went beyond the Western Front. The vast majority of German occupation units in the East and in the garrisons of the Home Army had also deposed their officers, established soldiers' councils, and declared their emphatic support for the revolution. While the front-line soldiers in the West seemed relatively unmoved by the news of the revolution, the soldiers in the rear areas in Belgium and France, in the occupation forces in Russia, and the garrisons inside Germany were active in proclaiming their common cause with the mutinous sailors who had started the revolution. The differing reactions continued through the ensuing weeks. While soldiers in the Field Army's rear areas often made their way home as individuals, improvising or confiscating what transportation they could find, the front-line troops marched west in well-ordered formations, following the demanding march schedule provided by the Field Army headquarters, the *Oberste Heeresleitung* (OHL) and its subordinate staffs.

The early stages of the German Revolution – the naval mutinies, the Kaiser's abdication, and the proclamation of the new republic – also provoked vastly different reactions from the front-line troops and the rest of the German Army. These disparate responses highlighted the divisions that existed in the *Kaiserheer* in the last stages of the war, divisions that would have profound importance for the course of the revolution. On one hand, during the critical weeks of November and December 1918, the soldiers and sailors of the German armed forces provided the revolution with much of its energy and almost all of its armed strength. Inside Germany, the institutions of the old empire crumbled in face of the militantly revolutionary garrisons and the soldiers' councils who led them. Many saw in these councils the same revolutionary potential as that manifested the year before in the soviets of post-tsarist Russia. On the other hand, the armed forces, in the specific form of the front-line divisions of the Western Front, also seemed to offer the greatest potential

---

[4] Hermann von Kuhl, in *Das Werk des Untersuchungauschusses der Verfassunggebenden Deutschen National Versammlung*, 4th series, *Die Ursachen des deutschen Zusammenbruchs im Jahre 1918* (Berlin: 1925–9), vol. VI, 23. Hereafter referred to as *UDZ*.

for counter-revolution. When the combat troops marched across the Rhine, they were led by the old officer corps, and they marched, almost invariably, under the banners of the old monarchy. The apparent political separation between "front" and "rear" could hardly have been more profound. The rank and file of the military provided much of the initial impetus of the revolution, and, paradoxically, in the units manning the trenches on the Western Front seemed to offer the greatest potential to undo the achievements of the revolution, most notably the abdication of the Kaiser and the establishment of a socialist-dominated republic.

To a certain extent, the German Army's complex and diverse responses to the revolution were to be expected. The German Army that fought the First World War was a complex and diverse social organism. Like the other mass armies of the war, it had evolved through the nineteenth and early twentieth centuries from the small, relatively simple regimental organizations of the dynastic period to a gigantic army with an abundance of organizational parts and functions, spread, by 1918, from the Caucasus to the English Channel. The size of the *Kaiserheer* and the lethal technology it wielded were based on an elaborate logistical and administrative organization. Whereas Frederick the Great's eighteenth-century army was able to deliver "tooth" to the battlefield with relatively little "tail," the front-line forces of the German Army of 1918 were significantly outnumbered by the support services, depot units, and homeland garrisons. These rear area support services included railroad engineers, bakers, truck drivers, nurses, supply clerks, signalmen, blacksmiths, and bridge builders, all of whom performed the vast number of tasks essential to the army's maintenance in the field.

This intricate differentiation in soldier function necessarily resulted in the evolution of unique subcultures within the German military. The truck driver behind the lines inevitably looked at his military role in a different way from the machine gunner on the Western Front. The supply clerk issuing uniforms to new replacements in Munich or Dresden naturally felt himself a different kind of soldier from the *Frontschweine* ("front-pigs"), as the men in the trenches called themselves. The fairly standardized regimental culture of the Frederician period gave way to separate subcultures within the wartime army, though this development befuddled the senior military leaders as well as the Kaiser himself, who persisted in believing that the only "true" soldiers were those who bore arms in combat.[5]

The army was geographically divided as well, most significantly between East and West. Of the 6 million soldiers in *feldgrau* in 1918,

---

[5] See, for example, Christopher Duffy, *The Army of Frederick the Great* (Chicago: The Emperor's Press, 1996), 77–85.

something like 3.5 million were deployed on the Western Front. The draconian terms of the Brest-Litovsk treaty had left Germany with an enormous protectorate carved out of the corpse of imperial Russia and, in order to secure this empire, Ludendorff left a massive army on the Eastern Front even as he was stripping that front of its best units to support his offensive plans in the West. Three-quarters of a million German troops served in outposts that reached from the Baltic coast to Georgia. Two hundred thousand troops were found in smaller German contingents that supported Germany's allies in such far-flung fighting fronts as Mesopotamia and Macedonia. Finally, the garrisons of the *Heimatheer* (Home Army) numbered 1.5 million men.[6]

The divisions in the German Army also reflected other aspects of the Second Reich's military demography. The one most scrutinized by historians has been the army's reflection of the iniquities within Wilhelmine society, with the noble class dominating the senior ranks, the middle class populating the junior and non-commissioned officer positions, and the proletarians and farmers' sons largely restricted to the enlisted ranks. Still other factors militated against the ideal of soldierly camaraderie, and a few generalizations suggest the nature of these divisions. For many, the concept of the German empire competed with their identification with the region of their birth. Bavarian soldiers were often suspicious of Prussians, and both Prussians and Bavarians were often very suspicious of Silesian Poles and Alsatians. Reserve officers outnumbered and envied the "active" officers of the prewar army, and both categories looked down on the "wartime" officers that dominated the junior levels of the officer corps by the end of the war. The older *Landwehr* soldiers tended to serve in quieter sectors than the other units of German infantry, but they had reason to be jealous of the even older *Landsturm* men in garrisons safely behind the line. Regular infantry envied the storm troop units which spent much of their time out of the line and were transported to the front by truck instead of foot march. The young replacements sent to the front in 1918 had a vastly different view of military service from their older brothers who had marched off to war in the fall of 1914. Finally, drill sergeants continued to find that Bavarian farm boys made more pliable (but less educated) human material than young fellows drafted from the industrial cities of the Ruhr.[7]

---

[6] German troop strengths from Richard Bessel, *Germany after the First World War* (Oxford University Press, 1993), 68–74. Erich O. von Volkmann put the number closer to 8 million, *UDZ*, XI (i), 241. See "A note on numbers" at the end of this chapter.

[7] The social patterns of front-line service are discussed in Benjamin Ziemann, *War Experiences in Rural Germany 1914–1923* (Oxford/New York: Berg Publishing, 2007), 29–71.

Military function, geographical stationing, regional origin, length of service, age, along with previous civilian occupation and social background, may all have been factors in determining how soldiers responded to the revolution. None of these divisions, however, was as crucial to the early course of the German Revolution as the chasm that separated those who served behind the line and those who had endured the terrible experience of service in the trenches of the Western Front in the last stages of the war. Yet the behavior of the front-line soldiers in the critical weeks of November and December 1918 presents a curious anomaly. Why would they be restrained in their response to the revolution? Why would they continue to obey the orders of officers who continued to lead them into harm's way in a war that was hopelessly lost? Certainly, the men at the front had suffered the most in the cause of German militarism. Thus, apparently, they had the most to gain from the revolution. The revolution promised the combat soldier more than political reform; a successful revolution would be the guarantee of their physical survival. Under these circumstances, one imagines the *Frontkämpfer* (front-line fighters) would celebrate the revolutionary achievements of the sailors whose mutiny launched the overthrow of the Second Reich. Instead, as we will see, upon returning to the homeland, the front-line soldiers often expressed a special contempt for the sailors they encountered (a contempt, incidentally, that was often mutual). One also imagines the troops of the Field Army would extend whole-hearted support to the soldiers' councils in the homeland. The political program of these councils aimed at preventing old elites from reasserting their traditional authority, and no men had endured more under the old elites than the men at the front. Yet the weeks after the end of the war saw countless fistfights and, in a few rare cases, pitched battles between returning front-line soldiers and the revolutionary garrisons inside Germany.

Thus, the seemingly anomalous actions of the *Frontkämpfer* during Germany's defeat and its subsequent political upheavals present two puzzling questions. Why was it so and did it matter? Why were the men who climbed out of the trenches on November 11 so different from the rest of the army? Beyond that, how and why did these differing perceptions shape the early history of the Weimar Republic? This study proposes to offer answers to these questions by looking at what the front-line soldiers went through before and after the end of the war and by considering how these soldiers were led, manipulated, supported, and feared by the leaders of postwar Germany. It will argue that the terrible ordeal endured by German soldiers on the Western Front in the last stages of the First World War set them apart from the remainder of army. It shaped their response to the dramatic political events that accompanied Germany's defeat, and thrust upon them, through their response, a decisive role in determining the outcome of the German Revolution.

The historiography of the German Revolution usually assumes that difference existed between the front-line soldiers and the rest of the army without exploring the question of why it existed. West German historians have tended to be much more interested in the soldiers' councils created within Germany. For years, they debated whether these councils might have served as the basis for a "third path"[8] for Germany's political destiny, offering an alternative, on one hand, to the Weimar Republic and its fatal compromises with the old elites, and, at the other extreme, the excesses risked in a Bolshevik-style regime. Though the front-line units often formed their own soldiers' councils, these associations rarely supported a revolutionary agenda and, thus, have seemed far less interesting to German scholars. When Western historians have looked at the political behavior of the front-line soldiers it was usually through the lens of what came almost two decades later, the ascent of National Socialism. However, the fact that the old *Frontkämpfer* seemed disproportionately represented in the early leadership of the National Socialists (including the *Führer* himself) overshadows the less conspicuous fact that most of the hundreds of thousands of combat veterans of 1918 marched back to their homes and returned, as best they could, to lives interrupted by the war, without involvement in extremist politics.[9]

Across the ideological divide of the Cold War, historians in the former German Democratic Republic were more attentive to the differences between front-line troops and the revolutionary soldiers in the rear. However, looking at these phenomena through a Marxist lens prevented them from examining the motivation of the *Frontkämpfer* with objectivity. Thus, East German accounts of the revolution portrayed the men who marched home under the control of their officers as ill-informed dupes or homesick pragmatists. That is, until some of these same men volunteered to serve in the *Freikorps*. At that point, the former front-line soldiers were transformed into bloodthirsty mercenaries and treacherous class enemies. There may be an important kernel of truth to this view, but, because of the ideological limits of East German analysis, it often seems more caricature than characterization.

[8] See, for example, Reinhard Rürup, "Demokratische Revolution und der 'dritter Weg': Die deutsche Revolution von 1918/1919 in der neuren wissentschaftlichen Diskussion." *Geschichte und Gesellschaft*, 9 (1983), 278–301.
[9] Bessel, *Germany after the First World War*, 257.

A completely satisfactory explanation for the way soldiers behave under specific conditions of extraordinary stress must necessarily be elusive. Through the course of modern warfare and, especially since the First World War, psychologists, officers, and historians have struggled to understand why men act the way they do when their circumstances are dominated by danger and uncertainty. Though dated, Ulrich Kluge's *Soldatenräte und Revolution* provided the most comprehensive description of the political behavior of German soldiers during the revolution.[10] Kluge suggested three material and political factors for the front-line troops' initially passive response to the revolution: (1) the German High Command successfully subverted the efforts of revolutionaries to agitate among the soldiers of the front; (2) the desperately difficult transportation situation during the return of the Field Army to Germany restricted the movement of revolutionary forces and prevented the coordination of revolutionary efforts; and (3) the soldiers' uncertainty over the situation in the homeland limited the appeal of political activists.[11]

While Kluge's three factors certainly contributed to the failure of revolutionary elements to gain political power among combat units of the West, they are not, by themselves, completely persuasive. Kluge's explanation seems to beg additional questions. Why were the efforts of the OHL to subvert the soldiers' councils (*Soldatenräte*) not successful elsewhere within the army? If the difficulty of the retreat from France and Belgium limited revolutionary agitation within front-line units, why was this not the case in the more difficult withdrawal from Poland and the Ukraine? Finally, if uncertainty over the situation within Germany provoked soldiers to shy away from radical appeals, why were the occupation troops in the East not similarly reticent?

We return to the argument that the soldiers on the Western Front represented a unique cohort and their political outlook was, likewise, unique. As the armistice approached, the political objectives of the men in the trenches may be summarized succinctly: early peace and the fastest return to home and family possible. They were indifferent to such issues as the rate of socialization in German industry, the role of the workers' and soldiers' councils in sharing power with the central government, or the federal structure in the new German state. Theirs was the agenda of war-weariness, homesickness and despair. When the

---

[10] Ulrich Kluge, *Soldatenräte und Revolution. Studien zur Militärpolitik in Deutschland, 1918/1919* (Göttingen: Vandenhoeck and Ruprecht, 1975).
[11] *Ibid.*, 104–5.

end of the war made the first goal a reality and the second a near-term possibility, the political views of the *Frontschweine* saw little alteration or evolution. Why? Even generalizations can be risky. Nevertheless, this study will use six factors – exhaustion, isolation, alienation, selection, cohesion, and management – to explain the peculiar response of the German front-line troops to the dramatic events that took place in a period of about ten weeks between late October 1918 and the end of that year.

Clearly, at this point further elaboration of these concepts is necessary to establish the framework of analysis; thus:

(1) *Exhaustion*, for our purposes, refers primarily to the mind-numbing fatigue that prevailed in German lines in the last months of the war, when incessant Allied attacks consumed German reserves and forced the OHL to leave units at the front for weeks without relief. It also refers to the profound war-weariness felt by front-line soldiers on both sides of No Man's Land in the fourth year of the conflict. By late 1918, two forms of exhaustion, physical and emotional, contributed to the dull indifference most front-line soldiers felt toward the world beyond the trenches.

(2) *Isolation*, as a factor, encompasses both the geographical and informational separation of the German fighting men from the sources of revolutionary agitation. While the young replacements in the homeland casernes were exposed to a full array of anti-war and anti-military propaganda, and the soldiers in the East often had opportunity to fraternize with Bolsheviks, the front-line soldier in the West faced a different situation. Unless on leave, or convalescing from wounds in a rear area hospital, he was relatively insulated from such influences. This was especially the case after the army cancelled leaves and the mail service broke down in the last days of the war. This condition of relative insulation persisted through the difficult return march across the Rhine in November and December 1918. (Where the isolation broke down, however, the behavior of the combat units would begin to resemble the other elements of the army more closely.)

(3) *Alienation* describes the sullen hostility felt by the *Frontschweine* towards those who did not share their misery and the constant danger besetting them. In broad categories, these included civilians on the home front (excluding, of course, the soldier's family), rear-area troops, and the officers who planned and directed operations on the various army staffs. It describes the phenomenon common to almost all modern armies in a lengthy war: the jealousy and resentment felt

by those exposed to lethal danger towards those who were not. This alienation manifested itself not only in attitudes but, as the *Westheer* marched across the Rhine, physical attacks on the representatives of the soldiers' councils within Germany.

(4) *Selection* includes two choices. The first is that choice made by the German High Command to put the most combat-effective units and the best-trained, most fit men on the Western Front. The second is the self-selection conducted by every front-line soldier when faced with the difficult choice of remaining with his unit under the command of his officers or, instead, seeking an escape from danger, a release from military coercion, and an opportunity to return home. For military reasons, the OHL put the men least susceptible to political agitation at the front (though this was far less the case in the last months of the war). War-weariness, homesickness, and despair pulled thousands of men out of the line when the last months of the war expanded opportunities for desertion, surrender, or some form of shirking. Thousands, however, chose to remain with their units up to the armistice and beyond.

(5) *Cohesion*, in this essay, will refer to several related phenomena: the camaraderie between men who share difficult experiences together; the loyalty felt by soldiers toward a specific leader, the *esprit* a soldier may feel toward a unit; the relationship between officers and men (either positive or negative). Finally, the term encompasses the limited and rapidly waning influence of national patriotism after the failure of the Ludendorff offensives.

(6) *Management* is the term used by this study to refer to what one Marxist historian called "special handling."[12] In the context of this argument, it will be the term offered in describing the active efforts of the German Army's chain of command to manage the perceptions and political outlook of the rank and file. The development of this factor will suggest the strength of Kluge's argument that the OHL "subverted" the effect of the revolution on front-line soldiers, but will extend this by attempting to show that every level of the officer chain of command had a role to play in this subversion.

A sociologist with an interest in military affairs could challenge the choice of terms and add or subtract from the six factors listed here. In the first place, these factors are interrelated and overlapping. As an example, an infantry battalion commander returning to Germany in

[12] Dieter Dreetz, "Rückführung des Westheeres und Novemberrevolution." *Zeitschrift für Militärgeschichte* (DDR), 1968, 586.

December 1918 might seek to *manage* the patriotic feelings of his men by taking defensive measures to *isolate* them from seditious agitation, and offensive actions, in the form of patriotic flyers and speeches to increase their *alienation* toward the agents of revolution. Similarly, a *Frontkämpfer* considering desertion (*self-selection*) would weigh the loyalty he felt toward his comrades (*cohesion*) against the anxiety he felt for his hungry family (in part, a failure of *management*) and the conviction that these worries and the worsening situation at the front had pushed him to the limit of human endurance (*exhaustion*). Nevertheless, I believe the use of all six factors will permit a relatively nuanced consideration of the dilemmas faced by German front-line soldiers and a useful analysis of the choices they made. They serve as "lines of analysis" that lead to a greater understanding of the 1.5 million front-line troops who marched back to Germany from the Western Front. When the six factors reappear in the narrative, they are periodically italicized as a reminder to the reader of their role in explaining the choices the soldiers made.

What kind of choices did the front-line soldiers confront? Consider, first, what the front-line soldier would experience in the last year of the war, for them a genuine *annus horribilis*. After spectacular but extravagantly costly victories in the spring of 1918, the German Army on the Western Front found its hard-won triumphs to be an illusion. From mid-summer on, the German forces in the West were subjected to a series of grinding and seemingly inexorable Allied counteroffensives. For the German soldiers at the front, the disappointment in the failures of the spring evolved into despair in the autumn as the Allies exerted their overwhelming superiority in manpower and *matériel*. Punch-drunk from fatigue though they were, the troops received the news of peace negotiations with reawakened hope, even as it undermined the credibility of the Reich's senior leaders. In November, rumors of revolution in turn provoked perplexity among the soldiers at the front as well as ill-informed anxiety over the situation inside Germany. After the ceasefire on the 11th, the front-line soldiers had little time to reflect on the defeat of the Reich, because the armistice terms demanded that they make a difficult forced march out of France and Belgium and across the Rhine. Returning to Germany, they were baffled, on one hand, by the heroes' welcome offered by the populace and, on the other, the open enmity of their comrades in the homeland garrisons. They were frustrated by the pace of a demobilization plan that seemed designed to keep them from returning to family and jobs before Christmas. By the end of the year, the bulk of Western Front veterans had found their way home as the old army disintegrated. Those who remained in the ranks of the Kaiser's old regiments experienced one final defeat and humiliation on Christmas Eve as a crowd of Berliners drove the tiny remnant of the Guards Corps out of the capital.

However, the *Frontkämpfer* were hardly the innocent victims of events and circumstances in 1918. With every significant development of that fateful year, the front-line soldiers had critical choices to make, and these choices drove events in a way that other accounts have overlooked. Consider the choices made in the last weeks of the war. In late September, after Bulgaria led the domino-fall of Germany's allies and Ludendorff had demanded the government seek an armistice, there could be no illusions about the outcome of the war: Germany had lost. Yet the German forces on the Western Front continued to hold the line for almost another month and a half, the thin *feldgrau* line bending but not breaking in the face of Allied attacks. Granted, during this period, thousands of German soldiers deserted, surrendered, or just did what they could to avoid danger. However, many thousands more remained at their posts along the four-hundred-kilometer front. By doing so, they spared the German generals the humiliation of a clear-cut and decisive defeat. By their desperate defense through October and into November, German combat troops would offer unjustified credence to the first great myth of the postwar period, that Germany was "undefeated in the field." This lie, of course, served as the basis for another, more pernicious lie, that Germany had been "stabbed in the back."

When, in early November, political unrest threatened the monarchy, the front-line soldiers in a number of handpicked units were given another opportunity to make an important choice. The OHL ordered two front-line divisions to seize Rhine crossings as the first stage of a campaign conducted by the Field Army to suppress the revolution. Another veteran combat unit received the mission of securing the key government buildings in the center of the capital. Finally, the army called its most famous storm troop formation to Spa, Belgium, to guard the person of the emperor himself. Pulled out of the trenches, the front-line soldiers in each of these units were asked to take arms against their fellow Germans. In each case, they refused. As the Kaiser lost his last hope of using the *Frontkämpfer* to crush the revolution, it was clear that the Hohenzollern monarchy was doomed.

A few days later, circumstances presented the troops on the Western Front with yet another dilemma. The war was over, the Kaiser was gone, and revolutionary forces were in charge in the homeland. Support units behind the line had already begun to dissolve and stream back across the Rhine in disorderly columns. Under those circumstances, should they, the combat veterans, remain with their units and continue to obey their

officers, or overthrow the chain of command and organize their own
withdrawal from the occupied countries, or abandon their formations
and seek the quickest road home as individuals? Almost to a man, they
chose the first option. Their reasons were overwhelmingly pragmatic
but the consequences were profound. The appearance of well-ordered,
disciplined units marching across the Rhine crossings and through the
cities of Germany added yet more unjustified evidence that the army
had not been defeated in battle. The success of the return march, the
Heimkehr, also encouraged the officer corps in a false hope that the old
army might yet be preserved. Finally, the appearance of the steel-helmeted combat veterans parading down the avenues of Germany's cities
sent a shudder through the revolutionary workers' and soldiers' councils and the leaders of the radical Left, the Independent Socialists and
the Spartacists. Here, it seemed, was counter-revolution on the march.

Yet the hopes of the officer corps and the fears of the Left began to
evaporate as the Field Army moved into the interior of Germany. At
this point, the war-weary veterans made another critical choice. The
circumstances of the army's demobilization offered them the option
of staying with the army to become part of a postwar military, waiting for an official discharge to be processed, or, if that took too long,
setting out for home on their own. The *Frontschweine* voted with their
feet, and, by January, the old army no longer existed. Some waited for
the money, the suit, and the stamped documents that went with an
official discharge, while many others did not. This phenomenon was
repeated in microcosm when the OHL ordered nine elite divisions to
march into Berlin in early December. Wilhelm Groener, the army's
First Quartermaster General, hoped these divisions would serve as the
government's powerful sword for suppressing its enemies on the Left.
Instead, the government prevaricated and the soldiers, after enjoy-
ing the welcome provided by Berliners, saw little reason to remain in
crowded casernes waiting on developments. Instead, they went home
for Christmas. Only a handful remained when the government finally
called for help, on Christmas Eve, 1918. After a pitched battle outside
the Imperial Palace, this handful of remaining front-line troops faced
one final dilemma: would they be willing to fire on a crowd of civilians
who stood between them and the government's enemies? They chose
not to fire. The last battle of the old army was an embarrassing defeat
that exposed the defenselessness of the provisional government and
emboldened its Spartacist opponents. Two weeks later, what Germans
had dreaded, civil war, began in earnest.

At a Great War conference fourteen years ago, Dennis Showalter
expressed the view that the German soldier in the trenches was a

sort of "invisible man." The enemy in *feldgrau*, he said, remained the "other" in English-speaking historiography, normally accessible only in the stereotypes presented by Erich Maria Remarque or Ernst Jünger. Meanwhile, ideological exploitation of the war experience by the Nazis and the attention demanded by the much greater disaster of the Second World War have served to undermine the efforts of German historians to give a fuller picture of the *Frontschweine* and their experience.[13] In the years since Showalter's call for a "recovery" of the German soldier of the Great War, however, German and British scholars have done much to correct this historiographical omission. Within the last decade, historians like Christoph Jahr,[14] Anne Lipp,[15] Bernd Ulrich,[16] Benjamin Ziemann[17] in Germany, and Alex Watson in Great Britain,[18] have made great progress in creating a more complete understanding the German soldier's experience of war between 1914 and 1918. They have made ingenious use of soldiers' letters and other original sources to broaden our understanding significantly. We now have a much fuller understanding of the Germans who manned the trenches in the Great War.

There is more work to be done. The study offered here attempts to extend the analysis beyond the experience in the trenches into the weeks immediately after the war.

However, unlike the work by authors cited above, the scope of the analysis and the limitations of available sources make this a military and political rather than a social history. The story of the front-line soldiers' role in the German Revolution of 1918 is told primarily through the relatively well-documented actions and attitudes of their leaders, political and military, as well as those that greeted them when the army came home, and, finally, those who feared them on the Left. The common soldiers had little opportunity during the last weeks of the war

---

[13] Dennis Showalter, "The German Soldier of World War I: Myths and Realities," in *A Weekend with the Great War: Proceedings of the Fourth Annual Great War Interconference Seminar, Lisle, Illinois, 16–18 September 1994*, ed. Stephen Weingartner (Wheaton, IL: The Catigny First Division Foundation, 1995), 63–80.

[14] Christoph Jahr, *Gewöhnliche Soldaten: Desertion und Deserteure im deutschen und britischen Heer, 1914–1918* (Göttingen: Vandenhoeck und Ruprecht, 1998).

[15] Anne Lipp, *Meinungslenkung im Krieg: Kriegserfahrungen deutscher Soldaten und ihre Deutung 1914–1918* (Göttingen: Vandenhoeck und Ruprecht, 2003).

[16] Bernd Ulrich, *Die Augenzeugen. Deutsche Feldpostbriefe in Kriegs- und Nachkriegszeit 1914–1933* (Essen: Klartext-Verlag, 1997).

[17] Benjamin Ziemann, *Front und Heimat: Ländliche Kriegserfahrungen im südlichen Bayern 1914–1923* (Essen: Klartext, 1997).

[18] Alex Watson, *Enduring the Great War: Combat Morale and Collapse in the German and British Armies, 1914–1918* (Cambridge University Press, 2008). Watson's book, comparing the experience of British and German troops, may well prove to be the definitive study of motivation and morale in the trenches.

and the first days of the peace to record their experiences and feelings, and few went back to reconstruct these events. The story, then, is taken from official documents, unit records, the memoirs of officers and politicians, and the observations of journalists. Nevertheless, this essay seeks to tell the story of soldiers who found themselves in very difficult circumstances.

Recently, historians have given enormous attention to the way memory is constructed and evolved, reconstructed and corrupted. It is certainly a worthy topic, but here it will receive only the briefest attention. Instead, this study attempts to recapture the events that memory would use as the raw material, material that became the basis for myth-making, propaganda, and historical revision. The *Frontschweine* were important actors in a decisive moment in modern German history. In large measure, their role has been skewed by the ideological filter of Nazism and Communism or overlooked by historians more interested in other aspects of the German Revolution. The role played by the men who marched home in November and December 1918 deserves another look.

More broadly, their story reminds us that the study of military culture requires an examination of the complexity of modern armies and the likely existence of numerous subcultures. It also serves as a case study in the role of armies in defeat and disintegration, and armies in times of revolution.

Chiefly, however, it is a story about how soldiers behaved in a specific set of extraordinary circumstances.

A note about numbers

Accounting for the strength of an army nearing its death throes is difficult. Throughout this study, I will use the figure of 1.5 million as the number of front-line troops on the Western Front. This number represents an educated but necessarily imprecise calculation. It represents approximately half of the German troops on the Western Front.[19]

---

[19] The total number of troops on the Western Front is also elusive and reflects, among other things, overlaps in accounting between the Field Army, occupation forces, replacement depots, and the rear-area support system. Richard Bessel, using figures from the Reich Demobilization Office, puts the number at 3.2 million (Bessel, *Germany after the World War*, 74), John Ellis and Michael Cox put the number at 3.4 million (John Ellis and Michael Cox, *The World War I Databook: The Essential Facts and Figures for All the Combatants* (London: Aurum Press, 1993), 245). Alex Watson, using British military sources, cites the figure of over 3.5 million (Watson, *Enduring the Great War*, 189–90). A German captain serving with the German delegation to the Allied Armistice Commission was probably exaggerating when he complained that his

It is derived first, by taking the "trench strength" (*Gefechtstärke*) of an infantry battalion at the end of 1918 as 350;[20] multiplying it by three battalions per regiment (adding several hundred additional men in machine and mortar companies[21] as well as regimental staffs and support personnel) for an approximate regimental strength of 1,400. Multiply this by the number of regiments in a division (three), add two thousand for division pioneers, artillery, headquarters and support troops (assuming these units were at approximately 60 percent),[22] add recruit depots,[23] and this yields a figure near 6,500 men per division, or just around half of the wartime strength for an infantry division.[24] Using this figure as the average strength of the 184 divisions on the Western Front yields a figure close to 1.2 million. Even using a smaller number for average battalion strength, if one adds non-divisional units found close to the front (artillery, storm troops, machine-gun units, signalers, medical staff, air defense, labor troops, etc.), the total readily seems to reach 1.5 million troops.

army had to feed 3.8 million men in its retreat back to Germany. (Extract from G-3: GHQ AEF: Fldr. 1207: Report dated Nov. 21, 1918, in *United States Army in the World War 1917–1919*, vol 10, part 1, *The Armistice Agreement and Related Documents*, 133.) One final, useful item of data comes from a staff officer with Army Group Crown Prince who recalled that his headquarters, which controlled almost exactly a third of the German divisions (61) and non-divisional artillery, had a strength of 1,220,000 at the moment of the armistice. Kurt Anker, *Unserer Stunde Kommt!* (Leipzig: Leipziger Graphische Werk, 1923), 70.

[20] There were dramatic variations; units in the path of Allied attacks were frequently well below this number. On the other hand, Allied observers at the Rhine crossings later counted infantry battalions of 500 and 600 men (US National Archives [hereafter NARA], RG 120, Box 5895, Third Army Intelligence Reports, December 1918). The average "trench" strength of infantry companies (three per battalion, down from four) of Army Group Crown Prince on October 21 was eighty-six. Adding machine-gun companies and headquarters brings the figure very near 350 (NARA, RG 165, Box 28, Folder X, Army Group Ib report of October 21, 1918, 44–6).

[21] A sample of strength reports from twelve divisions in Army Group Crown Prince on October 1 found an average of 110 men in each regimental machine-gun company and 149 in the mortar (*Minenwerfer*) company. NARA, RG 165, Box 28, Folder X, Group of Armies Crown Prince, Annexes (strength reports).

[22] At full strength, these combat support formations numbered just over 3,000. British General Staff, *Handbook of the German Army, April 1918* (London: Imperial War Museum and Nashville: Battery Press, 1996), 33–4.

[23] Using the twelve sample divisions cited above, the average strength in a divisional recruit depot at the beginning of October was 804.

[24] British General Staff, *Handbook*, 35.

2   The last ditch: German front-line soldiers in the final days of the First World War

The *Frontschwein's* dilemma

During the last weeks of the war, German officers on the Western Front were forced to acknowledge a painful reality. The tide of battle had clearly turned during the summer, and, increasingly, as the Allies asserted their material and manpower superiority, the German leaders found that their units were unable to sustain the battle against the onslaught of the British, French, and American armies. This was the situation of the 9th *Landwehr* Division defending a sector in the Argonne Forest. On October 8, the operations officer of the 9th sent this grim assessment to its higher headquarters, the I Reserve Corps:

> After the heavy fighting of the last several days the combat strength of the division has sunk even further. Because of severe losses the 116th Regiment has only about 100 men on the front line. Among the troops, who have been in 14 days of unbroken combat, there is manifested such an exhaustion that they are no longer in the condition to defend against an enemy attack.
>
> His Excellency, the Commanding General, has ordered me to report if I was of the view that the fighting strength of the division has come to an end. I believe this moment has arrived.[1]

Up to that point in the war, a third-rate unit like the 9th *Landwehr* Division would usually have held a quiet sector of the front. However, by the fall of 1918, German reserves were so exhausted that the middle-aged *Landwehr* men of the division found themselves directly in the path of Pershing's powerful offensive.

Elite units, too, were sounding notes of despair. The 2nd Guards Artillery Regiment facing the BEF on the Somme recorded ruefully on October 9 that any pleasure it could derive from its past victories were now clouded by "the foreboding signs of complete defeat." The front was giving way, and, what was worse, one could no longer count on the

---

[1] NARA, RG 165, Box 131, Folder: 9th *Landwehr* Division War Diary and Annexes, 119 (Division Autry Ia Nr. 5853, October 8, 1918).

"previously unshaken heroic spirit of the infantry."[2] On October 17, the war diary of the 6th Guards Brigade reported that the strain of prolonged combat and heavy losses had rendered the nerves of the troops *"kaputt"* and predicted that among them "the extreme measures that the officers use to hold them in place will completely fail."[3]

The signs of impending collapse seemed unavoidable, and, even though National Socialist mythology would later claim that the German Army was "undefeated in the field," the unit records of the *Westheer* in late 1918 suggest it was an army in desperate straits. Marshal Foch's strategy of continuous attack along the length of the Western Front had been designed to consume the German Army's thin reserves, and, if the policy was inelegant, it was, nonetheless, brutally effective.[4] Through the summer and fall, battlefield losses, desertion, disease, and malnourishment had sucked the strength out of the German divisions holding the line. The average strength of a German infantry battalion had plummeted from 800 men at the beginning of the year to 500 and below by autumn. The Kaiser's forces on the Western Front had been driven, seemingly, to the limits of endurance. On September 29, Ludendorff conceded the desperate situation when he demanded the German government seek an armistice. If this was a necessary measure, it was also an admission of defeat with a devastating effect on German home-front morale. Clearly, the war could not go on much longer.

Given these circumstances, the historian must contend with the fact that, when the armistice finally came, the German line was unbroken. What is more, the German troops on the Western Front continued to inflict heavy casualties on the attacking Allies up through the last days of the war.[5] Indeed, the German request for armistice caught Allied military leaders by surprise.[6] Moreover, just hours after the fighting had ended, the German troops picked themselves up out of the trenches and marched back into Germany in disciplined and orderly

---

[2] NARA, RG 165, Box 121, Folder II, 17 (War Diary of the 2nd Guard Artillery Regt., Oct. 9, 1918).

[3] *Bundesarchiv-Militärarchiv* (hereafter BA-MA), PH 8/I/67, Third Guards Division Annexes (Report of 9th Grenadier Regt., Oct. 17, 1918).

[4] The chief of staff of Army Group Crown Prince wrote, "The steadily widening battle ate reserves and even more reserves." BA-MA, Nachlass Schulenberg, N58/1, 212.

[5] One recent analysis finds estimates that the Germans on the Western Front inflicted over 1.1 million casualties on the Allies between the battles that turned the tide in the summer of 1918 and the end of the war. See James McRandle and James Quirk, "The Blood Test Revisited: A New Look at German Casualty Counts in World War I." *Journal of Military History*, 70, 3 (July 2006), 667–702.

[6] For a provocative, if not always convincing, discussion of the historical problem, see Niall Ferguson, *The Pity of War* (New York: Basic Books, 1999), 310–14.

formations, their bands playing the old marching songs of the Second Reich. It suggested to many that the collapse was not so imminent and the German Army's defeat incomplete.[7]

Assessing the actual condition of the German Army at the end of the war has proven to be an important historical problem. Could the tired divisions on the Western Front have continued to fight on? Could they have retreated back across the Rhine and prolonged the war into 1919? Would their remaining powers of resistance have been sufficient to wring better peace terms from the Allies? During the inter-war years these were questions central to the claim that the Kaiser's military had been "stabbed in the back" by the "November criminals."[8] In large measure, of course, the answers to these question were terribly complex and, perhaps, inaccessible. That, because in the last weeks of the war, continued resistance by the German Army hinged on decisions made by thousands of individual soldiers crouched in dugouts and shell holes along the front. In the fall of 1918, each of these men was confronted by a stark choice: continue to fight against overwhelming enemy forces in a war that was clearly lost, or abandon unit and comrades to seek some sort of life-preserving alternative in surrender, desertion, or mutiny. For the purposes of this study, the factors that shaped these decisions are crucial to analyzing their behavior in the final weeks of the war and the earliest weeks of the peace.

Exhaustion: the demands of *Materialschlacht*

Military historians tend to be fascinated by "first battles," and the special attention to the initial engagements of a war is understandable. First battles, as a phenomenon, allow the scholar to pass judgment on the foolish tactics, flawed assumptions, and inadequate organizations of peacetime militaries. To paraphrase Sir Michael Howard, peacetime armies usually "get it wrong." The campaigns of 1914 offer a conspicuous

---

[7] Four years after the war, the famous historian and scathing critic of Germany's war leaders Hans Delbrück wrote that, "[T]he front troops were weakened by thousands of deserters in the rear areas and even by those few who went over to the enemy. Nevertheless, with the exception of a very few, the army fought on flawlessly until collapse and kept itself in order even during the retreat following the armistice." Quotation from "Ludendorff's Self-Portrait," in Hans Delbrück, *Delbrück's Modern Military History*, trans. Arden Bucholz (Lincoln: University of Nebraska Press, 1997), 191.

[8] The Reichstag commission investigating the causes of German collapse during the 1920s considered these questions through thousands of pages and twelve volumes of testimony in the *UDZ* series cited in Chapter 1 (*Die Ursachen des Zusammenbruchs im Jahre 1918* [The Origins of the Collapse in 1918], Eugen Fischer, *et al.* [Berlin: Deutsche Verlagsgesellschaft für Politik und Geschichte, 1925–9]), again, hereafter *UDZ*.

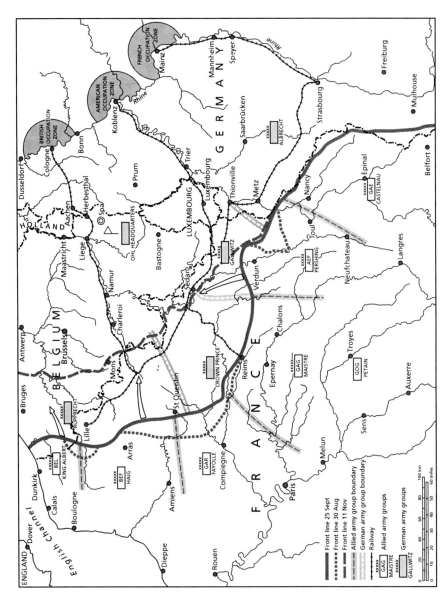

Map 1. Allied counteroffensive

case in point. The slaughter in Alsace-Lorraine, on the Marne, and at Tannenberg, in turn, exposed the glaring flaws in French tactics, German planning, and Russian leadership. Yet last battles have their own peculiar and interesting characteristics, especially in a long war. Though prewar cadres may have been decimated by the latter stages of a prolonged conflict, belligerent armies have usually refined the business of killing their enemies to a level they were incapable of at the beginning of the conflict. Last battles tend to be bloody. In the same way, last battles frequently feature one side fighting with its back to the wall, frantic to stave off defeat. Last battles tend to be desperate. Spotsylvania in 1864 along with Okinawa and Berlin in 1945 serve as grim examples of these two characteristics. "Bloody" and "desperate" certainly describe the fighting on the Western Front in 1918, where casualties surpassed those of the previous years. Though the opposing armies had not completely solved the tactical problem of exploiting a breakthrough of the enemy's trench systems, they had, nevertheless, largely solved the technical problem of destroying the men who held them.

In the summer and fall of 1918, the Allied armies demonstrated this lethal capability through their mastery of *Materialschlacht*, the battle of material.[9] Allied industrial production, fully mobilized and supported by American raw materials and American dollars, had provided the French and British Armies the engines required for a deadly program of attrition. General Pétain had captured the essence of it the year before when he warned the French Army, "Artillery conquers, infantry occupies." It was, of course, more than just artillery. *Materialschlacht* called for the orchestration of tanks, aircraft, poison gas, and small arms as well. Yet the delivery of overwhelming high explosive artillery fire was the key. The other weapons were complementary.

To be a German defender in the path of a major Allied attack late in the war was to experience the horrors of Dante's *Inferno*. The impact of the first rounds of a preparatory barrage was his signal that the next hours would be spent cowering under "drum-fire" (*Trommelfeuer*) with the chance of survival slim. By 1918, the Allies had enough medium and heavy guns to obliterate entire trench systems in a matter of hours. The BEF demonstrated the point in September 1918 by crushing the formidable Hindenburg Line under an avalanche of shells.[10] The stunned

---

[9] According to Hew Strachan, the terms dated back to the Germans' exposure to the BEF's lavish expenditure of ordnance at the Battle of the Somme. "The Morale of the German Army, 1917–1918," in *Facing Armageddon: The First World War Experienced*, ed. Hugh Cecil and Peter Liddle (London: Leo Cooper, 1996), 384.

[10] For a discussion of the techniques of *Materialschlacht*, see, among others, Shelford Bidwell and Dominick Graham, *Firepower: The British Army Weapons and Theories of*

survivors of such bombardments could usually offer little resistance after such a literal "storm of steel."

By late 1918, the British were probably the most proficient in delivering such destructive barrages, followed closely by the French, but even the inexperienced American Expeditionary Force could use artillery to annihilate entire enemy units. On November 1, just prior to a US attack, the German 52nd Infantry Division moved up to the Argonne front to relieve the 41st Infantry Division. Before the relief was complete, American artillery fire inundated the 52nd and destroyed it as an effective force. In the course of the fighting that followed, the division headquarters staff found itself in a blocking position trying to hold the gap blown in the German lines by the enemy barrage. At the end of the day, from a strength of perhaps 10,000 men, the division chief of staff could muster just 206 dazed survivors, whom he herded back behind the line to become the corps reserve. Most of the missing men had been killed or wounded by artillery fire.[11] The fate of the 52nd Infantry Division provided frightening testimony to the lethal effect of Allied artillery in the last year of the war.

Drumfire barrages brought much death and mutilation, and men that survived such barrages faced the prospect of nervous exhaustion. David Grossman, in his book *On Killing*, a thoughtful analysis of the behavior of men in combat, has given insights into why this was so. Grossman observed that one normally associates two human responses to mortal danger – *"fight* or *flight"* – but there are actually four. Along with fighting or fleeing, studies have revealed two further responses: *posturing* and *submission*. Posturing involves any activity by the threatened person designed to cow or discourage a possible assailant without actually attacking him. Thus, primitive tribesmen brandish weapons at each other in order to avoid the nastiness of close combat, and modern soldiers use wild, unaimed automatic weapons fire to make their enemies seek cover and cease their own fire. Submission, of course, means offering the aggressor gestures of surrender and indications that one intends no harm. Any of the four options – fight, flight, posturing, and submission – gives a threatened person an opportunity to act, to discharge the adrenaline and other chemicals his body produces at the approach of

War, 1904–1945 (Barnsley: Pen and Sword Books, 1982), 131–8; J.P. Harris, *Amiens to the Armistice: The BEF in the Hundred Days' Campaign* (London: Batsford, 1998); and Shane Schreiber, *Shock Army of the British Empire: The Canadian Corps in the Last 100 Days of the Great War* (Westport, CN: Praeger, 1997), 71–114.

[11] NARA, RG 165, Box 201, Misc. Folder: Correspondence with German officers and copies of *Reichsarchiv* documents on the effect of American artillery fire (Letter from Major Douglas to Colonel Sorley, dated October 14, 1923).

danger. In the presence of the threat of grievous bodily harm, action of
any type is preferable to inaction and, thus, therapeutic.[12]

Consider then, the poor *Frontschwein* sitting in a shelter with his comrades during an Allied preparatory bombardment of several hours' duration. None of the four options was available to him. He could not fight
the shells that caused the walls of his hiding-place to shudder. Neither
could he flee; to leave the shelter would probably have been certain
death. Posturing was of no use, and one does not surrender to a barrage. The soldier was forced to stew in his own fear, often for hours;
there could be no discharge of stress and nervous energy associated with
anxiety. J.F.C. Fuller later observed that, "what produced 'shell-shock'
much more than the sudden danger [was] prolonged danger in a static
position, where the man cannot get away from it."[13] For the German
front-line soldier of 1918, the consequences of enduring this prolonged
Allied bombardment was short-term nervous exhaustion and, in many
cases, long-term emotional problems. After such a bombardment, one
German soldier wrote, "No one can express what this means ... Our
battalion lost half its strength in a single day ... Many have had their
ear drum ruptured, without having a scratch, one man has gone crazy
from the explosion of a shell. One would think that almost everyone has
had a nervous collapse."[14]

Casualties and exhaustion: the effect of the nearly continuous Allied
offensives had a diabolical, two-edged effect. First, the enormous firepower and material superiority of the French, British, and Americans
ensured that wherever they struck a blow their enemy would suffer
heavy losses. From mid July, when Foch wrested the initiative from
Ludendorff, until the end of the war, the German Army lost approximately 420,000 men, killed or wounded. A further 340,000 were lost as
missing, some as prisoners of war, the others as deserters.[15] To this sum
one must add an estimated 1 million cases of sickness.[16] To measure

[12] Dave Grossman, *On Killing: The Psychological Cost of Learning to Kill in War and Society* (New York: Little, Brown, and Co., 1995), 1–15. Grossman can be taken to task for some of his sources, but his arguments are always provocative and often persuasive.

[13] Fuller quoted in Alex Watson, "Fear in Combat and Combating Fear: British and German Troops in Endurance Warfare, 1914–1918," unpublished paper.

[14] Soldier's letter quoted in Klaus Latzel, "Die misslungene Flucht vor dem Tod, Toten und Sterben vor und nach 1918," in *Kriegsende 1918: Ereignis, Wirkung, Nachwirkung*, ed. Jorg Düppler and Gerhard Gross (Munich: Oldenbourg Verlag, 1994), 187.

[15] Testimony of General von Kühl in Ewald Beckmann, *Der Dolchstoßprozeß in München vom 19. Oktober bis 20. November 1925* (Munich: Suddeutsche Monatshefte GmbH Verlag, 1925), 76.

[16] Wilhelm Deist, "Verdeckter Militärstreik im Kriegsjahr 1918," in Wolfram Wette, ed., *Der Krieg des Kleinen Mannes: Eine Militärgeschichte von unten* (Munich: Piper GmbH, 1992), 150.

the full effect of 1918 on the German Army, one must combine these figures with the nearly 1 million casualties suffered during Ludendorff offensives, losses that had fallen, very disproportionately, among the very best units of the German Army.[17] Given such casualties, it is little wonder that the *Westheer* was reeling at the end of the war.

The second effect created by continuous attacks was to ensure that those German soldiers that survived were pushed to the limit of endurance. As their casualties mounted, the Germans found themselves unable to make up the losses. As a result, the army asked fewer and fewer men to cover increasingly wider sectors of the line without relief. Those who survived the Allied drumfire were, by the last weeks of the war, numbed by physical and nervous exhaustion. Units found themselves constantly shuttled back and forth to cover new gaps in the line. On October 23, the First Army sent Army Group Crown Prince this report from the commander of the 51st Reserve Division, General von Kleist:

Since September 25, the division has been committed to defensive battles, found itself marching (with many night marches) or in inadequate quarters, usually in local bivouacs, at times in the rain and cold. Since October 16, the division has marched over 100 kilometers. It has been assigned since September 25, to six [different] armies and 15 [different] corps commands.

Due to the heavy fighting, the strenuous marches and the insufficient quarters in [un]imaginably unfavorable weather, the officers and men are completely exhausted. Despite the best will, the physical and spiritual strength has broken down. Under these conditions, the mood of the troops has suffered severely.

After complaining of the need for delousing, the increase in influenza cases, the inadequacy of replacements, and the requirement to consolidate his remaining infantry into provisional units, he concluded: "I believe that, at present, the division is no longer capable of defending against a serious enemy attack."[18]

While von Kleist's message spelled out the effects of prolonged combat, it also suggested the other circumstances that contributed to the desperate fatigue of the German combat units on the Western Front. The offensives of March, April, May, and June had pulled much of the German *Westheer* out of its well-prepared position. The German

---

[17] According to the official medical reports, between March and July of 1918, the German forces in the West lost 124,000 killed, 748,000 wounded, and 101,000 missing. Heeres-Sanitätsinspektion des Reichswehrministerium, *Sanitätsbericht über das Deutsche Heer im Weltkriege 1914/1918*, vol. III, *Die Krankenbewegung bei dem Deutschen Feld- und Besatzungsheer* (Berlin: Mittler und Sohn, 1934), p. 143 of Annexes.

[18] NARA, RG 165, Folder: Army Group Crown Prince, Doc. 192/193.

breakthroughs had penetrated deep enough into Allied positions to outrun supplies but not deep enough to achieve decisive results. The eventual outcome of Ludendorff's folly found the Germans defending from shallow, hastily dug trenches around the perimeter of three vulnerable salients.[19] Then, through the summer, the Allies had driven the Germans back to their original lines, and, by September, the Kaiser's armies had lost much of these as well. The last three months saw the Germans in a general retreat that forced them to abandon most of their comfortable, well-constructed, and well-sited defensive positions. During the weeks before the armistice, German infantry were defending from shell holes and slit trenches with little cover from either the elements or indirect fire.[20] Instead of resting or training, commanders were forced to commit the few units held in reserve to digging rearward defenses. The war of movement also meant that units saw less and less of the *Gulaschkanone* (field kitchens), delousing stations, or supply wagons with replacement uniforms and boots. The *Westheer* became a ragged, lousy, weather-beaten, and poorly fed army.

These conditions, poor rations, the absence of shelter, crushing fatigue, and worsening weather made the German front-line soldier especially vulnerable to illness. The first wave of the worldwide influenza pandemic reached the German lines in the summer, and the number of reported illnesses in the Field Army jumped from 350,000 in June to 630,000 in July.[21] As the impact of influenza abated in the fall, other illnesses – pneumonia, dysentery, trench foot, and even malaria – sapped the strength of the front-line formations.

The desperate shortage of men forced the German Army into a variety of stopgap measures. In the last months, divisions routinely pressed their pioneer companies into service as infantry. At a higher level, the army pulled the cadres of weapons schools out of the rear into front-line service. The OHL combed lieutenants and captains out of staffs to lead companies and battalions short of officers. It became routine for battalions to consolidate their four infantry companies into three

---

[19] The frontage the army had to cover increased from 390 to 510 miles. Strachan, "Morale of the German Army," 390.

[20] On October 30, the 16th Bavarian Infantry Division reported, "The health of the infantry is no longer satisfactory. Many colds have appeared as well as influenza. The reason lies, above all, in the relatively meager shelter of the people in the front line where they are forced to inhabit wet burrows for long periods. In addition there has been no opportunity for over a month to change underclothes or, above all, garments ... The infantry regiments are no longer able to meet the demands of a major battle." *UDZ*, II (vi), 324.

[21] *Sanitätsbericht*, vol. III, Annexes, 143. Influenza accounted for 375,000 of those cases (*ibid.*, 28).

Figure 2.1 German troops on the march near Albert in the summer of 1918. The fatigue seen in these men's faces would turn to exhaustion by the fall.

and for regiments to consolidate their three battalions into two. In August, the OHL directed ten divisions disbanded in order to flesh out the remainder on the front. By October, the army dissolved another twelve. Such measures inevitably meant a heavy blow to unit morale and cohesion.[22]

These measures did not suffice to fill the gaps and, as summer turned to fall, the average battalion strength continued to fall. The result, again, was fewer men holding wider sectors for longer periods of time. Something had to give. After the Second World War, research into the psychological effects of prolonged combat revealed that every man has a breaking point; that, when exposed to the stress of combat for an extended period, every soldier will reach a condition where he is unable to function and is useless to his unit. Whole battalions could be reduced to helplessness if not given rest periods away from danger. The armies

[22] Eberhard von Hofacker, *Der Weltkrieg* (Stuttgart: Verlag von W. Kohlhammer, 1928), 454.

of the First World War recognized this, at least implicitly. For most of the war, units on the Western Front were regularly rotated in and out of the line at intervals of about five to ten days. Through four years of war, front-line soldiers on both sides of the line came to expect regular rest periods as a normal condition of service. Despite the desperate nature of the fighting of late 1918, German *Frontkämpfer* felt cruelly used when left in the line without relief. The commanders of such units could take an almost petulant tone in demanding relief for their weary men.

What was possible for the other divisions in the army sector after the June attack, must indeed, henceforth, also be possible for the [3rd Bavarian] division, after making this attack with insufficient previous rest and training to the fullest satisfaction of all superiors *and* the immediately following stressful period in the trenches from June 6 to August 9 *and* carrying out the defense against the attack of August 10–14.[23]

For experienced troops, the lack of relief was an almost intolerable grievance. In his research on the mutiny of the French 5th Division in 1917, Leonard Smith proposed that in a long conflict the relationships between superiors and subordinates shift in an important way. Among veteran troops, the level of obedience to orders by the rank and file is dynamic. Over time, their willingness to comply is based on an implicit contract which remains in a constant state of negotiation. In combat, soldiers will evaluate every order to determine whether the value of the objective is proportional to the perceived risks involved in following the order. Is obedience worth the danger and suffering that may result? The point may seem almost banal, but in the leadership doctrine of most armies it remains a dirty little secret. The willingness of troops to follow the orders of an officer is conditioned by such things as previous experience of risk and the officer's demonstrated level of competence. Thus, if troops are ordered into an attack they see as hopeless, led by a lieutenant seen as untrustworthy or foolish, disobedience or even mutiny is a likely result. On the other hand, soldiers are willing to take risks when they see a reasonable chance of success, and when they have learned to trust their chain of command.[24]

Following the line of Smith's argument, by the fall of 1918, the unwritten contracts between leader and led in the German Army were unraveling. Complaints like the one above from the 3rd Bavarian Infantry

[23] NARA, RG 165, Eighteenth Army, 131, "Kampfwert der Truppe," report dated Aug. 15, 1918.
[24] Leonard Smith, *Between Mutiny and Obedience: The Case of the French Fifth Infantry Division during World War I* (Princeton University Press, 1994), 11–17.

Division were common; the rest units had come to expect was not available for the understrength formations holding the line. Rest periods, if they came, were shorter and subject to sudden interruption.

Before 1918, the German Army could rebuild units burnt-out in heavy fighting behind the line or in a quiet sector. Given time, battalions could bring themselves up to strength with a draft of replacements from the recruit depot and, given more time, the new men would be trained and integrated among the veterans. During the war's final campaigns, the system broke down. In the first place, there were few quiet sectors and too few divisions to stem the Allied tide on the rest of the front. The replacement pool was inadequate, and those sent forward at the end of the war – largely eighteen-year-olds from the year group 1900 – were virtually untrained. Almost no divisions could be spared from the battle long enough to turn the recruits into trained and useful members of a fighting unit. However, worse than that, the replacements of 1918 often brought with them an unmilitary disposition and hostility to the army that made commanders wonder if their units would be better off without the new men. On October 10, the 80th Reserve Division complained:

The newly arrived and deployed replacements have proven themselves completely unusable and unreliable. Daily, the number of cases increase that, with the approach of weak enemy patrols, the newly arrived men run or allow themselves to be taken captive ... The company and battalion commanders would rather fight with ten of the old remaining core of men (*Stammmannschaften*) that fifty of the new replacements.[25]

In the fall of 1918, the 80th Reserve Division, and every other German division on the Western Front, based their remaining defensive strength on their *Stammmannschaften*, a dwindling nucleus of tired veterans. These hard-pressed men had neither the time, the energy, nor the inclination to consider complex political issues. On October 30, the 16th Reserve Division commented, "morale improved, however the majority of men regard the most recent events [the exchange of notes between Wilson and the German government as well as the collapse of Germany's allies] with a certain indifference and mental stupor."[26]

Another example demonstrates the simple priorities of men pushed to the limit. The Crown Prince's chief of staff, General Friedrich von Schulenberg, wrote of the assignment to his army group of a highly regarded division. It had been burned out in a continuous month of fighting in another army group during the fall of 1918. Nevertheless,

---

[25] NARA, RG 165, Box 28, Folder X, Group of Armies Crown Prince, Annexes.
[26] *UDZ*, VI (ii), 325.

Schulenberg's headquarters had to send it into the line almost as soon as it arrived. Despite its exhaustion, it performed well. No sooner had it come out of the line, than the OHL committed to another battle. From there, it returned to Army Group Crown Prince where it became a "fresh reserve."

When we ordered the division forward [again] we received the report that the division had refused to comply and that the troops had explained that they wanted, for once, a chance to eat a hot meal and sleep under a roof, then they would allow themselves to be killed. The division had their hot meal, spent a night under a roof, and then, dead-tired, entered the trenches once again where they fought with the greatest bravery.[27]

Such privation led to apathy and a desire to end their ordeal, which, in turn, meant indifference to the political outcome of the war. In September, the Field Mail Censorship Office of the Sixth Army had observed:

War-weariness and dejection is universal. The letter writers accept as a naked fact – we cannot win – and connect that, in part, to the view that Germany must go under. Though, amid the ill feeling and dissatisfaction, a certain number argue for holding out [Durchhalten] with loyalty to the monarch and unchanged love for the Fatherland worth all the sacrifices. The number of letter writers who wish the death of the Fatherland is not much less. They say, with any further [battlefield] successes, the war could only be lengthened; with defeat we would achieve the desired peace![28]

In late October, a private wrote home:

After a short rest we were informed of the relief of Ludendorff. The news went through all of us with a great sigh, with the majority murmuring, 'Thank God that this man, who as a soldier has long meddled in politics ... that this obstacle ... has disappeared.' I hope another will soon take his place and give us peace.[29]

The front-line troops wanted an end to their ordeal and an opportunity to go home.[30] Nothing else really mattered, and that was a fundamental

---

[27] BA-MA, N 58/1, Nachlass Schulenberg, 226.
[28] Bernd Ulrich and Benjamin Ziemann, eds., *Frontalltag im Ersten Weltkrieg: Wahn und Wirklichkeit: Quellen und Dokumente* (Frankfurt: Fischer Taschenbuch Verlag, 1994), Document 58: "Report of the Sixth Army Field Mail Office Review Office," 203–4.
[29] Letter of Private Ludwig Schröder in *UDZ*, V, 239.
[30] "Political influences have no appreciable effects on troops that are fresh. Tired troops see no possibilities of relief without a quick peace." World War Records, *First Infantry Division, A.E.F. (Regular) German Documents, Meuse-Argonne*, vol. IV (Washington, DC: First Infantry Division Historical Section, 1933), Doc. 88: Report of the 37th Division, "Experiences during the Recent Actions" (report of October 13, 1918).

Figure 2.2 German troops on the defense. From the shallowness of the trench and the condition of the nearby village, this appears to come from the very last stages of the war after the Germans had been driven from their well-prepared positions.

reason why political agitation among the combat units fell largely on deaf ears.[31] Men overwhelmed by fatigue and war-weariness were more willing to surrender or straggle behind the line. However, they were not inclined to become energetic revolutionaries.

Isolation: the world within a shell crater

In her book *Armies and the Art of Revolution*, Katherine Chorley argued that fraternization with the civilian population is one of the most powerful "solvents" for an army in a revolutionary situation.

It refers to definite attempts on the part of civilians to seduce soldiers from their duty when they are under arms for a specific purpose, for example, in order to suppress a riot or insurrection. It is, of course, only an effective weapon when the troops are already hesitating in their allegiance, and if, at such times,

---

[31] This was a point conceded by the East German historian Dieter Dreetz in "Rückführung des Westheeres und Novemberrevolution," 578–9.

soldiers are themselves not only hesitating but hesitatingly led, the effect is deadly.[32]

The truth of Chorley's observation would be clear within the Home Army (*Heimatheer*) during the early days of the revolution in Germany.

Yet the solvent of fraternization could not work with the same effect on the Field Army. The soldier on the Western Front did not experience routine exposure to civilian misery and revolutionary propaganda that was regular fare for the homeland garrisons. Neither did he have the prolonged contact with Russian Bolsheviks that his comrades in the East did. Indeed, the case of the men returned from Russian captivity in 1917 offered a vivid example of the effect that fraternization could have on German soldiers. The soldiers on the Western Front called these former prisoners "*Bolsheviki*," for almost to a man, the experience in the Russian camps had changed these men. If not converted to pacifism or even revolutionary Bolshevism, they were imbued with a profound hostility to further service. Most had long held the belief that their war was over and exposure to the revolution in the East had given them a political lexicon to use in expressing their resentment toward further front-line service. Initially, the army put these men into quarantine camps where, it was hoped, they could be retrained and reacquainted with army discipline. When the replacement situation became acute, in late 1918, the army shipped many of the "*Bolsheviki*" west where they posed a huge problem to those responsible for getting them to the front as well as to the front-line commanders who received them.[33] Thus, the 87th Infantry Division reported on October 31, "The former prisoners of war coming from Russia mean, at this time, not an increase in strength, but, instead, a great danger. Especially pernicious is their conduct, which undermines discipline." The report went on to warn that the password of these men was "Lights out, knives out, beat him!" (*Licht aus, Messer raus, haut ihm!*) whispered or even shouted behind the back of officers.[34]

In contrast to the *Bolsheviki*'s direct contact with revolutionary influences, the conditions of combat in the West in 1918 dominated the

---

[32] Katherine Chorley, *Armies and the Art of Revolution* (Boston: Beacon Press, 1973), 153.

[33] The Deputy Commander of the V Army Corps complained that the prisoners of war returned from Russia were a "poisonous" influence not only on the young, impressionable replacements but also the civil population. Erich O. Volkmann, *Der Marxismus und das deutsche Heer im Weltkriege* (Berlin: Verlag von Reimar Hobbing, 1925), 193, fn.

[34] *UDZ*, VI, 350.

combat soldier's attention, and circumstances also served to discourage those who would seek to reach the front-line troops with the powerful effect of face-to-face agitation. The danger the *Frontschweine* faced almost daily served to insulate them from that form of revolutionary pressure.

Nevertheless, the insulation of the Field Army was far from total in the months prior to the revolution. The OHL and its subordinate commands were unable to prevent the circulation of pacifistic and revolutionary material among the troops. In vain, the military authorities attempted to choke off socialist influences through threats, censorship, the prohibition of political activity among soldiers, and the outright suppression of hostile newspapers.[35] The ultimate failure of such measures is indicated by a report prepared by Lieutenant Colonel Faupel of the General Staff in late October 1918. "[T]he circulation of newspapers and pamphlets of the Independent Social Democrats, openly and secretly inciting to revolution, has a demoralizing effect at present ... Measures must be taken immediately to prevent and render punishable the distribution of such pamphlets and newspapers in the Army."[36] Of course, by October, such measures, even if successful, would have had little effect on the outcome of the war.

The Allies also did their best to demoralize the German soldier. The impact of their efforts was recorded in the history of a field artillery regiment.

In the trenches the troops were bombarded with leaflets. At first, German troops were amused by the contents. But the repetition as well as the conditions under which the troops had to live, caused the propaganda to eventually have an effect. The propaganda emphasized the hunger in Germany, aggravation between Bavarians, Badenese and Württemburgers against the Prussians, the war aims of the Junkers and Pan-Germans and, above all, militarism.[37]

---

[35] For examples of such measures see *Quellen zur Geschichte des Parlamentarismus und der politische Parteien* (Düsseldorf: Droste Verlag, 1970), vols. I and II, *Militär und Innenpolitik 1914–1918*, ed. Wilhelm Deist (hereafter *Quellen*): threats (Document No. 404: Telegramm des Chefs der Nachrichtenabteilung im Generalstab des Feldheeres an das Kriegspresseamt. Anordnung von Massnahmen gegen den "Vorwärts." Dated June 11, 1917, 1091–2); prohibition of political activity (Document No. 416: Auszug aus den Aufzeichnungen aus der Pressbesprechung. Stellungnahme des Vertreters des Kriegspressamts zur Frage der Freigabe eines sowjetrussischen Funkspruchs. Dated December 31, 1917. 1120–1); and suppression (Document No. 429: Auszug aus den Aufzeichnungen aus der Pressbesprechung. Stellungnahme des Vetreters des Oberkommandos in den Marken zu den Verbot des "Vorwärts." Dated January 30, 1918, 1141–3).

[36] *The United States in the World War, 1917–1919: The Armistice Agreement and Related Documents* (Washington, DC: Center of Military History, 1991), Vol. XI, 459.

[37] Eugen Taischik, *Das kgl. Preuss. 2. Rhein. Feldart. Nr. 23 im Weltkrieg* (Altenburg, 1928), 245. Between May and July, for example, the BEF launched 4 million leaflets

The effect of Allied propaganda was greater than the German chain of command wished to admit at the time. After the war, Hindenburg conceded, "The enemy said in his innumerable leaflets that he did not mean to be hard with us, that we should only be patient and renounce all that we have conquered, then all would be well ... Such the soldiers read and discussed. The soldiers thought surely these could not all be lies, and permitted themselves to be poisoned and poisoned others."[38]

Throughout most the war, there was a continuous if limited contact between the front and the German homeland. The censors scrutinized the flow of mail though the *Feldpost*, while soldier leaves – with a good rail connection the *Frontkämpfer* could be home in matter of hours – along with newspapers and magazines, kept the lines of communications open. As the war dragged on, the flow of mail, leave-takers, and publications led to a curious war of words between the Field Army and the Deputy Corps Commanders who were responsible for order in the corps districts of the homeland. The OHL blamed the home front for undermining the morale of the combat units, while the military and civilian authorities inside Germany accused the soldiers who came home on leave of depressing the civilian populace with their stories of slaughter and futility. Both were justified. Thus, in a meeting of the imperial cabinet on October 17, when Ludendorff demanded a greater levy of replacements and complained of the depressing effect the home front was having on the Field Army, the Social Democrat minister Phillip Scheidemann responded, "I am willing to believe that hundreds of thousands of men can be mobilized for the army, but any man deceives himself who believes that these hundreds of thousands would raise the spirit of the army. It is my firm conviction that the contrary would be the case." After complaining of the depressing effect of the failed U-boat campaign, the clear evidence of Allied material superiority, and the collapse of Germany's allies, Scheidemann continued, "Men on leave come from the army with ugly stories; returning from home they carry bad news back to the army. This exchange of ideas depresses public spirit. We would be deceiving ourselves, if we tried to gloss it over."[39] Scheidemann's response to Ludendorff suggested the synergistic effect of homeland and front-line despair. As long as the army gave front-line troops opportunity to interact with the unhappy

---

at the German lines. Christoph Jahr, "Bei einer geschlagenen Armee ist der Klugste, wer zuerst davonlauft. Das Problem der Desertion im deutschen und britischen Heer 1918," in Düppler and Gross, eds., *Kriegsende 1918*, 259.

[38] Hindenburg's memoirs quoted in George Bruntz, "Allied Propaganda and the Collapse of German Morale in 1918." *Public Opinion Quarterly*, 2, 1 (Jan. 1938), 70.

[39] Ralph H. Lutz, ed., *Fall of the German Empire, 1914–1918* (Stanford University Press, 1932), vol. II, 481.

civilian population back home, there would be a corresponding depressing effect on the front.

The front-line soldier who had returned from leave in Germany was a critical source of information to his comrades in the trenches. The soldier in the line could scoff at Allied leaflets and socialist tracts, but he would certainly have listened closely to the reports on hunger, war-weariness, and political agitation the men in his unit brought back from the homeland.[40] Leave was, of course, the chance for the front-line soldier to put the strain of front-line duty behind him and the opportunity for exposure to the same revolutionary pressures faced by the troops in the homeland. Finally, leave allowed the *Frontkämpfer* the time to reflect on the nature of his experience and the prospects for the future. Only when the army halted leaves from the Western Front in the last weeks of the war, was this input to soldier attitudes cut off.

Under normal circumstances, the soldier at the front received news of events in Germany within several days of the actual event;[41] however, shortly after November 9, front-line units lost contact with the homeland as revolutionary activity and its attendant disorder interrupted the flow of mail to the front.[42] This interruption had two effects. First, it provoked anxiety among common soldiers over the circumstances of their homes and families. Secondly, the enlisted ranks became dependent on their superiors for information on events outside of the unit. It was a tense condition where rumors carried great weight. One soldier wrote in November, "The overall situation was lawless and we worried about what might be going on in our hometown. Rumor had it that some good and loyal divisions were fighting inside Germany to restore order."[43]

The last days of the war saw the troops on the Western Front cut off from news from the homeland. As we will see, the information vacuum during this pivotal time served to reinforce the efforts of the officer

[40] Wilhelm Groener, Ludendorff's replacement as the German Army's First Quartermaster General, emphasized this point in his memoirs. *Lebenserinnerungen: Jugend, Generalstab, Weltkrieg*, ed. Hiller von Gaertringen (Göttingen: Vandenhoeck and Ruprecht, 1957), 492.
[41] According to his diary, Lieutenant Herbert Sulzbach, an artillery officer at the front, knew within three days of Ludendorff's relief (October 26). He heard of the Kiel mutinies six days after the first outbreak. Herbert Sulzbach, *With the German Guns: Four Years on the Western Front, 1914–1918* (Hamden, CT: Archon Books, 1935, reprinted 1998), 235 and 246.
[42] German General Staff, *Die Rückführung des Westheeres* (Berlin: Mittler and Son, 1919), 28.
[43] Fritz Nagel, *Fritz: The World War I Memoirs of a German Lieutenant*, ed. Richard Baumgartner (Huntington, WV: Der Angriff, 1981), 106.

corps to insulate the *Westheer* from the infectious spread of revolutionary
sentiment.

Alienation: the uneven burdens of total war

In February 1918, Josef Huber, a soldier *"im Felde"* (in the field), wrote a
letter to the *Oberbürgemeister* of Düsseldorf. In the letter, Huber referred
to a speech of January 22, in which the lord mayor had asserted that
every child born to a German family represented a strengthening of the
nation. What are these children to be used for, Huber asked? The way
things were going, the boys will be used as cannon-fodder and the girls
will be pressed into service in an armaments factory. It was a fine thing
to demand a victor's peace in the current war,

[B]ut not for us in the trenches or the shell holes, in my case in Flanders, or
on the Somme, where almost all of us were. We in the field these past three
and a half years have slowly had our belly-full, not only of this dog's life [at the
front] but also with the victors and heroes behind mother's skirts at home, who
fight there so bravely as long as others are putting their lives on the line at the
front.[44]

Not every front-line soldier was ready to offer a public challenge to a
major government official, but Huber's letter represented an outlook
that was widespread in the German Army in the last year of the war.
Along with the war-weariness we have considered, there was a perva-
sive conviction that the war experienced by the men in the trenches was
vastly different from the war experienced by the rest of the German
nation.

Such feelings were, most likely, inevitable in what has been called
history's "first total war." The idea of "total war" is, of course, a the-
oretical construct; as Clausewitz once noted, no war makes absolute
demands on a nation's resources and no conflict sees the belligerents
able or willing to abandon all restraints on the use of violence. However,
the First World War came far closer to the "ideal" of totality than any
previous war, and, for Germany, this meant that a burden of sacrifice
and suffering was borne by every element of society. Yet the soldiers in
the trenches were well aware that the burdens were not shared equally.
As the "Great War" solidified the idea of a "front" and a "rear," those
in the trenches knew they were doing the dying as well as taking on
a disproportionate share of the suffering. As the war progressed, the
German front-line soldier, like his Allied counterparts on the other
side of No Man's Land, came to envy and often despise those who had

[44] BA-MA, PH 2/479 *Feldpost* letter dated Feb. 15, 1918.

not suffered what he had suffered and those who could not understand
what he had been through.

If such alienation is common to soldiers in modern war, it was exacerbated for German combat soldiers by the real and perceived abuses
of privilege and power in the rear areas of the army and the homeland.
A deep rift developed between men in the front-line formations and
the soldiers in the *Etappe*, the staffs, the Home Army, and those in the
civilian population perceived to be benefiting from the war. This rift
produced tensions that carried over into the postwar period.

Among those at the front, there was a special disdain for the troops
in the *Etappe*. Within combat units, stories of the plush life led by the
shirkers in the rear were legion. One soldier, a former miner who later
deserted, wrote bitterly that "the worst 'hyenas' of the battlefield are to
be found in the ammunition and transport trains ... Compared with
the soldiers fighting at the front, it is easy for them to find food ...
To them, war is a business, because they largely take possession of all
that is of any value."[45] Soldiers at the front circulated a poem entitled
"Etappenschweine" [rear-area swine]. It complained that those in the
rear had access to wine, women, and better rations while portraying
themselves as much-decorated heroes. The final stanza reads:

> With your flabby and pale faces,
> You bloated, cowering mob,
> We hope your loutish life
> Will give not one of you proud memories.
>   We are called by love and loyalty,
>   You remain sows of the rear![46]

Late in the war, an officer passing through the *Etappe* on the way to
the front observed with loathing, "Where do all these gray crowds come
from, seeing that leave has been entirely stopped? These are the slack-
ers who are always looking for their unit, but whose most fervent hope
is that they will never find it."[47] He and other front-line soldiers were
embittered by what they saw in the rear areas of the army in Belgium
and France. A union leader wrote Hindenburg:

If the men go on furlough, they are very much amazed to see that the line of
communications zone is swarming with men and that officers of all ranks are

[45] No author cited, *A German War Deserter's Experience*, trans. J. Koettgen (New York:
1917), 106.
[46] BA-MA, Msg. 2/930; poem taken from a *Feldpostbrief* (field letter), undated. I am
indebted to Alexander Watson for calling my attention to this bit of soldier doggerel.
[47] Anonymous diary entry of October 23, 1918 in *Why Germany Capitulated on November
11, 1918: A Brief Study Based on Documents in the Possession of the French General Staff*
(London: Hodder and Stoughton, 1919), 58.

to be seen whereas there is a lack of officers at the front … Much complaint is also heard about the poor quality and insufficient amount of rations at the front. The men compare it with in the food in the line of communications zone, where a great deal of buying and trading is done. Everybody lives well.[48]

Not everyone in the rear lived well; yet that was the prevailing perception among the troops at the front.

The scorn of the combat soldier was not restricted solely to the men of the supply depots and ammunition columns. The conditions of the war separated the front-line fighter from the higher-level staff and commanders. The relative safety of these high-ranking personnel as well as their ignorance of conditions at the front made them special targets of resentment by both officers and men in the trenches. Such staffs, wrote one critic, "became removed from all comprehension not only of the needs but also the physical and moral capabilities of the troops."[49] After the war, another observer wrote:

The officers in the trenches frequently had to share both dangers and meals with the rank and file. The close comradeship sometimes entailed a definite leveling process … Also there emerged an antipathy to a certain extent common to both soldiers and officers in the trenches against rear officers and the General Staff. These, for their part, blamed the trench officers for their narrow-mindedness.[50]

A particular grievance of soldiers in the line was the belief that higher-level staffs were deluded by excessively optimistic reports submitted by intermediate headquarters. They called the resulting situation *Frontfremdheit*, roughly "unfamiliarity with the front."[51]

By the end of the war, the front-line soldier's feelings of alienation transcended hostility toward the staffs and the "hyenas" of the rear

[48] Ludwig Lewinsohn, *Die Revolution an der Westfront* (Charlottenburg: Mundus Verlagsanstalt, 1919), 26. The men in the rear areas had some reason to reciprocate this ill will. With food scarce everywhere, the army allocated a greater share to soldiers at the front than those in the rear (though soldiers in *Etappe* were likely to have greater opportunity to "scrounge" additional food). War Office, *Statistics of the Military Effort of the British Empire during the Great War. 1914–1920* (London, 1922) and Kriegsgeschichtlichen Forschungsanstalt des Heeres, *Der Weltkrieg 1914 bis 1918*, vol. XIV, 31.
[49] Martin Hobohm in *UDZ*, IX (i), 244.
[50] Hans E. Fried, *The Guilt of the German Army* (New York: Macmillan, 1942), 163. See also Albrecht von Thaer, *Generalstabdienst an der Front und in der OHL* (Göttingen: Vandenhoeck und Ruprecht, 1958), 187–8. As the title suggests, von Thaer spent time at both the front and the OHL and his diary reflects the disgust of a front-line officer for the OHL's lack of awareness of true conditions at the front.
[51] Kurt Anker, *Unsere Stunde kommt! Errinerungen und Betrachtungen über das nachrevolutionäre Deutschland* (Leipzig: Leipzig Graphische Werk, 1923), 32.

area. In many cases, the soldier in the trenches felt abandoned by the homeland itself. Lieutenant Rudolf Binding wrote:

If one cast one's eyes from the Front, where there is certainly not much enthusiasm these days, back homewards, they meet a very pitiful sight. Many men will ask themselves whether there is any sense in going back, and some will envy those who have no home to go to. The only consolation to be derived from the prospect lies in the thought that all the screaming in Parliament and between parties is quite a superficial phenomenon, since all that is best, youngest and strongest in the country is at the Front.[52]

Another officer, Franz Schauwecker, home on leave in the last year of the war, wrote, "One appears alien in one's own country. It is best to go out there again. Out there, meaning the front."[53]

Both Binding and Schauwecker were officers. However, the German historian Anne Lipp has used an analysis of trench newspapers to refine our understanding of how the common German soldier viewed the "home front." She finds that the troops tended to put the civilian population into three categories: (1) immediate family, (2) war profiteers (*Kriegsgewinnler*) and "pub strategists" (*Wirtshausstrategen*), and (3) the striking workers and anti-war activists.[54] To the first two groups, the *Frontbürger* ("citizen of the front") maintained a consistently antagonistic attitude. Family members were adored and missed. On the other hand, the front-line troops felt special resentment for those on the home front who were enriched by the war. The older soldiers supporting a family held especially harsh feelings toward those being paid the inflated wages of the armaments industry. Also detested were those who sought to turn the conflict into a war of annexation. After the war an army doctor recalled:

The only war aim he [the front-line soldier] recognizes and can feel with his entire being was the motto: we fight a defensive war. Soon, though, in wide circles outside the front, the desire to defend gave way to the desire for conquest ... In every case, the troops responded negatively to efforts for 'securing of strategic position' and 'boundary rectifications' in the east and west ... And, when in the summer the successes that should have ended the war failed to occur, then the 'Front' lost all sympathy for the conduct of those circles who, even in July 1918, refused a peace based on *status quo ante*. The front-fighter showed

[52] Rudolf Binding, *A Fatalist at War* (New York: Houghton, Mifflin, 1929),189.
[53] Franz Schauwecker quoted in Eric Leeds, *No Man's Land: Combat and Identity in World War I* (Cambridge University Press, 1979), 206.
[54] Anne Lipp, "Heimatwahrnehmung und soldatisches 'Kriegserlebnis'," in *Kriegserfahrungen. Studien zur Sozial- und Mentalitätsgeschichte des Ersten Weltkriegs*, ed. Gerhard Hirschfeld, Gerd Krumreich, Dieter Langewiesche, and Hans-Peter Ullmann (Essen: Schriften der Bibliothek für Zeitgeschichte, 1997), 225–46.

an increasing exasperation against those in the homeland, in the army's rear areas, and with the high staff's active agitation for the goals of the Fatherland Party [a policy which included aggressive annexations].[55]

To the third group, striking workers and anti-war activists, soldier sentiment seemed to follow the arc of Germany's fortunes on the battlefield. In the spring of 1918, when the troops anticipated that the coming offensive would bring victory and peace, the men at the front were hostile to the striking workers inside Germany. They felt that the likely interruption of production of ammunition supplies and other war *matériel* undermined the possibility their attacks would end the war. ("Why shouldn't we turn our mortars and machine guns around for a day and make mincemeat out of these dishonorable and ignoble dregs of the German people?"[56]) Months later, after the Ludendorff offensives had foundered, the soldiers at the front were much more likely to see any form of anti-war activism in the homeland as a positive step in relieving their own misery.[57]

The men in the trenches in late 1918 had little opportunity for profound reflection on political matters; they nonetheless had cause and sufficient emotional energy to resent those who did not share their terrible experience. The alienation they felt toward those beyond the front would find expression in their response to the revolution and those who made it.

Alienation was a product of experience, and decisions made by the army and soldier himself shaped the nature of the soldier's experience.

Selection: the choices of the High Command and the choices of the individual

At the beginning of 1918, the "Second OHL," the duumvirate of Hindenburg and Ludendorff, made extraordinary efforts to gather the best possible human material for the decisive effort in the West. The average age, physical condition, and training of the combat troops on the Western Front marked them as the most "battle worthy" members of the Kaiser's army. As we shall see, these same factors, taken together as the basis of combat effectiveness, were seen by Germany's military leaders as guarantors of political reliability in a time of revolutionary turmoil.

The front-line soldiers of the German Army formed a relatively small elite within the Imperial Army. In an army of some 6 million

---

[55] *Ibid.*, 239.   [56] *Ibid.*, 240.   [57] *Ibid.*, 241.

men and a "Field Army" in France of at least 3 million,[58] probably no more than 1.5 million could be classified as "front-line" troops.[59] Two mechanisms determined the composition of this core force: (1) the policies of the OHL, which had aimed to supply the Western Front with the best available human material, and (2) the choices made by soldiers themselves during a period in the war when army discipline was collapsing.

The beginning of 1918 had seen the OHL struggling to cope with an acute manpower shortage. The losses of 1917 had just barely been made up, and Ludendorff's plans for a massive offensive in the spring meant that the army needed to strengthen the combat divisions deployed in France and Belgium by every available means. Ludendorff decided to centralize the control of manpower replacement within his own head-quarters. (Up to that point in the war, the replacement of losses had been the responsibility of individual corps and divisions and their respective *Ersatz* depots within the recruiting districts of the empire.) The First Quartermaster General used his new control to systematically strip the units outside the Western Front of their best soldiers.[60]

The occupation forces in the east felt the effects of the First Quartermaster General's manpower program even before the final sign-ing of the Brest-Litovsk treaty. As the best divisions of the *Ostheer* were ordered west to reinforce the upcoming offensives, they pulled all their soldiers over thirty-five and all fathers of large families out of the ranks and exchanged them for younger men from units remaining on occu-pation duty. Thus, the only soldiers under thirty-five remaining in the east were 150,000 recruits from the class of 1899 who were undergoing training. In the spring of 1918, Ludendorff began to make demands of this pool of youthful manpower as well. Also remaining in Russia were soldiers who, because they were recruited from the former French prov-inces of Alsace-Lorraine, were considered less than completely reliable. Thus, in October 1918, the High Command East (*Oberbefehlshaber Ost* or *Oberost*) indicated that a remarkable 14 percent of their reported strength was Alsatian.[61]

The impact of Ludendorff's selection process may be seen in the example of the 83rd Infantry Division stationed in Galicia in early 1918. From an authorized strength of approximately 12,000 men, the 83rd found itself short 2,000. From the men that remained, 1,785 were

---

[58] See "A Note about Numbers" at the end of Chapter 1.
[59] See footnote 4, Chapter 1.
[60] The replacement situation was described by General v. Kuhl in his testimony in *UDZ*, III, 43.
[61] *Ibid.*, 61.

between 36 and 41 years old, and 1,626 were over 42. Additionally, 1,353 of the divisions were fathers with more than 4 children, and 1,055 were from Alsace-Lorraine.[62]

Along with the pick of the men from the east, the *Westheer* also received the cream of the youthful replacement crop. When the army called year group 1899 to the colors in the autumn of 1917, it sent those considered most physically and mentally mature to the recruit depots in France and Belgium. As these conscripts completed their training, the Field Army fed them into front-line formations.[63] (Year group 1900 reported for duty in October and November 1918, though most of its members remained part of the Home Army during the revolution.)[64]

Other parts of the army were "combed out" for men capable of front-line duty. In the summer of 1918, Ludendorff told subordinate commanders that the situation made it necessary "to get every physically fit man to the combat troops and to use men fit only for garrison deployment and labor in the most economical manner."[65] Thus, the army attempted to reach down into the homeland garrisons and the *Etappe* to reinforce the front. The OHL even made claims on laborers in "essential" war industries and, as we have seen, prisoners returned from Russian captivity.

These measures proved insufficient to meet the ravenous requirements of the Western Front in 1918. The rear echelon commanders were able to procure exemptions for half the men chosen for front-line duty, while industrial leaders were largely successful in preventing the diversion of factory workers into uniform in any significant numbers.[66] Thus, some two-thirds of the replacements fed into the depleted front-line divisions in the last year of the war were wounded veterans from the Western Front judged sufficiently recovered to rejoin the fight.[67]

Those we consider *Frontschweine*, then, were predominantly the soldiers who were serving on the Western Front at the beginning of the year, selected conscripts from the class of 1899, and the best soldiers the Eastern Front had to offer at that stage in the war. Again, they tended to be younger than the rest of the army, more physically capable, and more

---

[62] *Ibid.*, 62–3.   [63] *Ibid.*, 59.

[64] Ernst Schmidt, *Heimatheer und Revolution: Die militärischen Gewalten im Heimatgebiet zwischen Oktoberreform und Novemberrevolution* (Stuttgart: Deutsche Verlags-Anstalt, 1981), 245–6.

[65] *The US Army in the World War, 1917–1919*, vol. XI, *American Occupation of Germany* (Washington, DC: Center for Military History; reprinted 1991), 327.

[66] Von Kuhl in *UDZ*, III, 71. In the first quarter of 1918 the number of those exempted for war work actually rose by 123,000 (*ibid.*, 66).

[67] *Ibid.*, 68.

completely trained.[68] With regard to the analysis that is presented in the following chapters, the key question then becomes can these characteristics be related to the front-line soldiers' political behavior during the overthrow of the monarchy and the days that followed that event?

The nature of military socialization as explored in recent military history may indicate a partial answer. For almost every modern army, the purpose of an inductee's initial training is to break the ties with civilian society. If the training is successful then the soldier's sense of personal identity is, to some extent, aligned to the institutions of the military. The more complete the soldier's socialization, the less likely he would be to rebel against the authority of those above him in the military chain of command.

Traditionally, armies have found that those most susceptible to military socialization are young men, preferably farm boys, just out of school, with relatively little experience of the world, in either creating their own families or establishing themselves in the world of work. Those least susceptible are likely to be older men with a more urbanized background who have had time to develop strong ties to family, work, and community, the kind of ties that would compete with the military's requirements for allegiance and obedience.[69]

The military socialization process, the alignment of personal values and behavior with the values and behavior required by the army, was more likely to be well advanced among the three groups found on the Western Front than among the other groups in the German Army. The process was certainly most complete among those survivors of the prewar army's active and reserve formations. With the exception of a handful of cavalry units on the Eastern Front, all of these prewar units were deployed on the Western Front.[70] Those that arrived on the Western Front as replacements between 1914 and 1917 might not be nearly as "militarized" as those who came from the prewar army. Nevertheless, one can assume that those who joined the army in the first several years of the

[68] This is a generalization which does not account for the older men in the *Landwehr* units on the Western Front. These, for the most part, held quiet sectors on the southern end of the theater. Not surprisingly, Allied intelligence rated all German units on the Eastern Front in 1918 as third- or fourth-class, while all first- and second-class divisions were deployed in the West. See Records of the Intelligence Section of the General Staff, AEF, *Histories of Two Hundred and Fifty-One Divisions in the German Army Which Participated in the War (1914–1918)* (Washington, DC: G.P.O. 1920). Hereafter, AEF G2, *251 Divisions*.
[69] The role of socialization is considered in Kurt Lang, *Military Institutions and the Sociology of War. A Review of the Literature with Annotated Bibliography* (Beverly Hills: Sage, 1972), 55.
[70] "The Break-up of the German Armies on the Russian Front in November 1918." *Army Quarterly* (UK), 34, 1 (April 1937), 34.

war had ample time for training and integration. They had also matured as soldiers in an environment where patriotism was still esteemed and the war was still viewed as righteous defense of the Fatherland. As John Keegan wrote in trying to explain the German Army's resilience during the First World War, the German soldiers of 1914–17 had been raised on "a diet of victory."[71] If they remained with their units into the waning days of 1918, they did so as much by positive choice as by compulsion. Meanwhile, among the conscripts of the class of 1899, there may have been time during the year for units to train them and integrate them among the veterans, although the class of 1900 was another matter entirely. The younger men transferred from units in the East were also an uncertain reinforcement. They shared the youth of many of their counterparts in the West, but many had been "tainted" by fraternization with the Bolsheviks. Like their comrades returned from captivity, their deployment to the Western Front proved a mixed blessing to army commanders there.[72] Reflecting on this, Crown Prince Rupprecht of Bavaria, serving as an army group commander on the Western Front, recorded in his diary a conversation with Colonel Wilhelm Heye of the OHL on October 20, 1918. Heye had proposed that twenty divisions would be brought from the East to reinforce the Western Front in order to remedy the desperate manpower situation. Rupprecht was dubious, telling Heye that most of these men were over thirty-five. Their most recent service had been "police duty," which meant they lacked any experience of war in the West. Worse, they had been tainted by "Bolshevik ideas."[73] Staffs at lower levels were making similar assessments. On September 24, the 213th Brigade offered this evaluation of its replacements.

The different forms of replacement – consisting partly of recruits, partly of old *Ostkämpfern* who had been exempt for years and who lack any knowledge of fighting methods in the West, partly of convalescents from other units, who, in part, have returned from the homeland with very poor attitudes – have, due to the lack of opportunity to train together and become acquainted with one another, created the most unfortunate relations [within the unit].[74]

[71] John Keegan, *The Face of Battle* (London: Jonathan Cape, 1976), 271–2. In the same section of the book, Keegan suggests that the armies of the First World War seemed to break, as the Russians, French, and Italians did in 1917, in their third year of war at the point where casualties had risen to equal the number of men in the prewar cadres. Neither the British nor German Army, he conceded, fits this predictive model.
[72] Kriegsgeschichtlichen Forschungsanstalt des Heeres, *Der Weltkrieg, 1914 bis 1918* (Bonn: Bundesarchiv, 1956 reprint), vol. XIV, 523.
[73] Rupprecht, Crown Prince of Bavaria, *In Treue Fest: Mein Kriegstagebuch*, ed. Eugen von Frauenholz (Berlin: Mittler und Sohn, 1929), diary entry for October 20, 1918, vol. II, 375–6.
[74] NARA, RG 165, Box 163, Folder 1, 107th Infantry Div. War Diary and Annexes, 27. Along with highlighting the poor quality of replacements, the report also reinforces

Clearly, the elements of the German Army beyond the front line fared less well against the test of military socialization. At the moment of the revolution in early November, the *Ostheer* was made up largely of older men from the *Landwehr* and *Landsturm*. For these graybeards, entry-level military training and socialization was a thing of the distant past, replaced in consciousness and the establishment of identity by ties with family, work, community and, frequently, party affiliation.[75] By contrast, the Home Army consisted predominately of young, untrained draftees as well as older men considered unfit for anything but garrison duty. For this mixed bag of men as well, either serving out the war in monotonous jobs or waiting in anxiety for the next troop levy for the front, socialization was often incomplete or unsuccessful. The Social Democratic leader, Gustav Noske, sent to bring order in the mutinous North Sea ports in November, wrote a description of the young soldiers he found in the *Ersatz* units. "In the casernes at the beginning of the Armistice, the youngest conscripts were billeted with the *Landsturm* people of the oldest year groups ... Already in Kiel, I was able to make the observation that all of the young people with little or no training were the most insubordinate elements. In Berlin this impression was sharper still ... Deputations of young fellows came to me demanding discharge and speaking with an insolence that one would have to experience in order to believe it."[76]

As for the older soldiers, one finds special significance in the leadership of the soldiers' councils formed after the overthrow of the chain of command in the homeland garrisons. They were, disproportionately, mature men with strong ties to their communities (bureaucrats, artisans, small businessmen, academics, etc.). Experienced Social Democratic Party leaders were an especially conspicuous element.[77]

The men at the front were younger and, if they had served for any length of time, were likely to be more adapted to the subordination

the argument made earlier about isolation. It seemed that the more contact a soldier had with the home front or foreigners with seditious ideas, the less reliable that soldier was going to be.

[75] In their famous study of German troops in the Second World War, Shils and Janowitz found that married men with large families had ties that "prevented insuperably strong ties to the army unit." Edward Shils and Morris Janowitz, "Cohesion and Disintegration in the Wehrmacht in World War II," in *Motivating Soldiers: Morale or Mutiny*, ed. Peter Karsten (New York: Garland Publishing, 1998), 286, fn. 9.

[76] Gustav Noske, *Von Kiel bis Kapp: Zur Geschichte der deutschen Revolution* (Berlin, 1920), 77. In a report of October 3, the 117th Infantry Division reported that, of the 900 replacements called forward to join the unit, some 115 were awaiting sentencing for breaches of military discipline. NARA, RG 165, Box 164, Folder I, 117th Infantry Division War Diary and Annexes, 12–13.

[77] Kluge, *Soldatenräte und Revolution*, 110.

found in military service. Such men made up the *Stammmannschaften* that units relied on to hold the line in the last weeks of the war. When that essential "core" was gone, then little could be expected of a unit. The 213th Brigade again: "It must be added, that the moral value of the troops is thus considerably diminished, because no good core (*Stamm*) is available that can take the new, badly influenced new men – note the report of the leader of the last March (replacement) battalion – and assimilate and prepare them without harm [to the unit]."[78] One senses, then, a generation gap on either side of the age cohort of these twenty-something veterans: on one end were the younger replacements, alienated teenagers who had grown up in the embittered and war-weary Home Front; on the other end; the older family men whose devotion to family, work, and political party competed with the loyalties demanded by military service. Holding a unit together in 1918 meant heavy reliance on the veterans in the "middle." In the unit records, one frequently finds orders like the one from the 80th Infantry Brigade that directed that straggler control points be commanded by an energetic officer supported by "several reliable, older soldiers."[79] The "older" men, of course were not the oldest in age, but rather those who had been at the front the longest.

Through the course of the war, the soldiers who formed the *Stammmannschaften* came to the front in units or as individuals on orders from army's chain of command. As we will see, if the men in this core element remained there until the end of the war, it was largely by choice rather than the coercion of military authorities. The bonds of discipline that held the German Imperial Army together began to loosen in late 1917 and early 1918, and this, coupled with the growing unpopularity of front-line duty, caused perhaps hundreds of thousands of soldiers to evade that duty in a variety of ways. With the decline in discipline and the chaotic situation at the front, leaving one's unit became both easier and less risky. The process of disintegration accelerated after the failure of the Ludendorff offensives, as German soldiers increasingly believed they were fighting for a lost cause. When armistice negotiations began, the process of disintegration gathered even more momentum; no soldier wants to be the last to die in a lost cause. Those who remained in the trenches could only hope to survive until their leaders made peace.[80]

[78] NARA, RG 165, Box 163, Folder I, 107th Infantry Division War Diary and Annexes, 28.
[79] BA-MA, PH/8/I-157, 15th Infantry Division Subordinate Units, Folder II, order of Sep. 29, 1918, 48.
[80] For a description of the discipline at and behind the front during the last days of the war, see Volkmann, *Der Marxismus und das deutsche Heer*, 202–4. For a more

Both during and after the war, conservatives and apologists for the officer corps blamed the socialist parties for undermining the discipline of the German Army. The critics made special note of such measures as the Reichstag amendment of April 25, 1917, sponsored by the socialists, which reduced the maximum punishments that could be awarded for military offenses. The amendment also directed all imprisonments be carried out within Germany.[81] Before that, the army had formed military prisoners into penal units for duty at or near the front. The amendment enabled a soldier at the front to avoid the dangers of combat if he was willing to endure a period of imprisonment. A front-line officer complained of the reduced punishments, writing that a deserter, "risks only captivity, and of long duration. A man with no sense of honor much prefers to find himself in captivity rather than a military penal company. After the peace he reckons with certainty on amnesty." Such attitudes, the officer continued, were contagious.[82]

Depressed morale, desertion, and localized acts of mutiny had cropped up already during the summer of 1917.[83] Even more evidence of the breakdown of German discipline came during the Ludendorff offensives as entire German units broke off their attacks to loot Allied stores.[84] As the situation worsened, the OHL appealed to the war ministry to take action. In July 1918, Ludendorff recommended more severe sentences, to include a more liberal application of the death sentence. In August, he cited a report from the *Jäger* Division that troop commanders "more and more demand the death penalty for repeated cowardice in the face of the enemy."[85] The war minister, von Stein, responded by directing that any sentence of over six weeks be served in

recent interpretation: Wilhelm Deist, "Verdeckter Militärstreik im Kriegsjahr 1918?" in *Der Krieg des kleinen Mannes: Eine Militärgeschichte von unten*, ed. Wolfram Wette (Munich: Piper, 1995), 146–67. (Both accounts must be read with caution, because both authors have ideological reason [albeit from different points of the political spectrum] to emphasize the disintegration in the German Army; Volkmann in order to emphasize the extent of defeatist subversion and Deist to highlight the bankruptcy of the Hohenzollern system.)

[81] Discussion of the penal system from Kriegsgeschichtlichen Forschungsanstalt, *Weltkrieg*, XIV, 520.
[82] *Quellen*, II, 1288, fn. 2.
[83] Using French general staff documents, Strachan refers to localized mutinies among Saxon, Württemburg, and even Prussian units in 1917. Strachan, "Morale of the German Army," 387.
[84] Alexander Griebel, "Das Jahr 1918 im Lichte Neuer Publikation." *Vierteljahrshefte für Zeitgeschichte*, 6, 4 (1958), 362–7. The article cites one battalion commander's belief that the failure of the spring offensives was largely caused by the alcohol looted by advancing German troops.
[85] Jahr, "Bei einer geschlagenen Armee," 245.

a front-line penal unit and that officers would henceforth be authorized to use weapons to correct insubordination. [86]

Despite these eleventh-hour measures, the military penal system of the German Army was, arguably, the most lenient of all the major belligerent nations. During the entire war, the Germans carried out only forty-eight executions. This should be compared to 346 executions in the considerably smaller British Army. The French executed forty-nine soldiers just in response to the mutiny of 1917,[87] while, in the aftermath of Caporetto, the Italians carried out daily executions. Significantly, the only death sentences carried out for desertion in the German Army were for those instances taking place "in the presence of the enemy ("*vor dem Feinde*").[88]

Clearly, the fearful or war-weary German soldier had relatively little to fear if he left a troop train and got "lost" on the way to the front. In 1918, the result was widespread increase in a phenomenon called "*Drückebergerei.*" The comprehensive *Collins German Dictionary* defines *Drückebergerei* as "shirking" or "skiving" (a British term).[89] In the usage of the German Army of the First World War, the word could mean anything from finding oneself a cushy job in the rear to outright desertion. Most commonly, it referred to the soldier who "became separated" from his unit somewhere in the rear area and never found his way back.[90] To German commanders, in the summer and fall of 1918, the term *Drückebergerei* represented a disastrous hemorrhaging of front-line strength. No certain figures can be given for the number of *Drückeberger* behind the line at the moment of the armistice, but after the war the Reichstag committee charged with investigating the causes of Germany's collapse in 1918 recorded estimates of between 300,000 men and up to a million.[91] The army's official history

---

[86] Kriegsgeschichtlichen Forschungsanstalt, *Weltkrieg*, XIV, 520.

[87] Smith, *Between Mutiny and Obedience*, 213.

[88] Execution figures from the testimony of E.O. Volkmann, in *UDZ*, XI (ii), 64.

[89] *Collins German–English English–German Dictionary*, ed. Peter Terrell *et al.* (New York: HarperCollins, 1991), 175

[90] German Army regulations made intent to stay away a necessary condition for proving desertion as opposed to "unauthorized absence." Jahr, "Bei einer geschlagenen Armee," 245–6.

[91] Martin Hobohm, who authored a study of social grievances in the German Army for the Reichstag Investigating Committee, judges the numbers of deserters behind the line at 300,000. Erich Volkmann, a retired officer who rebutted Hobohm in a companion volume, estimated the number at as many as a million. See Hobohm in *UDZ*, XI (i), 184 and Volkmann in *UDZ*, XI (ii), 66, respectively. Hobohm's findings have been reprinted in summary form in a more recent anthology, *Der Krieg des kleinen Mannes: Eine Militärgeschichte von unten*, ed. Wolfram Wette (Munich: Piper, 1995, 136–5.

put the figure as high as 1.5 million.[92] More recently, scholars have challenged these numbers as exaggerated. The research of scholars like Christoph Jahr and Alex Watson has suggested the problem of desertion and *Drückebergerei* was not as widespread as originally thought.[93] Nevertheless, enough anecdotal evidence exists in unit reports and eye-witness accounts to indicate, by late 1918, that the number of soldiers of leaving their units was growing.

One of the most common ways for a soldier to evade duty at the front was to leave a troop train somewhere in Belgium or France.[94] In one instance, in May 1918, a unit reported that, from a shipment of 76 NCOs and 555 men destined for the front, three NCOs and 80 men were missing by the time the train reached its destination.[95] A report from the OHL in June 1918 estimated that 10 percent of the replacements dispatched from Germany failed to arrive at their units.[96] Once separated from his unit, the *Drückeberger* would often remain around a nearby train station, for such installations offered opportunities to steal from supply trains and, if desired, catch a train ride to Germany. As a result, a major rail hub such as Namur might have as many as 40,000 deserters in its immediate vicinity. Other large stations such Maubeuge, Liège, and Brussels supported similar small armies of *Drückeberger*.[97]

That the German Army let the situation get so far out of hand is one of the puzzles of the war. In mid October, Ludendorff demanded that army commanders restore order in their rear areas. "The suspension of furloughs on the Western Front offers an opportunity to put a definite stop to the disorder which the overcrowding of railroad stations, the prevalence of unauthorized absences of troops, and the

---

[92] Kriegsgeschichtlichen Forschungsanstalt, *Weltkrieg*, XIV, 760.

[93] Christoph Jahr, *Gewöhnliche Soldaten Desertion und Deserteure im deutschen und britischen Heer, 1914–1918* (Göttingen: Vandenhoeck und Ruprecht, 1998) and Alex Watson. *Enduring the Great War: Combat, Morale and Collapse in the German and British Armies, 1914–1918.* (Cambridge University Press, 2008). The numbers were and are controversial. After the war, both the Right and Left in Weimar Germany were willing to accept high numbers. For the Right, a large number of deserters might be seen as proof of how deeply socialist and pacifist propaganda had undermined the fighting spirit at the front. For the Left, the number of deserters in 1918 would suggest that the troops in the field had finally realized their class interests and the bankruptcy of Germany's war aims.

[94] Desertions from rest areas behind the front and from the trenches themselves did become more common in the last weeks of the war. See *Why Germany Capitulated.*

[95] General von Kuhl in *UDZ*, III, 15. An example of the army's exasperation with the problem is seen in a secret memorandum of August 1918, in which the Deputy Commander of the Guard Corps, General Freiherr von Richtofen, threatened to take actions against officers in charge of replacement elements if those officers did not take stern measures to reduce indiscipline and unauthorized absences. BA-MA, PH 6/I/247.

[96] *Quellen*, 2 (i), II, 1226, fn. 1.

[97] Kriegsgeschichtlichen Forschungsanstalt, *Weltkrieg*, XIV, 760.

lack of discipline during rail movements produces in the rear areas."[98] However, the army's rear area remained an area where the chain of command had to be uncertain of its authority. There were reports that, "from trains shots and stones were directed at the station command-ers, and the troops took a threatening attitude towards the interpos-ing NCOs of the station guards, and answered orders with the call, 'Beat him!' The behavior bordered on mutiny. In fact, hand grenades were thrown from the trains into the station."[99] The disorder continued through the last days of the war and the first days of the peace.

For the front-line soldier seeking an escape from the trenches but lacking an opportunity to desert, there was another option. As the Allied general offensive forced the *Westheer* back through successive defensive positions, many German soldiers used the opportunity to give them-selves up to the enemy.[100] This was clearly a much riskier option than desertion.[101] Nevertheless, Allied intelligence noted that, in the last months of the war, even "first-class" divisions were giving up thousands of prisoners.[102] The situation was so bad that it forced the Germans to reconsider their celebrated "elastic defense" tactics. In a report enti-tled "Experience during the Fighting from September 25–30, 1918," the 233rd Infantry Brigade observed that, while dispersion in the for-ward areas of the defense undeniably reduced the number of killed and wounded, it also increased the number of missing in action. Describing soldiers in outpost positions, the report stated, "If he does not know where his comrades are, he will make too much use of 'the elastic defense [for fleeing or surrendering].'"[103] The 213th Brigade warned against putting new replacements up in forward outposts where they were only too willing to give themselves up to American patrols.[104]

---

[98] *The US Army in the World War*, XI, 434.

[99] Von Kuhl in *UDZ*, III, 15.

[100] Alex Watson argues that surrenders, including surrenders condoned by the chain of command, became the most salient characteristic of the German Army's disintegra-tion in 1918. He believes that surrenders undermined the front-line strength of the *Westheer* far more than desertion behind the lines. *Enduring the Great War*, 204–31.

[101] For an interesting recent analysis of the uncertain prospects involved in surrender-ing see Tim Cook, "The Politics of Surrender: Canadian Soldiers and the Killing of Prisoners in the Great War." *Journal of Military History*, 70, 3 (July 2006) 637–66.

[102] For examples see AEF G2, *251 Divisions*, 54 (2nd Guards Infantry Division), 163–4 (4th Bavarian Infantry Division), and 110 (5th Infantry Division).

[103] NARA, RG 165, Box 164, "Editorial Translation of 117 Inf. Div. documents", report dated Oct. 2, 1918, 1–4.

[104] NARA, RG 165, Box 163, Folder I, 107th Inf. Div. Subordinate Elms., War Diary entry of Sept. 22, 1918. 2. In other cases, soldiers might maintain their ties to a unit but avoid the dangers of combat by temporarily leaving the ranks just before their unit went into the line, and then returning when the unit returned to a rest area in the rear. Crown Prince Rupprecht described such a case in his diary entry of Oct 23, 1918. *Mein Kriegstagebuch*, vol. II, 468.

Whether surrendering, malingering, straggling, or deserting, in the fall of 1918, German soldiers were abandoning the war in their thousands. The unraveling of institutional discipline and the opportunities offered by a thinly held front meant those front-line soldiers who had decided their own war was over could act on that decision without the dangers that existed earlier in the war. Given what is known about conditions at the front, the miracle, perhaps, was that anyone remained to hold the line. Nevertheless, when the fighting stopped over a million men remained in the line. Ernst von Salomon, a student who joined the *Freikorps* after the revolution, found that many of his comrades were veterans of the Western Front. He wrote of them, "In the last years of the war, because of the diverse opportunities to avoid action, every front soldier was basically a volunteer and felt himself to be one."[105]

The "diverse opportunities to avoid action" had included exemption for war work, a safe job in the *Etappe*, as well as *Drückebergerei* or surrender to the enemy. Von Salomon may have overstated the case by calling the men who remained in the line volunteers. However, in late 1918, coercion alone did not suffice to keep soldiers in the trenches. Whether it was the leadership of strong officers, the bonds of comradeship, a sense of patriotic duty, or just dog-tiredness or unimaginative inertia, the *Frontschweine* on the Western Front on November 11 were the self-selected remnant after hundreds of thousands of other men had avoided the front, deserted, or surrendered themselves.

In the fall of 1918, then, the soldiers of the combat units of the *Westheer* were a relatively select group within a vast *Millionenheer*. Ludendorff had ensured the best of Germany's remaining soldiers were at the front at the beginning of that fateful year, and those who survived and remained with their decimated battalions until the armistice did so in spite of opportunities to evade the danger at the front. These circumstances, of themselves, suggest that many, perhaps most front-line soldiers used a different set of criteria to make their decisions about obedience and duty than the remainder of the army.

One key criterion was the soldier's relationship to his comrades in the trenches.

Cohesion: camaraderie and contradiction

Along with the emotional stresses of combat already discussed, much of what we know about the motivation of combat soldiers also comes from

---

[105] Von Salomon quoted in Hagen Schulze, *Freikorps und Revolution* (Boppard am Rhein: Boldt Verlag, 1969), 56.

research on the Second World War. In particular, the groundbreaking work of Edward Shils and Morris Janowitz introduced the idea that soldiers fight not for ideology or homeland, not for the patch on their shoulder or their regimental tradition, but for one another. In their investigation of why German units fought so tenaciously in 1944 and 1945 against overwhelming odds in a war that seemed clearly to be lost, Shils and Janowitz introduced the idea of the "primary group." The primary group was that small group of soldiers bonded together by experience and shared circumstances that formed the basis of an army's fighting strength.[106] Shils and Janowitz concluded that strong primary groups had been the basis of the German military's last-ditch tenacity.

Much of what Shils and Janowitz concluded about cohesion in the *Wehrmacht* in the last days of the Third Reich may be read back productively into an analysis of the *Kaiserheer* in 1918.[107] Both were armies that, despite a previous record of battlefield success, faced nearly certain defeat against enemies of overwhelming strength. Certainly, the record in both wars shows tenacious defensive fighting by German soldiers up until nearly the very end. However, between the two armies, separated by twenty-five-plus years (1918 to 1944), at least three crucial distinctions must be kept in mind: (1) despite its desperate circumstances, the German Army of 1918 was never driven back into its homeland; (2) despite efforts to "remobilize" the *Frontkämpfer* with "patriotic instruction," ideology did not play the same role in motivating the Germans of the First World War as National Socialism did in the Second World War; (3) as we have seen, the Imperial Army was unable or unwilling to use the murderous techniques employed by the Third Reich to enforce military discipline; i.e. there were no "flying tribunals" and summary executions in 1918.[108]

In the case of the *Westheer* of 1918, a consideration of the different aspects and venues of soldier motivation highlights the importance of

---

[106] Shils and Janowitz, "Cohesion and Disintegration," 267–8.
[107] Indeed, the two authors use a soldier's letter from the First World War to describe the true motivation of a front-line soldier: "[T]he idea of fighting, living, and dying for the fatherland, for the cultural possessions of the fatherland, is but a relatively distant thought. At least it does not play a great role in the practical motivations of the individual." *Kriegsbriefe gefallener Studenten*, quoted in Shils and Janowitz, "Cohesion and Disintegration," 270.
[108] In the last months of the war, the Prussian war ministry had authorized officers to use their personal weapons to enforce discipline, so cases of battlefield executions may have taken place. Jahr, *Gewöhnliche Soldaten*, 188. Manfred Messerschmidt has estimated the number of Wehrmacht soldiers executed during the Second World War at somewhere between 18,000 and 22,000. *Die Wehrmachtjustiz 1933–1945* (Paderborn: Militärgeschichtliches Forschungsamt/Schöningh Verlag, 2005), 453.

primary groups.[109] Sociologists identify three different areas where motivation is necessary in the life of a combat soldier. The first is the motivation that brings him into the service. This may be influenced by patriotism, parental expectations, peer group pressure, and, especially in a conscript army, governmental coercion. The second area where motivation is needed is that which keeps the soldier in the ranks or, in the case of the First World War, in the trenches. Here, lofty ideals give way more often to coercion, while the formation of primary groups serves to satisfy the emotional needs of the fighting man and to steel him to his soldierly duty. Finally, there is the motivation that keeps the soldier on the firing line in the presence of mortal danger. In this case, Shils and Janowitz argued, primary group loyalty trumps all other motivations.

As suggested above, in late 1918, the German front line was held by each unit's *Stammmannschaften*. These were the core of men who came into the army before war-weariness and the prospect of defeat had overcome patriotism and a sense of duty. These men had time to form primary groups, and these groups apparently sustained them even under the most fearful conditions. The replacements of 1918, on the other hand, possessed little or none of the motivation that serves to bring a soldier into the military and had not formed the bonds that would make them steadfast soldiers in the crisis the German Army faced in the fall of 1918. Four days before the war ended, the 75th Reserve Infantry Division's diary recorded that the division commander had gone forward to investigate the report that thirty men had refused to move up to the front. He found that they were replacements, just arrived. That night, in another regiment, another body of men disappeared. Of these events the staff officer in charge of the diary wrote, "The older soldiers still, in the main, show the loyal sense of duty and have not failed in the recent battles. In contrast, the young replacements coming from the homeland are completely unreliable, without discipline, and thus refractory."[110]

The OHL recognized the importance of cohesion and, as it was forced to disband divisions to provide manpower to others, it attempted to ameliorate the effects of the reorganization by keeping men of the defunct units with their old comrades. When the men of the 202nd

---

[109] Here I summarize John Lynn's summary of soldier sociology offered so concisely and clearly in his chapter "The Elements of Victory: A Theory of Combat Effectiveness," in *The Bayonets of the Republic: Motivation and Tactics in the Army of Revolutionary France, 1791–1794* (Boulder: Westview Press, 1996), 21–42.

[110] NARA, RG 165, Box 157, 75th Res. Inf. Div. War Diary and Annexes, report of November 7, 1918.

Infantry Division were divided up to strengthen three other divisions, the High Command ordered, "With the dissolution special attention is to be given to the tradition and the existing cohesion. As far as it is possible in the reinforced division, the troops from the dissolved units should be allowed to stay together in unified groups [regiments became battalions in their new assignments]." The gaining units were admonished to tell the OHL if they had been forced to parcel out the troops as individuals.[111]

Along with the loyalty of soldier for fellow soldier, the relationship between officers and men in the trenches further distinguished the army in the West from the remainder of the German armed forces. The key variables in determining the nature of these relationships were leadership, unit cohesion, and the extent of "social grievances."

When one seeks the sources of the growing disintegration within the German Army in 1918, the social grievances in that body cannot be overlooked. The expansion into a mass army during the war had stretched and twisted the relations between officers and men and had led to deep hostilities between the ranks. After the war, both critics and defenders of the army agreed that social grievances had played an important part in the demise of the Imperial Army. But if social grievances undermined authority, their influence was not uniform throughout the army. The physical conditions of trench life, as well as the nature of the leadership found in the front line, served to alter the relationship between officers and men and reduced much of the bitterness that might have developed between the two military strata.

The social grievances that undermined the army's cohesion reached into every aspect of a soldier's existence. Basic living standards became a particular sore spot. Officers received better food, pay, and lodging that their men did, and the powers granted to officers led to further abuse of privilege. Soldiers were routinely overtaxed on work details, humiliated in the barracks, and, at times, apparently exposed to needless sacrifice to win promotions and decorations for their superiors. The arrogance and inhumanity of many German officers and NCOs led, quite understandably, to widespread resentment within the ranks.[112]

The most flagrant abuses occurred in the *Etappe* and the *Heimatheer*. On this point, both the critics and advocates of the officer corps are in general agreement. The rear area was the home of the "*Etappenwirtschaft,*"

[111] BA-MA PH/8/I-511, Excerpt of OHL Order Ib # 11230 to Army Group Crown Prince, dated November 4, 1918.
[112] The extent of the grievances is illustrated in a survey reviewed in Hobohm's testimony in *UDZ*, XI (i), 210.

the "depot economy," where officers used their authority to create comfortable lifestyles and where corruption was widespread. In some places, officers lined their pockets by short-changing soldiers of their rations. Other descriptions cite depot commanders setting themselves up as lords with troops serving the role of serfs. A chaplain wrote, "In almost every assembly, the dissipated lifestyle of officers behind the front is mentioned ... The food provided the men does not compare with that of their superiors."[113] Another chaplain, assigned to occupation troops in Rumania in late 1918, expressed amazement that, while Germany was starving, the staff of his unit was being serving turtle soup, pastries, and caviar.[114] The corrupted nature of conditions behind the lines contrasted with the situation at the front. Speaking of the cases where officers supplemented their mess with rations taken from the troops, one officer admitted: "One should be open; it happened often. But it was energetically opposed in the field and more frequently at the lower levels than the upper. It occurred, I must honestly say, because the iron broom that would clean out such luxurious living was missing, but that [situation] was not allowed to begin in the field, but behind the lines where the abuse was greatest."[115]

The prevalence of complaints about unjust treatment finally compelled the highest levels of the German hierarchy to respond. In June 1917, the Prussian war minister, Hermann von Stein, exhorted the rear areas to set the example for the men by living a simple lifestyle. Thus, they might quell complaints, for example, of unfair provisionary practices.[116] In October 1918, von Hindenburg issued a memorandum that noted the number and nature of complaints against officers behind the line:

The complaint is made that the officers live better than the men at the expense of the latter. The accusations contained in such complaints are so serious I cannot help but challenge them. However, [even] the semblance of such a thing must be avoided. The troop officer lives and fights with his men and shares their joys and sorrows. The relationship to his men must be ennobled by an untiring solicitude for the welfare of every individual man in all matters within the officer's jurisdiction.[117]

That the field marshal, after four and a half years of war, felt the need to issue such a message is evidence of the severity of the problem.

---

[113] *Ibid.*, 60.   [114] *Ibid.*, 424–5.
[115] Kurt Hesse, *Das Marne Drama des 15. Juli 1918: Wahrheiten aus der Front* (Berlin: Mittler und Sohn, 1920), 53.
[116] Hobohm in *UDZ*, XI (i), 26–7.
[117] *The US Army in the World War*, XI, 450–1.

Hindenburg felt compelled to respond to charges that indicated a fundamental failing in the German officer corps. If officers had to be prodded to perform their basic duty, that is, caring for the welfare of their men, then something was badly wrong with the German officer corps in 1918.

The chain of command, together with those who investigated the social conditions in the army, was drawn to the same conclusion about the chief source of the problem. The bulk of the grievances were based on the conduct of the young officers commissioned into service during the war.[118] The old officer corps had been nearly annihilated in the first years of the war. By the end of the war, some 94 percent of the prewar cadres had been killed or wounded. But, while the ranks of the regulars were decimated, the size of the officer corps expanded almost sixfold by the end of the war, from 30,000 to over 180,000.[119] Such were the numbers required by the mass army that the new "wartime" officers were drawn, in part, from the upper, middle, and, in rare cases, the lower classes and thus represented a break from the relatively exclusive nature of the old officer corps.[120] The wartime officers obviously lacked the prewar experience of the active officers and received limited training before they found themselves holding positions of responsibility at the front and in the rear.

The complaints against them came from all levels. A unit pastor wrote, "in fact the young age of many wartime lieutenants has often complicated the achievement of good relations between officers and men."[121] A major wrote that the poor relations between officers and men came from "a period when too much young blood came in, whom no one had taught the duties of an officer."[122] The front line had its share of young officers, but one of the key factors that differentiated units in the trenches from the rest of the army, in terms of leadership, was the much higher percentage of active officers found there. These survivors of the old army served as examples to the younger leaders and were able to create a healthier atmosphere between the ranks.

In 1918, recognizing that their reduced numbers limited the impact made by prewar officers, the OHL attempted to comb out the staffs and *Etappe* for physically capable active officers. In this respect, the selection process that ensured the best soldiers were deployed to the Western Front was paralleled by an even more rigorous selection process for officers. The contrast in active presence at the front and rear

---

[118] See complaints in Hobohm, *UDZ*, XI (i), 61, 225–36, and 406–7.
[119] Volkmann in *UDZ*, XI (ii), 33–5. [120] Katzenstein testimony in *UDZ*, IV, 4.
[121] Neter, quoted in Hobohm, *UDZ*, XI (i), 228. [122] Hesse, *Marne*, 54

was significant. The active and reserve divisions serving on the Western Front at the beginning of the last year of the war had a ratio of wartime to active officers of 4.66 to 1 and 8.7 to 1, respectively, while *Landwehr* divisions, many of which were deployed in the East, had a ratio of 33 to 1. In the *Etappe* there were almost no active officers who had not been invalided out of the line for wounds or nervous exhaustion. Conclusive evidence that the prewar officers were disproportionately represented at the front was the fact the rate of battle deaths among active officers was four times the per capita rate for wartime commissionees.[123] Casualties among the active officers remained unusually high throughout the war.[124]

The positive influence of these active officers was often indicated in the same letters that criticized the conduct of the young wartime officers. One labor union leader, complaining of the treatment of his membership by wartime officers, wrote to Hindenburg, "The men, however, stress the faultless behavior of the majority of the active officers in this particular."[125] A member of the postwar Reichstag investigating committee spoke of hearing the complaint, "Yes, if we had our first captain, then all of this would not have happened, but when the public welfare student so-and-so who sat with me on the same school bench became a lieutenant, then one could see how poorly he handled us."[126] Even those hostile to the old army were forced to concede that the soldiers held the active officers in higher esteem. The reason, said one, was the nostalgia felt by the men for the "good old days" before the war and the first few months of victory when the officer–soldier relationship was the best.[127]

The clear advantages the active officers had over their wartime counterparts derived from training and experience. These two advantages gave the prewar officer confidence in his authority and allowed him to feel comfortable in looking out for his men without damaging the superior–subordinate relationship.

Already at the *Kriegschule*, the cadet was indoctrinated with the idea that the officer must be an example and caretaker for the men entrusted to him, and it would go badly for the lieutenant who, while on field training or maneuver and at a halt or a rest stop, took a draught of water before his men had quenched

[123] The statistics in this paragraph are drawn from Volkmann in *UDZ*, XI (ii), 111–12.
[124] Major von Bussche, in a report to the Reichstag quoted in E.O. Volkmann, *Der Grosse Krieg* (Berlin: Hobling Verlag, 1922), 239
[125] Letter of A. Leonhardt, quoted by Hobohm in *UDZ*, XI (i), 73.
[126] Bernhard Schwertfeger in *UDZ*, IV, 43.
[127] Hobohm in *UDZ*, XI (i), 226. For a useful analysis of the prewar German Army's development of a more paternalistic leadership style, see Dennis Showalter, "Army and Society in Imperial Germany: The Pains of Modernization." *Journal of Contemporary History*, 18, 4 (Oct. 1983), 607–12.

their thirst, or, who had retired to his quarters to rest before he had seen to the accommodations for his people.[128]

The survey of soldiers' letters mentioned earlier found that the peacetime active officer as well as the reserve officer trained in peacetime seemed to have better appreciation of the mood and outlook of their soldiers.[129]

If the example of the active officer was an important factor in reducing front-line grievances, the fact remains that, in 1918, the wartime officer carried the overwhelming burden of leadership in the trenches. When he was good, he was an inspiration to his troops, and when he was bad, he was the source of poor soldier morale. Whatever his qualifications, though, he was likely to be much closer to his men than the masses of wartime officers who staffed the Home Army and the *Etappe*. Going against the grain of much current German historiography,[130] British historian Alexander Watson has argued that the junior officers at the front did surprisingly well, given their relative youth and limited training. He finds that the endurance of the German Army on the Western Front is not explainable without accounting for the leadership of these wartime officers. To a large extent, the active cadres were able to transfer the paternalistic ethos of the prewar officer corps to those commissioned after 1914. Abuses were plentiful; however, many young officers sought to follow guidance like that promulgated in the field instructions of the Sixth Army: "The young officer must be constantly conscious of the responsibility-demanding task of constant care for his subordinates."[131]

The conditions of life at the front demanded a closer relationship and, in this respect, the German Army of the First World War was no different from any other army in the history of modern warfare. A text on military sociology indicates the universal nature of this front-line condition:

We state this cardinal rule: the closer a unit is to the line of actual combat and the more directly the men in it are engaged in action against the enemy, the more formal organizational control becomes diluted. Under the makeshift characteristics of front-line living arrangements with officers and men alike

[128] Anker, *Unsere Stunde*, 45.   [129] Volkmann, *UDZ*, XI (ii), 135–6.
[130] For example, Benjamin Ziemann writes, "The major sacrifices and danger which front-line service entailed made ordinary soldiers all the more aware that their relationship with officers was an unequal one." *War Experiences in Rural Germany 1914–1923*, trans. Alex Skinner (Oxford/New York: Berg Publishers, 2007), 74.
[131] Alexander Watson, "Junior Officership in the German Army during the Great War, 1914–1918." *War and Society*, 14, 4 (November 2007), 428–53.

exposed to very considerable risks and suffering extreme deprivations, the military social structure, as officially defined, undergoes a partial disintegration and is replaced by an emergency social system.[132]

Expression of this "emergency social system" includes disdain for all non-combat soldiers and the near-total disappearance of all etiquette surrounding rank, a tendency that has been noted by every observer of front-line behavior.[133]

During the First World War, German soldiers called the emergency social system *Frontkameradschaft*, the "camaraderie of the front." The miserable and terrifying conditions on the Western Front often broke down the barriers of class that were so strong in the prewar army. In modern historiography, it has become fashionable to dismiss *Frontkameradschaft* as a fantasy concocted by men like Ernst Jünger and later nurtured by the Nazis in order to carry on the myth that National Socialism was building on the social revolution that had taken place in the trenches.[134] Certainly, one must judge Jünger's depiction of the front-line troops as the "princes of the trenches" and, even more, Nazi propaganda with a skeptical eye. Yet Erich Maria Remarque, a friend of neither Nazis nor militarists, had this to say about the leveling effect of trench warfare:

[T]he things that existed before are no longer valid, and one practically knows them no more. Distinction, breeding, education are changed, are almost blotted out and are hardly recognizable any longer ... It is as though formerly we were coins of different provinces; and now we are melted down, and all bear the same stamp.

It is a great brotherhood, which adds something of the folk song, of the feeling of solidarity of convicts, and of the desperate loyalty to one another of men condemned to death.[135]

There is enough evidence to conclude that relations were different and that, in many cases, the order and discipline required of a functioning military hierarchy was based on a closer relationship between officers and men than the old army was used to. The officer was required

---

[132] Lang, *Military Institutions*, 73.   [133] *Ibid.*, 74.

[134] See, for example, Bernd Huppauf, "Schlachtenmythen und die Konstruktion des 'Neuen Menschen'," in *Keiner fühlt sich hier mehr als Mensch: Erlebnis und Wirkung des Ersten Weltkriegs*, ed. Gerhard Hirschfeld, Gerd Krumeich, and Irina Renz (Frankfurt: Fischer Taschenbuch Verlag, 1993), 53–103, and Peter Knoch, "Kriegsalltag," in *Kriegsalltag: Die Rekonstruktion des Kriegsalltags als der historischen Forschung und der Friedenserziehung*, ed. Peter Knoch (Stuttgart: J.B. Metzersche Verlagsbuchhandlung, 1989), 222–51.

[135] Erich M. Remarque, *All Quiet on the Western Front* (1928; reprinted New York: Ballantine, 1987), 235–6.

to be less the "superior" and more the "leader."[136] A front-line officer
wrote of this phenomenon, "In the last years of the war the only thing
that counted was personalities." The new superior–subordinate relationships, he said, would have astonished the "brass hats" of the staff
and the rear.[137] In the most famous shock formation of the war, troops
called themselves "Rohr men" (after their commander, Captain Willi
Rohr) instead of referring to the unit's official title (Storm Battalion
Number 5), and observers were shocked to hear officers and men using
the familiar "*du*" form with one another.[138] The effective leader developed a rapport with his troops and could instill a spirit in them that,
according to another officer, "would not be betrayed in the sternest
tests, although a large segment held the same political conviction as one
otherwise holds responsible for the collapse."[139] Adolf Hitler, the most
famous of the *Frontschweine*, recalled that the officers at the front were
"respected by the men in quite a different way from the commanders from the rear" for whom the "peculiarities" of the front-line soldier were totally incomprehensible.[140] One may rightly be suspicious of
Hitler's recollections, except that they track with much of the evidence
found in the archives.[141]

However strong the solidarity of the men at the front, officers were
forced to use a different kind of leadership to hold their units together
in the last desperate days of the war. When the 253rd Regiment was
ordered into the line on November 8, the men showed signs of unwillingness to go forward. They complained that they had served more
time on the front line than other units and had not had the rest they had
been promised. The war diary of the 76th Reserve Division recorded,
"Through explanations offered by the regimental and battalion commanders and a general staff officer from division that relief was not
available, the men were appeased." Officers assured the men that
"desires with respect to food and delousing will, if possible, be fulfilled." As an additional palliative measure, the unit set up a council of

---

[136] Schulze, *Freikorps*, 56. See also Hobohm, *UDZ*, XI (i), 242.
[137] Neter, quoted in *ibid.*   [138] Fried, *Guilt*, 165–7.
[139] Captain Muller-Brandenburg quoted in Katzenstein, *UDZ*, IV, 23.
[140] Adolf Hitler, *Mein Kampf*, ed. John Chamberlain *et al.* (New York: Reynal and
    Hitchcock, 1939), 250. Ernst Jünger, who would become the most famous of the
    young front-line officers, recalled the front-line camaraderie thus: "The gleam of
    many an ideal that shimmered for me over our war aims has been dashed to the earth
    by war. One [thing] remains forever: this fidelity [between front-line soldiers] that
    cannot be shaken." From Ernst Jünger, *The Storm of Steel: From the Diary of a German
    Storm-Troop Officer on the Western Front*, trans. Basil Creighton (1921; reprinted
    London: Allen Lane, 2003), 243.
[141] Again, see Watson, "Junior Officership," 26–30.

trusted men (*Vertrauensrat*) to advise the chain of command on rations issues. Through these actions, the diary reports, the unit was able to restore officer control of the unit.[142] The example of the 253rd demonstrates how far the German Army of 1918 had come from the old Prussian *Kadavergehorsam* ("discipline of the corpse"). To order tired and unhappy men into the line was no longer sufficient; German officers found themselves having to explain why and offer incentives. With the creation of advisory councils to deal with rations, the military hierarchy was driven to a small measure of power sharing that would have been utterly inconceivable in the prewar army.[143] Officers would find that such improvised methods to keep men in the line in difficult moments of battle would prove even more useful in the days after the revolution.

The solidarity the front-line soldier felt for his comrades in the trenches, especially when that *Kameradschaft* extended to his officers, must certainly have played a considerable role in the soldier's decision to stay with his unit or abandon it in the last days of the war. Abuses of power did occur at the front. However, one senses that such abuses were neither as widespread nor flagrant as they were a few miles to the rear, in the East, or back in the homeland garrisons. The argument here is not that the relationship of officers and men at the front was perfect, or even that it was "good" across the board; just that it was qualitatively different from that in the rest of the army. The terrible pressures of front-line combat pushed needy men together and, at the front, the common soldier was more likely to find officers willing to look out for the morale and well-being of his subordinates. Under such conditions, the existing authority relationships were more likely to hold, though modified by the conditions of a long war. The peculiar nature of officer–soldier relationships was another element in the unique response of front-line soldiers to the revolution.

Management: the manipulation of despair

Thus far, it has been argued that late in the war the German front-line soldier was sustained by the presence of comrades (and, perhaps, his leaders). Though tired, isolated, and bitter, he had decided to remain with the remnant of his unit's surviving core of veterans. In the heat of

---

[142] NARA, RG 165, Box 158, 76th Inf. Div. War Diary and Annexes, 22, entry of Nov. 8, 1918.

[143] In late 1916, the German Army authorized units to create "Food Committees" (*Menagekommisionen*) with enlisted representation to bring oversight to the quality of rations (*Quellen*, 6/II, 15, fn. 3).

combat, he fought for those comrades. In the intervals between battles, however, the chain of command owed him a reason to fight on. If some semblance of risk–reward relationship was to be maintained, the army needed to justify why it continued to resist in the face of Allied material dominance and inevitable defeat. As the war went on, the army sought to counteract the influence of socialist agitation and Allied propaganda through a program of "Patriotic Instruction." Launched in the summer of 1917, the purpose of the program was to rekindle devotion to the monarchy and instill new faith in Germany's ultimate victory. Within the Field Army, the "Patriotic Instruction" was conducted by a special information bureau staffed by officers chosen, in theory, for their competence and knowledge of the troops.[144] However, in the latter stages of the war, effect of the instruction was marginal; patriotic appeals rang hollow to the men in the trenches. One officer detailed to perform such instruction told a meeting of his fellow education officers, "If I tell the men at the front the things that have been proposed here, they will laugh in my face."[145] A recent historical assessment finds the instruction deficient because of its abstract and pedantic nature and its failure to address the urgent needs of the front-line soldier: better food, better housing, and a chance for survival.[146]

Those charged with maintaining soldier morale had other problems, as well. The premise that the Fatherland was fighting a defensive war and seeking a "peace of understanding" was badly undermined by the rapacious nature of the Brest-Litovsk treaty that Germany had imposed on Soviet Russia. Though German soldiers were sustained by the hope that the spring offensives of 1918 would bring a quick end to the war, the failure of the offensives and the obvious reversal of battlefield fortune in the summer led to a morale crisis and, as we have seen, a growing breakdown in discipline. Any illusions as to the outcome of the war evaporated at the beginning of October when Germany asked the Allies for cease-fire terms.

In the weeks that followed, senior army leaders understood that news of mutiny and revolution in the homeland would have an unsettling effect on the troops. In late October, the army warned those units with

---

[144] *Quellen*, 1/II, Document 328: "Befehl des Chefs des Generalstabes des Feldheeres an die Oberkommandos der Heeresgruppen und Armeen betr. Die Einrichtung einer Aufklarungsorganisation beim Feldheer," 835.

[145] Walther Lambach, *Ursachen des Zusammenbruchs* (Hamburg: Deutschnationale Verlagsanstalt, 1920), 81–2. Lambach believed most of the education officers were blind to the true mood of the troops.

[146] Jürgen Forster, "Ludendorff and Hitler in Perspective: The Battle for the German Soldier's Mind, 1917–1944." *War in History*, 10, 3 (2003), 325.

wireless communication to limit the distribution of news that came from Germany. Signal personnel were to deliver messages into the hands of officers only.[147] Yet the disturbing news still leaked out. One corps headquarters reported: "First interception of wireless messages coming from workers' and soldiers' councils with fantastic content or warnings to maintain order are the only news from home which, in spite of all radio discipline, gets through to the troops and cause them greatest worries concerning their families at home."[148]

Along with rumor control, the chain of command had to offer some sort of positive motivation to the *Fronttruppen*. Why should they fight on? One corps commander appealed to the soldiers' sense of honor: "The honor of the army which has achieved the highest level of performance must stand, at the end, pure and untarnished."[149] Such an appeal must have sounded hollow or bizarre to many. Other leaders emphasized that the final shape of the peace agreement depended on their resistance. As an example, on October 21, one finds a division commander telling his men that, though their desire for relief and rest are justified, the crucial nature of the situation demands that they hold the line:

The political leaders of France and England want no part of a conciliatory peace, though Germany has offered the greatest concessions. They want to destroy us, to lay our country to waste. They believe this goal is near. That this is not the case is known by every member of the division who has taken part and seen in the recent battles how the French and American are taken down by our machine gun and artillery fire ... [Until relief is possible] we must do our duty and hold on despite extreme fatigue and terrible weather.

The division commander, Major General Freiherr Quadt, finished on a grimly practical note by telling the chain of command to emphasize to their men that if the division was pulled out of the line at that moment, it would very likely be thrown into an even worse situation somewhere else.[150]

Still other leaders made more visceral appeals for their soldiers to hold the line. On November 1, the 15th Bavarian Infantry Division

---

[147] Second Division Historical Section, Translations: *War Diaries of German Units Opposed to the Second Division (Regular) 1918*, vol. IX, *Meuse–Argonne* (Washington, DC: Army War College, 1935), Doc. 13 (148th Infantry Regiment War Diary and Annexes), unit order dated October 27, 1918.

[148] *Ibid.*, Doc. 22 (88th Division Selected Documents), Corps Kleist report to Fifth Army, dated December 5, 1918.

[149] Corps Bernsdorf Commander, October 22, 1918, quoted in Anne Lipp, *Meinungslenkung*, 166.

[150] NARA, RG 165, Box 15, Folder I, 75; 76th Res. Div. War Diary and Annexes.

published a division order that included this warning offering the specter of rape, pillage, and destruction:

Comrades! You know all the regions – devastated, battered and smashed – over which this war has passed. That will be the fate of our homeland if our front yields and the confusing mixture of races [referring, most likely to French colonial and US African American units] which represent our enemy is set loose to swarm over the German countryside.[151]

One imagines that the impact of such exhortations depended largely on the remaining credibility of the chain of command and soldiers' perception that they were being treated with candor. Perhaps the most effective approach was recorded a day before the armistice in the war diary of the 2nd Battalion, 124th Infantry Regiment, a unit of Württemburgers: "Quiet on both sides. At 3.00 p.m., the Battalion Commander, Captain Wolters, addresses the battalion and requests the members to persevere because the Armistice was just around the corner. At 11.00 p.m. a strong hostile bombardment opens up."[152]

"Better a terrible end"[153]

In the 33rd *Landwehr* Regiment, reports of an upcoming cease-fire proved to be the signal for disintegration. On the morning of November 11, the Third Battalion's war diary recorded that much of the regiment's Second Battalion had vanished during the night. It noted that, unfortunately, some of the Third Battalion had apparently gone with them. Number 8 Company had gone from twenty men to two, and Number 7 Company, from twenty-eight to twelve. The diarist gave the following reasons for the troops' disappearance: (1) a week-long tour in the trenches in the anticipation of a major enemy attack, and (2) reports of chaotic conditions in the homeland and rumors that a cease-fire was impending. "Soldiers were heard to say that they had no desire to be shot now, just before the peace."[154]

That same morning, at seven o'clock, the headquarters of the 1st Guards Infantry Division received a request relayed through higher

---

[151] Second Division Historical Section, *War Diaries of German Units*, vol. IX, *Meuse–Argonne*, Doc. 35 (15th Bavarian Infantry Division War Diary and Annexes), div. order dated November 1, 1918.

[152] *Ibid.* War Diary of the 2nd Battalion, 124th Infantry Regiment from November 1 to November 11, 1918, entry for November 10, 1918.

[153] At the end of both world wars, Germans often used a rueful saying of uncertain origin which went (roughly), "Better a terrible end than terror without end" (*"Lieber ein schreckliches Ende als Schrecken ohne Ende."*).

[154] NARA, RG 165, Box 121, War Diary Extract of the 3rd Bn. 33rd *Landwehr* Regt., 201.

headquarters from the German armistice delegation. It asked that, in order to secure more favorable conditions, units should continue to offer strong resistance. Such resistance was necessary to convince the Allies that German forces were still capable of continuing the fight, if need be. An hour later, the 12th Company of the division's 4th Foot Guards Regiment attacked through the morning fog and overran a small French bridgehead over the Meuse near Nouvion. The guardsmen killed twelve and captured fifteen *poilus* along with several machine guns. A few hours later, the Germans allowed the French troops to return under a flag of truce to recover their dead. The war was over.[155]

Which incident accurately represents the condition of the German Army on November 11? In a curious way, both do; the *Landwehr* troops and the guardsmen represent opposite ends of a single spectrum of behavior. The flight of the 3rd Battalion men reflects the advanced state of disintegration in the *Westheer* late in the war. On the other hand, the attack of the 12th Company on the French bridgehead reminds us that the German Army was a ferociously lethal killing machine up to the very moment the war ended. The behavior of the war-weary *Landwehr* men tracks closely with Leonard Smith's prediction that soldiers constantly re-evaluate their level of obedience according to a calculation of risk and rewards. The missing men from the 7th and 8th Companies had decided that there was nothing to be gained from holding the line until the very end. The risks were still considerable; the rewards less than negligible. However, such an economic model of soldier behavior breaks down when attempting to predict the reaction of the 4th Foot Guards to the order to launch a last-minute attack. Were the guardsmen too punch drunk with fatigue to measure the value of the probable outcomes (the temporary capture of a small piece of ground) against the dangers involved in storming French machine guns (the likelihood of death or wounds for many)? Or were they motivated by their unit's proud tradition, or the quality of their junior officers, or just the simple desire to support their comrades on either side? Or perhaps the men of the Fourth Foot Guards felt that, at this stage, to refuse to go forward would be to disavow what they had experienced, the sacrifices of their fallen comrades and what they themselves had endured. The question is impossible to answer. Likewise, one is hard-pressed to explain the Allied description of the seemingly suicidal resistance offered by German rear guards during the last days of the war. How did those

---

[155] The German attack described in Wilhelm Reinhard, *1918–1919: Die Wehen der Republik* (Berlin: Brunnen Verlag, 1933). Though author of the book was the regimental commander at the time, he uses a French eyewitness account to corroborate the conduct of his men, 26–31.

machine-gun crews make their risk–reward calculation? In such cases, Smith's model of soldier behavior lacks predictive power.

By the same token, having reviewed conditions as they existed in November 1918, one must challenge Wilhelm Deist's now famous argument that the German troops on the Western Front were conducting a "covert strike" at the time of the armistice.[156] Certainly, that description one could apply to the many thousands of *Drückeberger* milling around railroad stations and supply dumps in northern France and Belgium. However, it fails to account for the more than 1.5 million men who remained on the front line in November 1918. Neither does it explain Allied reports of stubborn German resistance through September and October into November.

The German soldier at the front was forced to make difficult decisions in the fall of 1918. If one is pressed to pick one of the six factors as dominant in determining the outlook of German front-line soldiers as the end of the war approached, it must certainly have been exhaustion. Isolation certainly added to his anxiety about things at home. At the front, there was little opportunity for soldiers to express their resentment of the staff, the rear area, or the homeland except through the time-honored practice of grousing. Selection had brought them to the front; self-selection held them there. This was certainly important. There can be little doubt that loyalty towards comrades and unit had been a part of that self-selection. At that stage in the war, the various exhortations used by the chain of command to influence soldier behavior must have had relatively little impact.

Both the *Drückeberger* behind the line and *Stammmannschaften* in the trenches prayed that the politicians would work out a peace as soon as possible. Therefore, in the last several weeks of the fighting, whether a soldier stayed with his unit or abandoned it, the political considerations influenced the decision. Yet the decision to stay or flee was rarely a political one. By November 1918, issues such as the outcome of the war or the future of the German monarchy were secondary to life and death considerations, as well as the support of one's comrades, cover from the rain, and the prospect of hot rations. With the end of the fighting, however, that would change.

---

[156] Deist, "Verdeckter Militarstreik," 146–67. Anne Lipp attacks Deist's assertion in slightly different terms. She reminds us that desertion and surrender in the German Army in 1918 was usually an individual decision and suggests the term "covert strike" overdoes the incidence of disintegration in the army. She points out that characterizing the situation as a strike would require the presence of collective action, to include leadership, coordination, and "a recognizable set of objectives." Lipp, *Meinungslenkung*, 146.

This chapter has described the factors that made that body of front-line soldiers different from the rest of the German Army, considering, in turn, their terrible exhaustion, their isolation from revolutionary influences, their alienation from those who did not share their experience, the relative strength of their cohesion compared to the remainder of the army, and, finally, the efforts of the army's leaders to impose a form of management on the attitudes of the soldiers and the information they received. The chapters that follow will examine how those differences shaped their responses to the revolution in Germany and how that response proved critical to the revolution's outcome.

3 Caesar without legions: the Field Army and the abdication of the Kaiser, November 8–9, 1918

The Kaiser and his army

On November 4, 1918, Kaiser Wilhelm II left the Field Army headquarters to visit the front. His journey into exile was still five days away but, in a sense, Wilhelm was already in flight. A week before, he had already left Berlin, where recent constitutional reforms – "the revolution from above" – had stripped him of much of his power and where members of the Reichstag were openly debating his abdication. The Kaiser sought refuge with his generals at Spa, Belgium, but even here bad news followed him. There were reports of unrest in the High Seas fleet and the socialists continued to demand concessions from the government. The chancellor, Prince Max of Baden, urged the Kaiser to return to Berlin, while continuing to relay news of political unrest in the imperial capital. There seemed no refuge from the world of problems that surrounded the Hohenzollern throne.

Under these mounting pressures, a trip west toward the front line offered a form of relief. Colonel Alfred Niemann, the OHL liaison to the Kaiser's court, described the heady feeling that day. "Away from the idle waiting amid the poisonous atmosphere that threatens to kill every healthy feeling in the homeland. Out at the front, the breeze of noble patriotism will free the soul. With our *Feldgrauen* [troops in field-gray], the Soldier-Emperor will come back to the awareness of the way the Germanic tribes have joined into a single people to hold out for four years against the onslaught of the entire world," Niemann later recalled.[1] The Kaiser and his entourage traveled west, first by Wilhelm's personal train, and then by automobile convoy. In the course of a busy day, they visited front-line troops in the rest areas of fourteen different divisions. At every location, the Kaiser, putting on a cheerful front, spoke with the troops and took pleasure in handing out large numbers

---

[1] Alfred Niemann, *Kaiser und Revolution. Die Entscheidenden Ereignisse im Grossen Hauptquartier im Herbst 1918* (Berlin: Verlag für Kulturpolitik, 1928), 129.

Figure 3.1 The Kaiser leaves his residence in Berlin for the last time as he travels to the army headquarter in Spa Belgium on October 31, 1918.

of Iron Crosses. During his visits, the front-line officers present assured the Kaiser that their men had lost all fear of Allied tanks and that, in the face of stubborn German resistance, Allied infantry was showing increasing timidity. At one point, the ceremonies were interrupted by a report of approaching Allied aircraft, followed shortly thereafter by the loud roar of anti-aircraft weapons. The Prussian monarch made a show of indifference, continuing down the ranks, talking to soldiers about home and relatives. When the attack passed, Wilhelm turned to the men and said, "May you indeed feel how gladly I share every privation and danger with you!" Clearly, the whole business had a rejuvenating effect on him, and, when he returned to the headquarters in Spa, the Kaiser reported to those who stayed behind that his reception at the front had been enthusiastic.

To others in the party, the trip presented mixed signals. The front-line troops gathered to meet Wilhelm showed no signs of spontaneous joy at the presence of their emperor, although they had presented a reassuring display of steadiness and loyalty under extreme circumstances. However, what the party saw on the road back to the Kaiser's train had been a different matter. The farther they went back from the front, the more unsettling were the sights encountered. As the Kaiser's party passed supply convoys and baggage columns, the troops there offered intentional indifference, cold stares, and a studied unwillingness to offer the appropriate honors. It seemed that a different army existed behind the front, and for those who were paying attention the signs were ominous.[2]

Perhaps Wilhelm chose to overlook the surly reception he encountered behind the lines. As the end of war approached, the Kaiser expected the front-line army to be the last, most reliable bulwark of the monarchy.[3] Even if revolutionary sentiment had infected the navy and the rear echelon troops (the *Etappe*) of the army, the front-line forces (*Frontheer*) had stood steadfast against overwhelming odds in the battles of the summer and fall of 1918. Insulated from the seditious ideas sweeping Germany, and inspired by their leaders, who were the last remaining cadres of the "old army," the heroes in the trenches would prove themselves *kaisertreu* if called on to defend their emperor.

The Kaiser's faith in and reliance on the army of the Western Front would be shattered over the course of two days, November 8–9, 1918. During these two crucial days the failure of the front-line troops to rally to their warlord was given stark expression. Indeed, over the last weeks of the war, the failing morale of German units on the Western Front convinced Germany's senior military leaders the war had to be ended before the final collapse of the army in the West, even if this meant abandoning the Kaiser. When front-line troops seemed unable to secure the army's lines of communications against revolutionary forces, the High Command determined that logistical support of a counter-revolutionary offensive was impossible. At the same time, the unwillingness of front-line soldiers to fire on mutinous sailors and revolutionary demonstrators in Berlin virtually guaranteed the triumph of the revolution in the capital of the Reich. In fact, the sentiment of the front-line troops, represented by vote of several dozen

[2] Description of the Kaiser's visit from Neimann, *Kaiser und Revolution*, 129–31, and v. Restorff, "Bericht des Kapitans zur See v. Restorff," from Alfred Niemann, *Revolution von Oben – Umsturz von Unten: Entwicklung und Verlauf der Staatsumwälzung in Deutschland, 1914–1918* (Berlin: Verlag für Kulturpolitik, 1927), 389. Niemann's books are, arguably, the most valuable resources for the crucial events in Spa during November 1918; first, because he was an eye-witness, and second, because he included the accounts of other key eye-witnesses in *Revolution von Oben*.
[3] General von Plessen, as head of the Kaiser's military entourage, did his best to shield Wilhelm from the most depressing news in the latter part of the war. See Maurice Baumont, *The Fall of the Kaiser*, trans. E. Ibbetson James (New York: Alfred Knopf, 1931), 70–2.

regimental, brigade, and divisional commanders, further convinced the army's two senior leaders that the combat troops lacked the will to fight for the Kaiser against his enemies in the homeland. Finally, when the elite troops designated to guard the Kaiser showed signs of discontent, Wilhelm's courses of action were reduced to a single option: abdication and flight to Holland. Thus, when the Kaiser called on the front-line troops to rescue his throne, their indifferent response, expressed in the actions of several key combat units and the attitudes of a handful of their officers, convinced Wilhelm that he was powerless to preserve his personal rule and the monarchy.

Who were these men in whom the Kaiser had misplaced his trust? On November 8, when Wilhelm II called on his army to follow him into Germany and strike down the revolution, he addressed the front-line soldiers of the Western Front as the only true warriors remaining in uniform. The Kaiser's view of the army was a traditional one. The support troops, the garrisons of the interior, and the old men occupying the East were the necessary adjuncts to the heroes at the front, the "real" army. These others behind the line, the teamsters, the supply clerks, the telegraph operators, and others of their ilk, though in uniform, were hardly soldiers. They were men of lower quality, baser and more susceptible to the seditious ideas that had ignited the revolution inside Germany. In Wilhelm's view, the thin gray line of heroes in the trenches was the shield of the Hohenzollern throne. However, by the fall of 1918 these "heroes" were being severely tested.

The scapegoat general

On October 26, the chief of staff of Army Group Kiev in the Ukraine, General Wilhelm Groener, received a telegram from Field Marshal Hindenburg ordering him to report to Field Army Headquarters in Belgium.[4] An unenviable task faced Groener; the field marshal was summoning him from Kiev to take over the post of First Quartermaster General of the German Army. As the replacement for Erich Ludendorff, Groener would be charged with salvaging what could be rescued from a lost war.[5] As he left the headquarters in Kiev, Groener

---

[4] Nachlass Groener, telegram of October 26, 1918 (microfilm roll, Combined Arms Research Library (CARL), Ft. Leavenworth, KS).

[5] Ludendorff had inspired his own relief by announcing to the army that "for us soldiers" the terms of Wilson's "Third Note" were unacceptable and that Wilson's dishonorable terms required the army to continue resistance to the bitter end. To Prince Max this seemed an open attempt by the general to hijack German foreign policy. The effect on world opinion, when the prince's government was making a show of distancing itself

Figure 3.2 Lieutenant General Wilhelm Groener and his wife, 1917. Before replacing Ludendorff, Groener had a reputation as a skillful technocrat who could work with Majority Socialist leaders.

told his colleagues, "I understand very clearly that I will have to play the scapegoat."[6]

As the virtual dictator over Germany's war effort, Groener's predecessor had gambled the nation's last reserves of strength and lost spectacularly. The failure of Ludendorff's spring offensives had shaken Germany's enfeebled allies and, in the weeks just prior to Groener's appointment, the armies of Bulgaria, Turkey, and Austria-Hungary had collapsed. Meanwhile, on the German home front, the Allied blockade had pushed the war-weary populace to the point of starvation. Widespread strikes earlier in the year had given clear evidence of the extent of unrest across Germany, and rumors of revolution provided a backdrop to Germany's efforts to negotiate an "honorable" peace. If Germany were to achieve any sort of satisfactory settlement, the army would have to hold out in the main theater, the Western Front. Here the prospects were grim and clearly getting worse. This was the situation that faced Groener when he arrived at the *Oberste Heeresleitung* (OHL-Supreme Command) in Spa, Belgium, on October 30, 1918. Events at home and at the front had seemed to be picking up a dangerous momentum. The Kaiser and the new chancellor, Prince Max, both needed Groener's best-possible assessment of the army's prospects for holding out. To provide such an assessment, Groener needed to consider both quantifiable factors – manpower and *matériel* – and unquantifiable ones – morale and fighting spirit.

Groener seems to have been aware of the deplorable state of morale. In early 1918, as a corps commander on the Western Front, he had observed the first signs of unrest in the rear areas of the Western Front.[7] Later, as the Chief of Staff of Army Group Kiev from March to October of 1918, he had seen discontent building in the morale of German occupation troops in the Ukraine. And, while in the East, he had access to the disturbing reports of the situation in the West. There were personal contacts as well. After Groener arrived to take up his new

---

from militarism, was disastrous. At that point, Prince Max forced Wilhelm to choose between himself and Ludendorff. In a heated session with the Kaiser on October 26, Ludendorff had tendered his resignation for the third time that year. This time the Kaiser accepted, but required Hindenburg to stay on. See Siegfried Kaehler, "Vier quellenkritische Untersuchungen zum Kriegsende 1918." *Nachrichten der Akademie der Wissenschaften in Göttingen*, Philologisch-Historische Klasse, 8 (1960), 434–53.

[6] Helmut Heussler, *General Wilhelm Groener and the Imperial German Army* (Madison: University of Wisconsin Press, 1962), 118. (Heussler covers the period of Groener's life up to the end of the war. There is no current, complete biography, in German or English, of this important figure.)

[7] Groener's testimony, October 30, in the 1925 "stab-in-the-back" trial, cited by Christof von Ebbinghaus, *Memoiren des Generals von Ebbinghaus* (Stuttgart: Begers Literarisches Büro, 1928), 26.

duties, a personal acquaintance, the division commander of the 192nd Infantry Division, wrote him:

My dear Groener! I don't know if I may still risk this letter. But my lines are not directed to the First Quartermaster General, but from a friend to an old friend. I am writing you because perhaps from the Great General Headquarters the insight into the troops does not go deep enough to truly measure the combat power for its real worth ... The powers of resistance of the troops have come to an end. You know me well enough to know that I am no doomsayer. My division has not had a day of rest since May ... The battle situation and losses haven't allowed even the withdrawal of companies ... So far as I can see around me, it is the same with every other division. To this point, we have done our duty. The time of our collapse comes dangerously close. It has become a matter of weeks. There comes, finally, a time where every influence for relief fails. We are coming to this situation.[8]

Groener could also build an impression of the situation on the reports of the subordinate army and army group headquarters. Yet, as a realist, the general was aware of the time-honored military practice of putting the best possible face on situation reports sent up the chain of command. With that in mind, Groener sent a staff officer, Captain Loose, on a four-day inspection tour for the express purpose of reporting on front-line morale. Loose interviewed senior leaders up and down the Western Front and returned on November 3, 1918, with disturbing news. Everywhere, commanders and staff officers assessed the mood of the men as bad. The troops faced nervous exhaustion and a breakdown loomed. The men no longer tolerated pictures of the Kaiser, Hindenburg, and Ludendorff on the wall of their mess halls, and trust in the OHL had been badly shaken. The leaders in both Army Group Gallwitz and Army Group Duke Albert asserted the men would no longer fight if peace did not come quickly. "The men want peace at any price," Loose reported.

Even more disturbing were Loose's findings on the mood of the officer corps. Many officers sympathized with the democratic reforms in the government. Among the junior officers and even, in isolated cases, among older staff officers, there was an increasing mood of political indifference and, occasionally, hostility to the regime. Other, more senior officers seemed shaken by the fear of Bolshevism. Loose warned that urgent measures were required to steady the nerves and ensure the commitment of the officer corps.[9]

---

[8] Letter from Major General Loeffler quoted in Groener, *Lebenserinnerungen*, 457.
[9] Gerhard W. Rakenius, *Wilhelm Groener als erster Generalquartiermeister: Die Politik der Obersten Heeresleitung 1918–1919* (Boppard am Rhein: Harald Boldt, 1977), 29–30.

Could the monarchy be preserved? Groener had taken up his new post convinced that the Kaiser, as a symbol and object of the officer's oath, was essential to holding the army together. Though a Württemberger and more open-minded in outlook than the Junkers surrounding him at the OHL, Groener had been solidly monarchist in his views and supportive of the Hohenzollern dynasty throughout his career. Still, Groener acknowledged that the army's loyalty to the Kaiser had eroded as the war turned sour. On November 1, he wrote the vice-chancellor, Payer, that, in efforts to unite the populace, the phrase "fight for the Kaiser" would have to be replaced with "fight for the united German fatherland" since the cause of the Kaiser alone was not enough to motivate the men for a final, decisive battle.[10] Still, in Groener's initial meetings with the civilian leaders of the government, he demanded that calls for abdication be quashed, warning that the army's steadfastness at the front depended on rejecting Allied demands for Wilhelm's removal.[11] At this point, the general seemed steadfast, but his views on the Kaiser's place in Germany's future changed dramatically as the events of early November played out.

Wilhelm himself was defiant. Woodrow Wilson's "Third Note," delivered on October 23, called obliquely but unmistakably for the end of the German monarchy. Wilhelm responded with derision. When Dr. Wilhelm Drews, the Prussian Assistant Secretary of State, visited Spa on November 1 to sound out the Kaiser's views on abdication, the emperor turned him away. Insulated from the worst reports, the Kaiser remained convinced he could rely on the army to stand behind the throne.[12] More important, he thought, the army relied on him. If he were to abdicate, he would be leaving the heroic men at the front "in the lurch" [im Stich zu lassen]. The army would collapse and leave the homeland open to the enemy.[13]

The Kaiser's defiance was supported by the most trusted figure of the Second Reich, Field Marshal Paul von Hindenburg. Yet Hindenburg did not make devotion to the monarchy his central argument in resisting abdication. Instead, according to Drews, he rejected abdication primarily because of the effect it would have on the Field Army. Speaking

[10] *Quellen*, Document 500, "Auszüge aus dem Bericht des bäyerischen Militärbevollmächtigten an den bäyerischen Kriegsminister," 1356, fn. 4
[11] *Ibid.*
[12] On October 30, the Bavarian representative to Berlin wrote: "There are still so many people in his entourage who tell the Kaiser he has the people behind him. H.M. is simply not informed." Isabel Hull, *The Entourage of Kaiser Wilhelm II, 1888–1918* (Cambridge University Press, 1982), 289.
[13] Bundesarchiv Reich (Berlin-Lichterfelde; hereafter BA-R), R43/2403/6, Drews' report on his trip to Spa, 4.

in a tone of deep "inner conviction," Hindenburg argued that the army on the Western Front was being held together only through the authority of the officer corps. If that corps was to lose its *Oberste Kriegherr* (Supreme Warlord), the Kaiser, their authority would be weakened, thus causing, said the field marshal, "half the army to dissolve and scatter throughout the homeland as marauding robber bands. You can imagine the fearful result that would follow." The Kaiser must remain at the helm, he continued. He and every other officer would consider themselves scoundrels if they were to abandon their emperor. The army could still make a stand that would bring some sort of an acceptable peace.[14]

Significantly, Hindenburg's argument indicated that the *Feldheer* was the critical element in determining Germany's future. If the German Army held out, the Allies might be willing to offer tolerable peace terms. However, if the units at the front collapsed, then the homeland would be flooded by armed bandits or worse. According to Hindenburg's conception, the army was composed of men capable of both tenacious heroism and terrifying criminality. From the field marshal's vantage, the units at the front were a double-edged sword that must necessarily inspire both admiration and dread from the homeland. In a curious way, the Kaiser's role had been reduced to a symbol useful for rallying the support of the front-line troops.

Here and in repeated instances in the crisis of late 1918, Germany's military leaders used the soldiers in the trenches as both carrot and stick. By portraying the combat troops as both valiant heroes and latent brigands, the High Command appealed to the moral stature the *Frontschweine* had earned in German society in four years of war as well as their potential for armed violence against that same society. They would use this somewhat cynical application again and again in the days before and after the overthrow of the monarchy.

In the first days of November, the veterans holding the front seemed to be doing their duty, and the army's leaders were cautiously optimistic about the *Westheer*'s immediate future. Despite the strain, the front had not broken. Sufficient indications existed to convince some in high places that the army could hold out a while longer, perhaps until the spring. After all, the divisions on the Western Front had withstood

---

[14] *Ibid.* This view was seconded by Groener. The army, he had said, recognized "no *Kaiserfrage* [Kaiser question]." Wilhelm was especially gratified by the stance of the new First Quartermaster General. Observing that the normally quiet Groener had spoken forcefully on his behalf, Wilhelm exclaimed, "That it was indeed a south German general who stood up for the German Emperor and the King of Prussia, what good that has done me!" Niemann, *Kaiser und Revolution*, 126.

Foch's counteroffensives without breaking. The army was withdrawing in relatively good order to the Antwerp–Meuse position. The Allied armies, plagued by supply problems, were pursuing only with difficulty. Perhaps there were enough stalwarts left to stop the Allied advance and earn Germany an acceptable peace settlement. In the first days of November, at Berlin and Spa, there was still an opportunity for some optimistic souls to hold out hope for the monarchy's future. However, that situation changed dramatically on November 4 with the outbreak of full-blown mutiny in the High Seas fleet.[15]

No watch on the Rhine

The events following the mutiny at Kiel seemed to confirm all of the doubts Germany's leaders held for the troops behind the front. After the naval authorities failed to contain unrest among the sailors in the North Sea ports, armed uprisings spread rapidly across Germany. The marines, military police, replacement units, and other local garrison forces placed in the path of the revolutionary tide proved unable or, more often, unwilling, to stop the onslaught. As the mutinous sailors carried the message of revolution from town to town on commandeered trains, resistance collapsed. Instead of fighting, the soldiers of the Home Army hailed the mutineers as comrades. Within a few days, revolutionary soldiers' and workers' councils (modeled after the Bolshevik soviets) had replaced the imperial authorities in many of the cities of northern Germany and the industrial centers of the Ruhr.[16]

Against this avalanche of bad news the Kaiser declared himself resolved to remain with the army. On November 8, he announced his goal of marching at the head of reliable front-line troops to put down the insurrection. After all, Hindenburg and Groener had assured him of the army's continued loyalty.[17] Wilhelm continued to resist the urgent pleadings of the chancellor, Prince Max of Baden, to return to the capital, where he was needed to help make the key decisions that had to be

---

[15] Prince Max, in particular, thought the OHL was slow to recognize the decline in both army and home front morale. See "The Abdication of the Kaiser," printed August 9, 1919 in the *Berliner Tageblatt* (*BT*) and reprinted in Hoover War Library Publications, *Fall of the German Empire, 1914–1918*, ed. Ralph Lutz (Stanford University Press, 1932), vol. II, 529–30. According to the OHL's representative to the Kaiser, Lieutenant Colonel Niemann, Groener's initial report on the military situation was generally positive. See Niemann, *Kaiser und Revolution*, 123.

[16] The collapse of the Home Army is described in the impressive scholarship of Ernst-Heinrich Schmidt's *Heimatheer und Revolution*.

[17] The Kaiser's outlook from the first-hand accounts by the head of his military cabinet, Lieutenant Alfred Niemann, in Niemann, *Kaiser und Revolution*, 134.

made on the future of the monarchy. Wilhelm had also rejected suggestions that he seek the sort of heroic death that would inspire the German
people and arouse sympathy for the monarchy. When he had traveled
west from Spa on November 4, some of the emperor's advisors urged
that he venture beyond the division rest areas all the way to the trenches
where the joy he had expressed in sharing the dangers of the front-
line veterans could be fully realized by exposing himself to enemy fire.
Though such a scheme would unite him with the stalwart *Feldgrauen*
who had encouraged him a few days before, orchestrating the sort of
heroic wounding or death such a gesture required would be problematic on a 1918 battlefield. Hindenburg weighed in against the plan,
and, more importantly, such a step would have violated the prohibition
placed on suicide by the Kaiser's sincere religious beliefs. Rejecting the
idea of a "death ride" [*Todesritt*] at the front, the Kaiser remained with
the OHL and looked to them to prepare the *Heimatoperation*, the campaign to reconquer the homeland.[18]

The problem with the Kaiser's plan was that it was built without a
foundation. This became apparent to Groener when he returned to Spa
on November 7, after a disturbing two-day trip to Berlin.[19] While he was
in the capital the situation had worsened and Groener began to doubt
that the revolutionary tide could be dammed. He was skeptical of proposals that railway bridges be blown up and railway lines dismantled to
protect the interior of the homeland. As for putting loyal troops in the
path of the revolutionaries, the high-quality combat formations needed
for such an operation were committed to the bitter defensive fighting

---

[18] The chief advocate of the imperial "death ride" plan was Admiral Paul von Hintze, the
liaison between Prince Max and the imperial cabinet. He gained a measure of support
from Groener but was unable to convince Wilhelm of the necessity of such a measure.
Hintze, "Aufzeichnungen des Staatssekretärs v. Hintze," in Niemann *Revolution von
Oben*, 366–9. See also Isabel Hull, "Military Culture, Wilhelm II, and the End of the
Monarchy in the First World War," in *The Kaiser: New Research on Wilhelm II's Role in
Imperial Germany*, ed. Annika Mombauer and Wilhelm Deist (New York: Cambridge
University Press, 2003), 250–8. Hull points out that the "death ride" scheme represented another effort by Germany's leaders to "instrumentalize" the Kaiser. Groener
gave his views on the "death ride" in his testimony the "stab-in-the-back" trial of
1925: "His Majesty should go directly to the front and indeed not to parades, reviews,
or awards of Iron Crosses, but instead into battle ... [not to make a suicide attack,
but to] simply be at the front, in the trenches, there where hundreds of thousands
of German soldiers and officers also stood." Groener's testimony in *Der Dolchstoss-
prozess in München: Ehrenrettung des deutschen Volkes; Zeugen und Sachverstandigen
Aussagen – Eine Sammlung von Dokumente* (Munich: Druck und Verlag G. Birke and
Co., 1925), 214.

[19] Though Groener had told the Social Democratic leader that the army would not consider the matter of abdication, events suggest that at this point he may have begun to
see the Kaiser as expendable. He also told the chancellor the army needed an armistice within three days.

at the front.[20] The army in the West had no significant reserves. The OHL would need days, perhaps weeks to extricate any large force from the front and prepare them to march against the revolution.[21]

Nevertheless, in response to government's earliest calls for help, the German High Command had already pulled a handful of tired units out of the line. They included the 7th Cavalry Rifle Division, the 52nd Reserve Infantry Division, the 2nd Guards Infantry Division as well as a variety of smaller formations.[22] On November 8, Groener met with the staff sections of the OHL to consider how best to deploy the three divisions. Much depended on these units, especially since the OHL had reports that *Rotarmisten* (Red Army troops) had seized the Rhine bridges.[23] The army's line of communications, its lifeline to the interior of Germany, was in danger.

What happened to these three divisions is extraordinarily significant for the course of the German revolution and the Kaiser's decision to abdicate. We know relatively little about the 7th Cavalry Rifle Division. Presumably, the OHL chose it because of its limited exposure to combat.[24] The army had dismounted the division and converted it to an infantry division only a few months before. However, the 7th had seen enough action for Allied intelligence to give the division its lowest possible rating: "fourth class" (useful only in holding quiet sectors of the front).[25] On November 8, the OHL staff alerted the division for movement to the vicinity of Verviers.[26] The order was cancelled when the division's higher headquarters, Army Group Duke Albrecht, protested that the 7th was in no condition for deployment against the homeland.[27]

[20] Groener's testimony in the 1925 "stab-in-the-back" trial cited in Ebbinghaus, *Memoiren*, 29.
[21] See Groener's discussion in *Lebenserinnerungen*, 449.
[22] Somewhere between November 5 and November 7, the OHL sent a *Sturm* (assault) battalion, and two *Jäger* (light infantry) battalions to support the military authorities in the Ruhr (Deist, document 504, 1373, fn. 5). The government of Württemburg requested the elite Württemburg Mountain Regiment be released for internal defense. However, at the time of the request the regiment was unavailable as it was involved in heavy combat with US forces and had been reduced to below battalion strength (Schmidt, *Heimatheer und Revolution*, 139)
[23] These seem to have been unfounded rumors of uncertain origin.
[24] Albrecht von Thaer, a lieutenant colonel and a senior member of the OHL's logistic staff. In his diary entry for November 7, he recorded the view that the cavalry divisions were among the most reliable: Thaer, *Generalstabdienst an der Front*. The French Army had relied heavily on cavalry units in suppressing the mutinies of 1917.
[25] AEF G2, *251 Divisions*, 156. The estimate of the division's quality is rather vague: "Its use on the Cambrai and Belgium fronts in September and October indicates that it might have been considered a third-class division after its reorganization." Thaer identifies this unit as the 6th Cavalry Rifle Division, but this seems to be a mistake.
[26] Thaer, diary entry for November 8, 256.
[27] Deist, Document 503, *Quellen*, 1373, fn. 5.

More is known about the 52nd Reserve Infantry Division. Made up of troops from the Rhineland, the division had seen action on the Western Front since October of 1914. Allied intelligence rated it as "second class,"[28] though "probably not so good as other divisions similarly rated."[29] The 52nd Reserve had recently suffered heavy casualties near Courtrai, Belgium, and been pulled out of the line on October 25.[30] On November 5, the OHL responded to a request from the Prussian war ministry by earmarking the division for employment against the naval mutinies at Kiel and Wilhelmshaven. While the unit was waiting for transport, the OHL changed its mission, directing it instead to move by rail to Hasselt in preparation for securing the Rhine bridges.[31] As the unit began to arrive in Hasselt, a general staff officer from Spa, von Fischer-Truenfeld, left Spa to deliver further instructions to the division.[32]

He returned to Spa on the morning of November 9, a shaken man. Fischer-Truenfeld described the situation at Hasselt as "catastrophic." He reported that the troops of the 52nd Reserve Infantry Division were engaged in full-blown mutiny, fraternizing with the Belgians and selling or giving away their weapons. Officers had been deposed and the soldiers had fashioned red armbands for themselves to demonstrate their support for the revolution. Fischer-Truenfeld's report added to the growing gloom at the headquarters during the decisive hours of November 9. Two of the three divisions assigned to secure the army's supply lines had failed.

The staff expected better reports from the 2nd Guards Division. Both Germans and Allies alike considered it an elite division that had fought well in the toughest battles on the Western Front.[33] A veteran guards formation, it was rated one of the most reliable in the army by Groener and his staff. This division, they believed, would be up to the task.

The division commander, Lieutenant General von Friedeburg, was not so sure. He had seen signs of wavering and unreliability among his men as early as August.[34] Since then, the division had been cut

---

[28] Though not an elite "assault" unit, a second-class division could be used in an offensive role.

[29] AEF G2, *251 Divisions*, 506.   [30] *Ibid.*, 506.

[31] Deist, Document 503, *Quellen*, 1373, fn. 5.

[32] Thaer, diary entry for November 2, 257.

[33] AEF G2, *251 Divisions* described it as a "first-class assault division" but conceded it had taken very heavy losses between August and October: 54.

[34] Von Friedeburg had warned his division about shirking behind the line and the failure of infantry to secure supporting artillery in an order entitled "Relations of Infantry and Artillery during Fighting," dated August 27, 1918, found in *Why Germany Capitulated*, 51.

to pieces, losing the best of its experienced officers and NCOs. His depleted strength forced Friedeburg to consolidate the men in each of his three regiments to two battalions of 200 men each.[35] He even lacked sufficient artillerymen to man the division's remaining guns. Making matters worse, since coming out of the line on November 1, the few replacements the division received were of uncertain quality. On November 3, for example, the 2nd Guards received a replacement draft of 160 men, many of whom were *"Bolsheviki,"* men returned from captivity in Russia. Twenty of the replacements had deserted en route to the unit.[36]

The depleted condition of the 2nd Guards Division brings into focus the acute dilemma faced by the OHL as it struggled to develop countermeasures against the revolution. Those units with the best fighting record were also the ones assumed to be best suited for use against internal unrest. Yet these were the same units most likely to be involved in the heaviest fighting and, thus, most likely to be under strength and overtired.

The division's employment against the revolutionary forces began badly. In Berlin, the war ministry made anxious requests for reliable front-line troops to stiffen the local garrison. The OHL alerted the 2nd Guards, and the division hastily formed an advance party to prepare the division's movement to the imperial capital. The advance party included elements of the division staff, the veterinary section, engineers, and elements of the division's supply trains. As the remainder of the division awaited transport, the advance elements moved to the army training area at Zossen, just south of Berlin. As each train arrived, it was greeted by mutinous members of the garrison. The garrison troops isolated and disarmed the surprised guardsmen, who lacked instructions on how to deal with such a reception. Thus rebuffed, the advance party returned to join the remainder of the division at Herbesthal on the German–Belgian border.[37]

The incident, while relatively insignificant, tells us much about the frantically haphazard response the leaders of the old regime made to the revolution. Apparently, no one told the 2nd Guards that revolutionaries had seized Zossen. Instead of leading the deployment to Berlin

[35] The peacetime complement of an infantry regiment included three battalions of over 1,000 men each.
[36] Details of the condition and employment of the 2nd Guards Division from von Friedeburg's own account "Die 2. Gardedivision am 9. November 1918." Von Friedeburg recorded this account at Potsdam, on August 1, 1927. It is included as an appendix to Niemann, *Revolution von Oben*, 425–7.
[37] *Ibid.*, 425.

with combat troops, the division had sent it noncombatant support elements first, a routine procedure for an administrative move, but certainly not one to be used when resistance was expected. One can imagine the bewilderment of the guardsmen when attempting to detrain at Zossen.

By November 9, the division received a new mission. As it hurried to assemble around Herbesthal, the OHL ordered Friedeburg to secure the eastern approaches to the headquarters at Spa. The new guidance was based on reports of revolutionary units preparing to move on the Supreme Headquarters from Aachen. Herbesthal was a key rail junction between Aachen and Spa, and the 2nd Guards were tasked to provide security for both the emperor and the army's highest headquarters.

Even this order proved difficult to execute. On the way to Herbesthal, the men of the division saw increasing signs of unrest along the army's line of communications. Crowds of rear-area personnel crowded around the intermediate railroad stations demanding transportation home. Red flags decorated train cars, and railway personnel abandoned their posts, forcing the 2nd Guards to load and move themselves. At the train station in Liège on November 9, the Guards Fusilier Battalion of the Alexander Regiment repelled a crowd of drunken mutineers from boarding their train. Slowed by the growing turmoil and shortage of railroad cars, the only unit to reach its destination by November 9 was a part of the division artillery. The first infantry battalion did not arrive at Herbesthal until a day later.[38]

Nevertheless, Friedeburg's assertion that his division was well in hand through November 9 carries a special significance. His claim conflicts with reports that reached Spa on the morning of November 9, which indicated that, along with the collapse of the 52nd Reserve Infantry Division, the 2nd Guards Division was "totally unreliable."[39] The origin of this damning evaluation is unknown but seems in keeping with the spirit of exaggeration, rumor, and increasing hopelessness that seemed prevalent within the headquarters at Spa in the last days of the war.[40] By November 8, it already appeared to the OHL's harried staff that their efforts to use the three divisions to secure the Rhine bridges were unlikely to find success. The 7th Cavalry Rifle Division was unavailable, and the 52nd Reserve Infantry Division and the 2nd

---

[38] Details of the 2nd Guards Division's experience around Herbesthal from *ibid.*, 425–7.

[39] Thaer, *Generalstabdienst an der Front*, 263. This comes from an eye-witness statement of Thaer's written after the war, 259–64.

[40] See Thaer's description of the mood of the OHL staff on the evening of November 8, *ibid.*, 261.

Guards were closing on their designated assembly areas too slowly to make an immediate impact.[41]

This was the situation Groener faced when he called his staff sections together late on November 8 to review the prospects for marching the army against the revolution. Early in the day, the consensus among the staff was that the Field Army should turn its strength as rapidly and powerfully as possible against the revolutionary forces inside the Reich. As the day went on, that consensus seemed to fade. The Chief of the Operations Section, Colonel Wilhelm Heye, expressed the view that there were not enough reliable troops left to make a counter-revolutionary operation possible. On the contrary, by controlling the Rhine bridges the revolutionaries held the upper hand.[42] The Chief of the Quartermaster Section warned that the army had only enough provisions for eight days.[43] If the men at the front could not be fed, the army faced an even more disastrous prospect than the OHL staff had previously imagined.

The crucial meeting continued into the evening. By its end, Groener had decided the *Heimatoperation* (homeland operation) was impossible. The army could not pull enough divisions out of line until the armistice was in place. Neither was there enough transport, as the difficulties and delays in moving just the 2nd Guards Division had demonstrated. Beyond these difficulties, if the army was to march on Berlin, it faced the prospect of fighting across 600 kilometers of territory held by the revolutionaries. It would have to operate without access to the depots that fed the army. These lay within territory held by the rebels.[44] Other reports indicated that elements of the revolutionary forces were well armed and well equipped.[45] Even if all these problems were overcome – an unlikely

---

[41] Reports of the unreliability of the 2nd Guard and 52nd Reserve Infantry had already reached Spa by the 8th according to an article appearing in the *Neue Preussische Zeitung* on July 27, 1919 (1–2) and reprinted as Document 523, "The Events of November 9, 1918, at Great Headquarters in Spa, Belgium," in Lutz, ed., *Fall of the German Empire*, 537–48. Hindenburg and many of the more monarchist senior members of both the OHL and the Kaiser's entourage confirmed the article's veracity.

[42] Thaer, *Generalstabsdienst an der Front*, 261.

[43] Thaer wrote that, in the course of the meeting he challenged that view, reminding those present that field units routinely hoarded enough supplies to sustain themselves two or three times longer than what their reported stocks indicated. He also pointed out that international relief agencies had established stocks for the civilian population of Belgium. In an emergency, these could be used to provision the army. Groener rejected this last idea, saying it would jeopardize the armistice negotiations (Thaer, diary entry for November 8, *Generalstabsdienst an der Front*, 256–7).

[44] Niemann, *Revolution von Oben*, 280.

[45] This was totally unfounded but typical of the wild reports that circulated during this period. Niemann said such reports weighed very heavily on Groener and the staff. *Ibid.*, 279.

outcome – what remained for every officer to consider was the prospect of bloody civil war, *feldgrau* fighting *feldgrau*.

The discussion within Groener's staff had ranged over a variety of topics, but, in every case, those present avoided the question of abdication. Nevertheless, everyone realized the Kaiser would have to be told his beloved army could not, perhaps would not, march to save his dynasty. This weighed especially heavily on Groener and Hindenburg who, together, had assured the Kaiser of the faithfulness of the men in the trenches just days earlier. How to convince the Kaiser the army could no longer be relied on? Earlier in the day, Colonel Heye had recommended summoning a number of front-line commanders, from regiment, brigade and division level, to meet at Spa the next morning.[46] From them, the Kaiser could receive a true, unfiltered picture of the army's condition. Groener decided to await the outcome of this unusual poll and to put off any further decisions until he had heard these representatives of the men in the trenches.[47] They would defer the key decisions until the next day.[48]

The *Armeeparlament*

Heye's recommendation led to one of the most unusual and controversial incidents in all of German military history: the *Armeeparlament*[49] of November 9, 1918. In effect, several dozen middle-level front-line commanders voted on the fate of their emperor. For the purposes of this study, the true significance of the *Armeeparlament* is found in who was chosen to attend. There were to be no staff officers or senior commanders. Instead, Heye asked for five regimental, brigade, or division commanders from each of the ten armies closest to Spa.[50] What he and Groener wanted was a candid assessment of the willingness of the front-line soldiers to fight a counter-revolutionary campaign on behalf of the Kaiser. Groener, in particular, did not trust the corps, army, and army

---

[46] Walter Goerlitz, *November 1918: Bericht über die deutsche Revolution* (Hamburg: Gerhard Stalling Verlag, 1968), 167.

[47] The account of the November 8 meeting is taken from Thaer, *Generalstabdienst an der Front*, 256, and 261–2; Lutz, ed., *Fall of the German Empire*, Document 523, 538–9; and Niemann, *Revolution von Oben*, 278–81.

[48] After the war, critics on the right bitterly criticized Hindenburg and Groener for not informing the Kaiser immediately once they had decided the *Heimatoperation* was not possible.

[49] This was the name given the meeting by von Hintze, the government's representative at the OHL, Baumont, *Fall of the Kaiser*, 229.

[50] They came from the following army groups from north to south: Army Group Rupprecht (Crown Prince of Bavaria), Army Group Crown Prince (of Prussia), and Army Group Gallwitz.

group headquarters to relay such an assessment up the chain of command to the OHL. As we have seen, the First Quartermaster General already had reason to believe the worst news about soldier morale was being filtered out as it made its way to the Supreme Command.[51] Better to hear first-hand the opinions of the men who had day-to-day contact with the front-line troops. One can hardly imagine Frederick the Great or the elder Moltke relying on such an unusual council of war, but neither Frederick nor Moltke had ever found himself in the position Groener struggled with on November 8.

For those front-line leaders chosen to attend, the summons meant a long, cold ride with an uncertain object. One of the chosen fifty, a regimental commander named Major Hünicken, later described the trip. Alerted on the morning of November 8, Hünicken was picked up by a staff car in the early afternoon and taken to corps headquarters, where he was told he had been chosen to go to the Supreme Commanders because of his courageous and capable service during the most recent weeks of combat. Chosen for what, no one could tell him, though some speculated correctly that he was to be interrogated on the morale and condition of his men. The next morning at 4.30, Hünicken left for Spa with another regimental commander. Six hours later, traveling through wind and snow, they arrived at the Supreme Headquarters. After submitting to numerous identification checks, they were ushered into the great hall of the Hotel Britannique, which housed the OHL staff. There they found several dozen waiting officers, all in the same condition as themselves, tired, cold, unwashed, unfed, and uninformed. They greeted each other in whispers and speculated as to the purpose of their gathering.[52]

Sometime between ten and eleven o'clock, Colonel Heye of the OHL's operations staff greeted the front-line commanders: "On behalf of the field marshal [Hindenburg] allow me to welcome you here. The field marshal wanted to greet you himself, but is momentarily unavailable since he is with His Majesty in an extremely important, urgent meeting." Heye went on emphasize the gravity of the situation to the officers present. Unrest had broken out in the homeland. There were urgent demands for peace at any price. Deserters in the army's rear areas had seized several key rail junctions, threatening to cut off the

---

[51] State Secretary von Hintze wrote that the refusal of the 4th Bavarian and 18th *Landwehr* Divisions to go to the front had gone unreported by army group headquarters. See Hintze, "Aufzeichnung des Staatsekrataers v. Hintze," in Niemann, *Revolution von Oben*, 372.

[52] Hünicken's story from his article, "Das Frontheer und der 9. November: Erlebnisse eines Regimentskommandeurs in Spa," appendix to Niemann, *Revolution von Oben*, 437–44.

army's supply lines. Heye went on to tell them they would each, in turn, be asked two questions regarding the mood of their troops: "(1) How do the troops feel toward the Kaiser? Is it possible for the Kaiser to lead the troops in battle to recapture the homeland? (2) How do the troops stand on Bolshevism?[53] Will they take up arms to combat Bolshevism in their own country?"[54]

Before the assembled officers could be asked these questions, Hindenburg entered the room. Hünicken wrote that the old field marshal's eyes were red, his face pale, and his hands clenched with emotion. Behind him were Groener and General von Plessen, the Kaiser's General-Adjutant, who was dabbing his eyes with a handkerchief. Hindenburg greeted the front-line officers and offered them his assessment of the situation. As Heye had done, he emphasized the army's difficult situation, beset by enemies at the front and threatened by revolutionaries in the rear. The Kaiser, he said, wanted to turn the army around in the face of the enemy and march on Berlin in a difficult operation that would last at least two to three weeks.[55] The situation was grave and the old field marshal urged every man present do his utmost to maintain order and discipline.[56]

After this brief address, Hindenburg withdrew. There was a moment of stunned silence among the officers in the room. Their shock was exaggerated by the fact the front-line army had not received mail or newspapers for two weeks. In the words of one officer, they had "lived on rumors."[57] Gradually, as the impact of the field marshal's words wore off, individuals around the room began to react with outcries of anger and dismay. An unknown major from the general staff then warned them that they did not understand how bad things really were. Revolutionaries had overwhelmed the Home Army and telegraphic and telephonic communication between Germany and the army had been cut off. The army faced starvation since the depots east of the Rhine were being

[53] The army's leadership routinely used the word "Bolshevik" to describe the revolutionaries, indifferent to (and largely unaware of) the diverse shades of political ideology among those who opposed them.
[54] Heye's briefing from Hünicken, "Das Frontheer," 439. Questions from the "Westarp Protokoll" (Kuno Graf von Westarp) reprinted in conservative newspapers on July 27, 1919. Reprinted in Gerhard Ritter and Susanne Miller, eds., *Die deutsche Revolution, 1918–1919* (Frankfurt: Fischer Taschenbücher, 1965), 71.
[55] Hindenburg's briefing from the eyewitness accounts of Major Beck and Captain Roedenbeck, reprinted in Graf Kuno von Westarp, *Das Ende der Monarchie am 9. November,* ed. Werner Conze (Berlin: 1952), 64–5.
[56] Hünicken, "Das Frontheer," 439. Von Schulenberg later criticized the field marshal for painting too bleak a picture of the situation. "Denkschrift des Generals Graf von der Schulenberg von 26 August 1919," Niemann, *Revolution von Oben,* 347.
[57] Westarp, *Das Ende der Monarchie,* 65–6.

plundered by mutinous troops. Both the King of Bavaria and the Duke of Braunschweig had already abdicated. "One must reckon with a great catastrophe within the army." The effect of the major's words, when added to those of Heye and Hindenburg, was "shattering."[58]

In this distressed state, the officers were now called to answer Heye's two questions. When he had first greeted them, thirty-two of the antici- pated fifty commanders were present. During their briefing, seven more arrived. Breakdowns and bad weather delayed the remaining eleven officers and they did not take part. Starting with the representatives from the northernmost army, Heye called the front-line officers into an adjoining room where another staff officer recorded their individual answers. Sometime after midday, the vote was complete.

To question 1, on attitudes to the Kaiser, one officer answered yes, his men would follow their Supreme Warlord against the revolution. Fifteen officers believed it was more or less doubtful whether the troops would follow the Kaiser. Twenty-three said no, it was not possible. To question 2, on the troops' attitude to Bolshevism, eight discounted any possibility of employing their men against the Bolsheviks. Twelve officers believed the men would require an extended period of rest and training before such a campaign could be attempted. Nineteen consid- ered it doubtful whether any or all of their soldiers would be willing to fight against the Bolsheviks under any circumstances.

The overall impression, according to Heye, was that the front-line soldiers were totally exhausted and "fought-out." They wanted to go home and to have nothing but peace when they got there. Only a direct threat to home and family would inspire them to take up arms against their own countrymen. Heye swore the thirty-nine officers to secrecy and prepared to brief the Kaiser.[59]

In the years after the war, die-hard monarchists denounced Groener and Heye for the way the *Armeeparlament* was conducted. General Graf von der Schulenberg argued it was impossible to expect an impartial vote from men as physically exhausted and emotionally shaken as were the thirty-nine commanders on the morning of November 9. Even worse, Hindenburg's briefing to the front-line officers had described the situation in almost hopeless terms.[60] What is more, none of those summoned knew what the consequences of their answers would be.

---

[58] Hünicken, "Das Frontheer," 439. Some speculate the unknown officer was Major von Stulpnagel who later attacked Groener in the Court of Honor held in 1922.

[59] The conduct and results of *Armeeparlement* comes from Heye's own account quoted in Groener, *Lebenserinnerungen*, 457–8.

[60] Schulenberg, "Denkschrift," in Niemann, *Revolution von Oben*, 347. See also Colonel Max Bauer, *Der grosse Krieg in Feld und Heimat: Erinnerungen und Betrachtungen von*

Whatever Groener's motivations, the criticisms made by Schulenberg and others manifest an ironic element. If the officers called to Spa were too tired, cold, emotionally drained, and uninformed to answer impartially, what of the men they represented? On a daily basis, the front-line troops in the trenches faced even greater levels of stress, privation, and uncertainty. Did Schulenberg expect them to be more steadfast than their commanders?

Whatever the conditions, the vote was in. The past weeks had shown the men at the front were increasingly unwilling to fight on. The three divisions of front-line troops dispatched to the Rhine bridges had failed to rescue the desperate situation. Now, through their own commanders, the front-line troops had turned a "thumbs-down" on the Kaiser's plan to recapture his empire.

The case of the *Armeeparlament* suggests the lines of analysis used to assess the behavior of front-line soldiers may be applied to their officers as well. Certainly, emotional and physical *exhaustion* shaped the views of the thirty-nine officers who had traveled through the night to reach Spa and the *Armeeparlament*. *Isolation* played a role as well. For the tired officers summoned to the OHL, the initial briefing by Colonel Heye was their first exposure to news of the revolution within Germany. It was news they were unprepared for and it left them shaken and confused. By the same token, *selection* was clearly a significant factor: the officers chosen for the *Armeeparlament* were probably among the best combat leaders available to the German Army in 1918. However, their competence and leadership did not translate into a mindless devotion to the monarchy. On November 9, they were tired, cold, hungry, and frank in their estimation of what their soldiers were willing to do. *Cohesion*, in the form of loyalty by the officers to their men, seems to have been at work here, as well. The front-line commanders called to Spa refused to sugarcoat their assessment of the condition of their troops and what they could accomplish. In describing the weariness of their troops, they hoped to avoid having the OHL call on their units for missions they could no longer perform. Finally, Groener's handling of the thirty-nine officers who participated in the *Armeeparlament* features a clear example of the *management* of perception. By having his lieutenant, Heye,

---

Oberst Max Bauer (Tübingen: Osiander'sche Buchhandlung, 1921), 269. Groener argued that the vote was vindicated by subsequent events (Groener, *Lebenserinnerungen*, 458). Bauer, a bitter critic of those present at Spa, blamed Groener for the outcome of the *Armeeparlament*. He argued that the question posed to the front-line commanders should have been: "Who wants to abandon the Kaiser and who wants to help him save Germany from oath-breaking sailors, deserters, and other rabble?" (*Grosse Krieg*, 269)

paint a bleak picture of the army's condition and combining that with the enormous moral impact of Hindenburg's grim personal assessment, Groener ensured that the assembled commanders would not feel compelled to contrive an excessively optimistic assessment of the attitude and capabilities of their men. Groener, in turn, would use this outcome of the *Armeeparlament* to manage the perceptions of the Kaiser, who, until that point, had refused to believe the *Frontheer* would not march behind him to crush the revolution.

Who speaks for the "front"?

As the front-line officers arrived and cast their votes on the fate of the empire, the army's leaders were meeting with the Kaiser to consider the same issues. Groener apparently decided not to wait for the outcome of the *Armeeparlament*. This may have been due to reports received late the evening before from Berlin. One in particular, forwarded by the chancellery around midnight, was a warning from the moderate leaders of the Majority Socialist Party. It said that if the emperor did not reach a decision on abdication immediately, the authorities in the capital could not prevent the workers of Berlin from taking to the streets the next morning. Clearly, the Kaiser needed to hear the truth about the *Heimatoperation* as soon as possible. Together with Hindenburg, Groener confronted Wilhelm in the garden hall of the Villa Fraineuse, the Kaiser's quarters. Also present were the emperor's general-adjutant, von Plessen, the chancellor's representative to the OHL, von Hintze, and General Graf von der Schulenberg, the chief of staff of Army Group Crown Prince, as well as several others.[61]

Despite the urgency of the situation, neither Hindenburg nor Groener was eager to be the first to speak. As a Prussian of old-fashioned values, Hindenburg could not bring himself to deliver the bad news. Groener, in turn, believed it was not his place as a South German to urge the Prussian emperor to abdicate; that was properly the business of the Junkers in Wilhelm's entourage. However, as First Quartermaster General, Groener could lay out the military realities of the situation and leave it to Wilhelm to draw the appropriate conclusions.[62] He told the Kaiser that a counter-revolutionary operation was out of the question. The army could no longer be relied on, and the

---

[61] The account of the morning meeting comes from an eye-witness, Major Niemann, the OHL's representative to the Kaiser's court. Niemann, *Kaiser und Revolution*, 136–9. There are some contradictions between Groener, Westarp, Baumont, and Niemann on the exact sequence of discussions during the morning and early afternoon.
[62] Groener's taken views from Groener, *Lebenserinnerungen*, 459.

loss of the Rhine bridges put the supply situation of the Field Army
(*Frontheer*) in jeopardy.

Schulenberg stepped forward to offer a sharp challenge to Groener's
views. From this point through the remainder of the day, he led the
effort to block the Kaiser's abdication, and, as an army group chief of
staff and a staunch monarchist, his views had to be reckoned with.[63]
Schulenberg countered Groener's brief with his own estimate of the
situation, arguing that, even though the army as a whole was no longer
reliable, the *Feldheer* could find enough steadfast units to restore the
situation. He granted that gathering such units might need eight to ten
days. However, he said, once the army found out how its supply lines
had been threatened by mutineers and deserters, there would be no
problem in getting troops to fight the revolution. Groener replied that
the time was past for such measures. "Events have overcome us." The
situation within the army was so uncertain that a campaign based on
the slogan "Fight for the Homeland" might engulf the army in a bloodbath within its own ranks.[64]

As the argument went back and forth, Groener versus Schulenberg,
the underlying contest was clear – who spoke for the front-line army?
All other considerations were secondary. Between the two men,
Schulenberg had the advantage. As an army group chief of staff, he
was one rung lower in the chain of command and thus, by definition,
"closer" to the men in the trenches. According to the unwritten rules
of universal military culture, he had the moral authority to speak for
the men in the trenches. Against Schulenberg's assertions that the
front-line troops were loyal, Groener merely said, "My information is
different."[65]

As the exchange became more heated, the Kaiser intervened. After
four years of sacrifice, his goal, he said, was to lead the army in good
order back to the homeland. Groener's replied, "The army will march
home in peace and order under its generals, but not under the leadership of Your Majesty."[66] As First Quartermaster General, he admitted

---

[63] No one knew why von der Schulenberg was at Spa or who had summoned him. This
was one of the minor mysteries of November 9. Westarp suggested it was a telephone
call from the ubiquitous Major Stulpnagel. Westarp, *Das Ende der Monarchie*, 48–9.

[64] *Ibid.*, 136–9.

[65] Baumont, *Fall of the Kaiser*, 97. One imagines Groener referred here to the report of
Captain Loose and perhaps the letter from Major General von Loeffler.

[66] Groener, *Lebenserinnerungen*, 460. The Crown Prince wrote of this verdict: "He spoke
as if any further discussion was useless in view of the programme he had imposed
on the conference." Quoted in Baumont, *Fall of the Kaiser*, 98. On the other hand,
Groener wrote that the Crown Prince was not present (another mystery?). Groener,
Lebenserinnerungen, 459.

later, he had uttered a "monstrosity."[67] Nevertheless, in his own mind, he had offered the truth as he saw it. The Kaiser angrily demanded confirmation of Groener's views from the army's senior commanders. Hindenburg attempted to calm the increasingly emotional atmosphere by offering his own assessment that existing circumstances meant that neither he nor Groener could take responsibility for the army's reliability. Groener left shortly afterward, and the Kaiser continued to consult with his staff and the army's other leaders. The question of who would be the spokesman for the fighting men at the front had not been satisfactorily resolved. The army's senior leader, Hindenburg, the man known by many as the *Schattenkaiser*, "the shadow emperor," had come down decisively on the side of Groener and thus, implicitly, abdication.

The capital falls

While Groener and Schulenberg were arguing, momentous events were taking place in Berlin. That same morning, the Prussian war minister, General Heinrich von Scheuch, met with his staff to assess the situation in the imperial capital. Though Berlin was nearly surrounded by territory controlled by the revolutionaries, he remained convinced that the city's garrison remained loyal and that the OHL was moving to support him with troops from the front.[68] Scheuch told his adjutant, "We in Berlin are now like a besieged fortress. All depends on us holding Berlin. As long as that is successful nothing is lost."[69] The war minister's outlook changed dramatically over the next several hours. By midday, he was reporting to Spa that resistance against revolutionary forces had collapsed and that he no longer had any troops willing to defend the government.

On the face of it, Scheuch had ample means to defend Berlin. He and the military commander of the capital, Colonel-General von Linsingen, could call on an order of battle that included aircraft, armored trucks, tanks, and almost 60,000 men. However, what these numbers did not show was the quality of the troops. Most of the Berlin garrison was made up of replacement (*Ersatz*) battalions and, although the units often bore the names of the proudest guards' regiments in the army, they inspired little confidence in their leaders. The troops were either

[67] Groener, *Lebenserinnerungen*, 460. Groener wrote he would not have been surprised if, at that moment, one of those present would have shot him for what he had said.
[68] Schmidt, *Heimatheer und Revolution*, 333.
[69] Gustav Böhm, *Adjutant im Preussischen Kriegsministerium, Juni 1918 bis Oktober 1919; Aufzeichnungen des Hauptmanns Gustav Böhm*, ed. Heinz Huerten and Georg Meyer (Stuttgart: Deutsche Verlag-Anstalt, 1977), 59, fn. 225.

convalescents or young conscripts with less than ten weeks of training. All that remained to lead the *Ersatz* battalions were those officers considered unfit for the rigors of duty in the trenches. The OHL had earlier combed out the ranks of the officer corps to ensure that those fit for front-line service were in the trenches.[70]

As the threat of revolution grew through September and October, 1918,[71] Scheuch realized the need for high-quality troops to stiffen the resolve of the garrison and pressed the OHL for reinforcements. Through most of the war, the army had maintained two combat-ready divisions near Berlin to ensure the capital against internal unrest. In the spring of 1918, Ludendorff took these divisions away, claiming he needed every available combat formation to strengthen his upcoming offensive. When the offensive failed, the OHL did not replace the two divisions.[72] In early November, as we have seen, the Kiel mutiny had inspired the OHL to a failed attempt to move the 2nd Guards Infantry Division to Berlin.

The only truly combat-ready formations at Scheuch's disposal were three battalions of veteran light infantry (*Jägers*). They had last seen action in Finland, where they had fought as part of the German *Ostsee* Division against Finnish Red Guards. The three battalions had returned from Finland to Germany in August, where they were to be re-equipped and brought up to strength in preparation for reassignment to the Macedonian front. In September, when the Macedonian front had collapsed, the High Command decided the *Jägers* could be better used around Berlin.[73]

Though the three battalions of *Jägers* probably numbered fewer than 3,000 men,[74] Scheuch looked on them as the backbone of his security forces. In modern military parlance, they were the garrison's "center of gravity." They had already been in action against Bolsheviks in Finland. Thus, while General Linsingen deployed the less reliable *Ersatz* battalions in a thin cordon around Berlin, securing the capital against the onslaught of train-riding mutineers, he gave the *Jägers* the key postings in Potsdam and the center of the city. There, in small outposts, the three battalions of front-line troops set up defensive positions

---

[70] Schmidt, *Heimatheer und Revolution*, 145–52.

[71] Along with the estimated 20,000 deserters in the Berlin area (Böhm, *Adjutant*, 51), the authorities were also concerned with the considerable number of veterans who had been "reclaimed" from the army to work in the war industry. If it came to a fight, there would be front-line veterans on both sides.

[72] Böhm, *Adjutant*, 51–2.

[73] Schmidt, *Heimatheer und Revolution*, 254–5.

[74] In rifle strength they almost certainly outnumbered the depleted 2nd Guards Division.

around key buildings. A company from the most highly regarded unit, the 4th *Jäger* Battalion, or "Naumburger *Jägers*," guarded the war ministry itself.[75]

In the days just prior to the revolutionary outbreak of November 9, the *Jägers* gave a good account of themselves. On November 7, they disarmed and apprehended several hundred mutinous sailors who had arrived at the Lehrter and Stettiner train stations near the center of the city.[76] On the next day, November 8, the *Jägers'* display of sound morale and their disciplined appearance, as well as their heavily armed patrols, reassured the Kaiser's supporters in the capital.[77]

All that changed on the morning of the November 9. When thousands of workers took to the streets carrying signs pleading "Brothers, Don't Shoot," the *Jägers* refused to fight. Or perhaps they were unable to do so.[78] Between suspicious no-fire orders of uncertain origin and fraternization with the crowds, the reason fowr the *Jägers'* passivity is uncertain. What is clear is that, in their preparations for counter-revolutionary action, the chain of command in Berlin, from Scheuch down, had failed to act with either decisiveness or clarity. Instead of deploying his troops in impressive masses, von Linsingen had distributed them in small bunches in and around the city. The troops lacked adequate ammunition for any serious fighting, and, worse, the authorities proved unable to feed them regularly.[79] Instead of consistent guidance, constantly changing and contradictory missions confused the troops manning the guard posts. Instead of preparing the troops with detailed instructions, the chain of command left the garrison uncertain of when armed force would be used. The result was a debacle.

The troops responded to the uncertainty of their situation in contradictory ways. The Naumburgers around the war ministry responded to a no-fire order from Scheuch by destroying their weapons. Reportedly disgusted by the war minister's lack of resolution, the front-line troops felt it was better to break their rifles and machine guns than let them

---

[75] Schmidt, *Heimatheer und Revolution*, 353–5.

[76] Böhm, *Adjutant*, 55–6. Two companies of the Luebbener *Jägers* were used to guard the sailors until the morning of the 9th, when the irresolute local commander at Neuhammer released the prisoners. (Schmidt, *Heimatheer und Revolution*, 104)

[77] Testimony of Colonel Schwertfeger, in *UDZ*, IV, 37.

[78] Report received at the war ministry at 10.30 a.m., Böhm, *Adjutant*, 60.

[79] Payer, the vice-chancellor, reported that men of the Luebbener *Jägers* around the chancellery abandoned their post for lack of food. Friedrich Payer, *Von Bethmann-Hollweg bis Ebert: Erinnerungen und Bilder* (Frankfurt: Frankfurter Societäts-Druckerei, 1923), 161. A similar reason is given for the *Jägers'* abandonment of the Kaiser's family at the *Neues Palais* in Potsdam.

fall into the hands of the mob.[80] Later in the day another element of
the battalion, at the Alexander Barracks, responded positively to the
exhortation of a leading Social Democrat, Otto Wels, and sent a deputation to the left-wing *Vorwärts* newspaper to express their sympathy for
the revolution.[81]

Through the morning, Scheuch was bombarded with reports that
the units of the Berlin garrison were refusing to resist the crowds that
surged towards the center of the city. The failure of the *Ersatz* battalions
was distressing but perhaps to be expected. However, when the *Jägers*
gave way the effect on the remainder of the garrison was devastating.
Captain Boehm recorded at 11.00 a.m., "The report hit like a bomb. It
was clear the other troops would soon follow."[82] Prince Max wrote later,
"The action of the Naumburg *Jägers* had a most demoralizing effect on
the whole garrison."[83]

The news reached Spa via confused and exaggerated reports. Late
in the morning, Colonel von Thaer of the OHL staff heard that "blood
was flowing in the streets," and that there was fighting everywhere.
The "allegedly reliable" *Jäger* battalions had thrown down their arms.[84]
Linsingen's last message to the OHL said that he had absolutely no
troops left willing to shoot, and he was no longer able to defend the
public buildings in the center of the city.[85] In its capital, the old regime
had collapsed with much more of a whimper than a bang.[86]

Oaths under fire

The Kaiser struggled to remain calm in the face of the depressing news.
Up to that point, he had placed great faith in the loyalty of his front-
line soldiers, and the events of the morning were a crushing revelation.
First, Groener announced that the army no longer stood behind the
monarchy and, during the early afternoon, the elite troops of the Berlin
garrison had given way before the mob. After Groener had left the
morning meeting, Schulenberg's encouragement temporarily restored

[80] Schmidt, *Heimatheer und Revolution*, 354–5.
[81] *Ibid.*, 388–9.   [82] Böhm, *Adjutant*, 60.
[83] Prince Max of Baden, "The Abdication of the Emperor," Document 522, in Lutz,
ed., *Fall of the German Empire*, 534.
[84] Thaer, *Generalstabdienst an der Front*, 258. Thaer wrote later that reports of the *Jägers'*
unreliability were unfounded. They had not refused, they had been misused.
[85] Schmidt, *Heimatheer und Revolution*, 358.
[86] Officers from the Guards Fusilier Regiment did fire on the crowds, and there were
isolated instances of fighting around the city. The death toll for the day was fifteen.
Goerlitz, *November 1918*, 178.

Figure 3.3 After joining the revolution, the Naumburger *Jägers* prepare to secure the war ministry. Their relief at the bloodless outcome of the day's events is apparent.

the Kaiser's resolve, but more bad news awaited Wilhelm. At around 1.00 p.m., Colonel Heye arrived with the results of the *Armeeparlament*. After reading the results of the vote, the colonel summarized the results: "The troops are still true to Your Majesty, but they are tired and indifferent. They want only rest and peace. They will not march against the homeland; also not with Your Majesty at their head. They also will not march against Bolshevism. Above all they want an end to hostilities; therefore every hour is important."[87]

The Kaiser was shaken by this report but persisted in believing that cohesion and discipline among the front-line soldiers depended on their loyalty to their emperor. The Kaiser then asked if the army could make an orderly march home without him. Schulenberg said no, Groener said yes. Heye answered, "The army will march home alone under its generals. In this respect, it is still solidly in the control of its leaders. And if Your Majesty marches with them, it will seem proper and pleasing to

[87] Heye quoted in Ritter and Miller, eds., *Die Deutsche Revolution*, 71.

them. The army only wants no more fighting either inside [Germany] or outside."[88] The Kaiser clung to his belief in the fundamental loyalty of the troops. He said that, as their Supreme Warlord (*Oberste Kriegsherr*), he wanted to see the opinions of the army's senior leaders in writing. "Hasn't the army sworn an oath of loyalty (*Fahneneid*) to me?"

According to his critics, Groener replied, "In this situation such an oath is only a fiction."[89] Other versions of this exchange have Groener saying, "Oath to the colors? War Lord? These are only words, an idea."[90] Later Groener would not deny what he had said but wrote that he had offered this comment to an unnamed general who could not understand how the sailors and soldiers in the homeland could violate their oath.[91] No matter what the exact words or circumstances, Groener's statement branded him forever as a traitor in the minds of German monarchists.

Schulenberg was especially vindictive, writing later that, because Groener had not arrived at the OHL until October 30, he had no basis for judging the mood of the troops. Schulenberg wrote:

In the trenches and under fire is where one gets to know the moral[e] of the army. The favorite reading of the men is the Bible and certain of the Psalms. Their high sentiments of duty are coupled with a profound sense of religion. The army which for four and a half years has done its duty, and is permeated with such a spirit, would be incapable, even when foredone [*sic*] and exhausted by battle, of breaking its oath and deserting its King.[92]

Such remarks make it apparent Schulenberg, like the Kaiser, persisted in believing the myth of the unshakeable loyalty of the combat units long after the facts had exploded the myth. As he had in the morning debate with Groener, Schulenberg sought the moral authority associated with "knowing" the true nature of the men. Schulenberg believed such authority was reserved to officers who had extensive service at the front.

Groener's record gave him no such authority. His front-line experience was limited. As a division and corps commander, he had served on a relatively quiet sector of the Western Front from August 1917 to February 1918. Beyond that, his background did not fit the "warrior" pattern. Son of a Württemberg paymaster, Groener had made his reputation as a highly capable staff officer and chief of the railway section of the Great General Staff when the war began. Through the middle

[88] *Ibid.*   [89] Niemann, *Kaiser und Revolution*, 138–9.
[90] Baumont quoting the Crown Prince's account, *Fall of the Kaiser*, 112.
[91] Groener, *Lebenserinnerungen*, 461.
[92] Schulenberg quoted in Baumont, *Fall of the Kaiser*, 113. See also Westarp's criticism of Groener's lack of combat experience in *Das Ende der Monarchie*, 142.

period of the war he served as the head of the war office, the war ministry's agency for managing the economic support of the war. There, Groener had excelled, while establishing a name for himself as an officer with a unique ability to reach across party and class lines to deal with labor union leaders and party bosses from the MSPD. He was a technocrat with an uncommon feel for the mood and capacities of the workers who were carrying the war effort on the home front. These were among the skills sought by the Kaiser and Prince Max when looking for a replacement for the politically maladroit Ludendorff.[93]

From our vantage, it seems that the ability to see beyond the class prejudices of the noble officer corps was what set Groener apart from the other participants at Spa. Groener's skill in dealing with working-class representatives suggested an acute awareness of the "common man" that Schulenberg had not developed. Far better than Schulenberg and the others, Groener could sense that loyalty oaths had become irrelevant to men as desperately war-weary as the front-line troops were in the last days of the war. Groener sensed that, for troops cowering under Allied shellfire, old symbols carried little weight.

The Kaiser lacked any such awareness, but by early afternoon, November 9, he understood that some form of abdication was inevitable. He favored giving up his title as Emperor of Germany while remaining King of Prussia and allowed this announcement to go out.[94] As he prepared for a late lunch, a report came from Berlin that showed the tide of bad news had not ebbed. Without confirming the fact with Spa, Prince Max had announced the Kaiser's full abdication. This new "treason" aroused fury in Wilhelm, but clearly his options were beginning to dwindle. He spent the remainder of the afternoon consulting with his advisers. The triumph of the revolution and the failure of the army to rally its forces against the insurrection meant that now Wilhelm's personal safety had become an issue.

The case of *Sturmbataillon* Rohr

Responsibility for the security of the Kaiser, his entourage, and the OHL rested on the most elite unit in the German Army, Assault Battalion (*Sturmbataillon*) Rohr. Named after its commander, it was a famous

---

[93] Heussler, *General Wilhelm Groener*, 117–18. Interestingly enough, Schulenberg was also considered. He declined, saying he desired instead to stay with the Crown Prince.

[94] Baumont, *Fall of the Kaiser*, 114–16.

combat unit, not a ceremonial guard.[95] Created originally in 1915 as an experimental unit of combat engineers, the battalion's innovation in the development of storm-troop techniques had made it the model for the assault battalions across the German Army.[96] Rohr and his men had an outstanding combat record and a reputation that extended throughout the German Army.

To the leaders of the German Army of 1918, military virtue and reliability were synonymous with combat effectiveness. The hierarchy of effectiveness put the *Ersatz* battalions of the Home Army at the bottom, followed, in ascending order, by the *Landwehr* units guarding the Eastern Front, the "trench" divisions of the Western Front (useful only for holding quiet sectors), mobile divisions, and then assault divisions. Assault Battalion Rohr was at the very top of the hierarchy. In such a position, the army's leaders took the political reliability of the unit as a certainty. Thus, when the Supreme Command began to fear for its own safety, the battalion seemed a logical choice to take up security duties at the headquarters.

The battalion received the order to move to Spa on October 20. It had come out of the line on October 10 near Sedan after heavy fighting in the American sector. In the rear, the unit linked up with its 4th Company, which had been training replacements, and began loading on rail cars for the redeployment. According to the account of the adjutant, First Lieutenant Schwerin, the movement to Spa was the battalion's first exposure to the "face" of revolution. There were clear signs of indiscipline among other units pulled out of the line. The Guards Grenadier Regiment Elisabeth, encountered on the way, was, Schwerin subsequently wrote, the gratifying exception. Otherwise, the trip through the army's disordered rear area demonstrated why the Supreme Headquarters had called for the Rohr Battalion.[97]

The battalion's arrival on October 21, 1918, sent a sigh of relief through the staff sections of the OHL and cowed any Belgians who might have considered the German Army's impending defeat an opportunity for insurrection. The battalion announced its arrival by parading through the town of Spa, the troops impressive in their special,

---

[95] The ceremonial Life Guards had remained in Potsdam when the Kaiser "fled" to the front.

[96] Timothy Lupfer, *The Dynamics of Doctrine. The Changes in German Tactical Doctrine During the First World War* (Ft. Leavenworth, KS: Command and General Staff College, 1981), 28–9. Ludendorff had observed a demonstration of the battalion's techniques shortly after he came from the Eastern Front to become First Quartermaster General. He decreed that every army on the Western Front build a similar unit.

[97] Graf Eberhard v. Schwerin, "Der 9. November in Spa," in Niemann, *Revolution von Oben*, 428.

leather-padded assault uniforms and camouflage-painted steel helmets. Even more impressive were the machine guns, trench mortars, flame-throwers, and light artillery Rohr's men brought with them. After this initial demonstration of strength, the infantry companies were posted to key positions around the headquarters and the Kaiser's villa, while the horses, transport, and heavy weapons were quartered outside Spa. Major Rohr regretted the dispersion of his unit but found it necessary on account of the nature of its mission.[98]

Guard duty was not a routine to which the combat troops of the battalion were accustomed, and this led to an unhappy incident shortly after the battalion arrived. Groener discovered that a sentry outside the general's quarters had absented himself from his post for what Schwerin called "very human reasons" (the call of nature?). The lieutenant hypothesized that incidents such as this may later have influenced Groener to describe the battalion as "unreliable."[99] Meanwhile, the duties of the unit brought it into contact with the rear-area troops who supported the OHL, including a naval signals unit whose sailors had shown considerable sympathy with their comrades in revolt at Kiel.

Rohr's men received their first call to action on November 7. In response to reports of a revolutionary soldiers' council being formed in Spa, the commander dispatched his 4th Company to disperse it. Schwerin wrote that the willing response of the younger, unblooded members of the battalion, as well as their eagerness to seize the alleged mutineers, revived the confidence of the officers. However, the report turned out to be a false alarm.[100] The situation seemed more desperate the next day, when the OHL received reports of three trainloads of mutinous sailors arriving at Verviers with the intention of marching on Spa. Rohr offered to send out motor patrols to check the reports but nothing came of it. That night, the OHL staff ordered Rohr to prepare a demonstration of modern assault techniques for the general-adjutant of the Dutch queen in a training area 2 kilometers outside Spa.[101]

The following day, November 9, began uneventfully. Major Rohr left the battalion command post early in the morning to conduct the demonstration, which went on into the late morning. When he returned at 12.30 p.m., the major was summoned to the headquarters. He returned with the shocking news that the Kaiser was preparing to abdicate. At

---

[98] *Ibid.*, 430.   [99] *Ibid.*, 429–30.   [100] *Ibid.*, 431.
[101] *Ibid.*, 432–3. According to Schwerin, this little episode has caused some excitement for conspiracy theorists who postulate that certain individuals were preparing the Kaiser's abdication to Holland long before it was announced.

the direction of the OHL's deputy headquarters commandant, the battalion's priority mission became security for the emperor's special court train (*Hofzug*). In an atmosphere filled with rumors and uncertainty, the deputy commandant also directed that the Rohr battalion was not to use their weapons except in the event of a personal attack on the Kaiser. Both Rohr and Schwerin believed this last order would have a severe impact on the morale and steadiness of their unit. They protested to the deputy commandant, a Major Münchausen, but to no avail.[102]

The battalion spent the rest of the day preparing a defense around Wilhelm's train. The battalion headquarters pulled the heavy weapons companies in from the outskirts of Spa, and the battalion was united for the first time in days. At 3.00 p.m., members of the battalion encountered the Crown Prince, who was on his way back to his own army group headquarters. Assault Battalion Rohr had been a personal favorite of the Crown Prince, and he had visited the unit often. The Crown Prince assured the soldiers the Kaiser would neither abdicate nor desert the army. The men responded with a "hurrah" as he drove away.[103]

At this point, one leaves Schwerin's account to follow the discussion of Wilhelm's plans for abdication. The Kaiser could not return to Germany, since revolutionaries held the Rhine bridges. He might attempt a flight to Switzerland, but that was many hundred miles away. He could accept his son's invitation to come to his army group headquarters, but moving closer to the front increased the risk of capture by the Allies if the army fell to pieces. He could stay at Spa, but rumors of powerful Bolshevik columns advancing from Aachen had unnerved many in his entourage. Then, at 4.00 p.m., Major Münchausen reported to General-Adjutant von Plessen that, in the case of Assault Battalion Rohr, "no certain reliance remained."[104] The origin of the major's assessment is unclear, but soon the news of the Rohr battalion's unreliability spread around the headquarters.[105] What is known is that, by the late afternoon, Hindenburg, Plessen, and others were telling the Kaiser that Assault Battalion Rohr could not be relied upon and that he must urgently seek asylum. Hindenburg warned, "I cannot accept the responsibility of seeing the Emperor hauled to Berlin by insurgent troops and delivered over as a prisoner to the Revolutionary

[102] *Ibid.*, 432–3. [103] *Ibid.*, 423.
[104] Westarp, *Das Ende der Monarchie*, 104
[105] Colonel Bauer suspected the report of the battalion's unreliability was trumped-up. The Kaiser, he believed, should have had a chance to speak to the men of the unit himself. Bauer, *Grosse Krieg*, 269.

Government."[106] Wilhelm's cousin, Tsar Nicholas II, had died before a revolutionary firing squad just over three months before, and his fate was present in everyone's thoughts.[107] Through the evening and into the night, the former Kaiser vacillated between a stubborn determination to stay with the army and a wavering commitment to leave for Holland the next day.[108] The next morning the *Hofzug* was gone. To the surprise of many, including Hindenburg, Wilhelm had left at 5.00 a.m. For security en route, he took a seventy-man detachment from Assault Battalion Rohr.[109] The *Frontschweine* had played their last bit part in the drama of the Kaiser's abdication.

What role had Rohr's battalion played in the Kaiser's decision to flee? Certainly, reports of the unit's unreliability were the last straw in a series of events that had shaken the Kaiser on November 9. Was the unit truly unreliable? To certain key staff officers it was. To its own officers it was not. Perhaps the truth lies somewhere in between. One expects that the sentries of the Rohr battalion greeted their own officers with a friendly heartiness. Together they had shared the worst fighting of the Western Front. Theirs was camaraderie enhanced by their status as an elite unit. One the other hand, one imagines that Rohr's front-line troops must have looked on the manicured, red-striped staff officers of the Supreme Headquarters with more than a little disdain.[110] Unaccustomed to the dreary monotony of sentry duty, the front-line troops may have responded as soldiers have over the centuries, with a surliness characteristic of bored soldiers. Veteran storm troops were poorly suited to the stiff formality and rigid routine associated with guarding an emperor.

The Iron Division

Though not directly related to the Kaiser's abdication, the experience of the 7th Reserve Division (7th RID) offers an additional perspective on the problem the German army faced in using front-line troops to

---

[106] Baumont, *Fall of the Kaiser*, 137.   [107] *Ibid.*, 139.

[108] Naval Captain von Restorff, deputy chief of the naval cabinet, observed Wilhelm's internal struggle on the night of the 9th; see Niemann, *Revolution von Oben*, 394–5.

[109] Rohr later wrote that the no-fire order on the 9th had disturbed his men. However, signs of unrest in the battalion did not show up until the next day, after the abdication was announced and the OHL had ordered the creation of officially sanctioned soldiers' councils. Schwerin, "Der 9. November," in Niemann, *Revolution von Oben*, 433–4.

[110] For a description of front-line resentment of high-level staffs, see Thaer, *Generalstabdienst an der Front*, 187–8, and Fried, *Guilt*, 163.

suppress the revolution's initial outbreak. Raised in Prussia, the division had compiled an enviable combat record during the war and had been nicknamed "the Iron Division."[111] In late October, when the collapse of Austria-Hungary threatened to expose the Reich's southern frontier to Allied invasion, the OHL redeployed the 7th RID to southern Bavaria, where it would serve as "stiffening" for the odd units being assembled to protect the invasion routes from Austria.

One officer observing the arrival of the division was Captain Victor Mann, younger brother of the famous author Thomas Mann. Captain Mann served as the adjutant of an *Ersatz* unit quartered in southern Bavaria and was responsible for quartering the front-line veterans with his own troops. He awaited the arrival of the combat unit with skeptical anticipation. His own front-line experience suggested that titles like "the Iron Division" were rarely justified. Nevertheless, when the unit arrived, he conceded that the disciplined and battle-tested appearance of the Prussians made a powerful impression on his young Bavarian replacements.

During the next several days, Mann heard rumors of unrest in various parts of Germany. Then, on the night of November 8–9, his orderly woke him to take an urgent call directly from the OHL. The voice on the other end of the telephone line ordered him to alert the 7th RID. The unit was to prepare for an immediate march on Munich, where revolutionaries had seized power and announced that Bavaria had become a socialist republic. It was an emphatic order from the army's highest headquarters, yet Mann was reluctant to carry it out. He reasoned that sending Prussians into the turmoil of Bavaria's capital was an invitation to disaster. His commander agreed, "Madness! Arouse Prussia against Bavaria! Munich is our business!" Nevertheless, Mann and his commander carried the order to the Iron Division's commander, a cavalry general with a white moustache and a weather-beaten face.

The Prussian officer received the order with an air of unhappy resignation. "An order is an order, even if I must take on Munich," he grumbled. Both Mann and his commander sought to protest when they saw the general's head sink onto his chest, "I don't want to do it." At that point, Mann recalled, "I recognized that he was a tired old man and as ready for the finale as all of us. He had no desire to shoot our *Frauenkirche* into ruins, even if it was full of revolutionaries." Nevertheless, the next morning, the 7th RID prepared to march on

[111] The story of the Iron Division and its march on Munich taken from Mann's account in *Revolution und Räterepublik in München 1918/1919 in Augenzeugenberichten*, ed. Gerhard Schmolze (Düsseldorf: Karl Rauch Verlag, 1969), 116–20.

the Bavarian capital. Mann's commander asked for volunteers from his own officers to accompany the Prussians in a liaison role. When no one volunteered, the commander picked several officers from Munich, hoping that such men might serve to avert needless violence.[112] Meanwhile, when the young Bavarian troops of Mann's unit heard of the revolution in Munich, the response was "great equanimity." Most of the replacements were farmers' sons, and they "wanted neither further war nor revolutionary tribunals nor burning palaces. They wanted to go home to their fields and workplaces."

Despite the commanding general's misgivings, the 7th RID marched on Munich as ordered. The lead battalion, reinforced by a battery of artillery, reached the outskirts of the city by train and unloaded in good order. Then, as it moved into the city, the front-line veterans encountered revolutionary troops wearing sporting hats, garish scarves, and carrying their rifles slung over their shoulders in the classic revolutionary position, with the muzzle down. The "Reds" called out to the front-line soldiers, "Brothers, comrades!" and announced that the time of slavery was over, freedom was born, and a people's republic was being created. "Don't raise your weapons against your brothers! Throw them down." The battalion, almost to a man, laid their rifles on the street.

In a moment, the Iron Division's operation was stillborn. The officers attempted to rouse their men to obedience with no effect. Giving up the effort, the officers returned to the nearest train stations, where they sought a ride back to the garrison. The arrival of more units led to the same outcome.

The soldiers of the Iron Division would not take arms against the revolution. Their reluctance was similar to that of the Second Guards Division, Rohr's storm troops, and the 4th *Jägers* and lends itself to analysis using the factors already considered. For each of these units, *selection* for the counter-revolutionary mission had been based on their exemplary combat record. Used wherever there was a crisis at the front, they were even more likely to be numbed with *exhaustion* than the less elite units holding the line. To be fully effective in any combat role, Rohr's battalion and the Iron Division needed weeks in a rest area.[113] Instead, at short notice, their orders thrust them into an unfamiliar situation where the "enemy" was likely to wear *feldgrau*. On November 9, the 4th *Jägers* was probably in better physical condition than these other selected units. However, like them, they had seen enough fighting to want an end to it. When the *Kaiserreich* needed fresh troops to

---

[112] *Ibid.*, 118.
[113] Interestingly, Colonel Bauer attributes the failure of the 2nd Guards directly to their exhaustion after weeks of uninterrupted combat. Bauer, *Grosse Krieg*, 269.

defend itself against revolution, it had none. For each unit, the break-down of the front-line soldier's *insulation*, the first contact with those who had already joined the revolution,[114] was sufficient to undo the bonds of discipline and subordination.[115] The combat veterans so long isolated from the world outside the trenches were ill-prepared to chal-lenge the appeals to revolutionary camaraderie they faced at places like the government quarter of Berlin, the suburbs of Munich, or the train station at Herbesthal. Whatever bonds of *cohesion* remained between officers and men did not suffice to overcome the appeals of revolution-ary solidarity.[116]

The night after the failed march on Munich, the remnants of the Iron Division returned to Mann's garrison, where they sang, made speeches, and visited the local inns. He observed:

The Iron Division had melted like snow under the sun. They had defied week-long barrages and ducked under machine gun fire. At Verdun, and in Russia, in the Balkans and in Flanders, they had poured out their blood and covered themselves in glory, but now the cries of half-drunk louts suffice to turn them into a crowd of farmers, workers, and *petit bourgeois* who want to go home.[117]

After the abdication

The abdication drew mixed reactions from the front-line troops who had participated in the momentous events of November 8–9. Schwerin

[114] During the crucial days of November 8–9, alienation between front and rear prob-ably played less of a role than the other factors considered here. There are indica-tions of it, however. Consider the artillery battery of the Second Guards that sought permission to fire on the trainloads of *Drückeberger* traveling through Herbesthal, for example. If the Fourth *Jägers* would not fire on the crowds of Berliners on November 9, they were, nonetheless, willing to apprehend the sailors who arrived in Berlin during the preceeding days. Reinhard demonstrated a front-line veteran's contempt for the staff in his description of his trip to Spa. On the other hand, one might still imagine that the Naumburger *Jägers* and Rohr's storm troops were tactically and temperamentally ill-suited for the mission of guarding government buildings in Berlin or resort hotels in Spa. Nevertheless, the resentment of front for rear probably played relatively little part in the events surrounding the Kaiser's abdication.
[115] The chain of command in Berlin realized that crowd control was best accomplished when crowds were kept at a distance from soldiers. However, they failed to provide the barrier material – especially barbed wire – that would have given the security forces a measure of stand-off from the throng of Berliners that marched on the gov-ernment quarter on November 9. Schmidt, *Heimatheer und Revolution*, 226.
[116] In Groener's view, cohesion in the form of loyalty one German soldier felt for another played an important role in the failure of the monarchy's attempts to contain the revolution. In his testimony in the "stab-in-the-back" trial of 1925, he said that, at the time, he was skeptical of any measures taken that would use "reliable" troops against "revolutionary" troops because "field-gray will not shoot field-gray" (*aber Feldgrau wird nicht gegen Feldgrau schiessen*). Any plans to use *feldgrau* against *feldgrau* was based on a faulty psychological assessment that believed that, after four years of suffering and camaraderie, German troops would be willing to fight each other.
[117] Mann quoted in Schmolze, ed., *Revolution und Räterepublik*, 122.

wrote that Major Rohr's men were bewildered. On the day after the Kaiser's departure, some gave their support to the soldiers' council set up among the troops in Spa.[118] The council's chief demand was for the storm troops to be disarmed. The OHL refused. In the ensuing days, a handful of Rohr's men left the unit without permission, but enough of Rohr's men remained under the control of their officers to provide a security force for the headquarters until it returned to Germany.[119]

The news of the abdication had a powerful effect on the discipline and morale of the 2nd Guard Division as it struggled to regroup around Herbesthal. November 9 brought increasing signs of collapse among the rear-area personnel around the division assembly areas. The roads around Herbesthal were soon crowded with leaderless troops from these other formations, all of them making their way back to Germany. Abandoned weapons and equipment littered the roadsides. Local soldiers' councils demanded that the division disarm itself, and on November 10, the 2nd Machine Gun Company had to threaten violence in order to seize the machine guns of mutineers who threatened their trains. That same day, the division commander, Friedeburg, wrote that his own unit began showing signs of dissolution. Twenty guardsmen from a company guarding the train station deserted *en masse*. Individuals began to leave other units of the division.

The reaction of the divisions to the news of abdication was not unmixed. The men from two batteries of the 2nd Guard Field Artillery Regiment asked for permission to maintain their positions so that they would have the opportunity to fire on the trainloads of revolutionaries anticipated from Aachen. Friedeburg's artillerymen realized that revolution meant an early end to the war and a chance to go home, but they had no love for the men who had made the revolution possible. In their time in the trenches, the front-line troops had learned to despise the malingerers, deserters, and war profiteers in the rear area. In holding this view, they reflected the *alienation* the front-line soldiers felt from all those who had not shared their experiences.[120] The fact that these same revolutionaries threatened the food supply of comrades in the trenches may also have been on their minds. Weighing the prospects for violent confrontation on one hand and mass desertion on the other,

---

[118] On November 10, the OHL told the army to form councils that included officers and NCOs. See Chapter 4.

[119] Schwerin, in "Der 9. November," in Niemann, *Revolution von Oben*, 435–6.

[120] This phenomenon is seen in virtually every mass army of the twentieth century. What the German Army called the "hyenas of the *Etappe*," the US Army later would call "REMFs."

Friedeburg asked for and received permission to march his division home.[121]

By the end of November 9, troops from the Naumburger *Jägers* were providing military security for the *Vorwärts* building, home of the most influential socialist newspaper in Berlin.[122] The government had hoped that these front-line troops would cow the crowds with their military bearing. Instead, the Naumburgers had gone over to the revolution. Based on the events of 1918, one could argue that imperial Germany needed a force ethnically or geographically removed from the unhappy populace against whom they were to defend, and that General von Linsingen needed a force akin to the tsarist cossacks of the nineteenth century or the Bourbon Swiss guards of the eighteenth. Instead, he had relied on the Naumburger *Jägers*, recruited from a town approximately 100 miles from Berlin. The Kaiser's generals discovered that expecting front-line troops to fire on their countrymen was quite a different prospect from sending them to fight Finnish Red Guards.

After the *Armeeparlament*, the thirty-nine front-line voters were finally offered lunch. As they were eating, they were surprised by the news of the Kaiser's intention to abdicate. Some left for the front that afternoon, others spent the night before returning to their units. After the war, some had second thoughts about their role in the events of November 9. Major Hünicken wrote that he regretted the answers he had given. He came to believe the whole affair had been a set-up job staged by Groener to reinforce a conclusion that had already been reached.[123]

Colonel Wilhelm Reinhard, commander of the 4th Foot Guards, held a similar view. Selected as one of the fifty commanders to represent the front, he had been delayed by a series of minor traffic accidents as well as the security checkpoints of the Guards Cavalry Rifle Division outside Spa.[124] Reinhard recalled that at these checkpoints, for the first time, he heard rumors of revolution inside the homeland and the possibility that mutinous troops were marching on the army's headquarters. Because of the delays, he arrived well after the vote of the original thirty-nine officers. Nevertheless, he and three other latecomers were

---

[121] Details of the division's experience around Herbesthal come from Friedeburg, 425–427.

[122] Schmidt, *Heimatheer und Revolution*, 388–9.

[123] Hünicken, "Das Frontheer," in Niemann, *Revolution von Oben*, 442.

[124] Reinhard is the only source to mention the presence of the Guards Cavalry Rifle Division providing the external security to the headquarters at Spa. Apparently chosen for its political reliability, the unit would later feature prominently in the events leading up to the German Civil War (see Chapters 6 and 7).

summoned to a briefing by the ubiquitous Colonel Heye. As he had
done earlier, Heye described a desperate situation in the homeland and
behind the front, emphasizing that the revolution had cut the army off
from its sources of food and ammunition on the east side of the Rhine.
He then asked the four commanders whether, under these circumstances, the war could be continued. The unanimous answer was no.
The second question was whether the troops would stand behind the
Kaiser. The unanimous answer this time was emphatic and unanimous:
yes. Apparently surprised by this response, Heye dismissed it as of no
consequence. He informed the front-line officers that formerly reliable
units like the 4th *Jägers* in Berlin had gone over to the revolution, and,
more importantly, the Kaiser had already decided to abdicate and seek
exile.

For Reinhard, a die-hard monarchist, these events would become a bitter memory. "What would have been the result of the *Armeeparlament*,"
he reflected, "if the Kaiser had asked the thirty-nine officers himself
instead of taking the report from Groener?" He believed the result might
have been very different. Similarly, what had become of Wilhelm's order
that the army commanders be consulted, an order never carried out?[125]

The politics of despair

In his memoirs, published four years after the war, Wilhelm did not
blame the front-line troops for the loss of his throne. He did include the
obligatory accusations of betrayal by the socialists: "The conscienceless
agitators are the men really responsible for Germany's collapse. That
will be recognized some day by the working classes themselves."[126] The
Kaiser also explained his failure to crush the revolution: "Others say
the Emperor should have returned home at the head of the army. But a
peaceful return was no longer possible; the rebels had already seized the
Rhine bridges and other points in the rear of the army."[127] (One finds
it necessary to ask: which army? Weren't the rebels wearing *feldgrau*?)
He concludes his chapter on the war by praising the *Frontheer*, which
"after four and a half brilliant years of war with unprecedented victories ... was forced to collapse by the stab in the back from the dagger of

[125] Reinhard's trip to Spa described in Reinhard, *Wehen der Republik*, 16–19. On the
night of November 9, Reinhard was introduced to Groener and Hindenburg.
Reinhard recalled that Groener's reception was "extremely cool."
[126] Wilhelm II, *The Kaiser's Memoirs*, trans. Thomas R. Ybarra (New York: Harper and
Brothers, 1922), 340.
[127] *Ibid.*, 290.

revolutionists, at the very moment when peace was within reach."[128]
But the army in the west did not collapse.

Wilhelm's memoirs celebrate the battlefield achievements of his
army, and ignore the fact that, when the monarchy was threatened
from within, the front-line army did not come to its rescue. The men in
the trenches demanded a peace with or without the Kaiser. The three
front-line divisions selected to begin the army's counter-revolutionary
efforts at the Rhine crossings failed in their mission. The thirty-nine
front-line officers summoned to Spa denied the army's readiness to
fight for the Kaiser. The handful of front-line soldiers assigned to guard
the imperial capital submitted to the revolution without firing a shot.
The elite front-line unit assigned as the emperor's personal bodyguard
was judged unreliable in the moment of crisis. Finally, the man the
Kaiser selected to direct the final stages of a lost war proved himself
ruthlessly frank as a spokesman for the front-line troops. "Oath to the
colors? War Lord? These are only words, an idea."

The Kaiser and his entourage were shocked by these words because
they had held on to illusions about the German Army and the German
people long after reality demanded its due. During the course of the
long war, the Kaiser's role in the German nation had diminished dramatically. He was overshadowed by Hindenburg and relegated to the
status of figurehead by Ludendorff. When the Kaiser recognized the
sacrifices of his people with belated reforms, it was far too late. In 1918,
the Hohenzollern dynasty was not a cause to die for.

The Kaiser and those who surrounded him failed to recognize how
much the army had changed. In 1914, the Kaiser's army was a well-
trained force led by a professional NCO corps and an officer corps dominated by nobility. In 1918, it was a "militia army." The old NCO corps
was buried at Passchendaele and Verdun, and the peacetime officer
corps had been decimated. Shop foremen as NCOs and schoolteacher-
lieutenants led the front-line troops. When Wilhelm, Schulenberg, and
Scheuch expected the "spirit of 1914" from these men, they would be
disappointed.

On the other hand, at the point when the soldiers of the 2nd Guards
or Rohr's battalion, or the "Iron Division" refused their order, they
did not turn on their officers. The soldiers' resistance was passive and
did not seem to reflect hostility toward their own immediate chain
of command. In each case, the actions of the *Fronttruppen* resembled
more a work-stoppage than a mutiny. Significantly, the 2nd Guards
Division and the 7th RID returned to Prussia as units, and the nucleus

[128] *Ibid.*, 289.

of *Sturmbataillon* Rohr continued to act as the security force for the OHL into 1919.

Within the leadership of the monarchy, apathy and doubt overcame the will to rule. Thus, when the revolution erupted across Germany, only a handful of officers from the Home Army (*Heimatheer*) offered armed resistance, and in Berlin on November 9 perhaps only a single officer died defending the property of the Reich.

Schulenberg and others believed the front-line troops could be motivated to fight the revolution by emphasizing the way the revolutionaries had cut off the army's supply line. It was an appeal based on both the front's alienation from the rear and naked self-interest. That message would have appeal later but not on November 9, when the army still had supplies on hand, and the desire for peace at virtually any price dominated the combat soldier's *Weltanschauung*.

The soldiers who remained at the front in the last days of the war displayed a dogged endurance in the face of daunting danger and privation. However, when asked to fire on their countrymen, the German *Fronttruppen* re-evaluated the terms of their obedience and decided their orders were no longer binding. When pulled out of the line and thrust, with little or no preparation, into an internal security role, they acted in ways that confounded the expectations of their leaders. [129]

The events of November 8–10 were recounted by those leaders, whether it was the battalion commander Willi Rohr, or the First Quartermaster General himself. During the crucial two days, these leaders struggled for the right to "speak" authoritatively for the front-line soldier. In the event, however, the actions taken by the front-swine spoke for them. The men in the trenches were indifferent to any object but peace and the chance to go home, and, in November 1918; theirs was the politics of despair. By their unwillingness to fight for the monarchy on November 8–9, they became key agents in the revolution's first and greatest victory, the abdication of the Kaiser.

---

[129] The story is also complicated by a number of unresolved loose ends. If the 2nd Guards Division was still in good order on November 9, as its commander claimed, why was it reported unreliable at Spa the day before? If the Naumburger *Jägers* refused to fire on the crowds in the streets of Berlin, was it for lack of will or lack of guidance? If Assault Battalion Rohr was not ready to defend the Kaiser, why did Wilhelm take seventy of Rohr's men with him to the Dutch border? The final and most interesting question involves Wilhelm Groener. When did he decide the Kaiser was expendable and how did that shape his subsequent behavior? For example, did he, as Major Hünicken believed, anticipate the outcome of the *Armeeparlament* before the vote was taken? We are not likely to find definitive answers to these questions, but they are worth the continued attention of historians.

4 Legions without Caesar: the German Army's response to armistice and revolution, November 9–14, 1918

Armistice

The Kaiser's flight into exile on the morning of November 10, 1918, did not end the ordeal of the *Westheer*. Even without their "Supreme Warlord," the thin "spider's web"[1] of troops holding the front lines endured another day of misery and danger before the end came. They endured ignorance as well; revolution had interdicted transport from inside Germany, and the forces on the Western Front were cut off from news from the homeland. In this situation, soldiers relied on what seemed to be improbable rumors of revolution, abdication, and armistice. For most soldiers, only the last – the prospect of peace – really mattered. One officer remembered that in the last several days of the war, whenever his staff car – marked with the headquarters flag of the Fifth Army – stopped by a body of soldiers, the men would crowd around his vehicle. Their question was always the same: "Is it over?" Among these men, he recalled, "there was no trace of revolutionary spirit," but rather "exhaustion and the boundless desire for one word: cease-fire . . ."[2]

That desire was realized on November 11. The OHL announcement proclaimed baldly: "11:55 German time hostilities cease. Forward line will not be crossed in the direction of the enemy."[3] With a one-hour difference in their reckoning of time, the German forces observed the end of the war as five minutes before noon, not 11.00 a.m., as the Allied nations would remember it.

---

[1] Letter of Major Beck (future Chief of the Reichswehr General Staff) November 28, 1918, excerpted in Otto-Ernst Schüddekopf, *Das Heer und die Republik: Quellen zur Politik der Reichswehrführung, 1918 bis 1933* (Hanover: Norddeutsche Verlagsanstalt, 1955), 25: "History will eventually show that we fought for weeks on unbelievable frontages without a battalion reserve, having only a spider's web of fighters, not breaking despite the Entente's Generalissimo."

[2] Hermann Schützinger, *Zusammenbruch: Die Tragödie des deutschen Feldheeres* (Leipzig: Ernst Oldenburg Verlag, 1924), 79.

[3] G. Seiz *et al.*, *Geschichte des 6. Badischen Infanterie-Regiments Kaiser Friedrich III. Nr. 114 im Weltkrieg 1914 bis 1918* (Zeulenroda: Bernhard Spoern, n.d.), 516.

The silence that came at midday left soldiers wary. On the American front, the odd shell continued to come across the line as doughboy artillerymen vied to be the ones who fired "the last shot of the war." Finally, however, the front was quiet and German soldiers could consider the reality of survival and the prospect of going home. In violation of the OHL directive, some moved cautiously into No Man's Land to meet their former enemies, hoping to exchange their badges and decorations for food and cigarettes.[4]

In the command posts behind the line, unit journals, normally the most laconic of military documents, reflected the mixed emotions of front-line officers. The war diary of the 32nd Infantry Regiment observed: "The joy over the announcement [of the armistice] was lessened by rumors of the great severity of the cease-fire conditions imposed on us."[5] The November 11 entry for the Second Battalion of the 31st *Landwehr* Regiment read: "The report [of the armistice] was received with joy that the bloody war is henceforth at an end, and pride that, until the last moment, when weapons were laid down, the battalion was undefeated."[6] One battalion diary closed the daily entry with a simple, heartrending question: "What has all the sacrifice been for?"[7]

As troops along the front tried to make sense of their new situation, their officers were being called to orders briefs. The armistice conditions were indeed draconian and left no time in planning staffs or troop units for reflection or recuperation. German troops would have to be out of Belgium and France in fourteen days and across the Rhine in thirty-one.[8] In this difficult situation, to whom would the army answer? Who would lead this difficult march out of the occupied territories? The answer for the 7th Guards Field Artillery Regiment came as the fighting stopped. "At the same time, at the beginning of the cease-fire, came the news of the abdication of His Majesty, the Kaiser Wilhelm II, and the outbreak of revolution in Germany," its diary recorded. "A telephone call from the OHL confirms that General Field Marshal von Hindenburg, as before, remains at the head of the OHL and requires

---

[4] Stanley Weintraub, *A Stillness Heard Round the World: The End of the Great War: 1918* (New York: Oxford University Press, 1985), 324–5.

[5] NARA, RG 165, Box 163, Folder II, 103rd Infantry Division and Subordinate Units, War Diaries and Annexes, 26.

[6] NARA, RG 165, Box 121, Folder I, 1st *Landwehr* Division and Subordinate Units, 194.

[7] NARA, RG 165, Box 163, Folder I, 103rd Infantry Division and Subordinate Units (2nd Battalion, 32nd Infantry Regiment), 79.

[8] Frankfurter Zeitung, *Der grosse Krieg: Eine Chronik von Tag zu Tag. Urkunden, Depeschen und Berichte der Frankfurter Zeitung* (Frankfurt: Frankfurter Societäts-Druckerei, 1918), vol. XCVII, 9958.

all command authorities and officers to do their duty under the new government."[9]

For the army's chain of command, this proclamation was reassuring. Paul von Hindenburg, the old Prussian field marshal who had seemed Germany's pillar of strength through the long war, was still at the head of the troops. The old lines of authority seemed intact, at least within the army in the field. However, the report was misleading in one crucial respect. It suggested that the revolution in Germany had just broken out. In truth, by November 11, the revolutionaries had achieved their first major objective, the downfall of the monarchy and the acceptance of peace terms. A new government, led by socialists and proclaiming a German Socialist Republic, was already in power in Berlin.

The soldiers at the front faced a world turned seemingly upside down, and, in the days immediately following the armistice, they were forced to make important choices. Though exhausted and confused, they had to decide whether to obey the old chain of command or emulate many of their comrades in the rear areas who were abandoning their units and returning to Germany by the fastest means possible. Alternatively, those in front-line units might follow the example of the troops on the Eastern Front and in the homeland garrisons, who were overthrowing their officers and replacing their authority with that of newly created soldiers' councils. The choices made by the *Fronttruppen* during these first few days would be crucial to the future of the officer corps and the army, the popular perception of the new government, and the course of the German revolution.

The "six-headed chancellor"[10]

The new government of Germany was the product of a spontaneous and seemingly irresistible uprising that had overwhelmed the Reich's overstrained imperial structure. The pace of the upheaval had left the leaders of the socialist parties, supposedly the natural leaders of such a revolution, scrambling to stay ahead of the crowds in the street. The result of their efforts was a hastily contrived coalition government that would rule Germany for seven weeks, until January 1919, when national elections served to launch the Weimar Republic as a parliamentary democracy. The new government was an uncomfortable compromise

---

[9] NARA, RG 165, Box 179, Folder I, Guard *Ersatz* Div. War Diary and Annexes, 116.
[10] This description of the provisional government is taken largely from Erich Matthias' introductory chapter in *Quellen zur Geschichte des Parlamentarismus und der politischen Parteien*, Series 1, vol. VI, part i, ed. Erich Matthias, *Die Regierung der Volkbeauftragten, 1918/1919* (Düsseldorf: Droste Verlag, 1969), xv–lxxxviii.

Figure 4.1 Friedrich Ebert, former saddle-maker and leader of the Moderate Social Democrats, the first chancellor of the new German republic.

between two competing and largely irreconcilable visions of where the revolution should take Germany. Thus, through the end of 1918, it would be a government divided against itself. The turmoil within this temporary political arrangement and the hostility the government earned from its enemies on the Right and Left created a situation of political instability in which the troops of the *Westheer* would be able to play a central role in determining the future of the new republic.

The head of the new government was Friedrich Ebert, leader of the Majority Social Democratic Party (*Mehrheitssozial demokratische Partei Deutschlands* –MSPD) and co-chair, with Philipp Scheidemann, of the party's delegation in the Reichstag. Ebert had accepted the leadership of the new provisional government on November 9 as Berlin workers and soldiers of the capital's garrison marched through the city proclaiming the revolution. Driven by events in the street, Prince Max sought to give continuity and a semblance of propriety to a transfer of power by passing the chancellorship to Ebert.[11] Though the new arrangement lacked any constitutional precedent, in the days to come it conferred upon Ebert a certain amount of legitimacy in the eyes of the old bureaucracy and the officer corps.

While Max pursued continuity, Ebert sought unity. The new chancellor decided the government should be built on an alliance of socialist parties, his own Majority Socialists and the far less numerous Independent Socialists (*Unabhängige sozialdemokratische Partei Deutschlands* – USPD). The Independents had been the left wing of the old Social Democratic Party, but had broken away in 1917 over ideological differences and the immediate issue of war credits. Though the ill will created by the split remained significant, Ebert believed that bringing the Independents into the government would present a reassuring front of socialist political unity and might serve to tame the USPD leadership, which, as outsiders, had become increasing radicalized in the last year of the war. To this end, the leaders of the two parties agreed to a power-sharing relationship based on equal representation in a ruling Council of People's Delegates (*Rat der Volksbeauftragten* – RdV) that would serve as (and be referred to) as the "cabinet" of the provisional government.[12] The arrangement represented a considerable concession by the MSPD, whose membership vastly outnumbered that of the USPD at the time of the revolution.[13]

---

[11] The confusion of that day were epitomized by Scheidemann proclaiming the new republic from the Reichstag shortly after Karl Liebknecht, leader of the far-left Spartacist League, had proclaimed it from the imperial palace.

[12] The term "*Volksbeauftragten*" has been variously translated as "people's commissars," "people's deputies," and "people's commissioners."

[13] The conditions of the USPD's participation were that the membership of the cabinet be exclusively socialist, that the heads of the ministries, though remaining in office, would be supervised by representatives of both the MSPD and the USPD, and that the cabinet recognize the Workers' and Soldiers' Councils as the source of their

The cabinet would include three members from each party. Ebert led the MSPD delegation, which included his party co-chair, Philipp Scheidemann, and Otto Landsberg, all former members of the Reichstag. The USPD's three members were led by Hugo Haase, the party's leader, and included Wilhelm Dittmann and Emil Barth. Barth was the "outsider" in the group. He had been plucked out of relative obscurity from the middle ranks of the USPD to serve in the cabinet. He was younger than the other members of the cabinet and during the war he had avoided military service by feigning a nervous disorder. Though relatively well known among the workers of Berlin, he had not served in the Reichstag, as the other delegates had. While Haase represented the center of the USPD, Barth represented the left end of the deeply divided Independents. He had joined the cabinet with severe reservations, and, of the six delegates, Barth was the most openly hostile to any accommodation with the old Wilhelmine elites.[14] He was to be a key figure in shaping the government's troubled relationship with the Field Army in the west and the OHL.[15]

The most important member of the cabinet, however, was Ebert. Trained as a saddle-maker, Ebert had risen within the party ranks in the years before the war, and, in the words of a German historian, his ascendance embodied the "triumph of pragmatism over theory in the Social Democratic party."[16] Within the coalition government, Ebert retained the title of chancellor and was clearly the first among six nominal equals. In the division of responsibilities, Ebert took on the key jobs of overseeing the military and internal affairs.[17] Despite ideological differences, the Independents never challenged Ebert's dominant position in the cabinet. However, there was a price to be paid for this role. In the years after the revolution, both ends of Germany's political

---

authority. Heinrich Marx, ed., *Handbuch der Revolution in Deutschland, 1918–1919*, vol. I, *Vorabend 9–15 November* (Berlin: Alexander Grubel, 1919), 176.

[14] In the words of Scheidemann, Barth often turned the meetings of the cabinet into "political theater." Gordon Craig described him as an "impetuous man with small judgment." Gordon Craig, *Germany, 1866–1945* (New York: Oxford University Press, 1978), 406.

[15] During one of the first meetings of the cabinet, Barth proposed relieving the officer corps within the Field Army *en masse*, leaving in place only those few technical experts necessary to direct the *Westheer*'s homecoming and demobilization. Emil Barth, *Aus der Werkstatt der deutsche Revolution* (Berlin: A. Hoffmanns Verlag, 1919), 65.

[16] Waldemar Besson, "Friedrich Ebert's Political Road from the *Kaiserreich* to the Republic," in *Friedrich Ebert, 1871–1971* (Bonn: Inter Nations, 1971), 68–9. The Left nicknamed Ebert the "radish": "red on the outside, white on the inside."

[17] The remaining responsibilities were: Haase – foreign affairs and colonies; Scheidemann – finances; Dittmann – demobilization, civil rights, and public health; Landsberg – press and public information; Barth – social policy.

spectrum – Right and Left – would call him a traitor; traitor to the nation in the eyes of the Right, and traitor to the ideals of the revolution for the Left. Yet any judgment one makes of his actions during the period 1918–19 must take into account the many challenges he faced. They included negotiating a peace treaty with the vengeful Entente, feeding a nation on the verge of starvation, drafting a new constitution, repelling Polish incursions on the eastern frontier, guarding against a leftist *putsch*, and demobilizing a vast army and an economy geared for war. He would have to accomplish these tasks while dealing with difficult political partners and an officer corps that despised his ideals.[18]

Though a spirit of cooperation marked the initial work of the coalition cabinet, these ideological differences were important. The political goals of Ebert and the MSPD had largely been realized through the reforms of October 1918 (the "revolution from above"). At that point, Ebert had been willing to preserve some form of constitutional monarchy. However, with the Kaiser's abdication, he and his party looked to the election of a National Assembly to establish Germany as a parliamentary democracy led by the Majority Socialists but including the *bourgeois* and conservative parties. The MSPD's immediate goal, in the aftermath of the turmoil of November 9, was the re-establishment of "peace and order." The Independents, on the other hand, sought to preserve the suddenly dominant position of the German proletariat and pressed for an early socialization of industry. They viewed the idea of a National Assembly with suspicion and, instead, looked to the workers' and soldiers' councils (*Arbeiter- und Soldatenräte – A/S Räte*) established in every city and garrison in Germany to be the fount of political power. In the USPD's conception of the new order, the councils would follow the recent example of the Russian Soviets by supporting the ascendancy of the working masses while serving as the agents of social reform.

The workers' and soldiers' councils represented a force with which both the MSPD and the Independents would have to reckon. The power of the councils was expressed in the famous meeting in Zirkus Busch on November 10. Three thousand members of the various Berlin councils gathered to recognize the cabinet and the provisional government and to elect their own Executive Council (*Vollzugsrat* – VZR) empowered, they declared, to exercise the councils' controlling authority over the government. In theory, then, the Executive Council held a position

---

[18] Analysis taken, in part, from Holger Herwig, "The First German Congress of Workers' and Soldiers' Councils and the Problem of Military Reforms." *Central European History*, 1, 2 (1963), 162–4.

Der Rat der Volksbeauftragten

Figure 4.2 Ebert's cabinet: the "six-headed chancellor." From left to right: Wilhelm Dittmann (USPD), Otto Landsberg (MSPD), Hugo Haase (USPD), Friedrich Ebert (MSPD), Emil Barth (USPD), Philipp Scheidemann (MSPD).

superior to the cabinet; in practice, the *Vollzugsrat* rarely intruded on the authority of Ebert and the other five delegates. Moderates dominated its membership of the Executive Council and, because its members came exclusively from Berlin, many outside the capital considered its authority suspect. Nevertheless, the nominal power-sharing relationship between the cabinet and the Executive Council served to confuse and irritate the army's senior leaders in their dealings with their new political masters.

The secret pact

While the socialists were consolidating their power in Berlin, the Kaiser's flight on the morning of November 10 had left the OHL staff stunned and irresolute.[19] Some officers looked to arm themselves against the

---

[19] The importance of Wilhelm II was as a symbol, not a leader. By 1918, the senior leaders of the German military realized that the Kaiser was out of touch with the realities of modern war and lacked any sense of the true feelings of the troops. Similarly, Wilhelm inspired little affection among the army's rank and file. See Gotthard Breit, *Das Staats- und Gesellschaftsbild deutscher Generale bei der Weltkriege im Spiegel ihrer Memoiren* (Boppard am Rhein: Harald Boldt Verlag, 1973), 94–104

anticipated onslaught of the "Bolshevists," while others attempted to
negotiate a working relationship with the new soldiers' councils created
at the headquarters. Despite the revolution, the headquarters could
not cease to function; an armistice was being negotiated even as Allied
attacks continued up and down the front. The 180 divisions holding
the German line still needed guidance and provisions. The situation
demanded action, since much of the Field Army's rear area had collapsed into a chaotic state, while revolutionary formations had apparently interdicted the army's supply lines.[20]

Thus, the day Wilhelm departed for Holland, the army's First
Quartermaster General, Wilhelm Groener, confronted a desperate
situation and two critical questions. One question, though painful,
was relatively easy to answer. From the announcement of the armistice
conditions the day before, Germany had seventy-two hours to reply.
Would the army support the Allies' draconian armistice conditions?
Groener knew that, given the state of his army, the conditions could
not be rejected. "For us there remained no choice."[21] On the morning
of the 10th, the OHL signaled the new government that it supported
the acceptance of the terms.[22]

The second question involved the allegiance and internal cohesion of
the army. Could the army support the new government? With the abdication of the Kaiser, the oaths taken by the German officer corps had
become meaningless. To make matters worse, on the day of the Kaiser's
abdication, the OHL had issued an order calling for every unit in the
army to create soldiers' councils. Though Groener later disavowed the
order as an error made by a misguided staff officer, to many officers
at the front, it seemed that the OHL had already surrendered to the
revolution.[23]

In this chaotic environment, Field Marshal von Hindenburg had
chosen to remain at his post at the head of the army, and he became

---

[20] Such threats were most likely more chimera than reality; if supply trains were not
reaching the front, it was probably caused more by temporary lawlessness than purposeful interdiction by revolutionary forces.
[21] Groener, *Lebenserinnerungen*, 466.
[22] Conditions in Auswärtigen Amt, and Reichsministerium des Innern, *Amtliche Urkunden
zur Vorgeschichte des Waffenstillstandes 1918*, Document 105: Dr. Staatssekretär a.D.
v. Hintze im Grossen Hauptquartier an das Auswärtige Amt, message of November
9, 1918 (Berlin: Deutsche Verlagsgesellschaft für Politik und Geschichte, 1927),
262–3.
[23] Groener, *Lebenserinnerungen*, 469, fn. 5, cites a 1937 letter which puts the blame on
Lieutenant Colonel Faupel of the OHL staff. The hyper-conservative Colonel Max
Bauer later made the unpersuasive argument that Groener "could not socialize the
General Headquarters rapidly enough." Max Bauer, *Grosse Krieg*, 271.

a fixed point of reference for the many senior officers who felt themselves unmoored from the certainties provided by oaths, rank, and social class. Despite the downfall of the monarchy he had served for his whole life, the field marshal's name carried enormous residual authority within the army as well as among the entire German people. However, the victor of Tannenberg was unlikely to throw his willing support behind a regime made up of socialists, especially those who had helped to hound the emperor off his throne. Realizing this, Groener advised him that Ebert's MSPD was the only remaining political force that could achieve stability in the homeland and avoid a Bolshevik take-over similar to the one that had taken place in Russia the year before. Grudgingly, Hindenburg indicated his readiness to act in support of Groener's views.[24]

A few hours after the Kaiser's train had left for the Dutch border, Groener moved to solidify the position of the officer corps in the sudden power vacuum. Under the field marshal's name, the OHL broadcast the following message to its subordinate headquarters:

That the army might return home in steadfastness and order, though the Fatherland is threatened with civil war through the menacing danger of Bolshevism, all officers are morally obligated to do their duty without reservation, deferring any existing misgiving of conscience with regard to the oath sworn to His Majesty the Kaiser and King, in order to save the German lands from the greatest danger.

On the same basis, I have decided to remain at my post and take over the supreme command of the German Field Army, in accordance with instructions spoken to me by His Majesty the Kaiser and King.[25]

In the remainder of the message, Hindenburg advised the army to withdraw its resistance to the creation of soldiers' councils and, instead, encourage the creation of "trustees' councils" (*Vertrauensräte*)[26] for the purposes of advising the chain of command. He admonished the men to continue to obey their officers and announced that the OHL intended to work with Reich Chancellor Ebert to restrict the spread of Bolshevism. The field marshal closed by advising officers that in the current circumstances they would have to use tact in dealing with enlisted men, in order to avoid disturbances among the troops.

---

[24] Groener, *Lebenserinnerungen*, 468.

[25] Lothar Berthold and Helmut Neef, *Militarismus und Opportunismus gegen die Novemberrevolution* (Frankfurt am Main: Verlag Marxistische Blätter, 1978), Document 21: Befehl Hindenburgs an das Feldheer vom. 10. November 1918, 150–1.

[26] Also translated as "councils of trusted men," and "confidential agents' councils."

Significantly, Hindenburg's message addressed "the army" but it was apparent that the army to which he referred was the army in the field; no other units faced a difficult march back to the homeland. The front-line troops in the West and, to a lesser extent, those in the East, had become "the army." The millions of men under the authority of the soldiers' councils in the homeland still wore the uniform, but, in the eyes of the OHL and, increasingly, Ebert's government, they had become something else. Redefining the word was an important, even if initially an unconscious adjustment: if the "army" was the only institution with the right to bear arms in postwar Germany, the OHL, and Ebert's government would benefit by limiting the scope of that term's usage to the men returning from the front.

The message also reprised several themes that the High Command had used frequently in the last weeks of the war: perseverance in the face of adversity (*Durchhalten*) and fulfillment of duty (*Pflichterfüllung*). Peace might be at hand, but, for the officer corps, these two themes were still powerful and necessary for an army facing the uncertainty of the postwar period.[27] Now, instead of the Allies, the enemies were disorder, hunger, and Bolshevism.

Groener's influence is evident throughout the message of November 10, but he relied on the enormous residual power of Hindenburg's name to assert the continuing authority of the OHL. The power of the officers' oaths was transferred to the field marshal, and, in announcing its cooperation with the Ebert government, the OHL was giving itself legitimacy in the eyes of those soldiers who had welcomed the revolution. Thus, the message could call on soldiers to obey their officers on the authority, not only of the old chain of command, but also of the new government. That was not all. By announcing the creation of trustees' councils, Groener hoped to undermine the position of the soldiers' councils formed or forming at the front.

Groener's next move was crucial. Without Hindenburg's knowledge, the First Quartermaster General acted to bind the OHL and the Field Army even more closely to Ebert's government. Late on the night of November 10–11, using a secret telephone line that bypassed the central switchboard at Spa and the chancellery's switchboard in Berlin, Groener called Ebert to offer the army's support to the new government.[28] In return for this support, the general wanted the chancellor's assurance

---

[27] Discussion of themes from Lipp, *Meinungslenkung*, 167.
[28] In Groener's memoirs, he confides that his objective, shared by his staff at the OHL, was to preserve the influence of the army and the officer corps, "the strongest and best element of the old Prussiandom (*Preussentum*)," *Lebenserinnerungen*, 469.

that the government would act to fight Bolshevism and the power of the councils and that it would support an early election for a National Assembly that would lay the basis for a representative parliamentary democracy. Ebert accepted the terms readily and thanked Groener for his support.[29] The chancellor's agreement established one of the most fateful unions in modern German history.

It was also one of the most controversial. In establishing the details of the alliance, history has only the testimony of Groener, offered well after the event. There were no corroborating accounts, since neither Groener nor Ebert confided the existence or nature of their pact to anyone else during the turmoil of 1918–19. Instead, Groener first revealed the alliance in testimony before the "stab-in-the-back trial" of 1925, shortly after Ebert's death. What makes the general's account plausible, however, is that from November 11 forward the two men cooperated closely to achieve the goals set for their alliance. Indeed, Groener recalled that, during the critical period that followed, he and the chancellor made nightly use of the secret telephone line to confer with one another.[30]

The union between the life-long monarchist and the socialist party leader was not as unlikely as it may have appeared. In the first place, it was not a union of strangers. The two men had met and talked only three days before in Berlin, when Groener had refused Ebert's proposals for the Kaiser's abdication. They had come to know each other during the middle of the war during Groener's tenure as head of the war office (*Kriegsamt*). In that post, he had been responsible for the allocation of resources within Germany's wartime economy. As a result, Groener became deeply involved in labor negotiations, and over time, had come to know Ebert well. The two had developed a relationship of mutual respect.[31] Beyond that, Ebert's political views were anything but revolutionary ("I hate it [social revolution] like sin."[32]), while Groener had the reputation in the army for holding "progressive" views.[33] Both

---

[29] *Der Dolchstoss-prozess in München: Ehrenrettung des deutschen Volkes,* 223–4.
[30] *Ibid.,* 223. The Groener–Ebert Pact opened the general to bitter attacks from the Right (for compromising with the "November criminals") and the chancellor to attack from the Left (for selling out the revolution).
[31] *Ibid.* Groener described Ebert as an honorable and reliable man during the "stab-in-the-back" trial and defended the former chancellor against accusations of treason. *Ehrenrettung,* 200–3.
[32] *"Ich hasse sie wie die Sünde."* Ebert's statement came two days before taking power as he warned the government of the consequences of delaying the Kaiser's abdication. Peter-Christian Witt, *Friedrich Ebert: Parteiführer, Reichskanzler, Volksbeauftragter, Reichspräsident* (Bonn: Verlag Neue Gesellschaf, 1987), 88.
[33] Groener's views were indicated in the "stab-in-the-back trial," when he offered a document he had written during the war that stated that the struggle between the

feared "Bolsheviks" might hijack the revolution. Both also shared the nightmarish vision of what might happen if the Field Army escaped the control of its officers and returned to Germany as an unruly and heavily armed rabble ready to prey on the populace. For Groener and his colleagues, this would be the officer corps' final dishonor. For Ebert, such an outcome might fatally discredit his government. Perhaps worse, the resulting anarchy might provoke an Allied intervention into Germany's interior under the pretext of restoring the situation.[34]

The two men believed they needed each other. Neither man, however, could deliver the complete support of the institution they represented. For his part, Groener's headquarters could only claim control (and that uncertain) over the front-line forces of the *Westheer*, at best about a quarter of the army's 6 million men. On the other hand, Ebert could offer only the support of his half of the ruling coalition. Yet, despite the limitations of the pact, Ebert's support gave Groener a vitally important weapon to use in his campaign to maintain control of the army in the field. Ultimately, however, the outcome of this struggle would depend on the general's ability to deal with the soldiers' councils already created or forming throughout the army.

The soldiers' councils

As an earlier chapter has suggested, the German Army of 1918 was an army of disparate elements. Behind the front there was the *Etappe*; behind the *Etappe*, the homeland garrisons. Beyond the homeland garrisons, there was the occupation army in the East. Each part comprised significantly different types of personnel, and the troops in each part served under dramatically different circumstances. Not surprisingly, the different elements of the German Army responded to the revolution in significantly different ways. The units at the front were slow to create councils, and, in the case of some units, never created them at all. Among the combat units, the councils had less influence than anywhere else in the German Army, and, in virtually every front-line unit,

---

Allies and the Central Powers had contributed to a "democratic torrent going over the world and it is madness to stand opposed to it because those who oppose it are thrown completely on the trash heap. The way to deal with this democratic wave is to steer it, consequently to choose the pilot and the course so that we can ride the wave and come into port, even if the war goes badly." *Ehrenrettung*, 202. Groener may have lost his job at the *Kriegsamt* in part because of the sympathy he had shown for workers during labor negotiations.

[34] An Allied intervention was a genuine fear of the provisional government. See Colin Ross' speech to the first session of the Greater Berlin soldiers' council, Marx, ed., *Handbuch*, 191–2.

the old lines of authority – from officer down to soldier – remained in place during the first days after the armistice. In these respects, the units at the front were different. However, to appreciate the unique behavior of the front-line troops in the West, one must consider the response of the rest of the army.

The Home Army (*Heimatheer*) was a polyglot organization of railway troops, garrisons, training, and administrative formations. Much of the manpower in this horde was found in the replacement (*Ersatz*) depots. Every regiment in the field had a corresponding *Ersatz* unit charged with in-processing, training, and shipping conscripts to the parent formation at the front. In late 1918, the *Ersatz* units had responded to the urgent demands of OHL by shipping off most of the soldiers who had received at least a minimum level of training.[35] What remained were hundreds of thousands of untrained men from the youngest classes; eighteen- and nineteen-year-olds. The army shoehorned these raw recruits into overcrowded casernes where facilities had often been badly neglected since the beginning of the war. Once there, they were placed under the supervision of officers and NCOs incapable of front-line duty because of their age, nervous condition, or physical handicaps. Alongside them in the *Ersatz* barracks were thousands of men in convalescent formations, recovering from wounds and often none too eager to return to the trenches. Prior to the revolution, the generals who commanded the homeland garrisons had considerable doubts about the reliability of the *Ersatz* battalions under their command.[36] One officer described the replacement formations as "bloodless, consumptive figures without any value."[37] These doubts were significant since the homeland garrisons played a central role in the Home Army's contingency plans for putting down revolutionary uprisings.

The misgivings of the Home Army's leaders were amply borne out in the first week and a half of November. When army units from local garrisons were sent to quash the sailors' mutinies in Kiel, the results were brief clashes followed by a complete defection of the army units over to the cause of the mutineers. As the sailors of the German fleet spread the news and the spirit of the revolution, the story repeated itself again and again, though, after Kiel, there was almost no bloodshed.[38]

[35] Schmidt, *Heimatheer und Revolution*, 19.
[36] See, for example, Ebbinghaus, *Memoiren*, 32. Ebbinghaus, a Württemburger, deplored the army's 1918 "combing-out" of cadre with over two years' experience in the training formations. By doing so, the OHL shipped to the front those officers and NCOs with the most experience in managing young recruits and convalescents.
[37] Schmidt, *Heimatheer*, 18–19.
[38] Sebastian Haffner, *Failure of a Revolution*, trans. George Rapp (New York: Deutsch, 1973), 58.

In the span of just a few days, the military command structure of the homeland was completely overthrown. Everywhere local soldiers' councils replaced the authority of the various army headquarters, while the garrisons in the homeland provided the new revolutionary order with its armed strength. Yet the transfer of power was not attended by widespread disorder and violence. In a number of cases, officers were harassed and beaten. More often, revolutionary soldiers ripped decorations, cockades, and shoulder straps with badges of rank off the uniforms of officers either bold or foolish enough to appear in public wearing these symbols of the old regime. Nevertheless, instead of chaos, the soldiers' councils of the *Heimatheer* usually became agencies for the re-establishment of order after the outbreak of the revolution had created an initial outburst of lawlessness.[39]

The immediate political program of the soldiers' councils reflected the general desire of the German people for peace, voting reform, and the abdication of the Kaiser. Beyond these common goals, the soldiers' councils reflected the aspiration of the rank and file to overhaul the trappings of militarism and the superior–subordinate relationships within the army. As an example, on November 12, the Munich soldiers' council described the new order for officers and men remaining on duty:

On the order of the [new] Minister Rosshaupter, officers come with good intentions to supply the hundreds of thousands of comrades at the front and to discharge them in the homeland. The officers come, not as your superiors, but as soldiers who desire to work for the welfare of the people. You are not required to salute officers, on duty or off. Also, what officers order can only be ordered in agreement with the council you have elected for your caserne.

Be assured, that your soldiers' council will watch carefully that the officers do not exceed their authority.

The proclamation went on to warn officers to remain constantly aware of the "new spirit" of the Bavarian People's State, to strip off their badges of rank, and work along with the enlisted soldiers to ensure order.[40] This last point was important. In general, the Home Army's councils cannot be described as radical, though some were dominated by the USPD and by its extreme left wing, the Spartacists.[41]

---

[39] This was one of the major conclusions drawn by the revisionists of the 1960s and 1970s. See Eberhard Kolb, "The Revolutionary Origins of the Republic," in Eberhard Kolb, *The Weimar Republic*, trans. P.S. Falla (London: Routledge, 2001), 138–47.

[40] Berthold and Neef, *Militarismus und Opportunismus*, Document 38: Aufruf des Soldatenrates München vom. 12. November, 1918, 171.

[41] This paragraph and the previous discussion summarize Ulrich Kluge's discussion of the program of the soldiers' councils found in Kluge, *Soldatenräte und Revolution*, 113–18.

Within Germany, many leaders of the newly formed soldiers' councils realized the need for some sort of central direction in order to secure the "achievements of the revolution." To this end, the Executive Council of the Soldiers' Councils of Berlin claimed the right to speak for all the council movements within the Home Army. The provisional government recognized this authority on November 10.[42]

Despite this acknowledgement, the local Home Army councils were jealous of their local authority. Inside Germany, even when officers remained at their post to conduct administrative functions, they were required to recognize the authority of the local councils. This new arrangement contrasted sharply with the continued dominance of the officer corps in the combat units. This contrast would serve as an inevitable source of conflict as the Field Army reached the borders of Germany.

In the East, the response to the revolution took yet another form. The German occupation army in the East numbered almost a million men scattered across a vast expanse of territory that included the Ukraine, Poland, the Baltic coast, and parts of White Russia. These garrisons were created from third- and fourth-class units made up almost predominantly of the oldest classes, the units the OHL felt it could most easily spare from the fighting in the West.[43]

The frontier of Germany's eastern empire brought its occupation troops into contact with the Russian Communists (as well as Polish, Ukrainian, and other nationalist forces) and this proximity did much to shape the response of the German garrisons to the revolution in their homeland. Even before the peace treaty of Brest-Litovsk in March 1918, the Bolsheviks had undertaken an active campaign to undermine the military effectiveness of the German forces inside Russia. The dispersion of the German forces made it difficult for the German chain of command to maintain close supervision over its troops, and, in 1918, fraternization between the Bolsheviks and German soldiers became a regular occurrence.[44] Even before the armistice, the effect of Bolshevik agitation was reflected in the mutiny of German troops in Kiev, Kharkov, Odessa, and other locations.[45]

The difficulty of communication over long distances delayed the news of the revolution from reaching the far-flung German garrisons

---

[42] *Ibid.*, 138–9.
[43] Kriegsgeschichtlichen Forschungsanstalt, *Weltkrieg*, XIV, 753. The troops in the north along the Baltic coast were commanded by the Eighth Army; those in White Russia and Poland by the Tenth Army, and those in the Ukraine by Army Group Kiev.
[44] "Break-up of the German Armies," 34–5.   [45] *Ibid.*, 34.

in the East. However, by the second week of November, almost every unit of the occupation army had created a soldiers' council. These councils were similar to those inside Germany in that the MSPD party men dominated the leadership and served as a moderating influence.[46] However, the soldiers' councils in the East held a much stronger position in relation to the old military authorities than their counterparts on the Western Front.[47] Thus, point 3 of the Kiev soldiers' council stated: "Officers remain at their posts as long as they accept the program of the Soldiers' Council and enjoy the trust of their troops."[48] Similarly, the soldiers' council of the Tenth Army announced, in the days following the revolution, that they alone "held in their hands the supreme power in the Tenth Army and therefore, carried the supreme responsibility."[49]

What the *Soldatenräte* in Russia, Poland, and the Ukraine shared with the units on the Western Front was the urgent desire to return to Germany as quickly as possible. The homeward retreat of the German forces in the East began almost immediately after the conclusion of the armistice. However, the conduct of the retreat in the East differed significantly from the orderly withdrawal of German units from France and Belgium. In particular, Army Group Kiev, which controlled all German forces in the Ukraine, left thousands of men and much of its equipment behind in its frantic attempt to extricate itself from the occupied territories. The war diary of this headquarters recorded: "Under the rigid discipline of their officers, the German troops proved themselves the best in the world. No sooner had they shaken themselves free from this than they showed themselves more slovenly in their behavior and more cowardly in battle than the half-trained Ukrainian and Bolshevik troops."[50]

As this excerpt from the war diary suggests, in a number of instances, the withdrawal was accompanied by fighting. Skirmishes, in some instances against the Poles, in others the Ukrainians or the Red Army, hastened the disintegration of the German forces. The 20th *Landwehr* Division, for example, refused to advance against the Bolsheviks and deserted *en masse*. When the Tenth Army headquarters in White Russia attempted to create a security unit for the East Prussian frontier, it was able to collect only a handful of volunteers.[51] And, although the

---

[46] Kluge, *Soldatenräte und Revolution*, 95.
[47] Roland Grau, "Zur Rolle der Soldatenräte der Fronttruppen in der Novemberrevolution." *Zeitschrift für Militärgeschichte* (GDR), 5 (1968), 555.
[48] *Ibid.*, 562.   [49] *Ibid.*
[50] "Break-up of the German Armies," 42.   [51] *Ibid.*, 38–9.

Allies, the Ebert government, and the OHL wanted to maintain a German presence in the East – albeit for different reasons – the Germans finally had to request relief from this responsibility. As they admitted to the Allies in early December, the new government no longer had effective control over their troops in the Ukraine.[52] Indeed, some of the soldiers' councils in that area had opened independent negotiations with Lenin's government.[53]

Clearly, the contrast between the conduct of the Field Army's troops in the West and those of the occupation forces in the East was marked. The troops in the East created their councils spontaneously and, in their relationship with the officer chain of command, reserved the dominant position for themselves. The eastern councils also asserted their independence when dealing with the Soviets and the new Polish government. Cooperation between the soldiers' councils and officers, when it did occur, could not prevent the disintegration of many units. Finally, for some units the retreat from Russia became a rout.[54]

The soldiers' councils also held the upper hand in the *Etappe*, the rear areas behind the line in France and Belgium. They frequently operated from a position of real strength: when support units and garrisons are added together, the troops assigned to the *Etappe* amounted to over a million men and they controlled access to the supplies the front-line forces relied on for sustainment. In the last year of the war, morale was poor and discipline had become notoriously lax within the *Etappe*. The chain of command often feared to exercise its authority, and, in some places, covert soldiers' councils may have formed as early as August 1918.[55] Front-line officers had been appalled by what they found behind the lines. A diary entry by an officer of the Guards recorded:

[A] crowd of back-of-the-lines soldiers, cynical and insubordinate, squatting in wagons without lights, smoking and talking. I always feel I should like to clear them out and move them on, but they would probably fly at your throat if you attempted to do so. They are constantly roaring, 'Blow out the lights.' 'Out with the knives!' 'Three men to cut him!' and things of this kind. This may only be barracks room bluster, but such cries are significant and indicate the degree of savagery these men have reached.[56]

---

[52] *The US Army in the World War*, X, 229.
[53] Kurt Fischer, *Deutsche Truppen und Entente-Intervention in Südrussland, 1918–1919* (Boppard: Vandenhoeck und Ruprecht, 1973), 71.
[54] "Break-up of the German Armies," 41.
[55] Bauer, *Grosse Krieg*, 260. Bauer was predictable in his claim that Jews were heavily represented in the leadership of these secret organizations as well as the councils that formed after the revolution.
[56] *Why Germany Capitulated.*

The chief of staff of one army group commented on the potential for unrest: "The danger of Bolshevism is great ... One of the greatest sources is [found in] the train stations and assembly areas. Here, where men of all branches are assembled in great numbers, away from their units and unsupervised, those who would do ill have the opportunity to find a willing audience."[57]

The apparent collapse of discipline among the rear-area formations made for a volatile situation. Add to that, the hundreds of thousands of *Drückeberger* clustered around major towns and depots, and the upheaval that took place with the news of the armistice is not surprising. General von Kuhl may have exaggerated only slightly in writing, "all bonds of discipline and order were loosed in a single moment."[58]

If von Kuhl had been inclined to hyperbole, nonetheless his observations were confirmed by observers from the American Expeditionary Force (AEF), who sought to develop an accurate and coherent picture of the German Army's condition in the weeks following the cease-fire. Using interviews with German soldiers as well as with citizens of France and Luxembourg, one American report read:

From the moment it became known Armistice negotiations were under way, some unruly elements of the German Army, coming especially from troops of the rear billeted in Brussels, met of their own accord and abandoned themselves to all sorts of excesses: corteges flaunting the red flag, soldiers disregarding their officers and ransacking local supplies to make money, etc. No resistance whatsoever seems to have been offered by the terrorized officers.[59]

Another AEF intelligence summary of the same period quoted a "reliable source":

The [train] stations and particularly the one in the city of Luxembourg were the scenes of much disorder. Officers had no control over their men, those who were on the trains or at the stations being treated with gross disrespect. While he [the source] had heard of cases of assault made upon the officers, he had no knowledge of specific cases. He had, however, heard that officers had been compelled to remove their insignia of rank and were openly disrespected by their soldiers. Pillaging of military stores was open.[60]

In some cases, these scenes of disorder occurred only a few miles behind the front.

The first priority for most of the men in the disintegrating formations in the *Etappe* was a speedy return home. Where the means were

---

[57] Kuhl, *UDZ*, III, 23.   [58] *Ibid.*
[59] *The US Army in the World War*, X, report of November 25, 1918, 157.
[60] *The US Army in the World War*, XI. 36.

available, as in the case of transport units, the soldiers frequently took matters into their own hands and made their way east. Elsewhere, crowds of deserters and mutinous troops hijacked trains and rerouted them toward the German frontier.[61]

Among those who remained, the news of the revolution inside the homeland led to the spontaneous creation of soldiers' councils. Prominent among these were the councils created in the major cities of the occupied areas: Brussels, Namur, Antwerp, and Beverloo. On November 10, the Brussels soldiers' council announced that it had taken control of the garrison newspaper and the local telegraph service. It offered comradely greetings (*Kameradgrüße*) to the homeland and the new government and declared that a commission under its control would assume responsibility for ensuring adequate food and lodging for the garrison and a speedy return to the homeland. While calling for order and discipline within the garrison, it added that only soldiers "on duty" need offer obedience and salutes to officers. Such messages suggested that the rear area councils could serve as a force for stability. However, among the large garrisons, anonymity and an absence of danger had offered ample scope for revolutionary agitation, and, according to Ludwig Lewinsohn, a veteran of the MSPD and the leader of the Fourth Army's soldiers' council, these rear-area *Soldatenräte* became a source of radical propaganda and a threat to the orderly retreat of the *Westheer*. Conflict between these councils and the front-line troops seemed inevitable.[62]

The history of the soldiers' councils of the *Etappe* in the West is relatively sketchy. The most likely reason was that the units and garrisons represented by these councils disbanded themselves shortly after the armistice in order to return to Germany well ahead of the combat formations. To linger after the front-line troops had departed would have put them in danger of reprisals from the hostile Belgian and French populations and capture by advancing Allied troops. When the rear area councils did come into contact with the withdrawing *Fronttruppen*, the results suggested the gulf between the men in the trenches and the support troops. The American Third Army staff noted:

A Soldiers' Council (*Soldatenrat*) was established in Luxembourg. Among its member were several marines [*sic*; read sailors]. They were never very active here except in the first days of the withdrawal. The S.O.S. troops [Service of Supply; the AEF's synonym for *Etappe*] were the first to go ... When the troops began coming back from the front, the council sank into insignificance. Many of the S.O.S. troops remained behind to influence the troops from the front. They met with a cold reception from many of the divisions coming back. They [the front-line soldiers] knew nothing of the political changes at home. In Luxembourg, for example, one regiment put up a machine gun to keep the damned S.O.S. troops away.[63]

Anecdotal evidence such as this suggests that the council movement in the rear areas of the Western Front played a relatively minor role in the course of the revolution. What is clear, however, is that, behind the lines the troops overturned the established military authority and set up councils on their own initiative. And, on their own initiative, many of these men returned to Germany using whatever means were available. Their behavior, as with that of the homeland garrisons and the troops in the East, contrasted sharply with that of the front-line formations. Indeed, where the front-line troops were initially confronted with the revolution, its appearance was often one that induced resentment. One corps headquarters reported:

Mechanics of an army transport park (to cite one example) drive with red flags squarely through all of the marching columns, hindering the smooth progress of the movement, calling themselves the Soldiers' Council of the Fifth Army. The [front-line] soldiers look upon this as the grossest misconduct on the part of men who have never seen the enemy and hardly deserve the honorable name of soldier.[64]

In such instances, disorder in the *Etappe* served to increase the *alienation* between front and rear while discrediting the goals of the revolution.[65]

For most soldiers in the trenches, however, the revolution was a long way off. While the men in the trenches greeted the news of armistice with dazed relief, their officers waited anxiously to see if the rumors of turmoil in the homeland would provoke their men into denouncing the authority of the chain of command and proclaiming the formation of independent soldiers' councils. Instead, to the surprise of officers and men, the initiative to create *Soldatenräte* came from above. On November 9, the OHL issued the order calling for the establishment of soldiers' councils within the units of the Field Army, and on the same day, another order, signed by Hindenburg, cautioned the officer corps

---

[63] *The US Army in the World War*, XI, 28.
[64] *Ibid.*, selected documents from the 88th Division, Doc. 22, Corps Kleist retrospective report dated December 5, 1918.
[65] Rumors of peace negotiations had preceded reports of revolution so that few soldiers could identify the revolution as a proximate cause for the ending of their ordeal in the trenches.

to the effect that "understandings with existing workers' and soldiers' councils will be achieved through amicable means."[66]

As indicated already, Groener believed this call for the creation of soldiers' councils within the front-line formations was an egregious blunder. He immediately set about retrieving the error. On November 10, he sent a message to the officer corps advising them to take the council movement "in hand." On the same day, he issued an order calling for the establishment of "trustees' councils" (*Vertrauensräte*) in every company, battery, and squadron-sized unit and greater.[67] The *Vertrauensräte* represented a thinly veiled ploy to undercut the soldiers' councils. Their organization featured a top-heavy membership that usually included one officer, one NCO, and two enlisted men for each council. As for their role: "The Trustees' Councils are suitable for the closest cooperation with unit commanders in dealing with all economic and social questions [rations, accommodations, leave, etc.], as long as order remains in the army. The leadership of the troops must, therefore, remain firmly in the hands of the commanding authorities."[68]

Whether they were called trustees' councils or soldiers' councils, the *Räte* [councils] movement among the front-line units was largely based on the orders of the High Command. In this respect, then, Ulrich Kluge's assertion that the OHL and its subordinate headquarters conspired to subvert the influence and revolutionary orientation of the soldiers' councils was correct.[69] Indeed, on November 16, the OHL distributed among officers a secret policy letter that admonished them to look on the councils as an "inoculation" designed to immunize the troops against more extreme influences. "The blunt reception of radical elements from the homeland is accomplished more smoothly through soldiers' councils of the troops than through the officers."[70]

Not surprisingly, the character of the front-line councils was often determined as much by officers as their soldiers. In the Seventh Army, for example, an officer organized the Central Soldiers' Council.[71] The Fourth Army soldiers' council held its first meeting at a time and place determined by the army's chief of staff. He issued a summons requiring representatives to report to the meeting in small groups so as not to run afoul of military patrols given the mission of dispersing soldiers in large gatherings.[72] One officer elected to serve on a unit council

---

[66] Kriegsgeschichtlichen Forschungsanstalt, *Weltkrieg*, XIV, 718.
[67] Groener, *Lebenserinnerung*, 469.   [68] *Ibid.*, 469.
[69] Kluge, *Soldatenräte und Revolution*, 103–4.
[70] Grau, "Zur Rolle der Soldatenräte," 555.   [71] *Ibid.*
[72] Details of the Fourth Army's council from Lewinsohn, *Revolution an der Westfront*, 7–8.

observed in his diary, "Shop stewards' committees [another translation of *Vertrauensräte*] are now being formed in all units ... No one in the Regt. feels inclined for such things, but we are still ordered to have them."[73] In some units – conspicuously among the Guards divisions – councils were never elected at all. In the Crown Prince's army group, the command forbade soldiers' councils and allowed trustees' councils only when soldiers specifically asked for them.[74]

The composition of the front-line councils reflected their moderate, unrevolutionary character. This was indicated by the disproportionate number of officers and NCOs serving on them when compared with the soldiers' councils of the Home Army and the East. The council of the 414th Infantry Regiment, for example, consisted of four officers, five NCOs, and four enlisted men.[75] Even more significant was the dominant position of MSPD party members within the front-line councils of the Field Army.[76] Fully one-third of the representatives sent by the *Fronttruppen* to the First Congress of Soldiers' and Workers' Councils in Berlin (December 16–21) were MSPD party functionaries or editors of MSPD newspapers before the war.[77]

From their inception, the front-line soldiers' and trustees' councils cooperated readily with the officer corps in maintaining order and discipline in the Field Army. The first proclamation of the Fourth Army's *Soldatenrat*, for example, called for every soldier to remain at his post and to guard his weapon from falling into unauthorized hands. "Our objective," the council asserted, "consists of protection for our loved ones at home, in the protection of jobs, and the securing of means of transportation and transportation routes in the interest of an orderly demobilization."[78] Such objectives were typical for the front-line

---

[73] Sulzbach, *With the German Guns*, 249.
[74] BA-MA, N 58/1, Nachlass Schulenberg, 243–4. Schulenberg wrote that the original order calling for soldiers' councils was evidence of the OHL's unnecessary submission to the forces of revolution. The war diary of the 3rd Battalion, 32nd Infantry regiment recorded that, on the evening of November 10, the headquarters received an order for subordinate formations to elect soldiers' councils. A division order followed a few hours later rescinding the previous directive. NARA, RG 165, Box 163, Folder II, 103rd Division Headquarters and Subordinate Units, 51.
[75] Grau, "Zur Rolle der Soldatenräte," 558.
[76] Kluge observed that leaders within the MSPD had been surprised by the speed and extent of the government's collapse. Nevertheless, they proved remarkably flexible in riding the revolutionary wave. Kluge, *Soldatenräte und Revolution*, 119–22
[77] Records from the seventy-five representatives dispatched to the congress from the *Westheer* list the prewar occupations of fifty-nine. Of these, twenty-five had been SPD functionaries before the war, nineteen were classified as "intellectuals" (attorneys, doctors, engineers, etc.), five had been civil servants, six were merchants or artisans, one was a professional officer, and one was a factory foreman. Only two were workers. Grau, "Zur Rolle der Soldatenräte," 564.
[78] Lewinsohn, *Revolution an der Westfront*, 23.

councils, and often their achievement meant that some councils were little more than adjuncts to the old command structure.[79] One young medical officer noted, "The functions of these councils were very vague; officially they had to approve the orders given by the commanding officer, but in practice they confined themselves to supervising the distribution of rations, and to putting a stamp on any document, as nothing in Germany was recognized as valid without at least one stamp and several illegible signatures."[80]

According to the newly established protocols for revolutionary authority, the soldiers' council of a senior headquarters had a span of control that corresponded to the headquarters from which it was formed. Theoretically, then, the soldiers' council of the OHL was a powerful agency that spoke for and guided the efforts all the councils within the Field Army. [81] In reality, its authority and impact on events is debatable. On one hand, Groener pointed to the composition of the council, which included his own orderly sergeant as well as the enlisted servant of Admiral Scheer, and claimed that the OHL council served as a willing "mouthpiece" for the policies of the High Command.[82] On the other hand, Marxist historians emphasized the memorandum the OHL council delivered to the Congress of Field Army Councils on December 1: "The creation of soldiers' councils is the final and total conquest of militarism."[83]

If it took the proper revolutionary attitude toward militarism, nevertheless, the soldiers' council of the OHL was hardly a radical organ. Men with middle-class backgrounds dominated its seven-man executive committee.[84] Upon meeting the membership of the senior

---

[79] Volkmann, *Marxismus und das deutsche Heer*, 253.

[80] Stephan Westman, *Surgeon with the Kaiser's Army* (London: William Kimber and Co., 1968), 179.

[81] Volkmann, *Marxismus und das deutsche Heer*, 254. The original initiative for creating the OHL council apparently came from a Captain Meunier, a member of one of the intelligence departments on the staff. The German Historical Museum, Exhibit Item Do2 92/200 "Ausweis fur Hauptmann Meunier, Mitglied des Vollzugsausschusses des Soldatenrates bei der OHL, Spa, November 13, 1918." Meunier may have been the one who told the generals on November 9 that the troops around the OHL would not fire on their *feldgrau* comrades. Marx, *Handbuch*, 82.

[82] Groener, *Lebenserinnerungen*, 470. Colonel Bauer recorded that the initial demands of the OHL council indicated its frivolous character: the members wanted a certain lieutenant colonel to be more prompt in returning military greetings and they wanted ten trucks put at their disposal to transport their members around. Bauer, *Grosse Krieg*, 271.

[83] Grau, "Zur Rolle der Soldatenräte," 557. One suspects that, at first, the council members were inclined to offer a degree of deferance to officers while at the OHL but later mimicked the sentiments of their more radical peers when away from the headquarters.

[84] *Ibid.*, 555.

council, Ludwig Lewinsohn, the chairman of the Fourth Army's council, was gratified to find that they reflected the same Majority Socialist outlook as his own army-level council. In particular, the OHL *Soldatenrat* supported the MSPD's fundamental goal of replacing the rule of workers' and soldiers' councils with an early convention of a National Assembly.[85] Thus, in a curious fashion, *selection* had played a new role in distinguishing the front-line response to revolution from the remainder of the army. Within the Field Army's councils, officers, NCOs, and MSPD party veterans were overrepresented in the councils of the combat units and the MSPD was similarly dominant in head-quarters' councils. The presence of these men served to shape the generally moderate outlook of their councils.

Moderate did not always mean compliant. While Groener found the OHL council useful, it was also a nuisance and, over time, his relationship with the council's leaders grew strained. For its part, the council made a great show of red armbands and banners, and demanded workspace and vehicles to support its activities, which, it believed, included monitoring the officers on the staff for signs of counter-revolutionary activity. For Groener, there was further aggravation. In accordance with the council's efforts to create a parallel chain of command, it required that no order or policy could leave the headquarters without the approval of the council's executive committee.[86] To circumvent the council's interference, Groener asked the cabinet to send him a representative to act as the government's sole conduit for its dealings with the OHL.[87] Ebert responded by empowering a representative, one Herr Giebel, who proved much more amenable to the efforts of the OHL.[88]

Whatever their political aims, the OHL council usually proved willing to cooperate with Groener's goal of maintaining order in the front-line formations during the army's retreat from France and Belgium, even if this put the OHL's council in conflict with the *Soldatenräte* in the homeland. Both Groener and the OHL council needed the other's cooperation if they were to convince the Field Army's rank and file

[85] Lewinsohn, *Revolution an der Westfront*, 64.
[86] Volkmann, *Marxismus und das deutsche Heer*, 254.
[87] BA-R, R43/2485, f.1, Document 35, Telegram: "Vorschlage der OHL fur Zusammenwirken zwischen Armee und Zivilstellen."
[88] The bulk of Giebel's correspondence with Berlin seems to consist of reports of misbehavior by homeland *Soldatenräte* or inquiries about his stipend. For the soldiers' council complaint that Giebel was insufficiently vigilant in his duties see, BA-R, R43/2500/4, "Überwachung der OHL" (Memorandum from the Soldiers' Council of the OHL to the "Reich Leadership"), December 24, 1918 (#5598).

that the existing command structure had to be maintained in order to accomplish the difficult retreat across the Rhine.[89]

The fruits of collaboration

If the *Westheer* was to meet the demanding deadlines of the armistice agreement, it also needed uninterrupted supply lines with the homeland and the cooperation of officers and men within the front-line units. On November 10, the OHL had already invoked the name of Hindenburg in a telegram calling on the new government to secure these objectives. "The Field Marshal expects from the new government that it will use every means to secure the provisioning of the army and, to this end, prevent any interruption of railway traffic ... Further, the troops must remain obedient to their officers; the Field Marshal expects support from the government in this respect."[90] If the cabinet resented the tone of this communication, it was not evident in their response. The day before the cease-fire, the cabinet had issued a proclamation aimed at those who might disturb the supply apparatus of the troops in Belgium and France.

The provisioning of our comrades on the Western Front is in great danger. At precisely this moment it be must be absolutely maintained. We owe that to our comrades ... Every act of plunder or confiscations of rations and fodder loaded on transportation allocated for the Field Army, every diversion or delay of transportation, every cessation of the loading process, must cease unconditionally.[91]

On November 11, the OHL sent the cabinet a telephone message that described the desired conditions of authority within the front-line units.[92] Two days later, Ebert and his colleagues issued the troops a virtual verbatim draft of the OHL's message under their own signatures. It read:

The People's Government expects from you the strictest self-discipline, in order to avoid immeasurable harm. [To this end:]

---

[89] For a Marxist interpretation of the significance of the retreat see Dreetz, "Rückführung des Westheeres."

[90] Berthold and Neef, *Militarismus und Opportunismus*, Document 20: "Telegramm Groeners an den Reichskanzlers und die neue Regierung am 10. November 1918," 148–9.

[91] Marx, *Handbuch*, 167. The next day Groener sent his liaison with the cabinet, Colonel Haeften, another message requesting that the government intervene to keep the homeland soldiers' councils from interfering with the army's demobilization. BA-R, R43/2485, f.1, Groener message to Haeften, November 11, 1918.

[92] BA-R, R43/2485, f.1, transcript of telephone message from the OHL to Berlin, 12 November, 1918.

1. The relationship between officer and soldier is built on complementary trust. For this, the willing subordination of the soldier under the officer and the comradely handling of the soldier by superiors are the prerequisites.
2. The superior relationship of the officer remains in place. Unconditional obedience in service is of decisive importance for the return to the German homeland. Military discipline and order in the army must, therefore, be maintained under all circumstances.
3. For the maintenance of trust between officer and soldier, the soldiers' councils have advisory voices on questions of rations, leave, and the imposition of military punishment. Their highest duty is to effect the **prevention of disorder and mutiny** [emphasis in the original].
4. The same rations for officers, warrants, and men [as well as the same quarters].
5. Weapons are to be used against members of the public only in emergency and for the prevention of plundering.[93]

For those willing to read between the lines, the message was clear. The tone of leadership in the German Army had changed, the perquisites of rank were now subject to question, and the soldiers' councils had a useful role to play. But one should make no mistake, the officers were still in charge and to disobey the chain of command was to betray the new revolutionary order.

Meanwhile, in its own communication with the rank and file, the OHL and it subordinate headquarters harped constantly on the theme that order and discipline was going to be needed to get the army home safely. Army Group Gallwitz told the officers of its command to relay to their men that those who would desire to get home ahead of other men were violating the comradely trust soldiers should have for one another and undermining the well-being of all.[94] In a division order issued on November 11, the 1st *Landwehr* Division reassured its soldiers that the same spirit that they demonstrated in four years of fighting would need to be maintained in the difficult march that lay ahead and the "oppressive uncertainty over the fate of our loved ones in the homeland." The chain of command assured the men that everything possible was being done to give them some rest after the exertions of the previous weeks, to find them fresh clothes, and to restore postal communication with Germany.[95] On the day of the armistice, the 255th Division headquarters warned its officers that for "the approaching return of the army

---

[93] BA-MA, PH 8 I/511, proclamation of the People's Government, November 13, 1918.
[94] BA-MA, PH 8 I/511, Fifth Army transcript of message from Army Group Gallwitz, November 11, 1918.
[95] NARA, RG 165, Box 121, Folder I, 1st *Landwehr* Division Order, November 11, 1918, 20.

to the homeland it is of extraordinary importance that leaders keep
the troops firmly in hand." It ordered that, within the division, staffs
would be stripped of officers in order to reinforce the chain of command
among the troop units, which would be consolidated under "energetic,
experienced officers."[96] The day after the fighting had stopped, Colonel
Reinhard had recovered from his frigid trip to Spa and back and had
assembled the men of the 4th Guards Regiment at the palace of Bouillon
for a brief address. After calling on his troops to remember their fallen
comrades and leading three cheers for the Kaiser, the colonel warned
his men that if they were to make an orderly march back to Germany,
they must remain steady, disciplined, and loyal.[97] So it went, up and
down the chain of command. Though one officer recalled that the men
understood "instinctively" that the return home would be perilous and
required old-style discipline, the officer corps was taking no chances
that any soldier might misunderstand the point.[98]

Along with reinforcing their own authority, the chain of command
had to act quickly to quash the torrent of rumors that threatened to
unsettle the troops.[99] The 88th Division ordered: "First interception
of wireless messages coming from workers' and soldiers' councils with
fantastic contents or warnings to maintain order are the only news
from home, which, in spite of all radio discipline, get through to the
troops and cause them greatest worries concerning their families at
home."[100] Even if revolutionary sentiment did not create mutiny among
the troops, their fear for wife and children might undermine good order
and discipline. With this in mind, Groener sent a radio message to the
Field Army on November 12 emphasizing that the food situation in
the homeland was under control and that no soldier should fear for the
well-being of his family.[101] That same day another message came from
Spa aimed at reassuring the troops by reporting that chaos had not
overtaken the homeland, that the violence accompanying the revolution

[96] NARA, RG 165, Box 179, Document 54, 255th Infantry Division War Diary, entry
for November 11, 1918, 145.
[97] Wilhelm Reinhard, *Das 4. Garde-Regiment zu Fuss: Nach den amtlichen Kriegstagebüchern und personlichen Aufzeichnungen bearbeitet* (Berlin: Gerhard Stalling Verlag, 1924),
394. During the war the regiment had lost 4,700 men killed and 11,800 wounded.
[98] Volkmann, *Marxismus und das deutsche Heer*, 253.
[99] BA-R, R43/2500/5, transcript of telephone call from Major [?] of the OHL to
the Reich leadership requesting news media – flyers, newspapers, etc. – to allay the
absence of information and to call for the unhindered transport of supplies to the
army.
[100] *Second Infantry Division*, Vol. IX, Intelligence Documents: Doc. 22: Corps Kleist
report to Fifth Army, dated December 5, 1918,
[101] BA-MA, PH 8 I/511, transcript of radio message "An Gruppe Soden," November 12,
1918.

had been isolated, and that the Spartacists were not part of the new coalition government.[102] Finally, yet another radio transmission on November 12 called on the chain of command to stamp out rumors that Field Marshal von Hindenburg had fled to Holland along with the Kaiser.[103]

While officers on the Western Front worked toward the common goal of maintaining order and discipline within the Field Army, their efforts did not necessarily reflect the solidarity of unanimously shared views. Some officers in the *Etappe* had abandoned their posts for the relative safety of the homeland. In the front-line units, many officers were dismayed by the order to create councils within their units. Reinhard of the 4th Guards believed that because the OHL was located deep in the *Etappe*, it was far too submissive in its relationship with the soldiers' councils, while unaware of how solid discipline remained among the combat units.[104] At a much higher level, the war diary of Schulenberg's headquarters, Army Group Crown Prince, was scathing in its criticism of the OHL for its failure to act decisively against the chaos in the rear areas.[105]

Yet few at the front fully appreciated the difficulties Groener faced. In particular, he anticipated a collision between the front-line forces and the homeland councils and urged the chancellor to bring councils under tighter control. In spite of the efforts of the officer corps, the general feared that agitation by the Home Army's *Soldatenräte* might undermine the relatively fragile bonds that held the *Westheer* together. With this same concern in mind, Ebert had already ordered the *Heimatheer* to render the returning field formations all possible assistance in their return to Germany.[106] Apparently, Groener was not completely satisfied with the government's efforts, because he sent an additional telegram on November 11 asking the chancellor to appeal to the *Soldatenräte* in the homeland to support the orderly withdrawal of the *Westheer*. This message also contained a threat. If order is not maintained in the Field Army, the general wrote, it will be like a "storm flood (*Sturmflut*) flowing over the fields of the homeland and the army and the homeland will

[102] BA-MA, PH 8 I/511, 213th Infantry Division message (unnumbered), "Reports from the Homeland," November 12, 1918.
[103] BA-MA, PH 8 I/511, transcript of radio message from Fifth Army 1a #777, November 12, 1918.
[104] Reinhard, *Wehen der Republik*, 36.
[105] NARA, RG 165, Box 27, Folder IV, War Diary of Group of Armies Crown Prince, entries for November 13, 1918, 8–10.
[106] Berthold and Neef, *Militarismus und Opportunismus*, Document 22: "Aufruf des Reichskanzlers Ebert an das deutsche Heimatheer vom 10. November 1918," 151–2.

dissolve into chaos." He went on to observe gravely that no one who called himself a German would want to take responsibility for such a disaster.[107]

In dispatching such a warning to the head of government, Groener demonstrated his readiness to use the men returning from the front as a political weapon. The government depended on the officer corps to bring the *Westheer* home, and that reliance made the troops and their good order vitally important in the officer corps' struggle to maintain their status and influence. In the same way that the Kaiser had warned that his abdication would lead to anarchy in the Field Army, Groener portrayed the front-line troops – according to his objectives of the moment – as either a force for renewed stability or a source of potential chaos. The message he repeated to Ebert and his colleagues was that unless the officer corps was supported and the radicals suppressed, the OHL could not take responsibility for the consequences. Clearly, the *Frontschweine* were the essential pawns in the game being played by the old elites.

Closely tied to the OHL's efforts to maintain their grip on the Field Army was a battle over symbols. The most conspicuous of these was the red flag, the symbol of revolution. The soldiers' councils inside Germany and in the Field Army's rear had taken up the red flag and red armbands as the symbol of their victory over militarism. Yet these symbols were slow to appear in the Field Army. In some cases, this was a result of official policy. In Army Group Crown Prince, for example, red armbands and flags were banned. Instead, the headquarters encouraged the troops to display their *Landesfarben*, the colors of their home state (for example, Bavarian blue and white). As the troops began to pull back into the rear areas, the same headquarters complained that troops in the *Etappe* used the red flag as cover for plundering and other excesses. Commanders urged the OHL to ban the red symbols across the army.[108] However, whatever the officers may have felt, there were members of the new government who believed that banning the red flag would be denying the revolution. In mid November, it remained to be seen what banner the Field Army would carry when it crossed the Rhine.

Other symbols included the vestiges of monarchy that lingered on in the army after November 9. Though Wilhelm was in Holland and most

[107] *Ibid.*, Document 27: "Telegramm Groeners an den Reichskanzler Ebert am 11. November 1918," 160. The same text is found in BA-R, R43/2500/5, telegram from the OHL to Ebert, but dated November 13, 1918.
[108] NARA, RG 165, Box 27, Folder IV, War Diary of Group of Armies Crown Prince, entry for November 14, 1918, 10.

of the twenty-odd remaining ruling houses in imperial Germany were in flight or preparing to flee, the immediate aftermath of the revolution found the two largest of the four army groups on the Western Front commanded by crown princes. In the north, Rupprecht of Bavaria commanded the armies facing the British and Belgians, and south of him, facing the French and part of the AEF, was the Kaiser's son, Wilhelm of Prussia.[109] Both princes wanted to lead their soldiers back into Germany. If they had no thrones to occupy, then they would still take their place at the head of the front-line troops. On November 10, Rupprecht send a message to the revolutionary government led by Kurt Eisner and to the Bavarian commanders at the front:

Along with the royal house that had been joined with them for hundreds of years, the Bavarian people have a right to demand that a constitutional national assembly chosen by a free and universal vote decide the new form of government. It is a self-evident demand that the soldiers returning home be given the opportunity to present their voice. Bavarian soldiers can then decide, in unified harmony with the Bavarian citizenry at home, how the future cooperation with the ruling house will be decided.[110]

Rupprecht had a reputation for political moderation and military insight, but he was grasping at straws. Meanwhile, Crown Prince Wilhelm had offered his services to the new government and asked Ebert for permission to continue "as a soldier to do his duty." Ebert denied his request, and both he and Rupprecht followed the Kaiser into exile in Holland.[111] Neither Ebert nor the more radical Eisner could afford to allow the crown princes, symbols of the old order, to lead their troops into the new republic.

The princes had left, but the generals remained. In the first few days after the revolution, Hindenburg, Groener, and the rest of the officer corps had moved decisively to assure the support and cooperation of the new government. And from the highest level, where Field Marshal von Hindenburg issued the warning to the troops that "The Armistice agreement requires a rapid return march to the homeland – under the prevailing conditions a difficult task requires self-discipline and the most loyal performance of duty from every one of you," down

[109] South of Crown Prince Wilhelm, facing the bulk of the AEF, was Gallwitz's group of armies, and south of Gallwitz was the army group commanded by Duke Albrecht of Württemburg.

[110] Rupprecht [Crown Prince of Bavaria], *Mein Kriegstagebuch*, vol. III, 369–70.

[111] NARA, RG 165, Box 27, Folder IV, War Diary of Group of Armies Crown Prince, entry for November 11, 1918, 8, and Wolfgang Zorn, *Bayerns Geschichte im 20. Jahrhundert: Von der Monarchie zum Bundesland* (Munich: Verlag C.H. Beck, 1986), 140–1.

to Colonel Reinhard's address to the 4th Foot Guards requiring them
to maintain the strictest order and discipline, the chain of command
was reinforcing the idea that the only sure way for a front-line soldier to
guarantee this expedient return to home and loved ones was by obedience. However, it was not to be the obedience of the old, prewar army.
The chain of command had made it clear that soldiers would have a
say in such things as rations and leave. Commanders were encouraging
their officers to handle their men with tact, to make regular demonstrations of concern for their soldiers' welfare, and to remind their men
why their compliance with orders was necessary for a successful return
to the Fatherland.[112]

The case of the 115th Division

Within a Field Army of 180 divisions, one would be hard pressed to
describe any single unit as "average." However, one could certainly
describe the 115th Infantry Division as unremarkable. Formed in April
1915, it was a South German unit, recruited primarily from Baden
and the provinces of the Rhineland. The 115th had arrived on the
Western Front in February 1918 after duty in a relatively quiet sector
in Rumania. Like so many other divisions, it had suffered heavy losses
in the last months of the war, and though it had fought well enough to
receive mention in official German communiqués, Allied intelligence
rated it as mediocre ("third-class"). A prisoner from the division told
an interrogator from the AEF's First Division: "The desire to be taken
prisoner is universal. The Prussians dare not desert because of consequences after the war. The Alsatians, on the other hand, are anxious to
cross the lines but often hesitate because of reprisals inflicted on their
families by the authorities."[113]

What is remarkable about the 115th is that a near-verbatim transcript has survived from the first meeting of the soldiers' trustees
(*Vertrauensmänner*) and the division's senior officers on the morning of November 14, 1918, in Lorentzweiler, a small town in central
Luxembourg.[114] The document offers a unique snapshot of the mood of

---

[112] See, for example, NARA, RG 165, Box 179, Folder 54, 255th Infantry Division War
Diary, entry for November 11, 1918.

[113] Description of the 115th Infantry Division from AEF G2, *251 Divisions*, 606–8, and
World War Records. 1st Division AEF, *Summaries of Intelligence*, vol. IV (December
25, 1917 to November 30, 1918), G2 Memorandum, September 26, 1918. Subject:
Enemy Information.

[114] NARA, RG 165, Misc. Records: "Documents of the 115th German Infantry
Division on Conferences Nov. 10 and 14, 1918, of Staff Officers with Confidential
Representatives of the Enlisted Men." I am indebted to Gerhard Weinberg's guide to

the troops, their concerns, and their relationship with their superiors. Particularly fascinating is the record of the trustees airing their grievances before the division "First General Staff Officer," a remarkable individual named Captain Römpler. The exchange between Römpler and the representatives of the division's soldiers records the negotiation of the new terms of authority in a front-line unit three days after the war had ended. Neither the officers nor the men were certain of their position in the exchanges and the dialogue necessarily contained a certain amount of probing and testing. It was a reflection of a new and uncertain order.

On November 10, 1918, following the guidance of the OHL, the division commander, Major General Friedrich Kundt, had issued an order for the establishment of trustees' councils. He began the order by praising the men for their bravery and endurance and asserting that the division's success on the battlefield had been based on the mutual trust between officers and men, a bond which needed to be strengthened given the uncertain situation in the homeland. He then gave specific guidance for the number of trustees to be elected in each unit; for example, one NCO and three men in each of the battalion, regimental, and brigade staffs; one NCO and three soldiers from each of the infantry regiments; one NCO and one enlisted man from each artillery battalion, one NCO and two soldiers from the pioneer battalion; with a similar representation from the rest of the division's units.

These trustees will remain regularly housed and fed with the staffs to which they are assigned. They have the right all times to directly approach the respective commander to present the wishes of their comrades. In order to be familiar with these wishes, the trustees must remain in continuous contact with their comrades. The trustees have, as their highest duty, to perceive and to contribute to the prevention of the advent of every grievance within the established confines of the division, and, if they arise, to remedy them. Trust for trust! [*Vertrauen gegen vertrauen!*]

Three days later, at 10.00 a.m., General Kundt opened the first public meeting of the newly elected trustees. Present also were the various unit adjutants and Captain Römpler. The division commander promised the

the German records in NARA for highlighting this document. A particularly interesting feature of this transcript is the comment in the cover letter sent from the *Reichsarchiv* at Potsdam by Colonel Sorley of the US Army Historical Section to his chief, Colonel Spaulding (June 6, 1923): "These documents are not 'operative' in the sense of our authority for publishing; indeed I don't think it would be a good idea to publish the picture of the town meeting in the German Army in our country anyway ..." One wonders if he believed the document might have a subversive effect on officer–soldier relationships in the US Army.

gathering a brief word before he turned the meeting over to the captain. He reviewed his purpose for bringing the representatives together and cited Hindenburg's proclamation in which the field marshal appealed to the Field Army not to "let him down." Kundt also referred to a directive by the Fifth Army commander that emphasized the difficult supply situation and the need to avoid an "every man for himself" situation. He closed by admonishing the men to warn their comrades that deserting the unit at that point would have dire consequences. Deserters would soon find themselves without food, and soldiers lacking proper discharge papers would not have access to government relief. With a final appeal to "trust and order," the commander turned the meeting over to his "Ia," Captain Römpler.

Initially, Römpler continued in the same vein as Kundt, by citing official proclamations. He read Ebert's telegram thanking the OHL for their support and the text of another message signed by every member of the cabinet:

Telegram from the new government to the OHL: To General Field Marshal v. Hindenburg: We request for the entire Field Army to be ordered, that military discipline, peace, and strict order in the army be maintained under all circumstances, that therefore the orders of military superiors be obeyed completely until a successful demobilization has been carried out, and that the discharge of soldiers from the army only proceed on the orders of military superiors. The superiors will retain their weapons and insignias of rank. Where soldiers' councils or trustees' councils have been formed, they will wholeheartedly support their [chain of command's] efforts to maintain discipline and order. Signed: Ebert, Haase, Scheidemann, Dittmann, Landsberg,Barth.

The captain followed this with supporting communications from Army Group Gallwitz and the Fifth Army headquarters. By now, it was clear that Römpler was reinforcing the theme introduced by the division commander: the army's chain of command supported the new government and the new government supported the chain of command. He quoted a Fifth Army order which made this point along with an emphatic warning against desertion:

1. All orders of the OHL and all military command authorities are given in the name of the present government. This government has repeatedly emphasized that these orders will be obeyed unconditionally.
2. It is the desire of the government that only those discharged with appropriate documents can make requests for subsistence support.
3. A citizen's militia (*Bürgerwehr*) is being formed at the Rhine crossing sites that will let no one without sufficient documentation pass.

People stopped without the necessary papers will be the last in the demobilization to receive discharge.

At this point, Römpler finished his recitation of official message traffic and focused his comments on conditions inside the 115th Division. All these orders, he told the trustees, were already in effect with the division. Their common duty was to ensure that the 115th "remains a superb, reliable instrument for order in the new life of the state." Against possible rumors of counter-revolution, he reassured the gathering that there was no plan for the division to take up arms against its countrymen ("... assuming we are not forced that way by others").

He informed the men that he had a number of important topics to cover before reaching the point in the meeting where he would entertain their questions and issues. By opening with subjects of immediate concern to the troops, it appears Römpler sought to retain the initiative and prevent a free-for-all "gripe session." But, first, he revisited the issue of unauthorized departure from the division and asked the trustees to help ease the natural anxiety that every man had for his loved ones and the desire for the earliest possible homecoming. The soldier, he said, must remain "master of the human in every one of us." The fastest way home was to remain with the unit.

Römpler then turned to a new issue, the fate of the men from Alsace-Lorraine and the west bank of the Rhine. By this time soldiers were aware that Alsace-Lorraine would be returned to France and that the western Rhineland would come under Allied occupation. With this in mind, the captain called on the trustees to talk with these men from the soon-to-be occupied areas, calm their fears, and pass on to them the news that their separation would be accomplished as the division approached the Rhine and the difficult rail situation began to sort itself out. Hearing this, a soldier spoke up: "What will be the condition of the Alsatians and those returning to the left bank of the Rhine? Will they be treated as prisoners?" The captain answered no; there was no reason to believe that. The armistice required the Germany army to leave those areas. "But legally discharged soldiers no longer belong to the army." (Here, again, Römpler missed no opportunity to reinforce the need for soldiers to remain with the division until properly discharged.)

After a brief discussion of subjects that had been important to soldiers for as long as there had been armies – leave, mail, and curfew[115] – Römpler

[115] On leave, the captain assured the men he understood their concerns; however, the disorder in the railway system made normal leave impossible. What about emergency leave, one soldier asked? The captain promised that each case would be examined on its merits, but in general, any form of leave would be difficult. Römpler offered

turned to a critical topic: what were trustees expected to accomplish? He told the group that the trustees would remain with the staffs to which they had been assigned. Even though this might put some distance between the trustees and the troops they represented, they must miss no opportunity to communicate with their comrades in their old units. A trustee protested that many trustees wished to remain with their units. Römpler replied that he would take this up with the division commander.

Before opening the meeting to issues raised by the trustees, the captain made a final point – one that was, to him, perhaps the most important. It had to do with the role of officers in the post-revolutionary army and the crucial struggle over symbols. He reminded them of the cabinet's message announcing that officers would retain their weapons and badges of rank. This, he asserted, was connected with maintaining the appropriate relations between officers and men even though Germany's form of government had changed dramatically. He made a cunning argument by referring to Germany's recent enemies. He pointed out that French and American soldiers, though members of "republican" armies, behaved "properly" in the presence of their officers and observed military customs and courtesies very similar to those of the old Imperial Army. He finished this point with an appeal to solidarity. Work with your comrades, he said, "so that slackening does not intervene and, again, recognize that the one who serves as leader is, first of all, a soldier!" The trustees needed to make this point not just to their own comrades but also to the "host" of smaller units that

commiseration for the lack of mail (*Feldpost*) and reported that almost nothing was going to or coming from the homeland. Mixing metaphors, he then took a swipe at those who had created disorder inside Germany. "The reason for that [the interruption of mail] is that, at the moment of the upheaval in the homeland, the baby was thrown out with the bath water and that the reins dropped on the ground have still not been restored to the hands of the drivers." When no one followed this up with questions, Römpler abruptly changed the tone of the discussion. He was going to seek the advice of the trustees in setting an evening curfew (*Zapfenstreich*) for the division. This was a clever maneuver. Whether the curfew was set for eleven o'clock, eleven-thirty, or even twelve, was not crucial. However, by soliciting input from the representatives, the captain offered the men the idea that they had a voice (or at least the illusion of a voice) in the management of the division's affairs. A soldier spoke up, suggesting eleven, but proposed that the curfew should apply "to all classes." Römpler asked if "all classes" meant officers, NCOs, and men. "General answer: Yes, indeed." At this point, Römpler may have been taken aback, but he promised to bring the matter up with the division commander. Another trustee urged that men on official duty be exempted from the curfew. The captain responded that that would be understood: "Perhaps we can define the matter so: after eleven in the evening no one may remain outside quarters, if they are in pubs or clubs or whatever one will call them, except where official duties require this." The transcript records general agreement.

were being attached to the 115th for the purposes of movement control. These included several recruit battalions, a pioneer battalion, and an airship unit. The captain asked the men to accept the new arrivals and communicate the common desire to maintain the reputation of the division as well as the importance of supporting the new government with proper behavior. With that thought, he ended his prepared remarks with a flourish:

The orders for the onward march of the division are issued. It begins today and will, as I hope, incur no further delay. Rest days are necessary for resupply and for organizing units and resting our exhausted horses. But I hope in the briefest possible time to see the waves of the river that we have defended with life and soul, belongings and the blood of our comrades for 4½years! [116]

At that point, Römpler announced he was prepared to entertain the questions and concerns of the trustees. He encouraged them to be frank. He also told them that at noon field kitchens would be operating outside the meeting area. "It gives me pleasure to be able to eat a bowl of soup together with you."

This scenario reflected a superb piece of stage management by Römpler and the division staff. The presence of the field kitchen ensured that the exchange of views between the captain and the trustees would be followed by a pleasant experience, emphasizing the renewed solidarity of the 115th, officers and men breaking bread together. By eating with the men, the officers present would undermine rumors that they ate far better than the soldiers did. More important, the presence of the *Gulaschkanone* would ensure that the trustees would not turn the meeting into an endless airing of grievances. The meeting would certainly end before noon. For men who had endured much privation, the prospect of a hot midday meal was likely to override most other concerns.

However, the first grievance raised by a trustee threatened to undo all of Römpler's plans for an amicable dialogue between subordinates and superiors. In response to the captain's call for a candid presentation of issues, an artilleryman stepped forward. "The comrades of the 1st Battalion/229th Field Artillery Regiment have tasked me to express the desire that Lieutenant Cypionka be relieved from the battery [command]."

This was a moment of truth. The entire tone of the meeting and the subsequent relations between the trustees and the officers might hinge on Römpler's response. If he promised the artilleryman that the chain

[116] Presumably, he meant the Rhine.

of command would consider Lieutenant Cypionka's fitness for command, he risked undermining the authority of all officers. The captain would be suggesting that the trustees could have a say in who qualified to lead the units within the division. Similarly, had Römpler asked the trustees for more information about Cypionka's failings, he might have risked an embarrassing public dialogue on what was acceptable behavior by junior officers. At the other extreme, had he dismissed the trustee's concern as frivolous or, worse, insubordinate, Römpler risked insulting the complainant and, worse, exposing the whole business of the trustees' councils as a sham.

One imagines that the room grew very still as the trustees strained to hear the captain's answer. When he spoke, Römpler said precisely the right words: "I request that you see me afterwards. I will remain here at your disposal." It was an answer respectful of the trustee's concerns, but it conceded nothing and avoided further consideration of a topic that might have taken the meeting in an ugly direction.

The discussion turned to rations as the adjutant of the 229th Brigade asked about rumors of a cut in officer rations. Here was a topic that Römpler must have anticipated. Officer rations, he told the group, were the same as those of the men. If the officers' mess, with its tablecloths and napkins, looked different from the conditions experienced by the troops, it was a function of the small group involved, not preferential treatment. This answer did not satisfy another trustee. "It has been observed that the portions of officers are considerably bigger and that the troops receive less meat. If one speaks with the cook about it, it turns out, that there are also bones with it." Römpler promised that both adjutants and supply officers would look into this question in order to ensure such [appearances] did not continue.

A soldier named Wicklein, a trustee from the 136th Infantry Regiment, complained that the commander of the Second Battalion required the men to execute an excessive number of "passes-in-review" during the unit's marches. Again, Römpler's response was deft. It was good practice to have the unit execute such a review at the beginning of a march and at the end, when the unit arrived at its quarters. However, there could be "different opinions" about whether it might be overdone. He promised to have the adjutant bring the issue up with the commander.

The line of questioning returned to rations. One soldier complained that the battalion canteens were in bad shape and that officers bought out the luxury items. Another soldier complained that some units had better conditions in their canteens than others. Finally, a trustee suggested that the *Vertrauensmänner* should have the right to check supply conditions. Römpler responded that the units had mess councils (*Menage-Kommissionen*) to perform such functions.[117] Several voices objected that some units did not have such councils. The captain promised that they would be reinstated immediately.

The next several questions concerned the division sutler and access to cigarettes, condensed milk, and other supplements to rations. Römpler used this topic as an opportunity to return to his own agenda, the need for discipline and order. He told the men that the division sutler had retreated in the direction of Mainz. As for the sutler's wares:

[W]ho can say whether or not a horde of misguided people have already seized it as booty. Along these lines, I will mention an example of the experience of the last several days: We should have met a supply train en route, in order to spare the troops the long way to Luxembourg. The train was stopped in Luxembourg and robbed, completely plundered. You can imagine what kind of difficulties that brings with it for a relatively small formation, such as a division. We must keep our own house clean.

To this, a trustee responded: "One should promulgate a proclamation for peace and order in the division." One can imagine the captain's pleasure at this comment. "That is why the trustees are there, to deal with such subjects with the troops. Things will have gone to the devil, if we can't manage to prevent such things with our men, the ones who have endured such battles." Another trustee suggested the staff make a transcript of the meeting available to the representatives so that it could be used to inform the men. Römpler readily agreed.

A trustee asked if it might be possible to change the form of greeting between officer and soldier, perhaps replacing the salute with merely an erect bearing. The discussion had returned to the struggle over symbols. In some units in the *Etappe* and the homeland, the soldiers no longer saluted, though the men of the 115th were probably not aware of this. This may have been an awkward moment for Römpler. However, the transcript records that when Römpler said that, for the time being, there would be no change, his audience responded with "general joviality." Apparently, this was not a compelling issue to most of the front-line trustees.

The soldiers' questions ranged over a variety of issues. One asked if the division could carry the troops' baggage. Römpler said no, for transport was too limited. Could the men dispense with their gas masks, helmets, and other gear? No, they would have to be carried, at least to the German border. At that point, the division staff would look

---

[117] Unit-level councils set up late in the war to advise the chain of command on rations issues.

into depositing such equipment in army depots. What about clothing at the point of discharge? Römpler assured the men that no one would go home naked. This and other comments introduced a lighter tone.

A trustee: It is desired that the company commander wish the company "Good morning" at the beginning of the march. Dr. Rapmund of Medical Company 115 has not introduced himself to the company [*laughter*], and never says a word to the company, while Dr. Keller and Senior Lieutenant Veith never neglected it.
Captain Römpler: This suggestion will also be complied with.

In an earnest tone, a veteran complained, "Someone should have directly warned the young comrades about order and prudence, because they are flighty. If an older comrade influences them a lot of good can be done. Now is not the time to pour oil on the fire." Another veteran suggested that, "if the troops had to carry three iron rations during the next three days, the younger troops would have eaten all of theirs within two days and the 'older, sensible folk' would be forced to look after them." This complaint and several similar ones allowed Römpler again to exhort the trustees to be a stabilizing influence, especially among the younger men and new recruits. When a trustee suggested that an occasional missed salute should not be punished too severely, the captain answered carefully: "It is essential military appearance be maintained as much as possible and that the troops do not descend into a gang of little rascals [*Rasselbande*]. There is no one so careful that he does not miss a salute on occasion. However, it should not be made obvious that an officer is not being acknowledged simply because he is an officer." In other words, the rigid discipline of the prewar army would no longer obtain; however, the chain of command would tolerate no open expressions of contempt for superiors. By this point, the meeting was winding down. Perhaps the field kitchens had added the aroma of freshly cooked rations to the proceedings. The transcript records that the meeting ended at 11.45 p.m., when there were no further questions.

By any standard, Captain Römpler's performance must be considered a *tour de force*. He had answered every question carefully and respectfully, without compromising the authority of the chain of command. Instead, he had used the meeting to recruit the trustees as allies in maintaining "peace and order" in the division. He had offered them the opportunity for input to relatively tangential issues without conceding any of the decision-making power held by the officer corps. In the uncertain environment created by armistice and revolution, the First General Staff Officer of the 115th Division had shown himself to be a nimble tightrope walker.

How does one explain Römpler's clever handling of the trustees? Several possible answers suggest themselves. (1) Römpler was a uniquely gifted officer with special insights into the motivation and concerns of the soldiers of his unit. (2) The 115th was unique in the willingness of its men to be co-opted into support of the chain of command. (3) The tone of the meeting between the captain and the trustees reflected an on-going evolution of a much more flexible and negotiable relationship between officers and men, an evolution which had been under way across the German Army during the last year or two of the war. Given what is known about the conduct of front-line soldiers, both before and after the armistice, one is drawn to a combination of (1) and (3) above. Römpler was, indeed, a clever officer, and General Kundt was fortunate to have him as the division's principal staff officer. One imagines that staff colleges around the world could use the captain's handling of the meeting as a leadership case study in the management of wavering and discontented troops. However, Römpler's readiness to acknowledge the concerns of the men and their willingness to accept his responses suggest that the two sides came to the meeting ready to listen to each other. One is reminded of Leonard Smith's thesis that obedience among veteran troops is a behavior that must be constantly negotiated, especially in a long war. At the meeting at Lorentzweiler on November 14, the officers and men came together in a mood to negotiate. In this respect, they seem to exemplify changes that had already been under way in the army for a considerable period. And, as the following chapters will show, if the 115th Infantry Division marched home in good order under the control of its officers, it was far from unique.

The end and the beginning

With the war ended, the officers and men at the front found themselves looking homeward into a sort of vacuum in which rumors, reports, and uncertain emotions mingled with the prospect of a long, difficult march. "When on the evening of November 11 the German march columns crossed the Chier Valley in the direction of the Rhine, many of the brave fighters from those bloody years had tears in their eyes," a veteran recalled. "However, soon the vitality of youth won out over all. For us, the revolution was an imaginary cloud-image [Nebelgebild]."[118]

In the post-revolutionary struggle for control of the Feldheer, the first round apparently had gone to the officers. Between November 9 and the armistice, the bulk of the front-line divisions stayed in the trenches.

[118] Schützinger, Zussamenbruch, 78–9.

There were instances of indiscipline and refusal at places along the front, but these were the exceptions.[119] In the aftermath of the armistice, the weary *Fronttruppen* obeyed their officers, formed up behind the lines, and prepared to move east toward the homeland. The timetable for withdrawal meant that they would have little time to recover from their *exhaustion*; revolutions require energy and there would little to spare at the front. A few miles behind them, officers in the *Etappe* were in flight or serving with their rank and cockades removed from their uniforms under the authority of local soldiers' councils. Yet the revolution had approached the front but had not reached it, at least not yet. Römpler and thousands of other officers up and down the Western Front had taken advantage of the *isolation* of the front-line troops and carefully *managed* what those soldiers believed it would take to get home safely. Where higher headquarters often appealed to the *cohesion* built on shared adversity and danger, Römpler and others closer to the soldiers appealed to a *cohesion* built on shared objectives. Thus, for hundreds of thousands of front-line soldiers, their perception of the circumstances that prevailed in the aftermath of the armistice made their first important decision a simple and straightforward one: they would march home with their units under the control of their officers.

Nevertheless, though the front-line officers may have been gratified at the initial conduct of the rank and file as they emerged from the trenches, maintaining control of the Field Army was only the first of several challenges facing those officers. While the first question, how would the troops respond to events, had been answered, the questions that still remained were, perhaps, even more daunting. Could the planning staffs solve the puzzle of moving the great masses of troops and vehicles down a limited number of routes? Would their tired soldiers be able to make the exertions required by the demanding march schedule? Would the Allies or the French and Belgian populations in the occupied areas intervene to slow or block the march? What interference could be expected from the revolutionaries holding the Rhine bridges?

The day after the armistice found most of the *Feldheer* on the move. The staff of Army Group Crown Prince, soon to be known as Army

---

[119] In some cases, front-line units were called out to suppress disorder in the rear. For example, on November 8, the 31st Bavarian Division was tasked to send 200 men and twelve machine guns to Arlon to suppress a mutiny among a trainload of replacements from the 75th Reserve Division. The division's war diary records the mission accomplished without bloodshed. The next day, it disarmed elements of the 20th Pioneer Battalion, with one of the Bavarian regimental commanders and his adjutant personally disarming the ringleaders. Second Division Historical Section, *War Diaries of German Units*, vol. IX, *Intelligence Summaries*, Doc. 37, War Diary of the 31st Bavarian Division, entry of November 8, 1918.

Group B, made a terse daily report: "The Field Army begins its march ... Conduct and morale of front troops good. Disorder and confusion reign within the units of the *Etappe*." After briefly noting the slow progress in building trustees' councils and the increase in desertions, the diary recorded gravely: "Once again, the OHL emphasizes that the future of the Fatherland depends on the orderly return of the army."[120] That aim remained in doubt.

[120] NARA, RG 165, Box 27, Folder IV, Group of Armies Crown Prince, War Diary and Annexes, entry for November 2, 1918, 8.

5   The last march: the German *Westheer*'s march to the Rhine, November– December 1918

> Along the road, step upon step, in their faded, dirty uniforms tramp the gray columns ... Old men with beards and slim lads scarce twenty years of age, comrades without difference. Beside them their lieutenants, little more than children, yet the leaders of many a night raid. And behind them the slain ...
>
> Erich Maria Remarque, *The Road Back*

The Field Army and the Fatherland

The war's conclusion left the German forces on the Western Front with one last, difficult operation to conduct – their long march home. The timetable for their journey was driven by harsh terms the Allies had imposed as part of the armistice agreement. With more than 3 million men in its front-line and support units, the *Westheer* was required to vacate northern France and Belgium and march beyond the Rhine in less than a month. In a further eleven days, German troops would have to vacate a 30- to 40-kilometer neutral zone on the east bank of the Rhine.[1] It was a timetable that would have tested a fresh, confident, well-supplied army. In November 1918, the German Army in the West was none of these things.

Many Germans believed their nation's future might depend on whether the Field Army in the West could return home intact. The day after the armistice, an officer in the war ministry in Berlin wrote, "Anger, shame, loathing, and sorrow – that is how it all appears ... What more can happen? Who can know? Perhaps – or probably – when this letter is in your hand Bolshevism will already be on top. If only the Field Army can remain peaceful."[2] This was the view within the old

---

[1] Auswärtigen Amt, and Reichsministerium des Innern, *Amtliche Urkunden*, Document 105: State Secretary Hintze, telegram to the Foreign Office, November 9, 1918, 262–3.

[2] *Adolf Wild von Hohenborn: Briefe und Tagebuchaufzeichnungen des preussischen Generals als Kriegsminister un Truppenführer im Ersten Weltkrieg*, ed. Helmut Reichold (Boppard am Rhein: Harald Boldt Verlag, 1986), 250.

officer corps and its conservative allies who hoped enough of the Field
Army could be preserved intact to re-establish order in the homeland
and suppress what appeared to be the growing threat of Bolshevism. For
the new coalition government of Friedrich Ebert, the Majority Socialist
(SPD) leader who headed the ruling Council of People's Delegates, the
safe homecoming of the troops represented a huge, inherited responsibility. If the troops returned in disorder, or if thousands were captured by the Allies, his government would be held responsible. On the
Left, the Independent Socialists (USPD) and the Spartacist League
feared that the returning front-line formations would be a potential
White Guard, a force to be used by a reactionary officer corps and
their Majority Socialist accomplices to crush the revolution. Finally,
the German populace feared that if the brutalized men from the front
were not kept in check that they might return as a mob of armed and
embittered marauders, looting and destroying as they moved.

As it turned out, the majority of front-line soldiers crossed the Rhine
under the control of their officers. The operation succeeded and, in this
last transitory triumph, the old army played an important role in shaping Germany's political future. In the short term, the successful march
rebuilt the shaken confidence of the officer corps. For those senior
officers who entertained ideas of reversing the tide of revolution, the
performance of the front-line troops in the last two weeks of November
and the first days of December gave renewed hope that the old army
could be used to strike down the revolution's most dangerous elements.
For the left wing of the USPD, the Spartacists, and the more revolutionary workers' and soldiers' councils of Germany, the Field Army's
arrival on the west bank of the Rhine, often marching under the flags of
the old empire, meant the revolution faced an impending crisis. *Die Rote
Fahne*, the newspaper of the Spartacus League, observed: "Militarism
in the Field Army was weakened at the outbreak of the revolution, but
still not completely overthrown; it has not been completely destroyed
by the revolution and, since then, it appears, it lives again; that is where
the counter revolution can be expected."[3] Finally, to the millions of
Germans shaken by the confusion and uncertainty that accompanied
the revolution, the appearance of well-ordered front-line units was a
reassuring, even joyous, occasion and a cause for celebration.

The uncertain road home

For German forces in the West, the clock started at 12 noon,
November 12. From that point, the Allies gave the German Army two

---

[3] *Die Rote Fahne*, "Rüstung der Revolution," December 2, 1918.

Map 2. Withdrawal plan

weeks – fourteen days – to be out of France, Belgium, Luxembourg, and Alsace-Lorraine. The Allies allowed a further seventeen days for the army to cross the Rhine and move beyond the occupation zones the Allied forces would occupy on the west bank at Mainz, Coblenz, and

Cologne.[4] It was a gargantuan task under the best of circumstances. With over 3 million men, including many sick and wounded, hundreds of thousands of horses, and thousands of vehicles, the divisions on the Western Front would have to march up to 200 miles on a limited number of roadways and cross a major river at a handful of crossing sites, before finally dispersing to railheads and demobilization points. What was worse, the initial stage of the movement took the army through a hostile populace embittered by four years of occupation. Throughout the march, Allied advance guards would follow only a few miles behind, ready to take stragglers as prisoners of war.

The daunting nature of the task was made even more extreme by the condition of the units at the front. The last months of the war had seen the infantry and artillery fighting for weeks without relief. On November 11, the *Frontheer* was physically and emotionally spent. Beyond that, four years of trench warfare meant that no units were conditioned to long, sustained marches. Finally, while moving healthy men would have been difficult enough, heavy fighting and the worldwide influenza epidemic had overfilled the army's aid stations and field hospitals, adding a major transportation requirement to the operation.[5]

The supply situation was equally grave. The final days of the war found the two northernmost and largest army groups on the Western Front, Army Group Rupprecht and Army Group Crown Prince, in the process of withdrawing to defensive positions on the Antwerp–Meuse Line. As they withdrew into eastern Belgium, these two formations abandoned the fixed shelters, supply points, and depots that had provisioned them for years. Thus, even before November 11, the bulk of the army had to rely on makeshift logistical arrangements. Virtually none of the front-line divisions had enough horses to move their baggage and equipment, and the horses available were often broken-down, underfed, and unable to pull a normal load. The truck fleet was in similar condition and critically short of fuel. To make matters worse, the backbone of the army's support structure, the railroad system, was overtaxed and on the verge of collapse.[6]

The withdrawal was further complicated by the conditions the Allies had imposed on the German forces to ensure that Germany was unable

---

[4] Foch originally demanded that the Germans be out of the Rhineland in eleven days. Armistice conditions from Deutschen Waffenstillstandkommision, *Der Waffenstillstand, 1918–1919, I. Der Waffenstillstandsvertrag von Compiegne und seine Verlängerungen nebst den finanzielle Bestimmungen* (Berlin: Deutsche Verlagsgesellschaft für Politik und Geschichte, 1928), 23–35.

[5] Army's condition described in German General Staff, *Rückführung des Westheeres*, 2–3.

[6] *Ibid.*, 3–8.

to resume hostilities at the end of the armistice's term of thirty days. In addition to turning over 5,000 artillery pieces, 30,000 machine guns, 3,000 mortars, and 2,000 aircraft, the Germans were also required to surrender 5,000 locomotives, 10,000 wagons, and 10,000 trucks to Allied forces.[7] The transfer of all this equipment posed an enormously complex problem. In particular, such a mass of weapons and vehicles would require thousands of drivers and crew to move them and a large security force to prevent such equipment from falling into the wrong hands. Any troops detailed to such missions would face danger from a hostile civilian populace and the possibility of capture by the advancing Allies.[8]

Even without surrendering thousands of vehicles to the Allies, supporting the withdrawal of the Field Army represented an incredibly difficult task for the transportation, communication, and supply systems in the *Etappe*. Of course, the fact that much of this support structure had collapsed with the news of the revolution magnified that difficulty enormously. In the first three or four days after the abdication of the Kaiser, much of the service and support structure simply disappeared. The thousands of deserters in the army's rear area joined with lawless support troops to plunder supply dumps, terrorize their officers, sell their weapons to the local populace, and commandeer eastbound trains to Germany.[9]

The unrest also spread to units closer to the front. A sergeant on the staff of the Fourth Army, Ludwig Lewinsohn, observed the displacement of the headquarters by train from Alost to Mechelen, in Belgium. As his train stopped alongside a column of supply wagons, soldiers from the headquarters staff began to plunder food and liquor from the wagons. None of the officers present had the courage to protest or resist. At first, only a few soldiers took part, but soon almost all joined

---

[7] Auswärtigen Amt, and Reichsministerium des Innern, *Amtliche Urkunden*, Document 105, 262–3.

[8] The following day, the OHL sent a protest note to the German government stating, among other things, that it had only 18,000 trucks (only half of which were running), and such a shortage of railway assets that any surrender of equipment made to the extent demanded by the Allies would mean a "complete collapse of the army's supply system." Auswärtigen Amt, and Reichsministerium des Innern, *Amtliche Urkunden*, Document 107: Hindenburg to the Prussian war ministry and Armistice Commission, 265.

[9] *Ibid.*, 14–15. See, for example, the interview of civilians found in AEF G2, *251 Divisions*, vol. IV, "Report on the Retirement of the German troops through Gravenmacher, [Luxembourg] November 12–22," and BA-R, R43/2500/5, Transcript of telephone call between Ebert and the OHL, November 13, 1918. The conversation included descriptions of disorder behind Army Group Gallwitz, as drunken teamsters took empty wagons "at a reckless pace" in the direction of Germany.

in. What followed was an "orgy" as drunken soldiers pronounced death sentences on all officers.[10] Widespread disorder also affected the army's source of supplies in the Reich. In some cases, workers' and soldiers' councils within Germany confiscated supplies headed for the front and encouraged workers in depots and magazines to discontinue their work. At first, local authorities seemed powerless to intervene.[11]

Taken together, the obstacles to a successful return march were enormous. However, the consequences of failure were equally great. If the army could not meet the Allied timetable, it risked having thousands of soldiers taken prisoner by Allied forces.[12] If supply arrangements collapsed, then the march was likely to turn into an affair of "every man for himself." Instead of a disciplined army, a desperate, hungry rabble would arrive on the frontiers of the homeland.

The question of authority

In the initial confusion that followed the outbreak of the revolution, the question of who would control the march seemed settled in favor of the old chain of command. Hindenburg had stayed at his post, and, under the uncomfortable scrutiny of the headquarters soldiers' council, the OHL staff continued to issue orders to the army in the field. In the assembly areas behind the front, the officers seemed to have the combat units in hand. Perhaps even more important, the soldiers' and trustees' councils among the front-line units appeared to be willing to work with the traditional chain of command to ensure the progress of the retreat from France and Belgium. While the revolutionaries in the homeland claimed sovereignty over the organs of the Second Reich, the practical men of the *Frontheer*'s soldiers' councils realized that if the army was to overcome the obstacles of the return march they would need to share authority with the old chain of command. Therefore, the role of the councils was limited by a power-sharing relationship that left the planning and execution of the march to the staffs of the divisions, corps,

[10] Lewinsohn, *Revolution an der Westfront*, 5. Lewinsohn's booklet must be considered one of the best eye-witness accounts of the march back to Germany. One must make allowances for his Majority Socialist outlook, which tends to amplify the role played by soldiers' councils of the Field Army.
[11] German General Staff, *Rückführung des Westheeres*, 8.
[12] This was the case with the Austro-Hungarian Army on the Italian Front in 1918. The Austrian staff muddled the cease-fire arrangements and hundreds of thousands of their troops were captured by the advancing Allies. Some 30,000 of these last-minute captives would die in Italian captivity after the war. See Bundesministerium für Landesverteidigung, *Österreich-Ungarns letzter Krieg, 1914-1918* (Vienna: Militärwissenschaftlichen Mitteilungen, 1930-8) [the Austrian official history], vol. VII, 598-603 and 758.

and armies. In the first place, councils recognized that they lacked the clear lines of communication and authority inherent in the traditional chain of command. The councils had no signal equipment of their own, and there was no binding, legal reason why the soldiers' councils in a division, for example, had to abide by the guidance issued by the corps council above it in the chain of command.

A more important basis for power sharing was the army's dependence on the technical skills of the officer corps. While the Ebert government had granted the officer corps a degree of political legitimacy, the leadership and staff planning skills of the officers gave them professional legitimacy among the *Fronttruppen* so eager to be led home. This point was illustrated when the newly constituted executive committee from the soldiers' council of the OHL arrived at the operations section of the headquarters on the evening of November 10. Met by a Major Wilhelm Faupel of the General Staff, the seven-member delegation demanded a supervisory role in the direction of the army's return to Germany. Faupel ushered the members of the committee into a room equipped with vast maps marked with unit boundaries and locations, complex transportation timetables, and stacks of marching orders. Faupel proceeded to offer an elaborate briefing emphasizing the vast complexity involved in bringing the army home and the danger that threatened if even minor parts of the plan miscarried. The committee members were suitably impressed and withdrew their demands, while expressing a desire to cooperate with the efforts of the OHL staff.[13] Later, two members of the OHL soldiers' council told a British general on the Armistice Commission "they were permitting the German High Command to get the Army back to Germany because they could best do it."[14]

Nevertheless, given the difficult conditions of the return march, the soldiers' councils in the front-line units had an important role to play. In particular, the initial disorder that followed the news of abdication and armistice required urgent action. Wilhelm Kaisen, for example, spent his first days as chairman of his regimental council squashing rumors, encouraging men not to take off on their own, and warning his

[13] Erich Volkmann, *Revolution über Deutschland* (Oldenburg: Gerhard Stalling, 1930), 69–71. Much of Faupel's exhibition may have been something of a sham. According to Schulenberg, the OHL delegated the most difficult aspects of the operation to its subordinate headquarters. It issued the timeline required by the Allies and established the boundaries that the four army groups would observe as they withdrew. Preoccupied, perhaps, by political issues, the Supreme Headquarters left the details of the march planning to the four army groups and their subordinate staffs. BA-MA, N58/1, Nachlass Schulenberg, "Erlebnisse," 244–5.
[14] Rhodes to Pershing, dated November 17, *The US Army in the World War*, X, 106–7.

comrades of the danger of capture by the Allies.[15] In a similar vein, the soldiers' council of the Fourth Army issued a leaflet that proclaimed:

Comrades! The return march home has begun. Do you understand what that means? Do you know that the Fourth Army's 500,000 men, 100,000 horses, and uncounted vehicles must move at prescribed times and places so that they can be quartered and fed? And did you know that these millions of men, horses, and wagons stand on a sector of fifteen kilometers width with only three available roads and bridges? Seek to understand what all this means.

The leaflet went on to tell the men that the soldiers' council was working along with experienced officers to control the march and that discipline was the key to making the operation successful. The clear purpose of the leaflet was to shock the soldiers of the Fourth Army into understanding how disorder jeopardized their chances of getting home safely.[16] The OHL council put out similar flyers warning of the consequences if discipline broke down. One issued on November 17 began, "Through the spread of disorder all our achievements come to nothing. Maintain discipline and order throughout the entire return march." It went on to urge soldiers to protect the trains, supply columns, and depots from thefts that could threaten the provisioning of the army.[17]

The emphasis on good order and discipline did not mean that relationships between officers and men were completely unchanged. As the army moved east, some unit councils demanded oversight of rations, leave, and punishments at the unit level.[18] Within some units, soldiers were not required to render salutes to officers while off duty, following the spirit of the guidance that relations between officers and men were to be based on a "spirit of camaraderie" and mutual trust.[19] From Groener on down the chain of command, officers often had little choice but to grudgingly accept these new revolutionary protocols.[20]

The officers also had to acknowledge the soldiers' indifference to the fall of the old regime. One officer noted the words to a tune sung by

[15] Wilhelm Kaisen, *Meine Arbeit, mein Leben* (Munich: List Verlag, 1967), 74.
[16] Lewinsohn, *Revolution an der Westfront*, 10.
[17] Groener, *Lebenserinnerungen*, 470.
[18] Army Group D suggested bringing the representatives of the soldiers' councils into the military justice proceedings at the division level and below. The OHL responded that such adjustments to the established practice of military law were unnecessary. BA-R, R43/2500/5, transcript of Representative Giebel's message to the cabinet (*Reichsleitung*), dated November 23, 1918.
[19] Lewinsohn, *Revolution an der Westfront*, 36.
[20] In still other units, the chain of command used the difficulty of the return march to enforce a standard of discipline higher than that practiced in the trenches. See, for example, the Gruppe Soden (V Reserve Corps) order saying that behavior must be beyond reproach in order to avoid an Allied march into Germany. BA-MA, PH 8 I/511, order of November 16, Ia/IIa # 473.

his men as they marched: *"Den Kaiser haben wir verloren./Den Kaiser brauchen wir nicht mehr."* ("We have lost the emperor./We don't need the emperor any more.")[21] Another officer observed of his men a "seemingly indifferent resignation to the existing situation; no special excitement, no fatal hate for the monarchy, but also no feeling for the tragedy of their defeat."[22]

Yet, though the world had been turned upside down, one still senses a spirit of deference in the front-line councils that contrasted with the revolutionary spirit prevailing elsewhere in the German Army. When Ludwig Lewinsohn, the chairman of the soldiers' council of the Fourth Army received a summons to the army headquarters to negotiate the role of his new council, he found the commander, General Sixt von Arnim, an intimidating figure. Lewinsohn remembered that the old general exuded a steely strength and nobility and a firmness of character that "extorted" a response of enormous respect from all present, even though, Lewinsohn added, the army commander represented a "collapsed system."[23] In another incident, members of the OHL council came to Groener unexpectedly to express their uncertainty over reports that Ebert had been dismissed from the government. Groener replied he was not aware of such a change in the government, but that he could readily determine the truth of the matter. With that, Groener telephoned Ebert and explained the concerns of the council members in his office. Groener then invited the men to verify the presence of Ebert at the other end of the line. The soldiers declined and excused themselves, apologizing as they went for wasting the First Quartermaster General's time.[24]

If the relationship between the front-line councils and the officer chain of command was often uncertain and uneasy, what was not ambiguous was the attitude of the *Westheer*'s councils toward the new government. The front-line councils stood solidly and overwhelmingly in support of Ebert and the Council of People's Delegates. The archival record contains dozens of messages from these councils expressing support for both the new government and the prospect of national elections, while denouncing the agenda of the Spartacists. This message, which came from the Field Army to Berlin on November 20, is typical:

The artillery of the 16th Infantry Division stands fully and completely behind Reich Chancellor Ebert and the current government which desires to lead us home in peace and order, represents the majority of the German people, and will establish peace with our enemies. We condemn the machinations of the

---

[21] Leed, *No Man's Land*, 198.   [22] Anker, *Unsere Stunde*, 66–7.
[23] *Ibid.*, 11.   [24] Groener, *Lebenserinnerungen*, 471.

Spartacus Group which disrupts the current government while wanting to bring power to itself in order to create a reign of terror.[25]

The same day, the council of the 71st Infantry Brigade staff telegrammed, "We make the sharpest possible protest against the resolution of the Executive Council of the Workers' and Soldiers' Council of Berlin calling for the creation of a purely proletarian government, which would express the will of a small minority, and demand the convocation of a National Assembly."[26] The next day, this telegram reached Berlin from the soldiers' council of the 167th Infantry Regiment: "We front troops want nothing to do with a Bolshevist government. After four and a half years of the hardest sacrifices, we want to live in a homeland of peace, order, and freedom. Only the current government can bring that to us."[27]

What is abundantly clear in these messages is the decisive victory of the MSPD in establishing the political agenda of the front-line councils and the relationship of the councils to the new government. Though each message encountered in the archives is different in detail, the essentials are the same: full trust in the current government, denunciation of those who would challenge Ebert's coalition, and the insistence by the front-line troops that they have a say in the final construction of the new German state. The telegrams come from every kind of unit, from army headquarters to medical company to provisional march units, but the similarities are striking enough to suggest that the Majority Socialist message was being promulgated from the higher-level councils at army group and army level, down to the division, regimental, and battalion councils. This, in turn, implies the support of the officer staffs in making the Field Army's communications channels available for use in the MSPD's "information campaign."[28]

---

[25] BA-R, R43/2486/17, telegram from trustees' councils of field artillery regiments [illegible; all from the 16th Infantry Division], dated November 20, 1918.

[26] BA-R, R43/2486/17, telegram from the soldiers' council of the staff of the 71st Inf. Bde., dated November 20, 1918.

[27] BA-R, R43/2486r, telegram from the soldiers' council of Inf. Regt. 167, dated November 21, 1918.

[28] Enough of these messages are signed to give the dominant, and none too surprising, impression that most councils were led by NCOs and junior officers. Such men had often held leadership positions in the prewar SPD, making them natural candidates to lead the soldiers' councils. For the importance of these men in the Eastern Front councils, see Dennis Showalter, "The Homesick Revolutionaries: Soldiers' Councils and Newspaper Propaganda in German-occupied Eastern Europe, 1918–1919." *Canadian Journal of History*, April, 1976, 69–86. One may, perhaps, hypothesize that the anti-war platform of the USPD might have encouraged their leaders to avoid front-line service in a war their party had disavowed.

Figure 5.1 Germans retreating through Luxembourg, November 1918.

There were more battles ahead. Perhaps they would only be political battles, perhaps not. Anticipating the possibility of open conflict Ebert and his allies had been strikingly effective in building support among the *Fronttruppen* as the army began its march back to the Fatherland. The strife between radicalized and moderate elements that divided the new government was not reflected among the troops of the Field Army.

The evacuation of the occupied territories

The German Army's evacuation of the occupied areas of northern France, Belgium, and Luxembourg was a race against time under the most difficult conditions. On one hand, Allied advance guards would march close on the heels of the retreating army, ready to capture those who failed to meet the required pace of withdrawal. The Germans also had to be concerned about the civilian inhabitants of the occupied zone. German wartime occupation policy had hardly been enlightened, and no one could say how long it would be before the resentment of the French and Belgian people against their former masters exploded into anti-German violence.

Fortunately for the Field Army, the danger from its own rear areas receded almost as suddenly as it had appeared. The disorder in the

Etappe seemed to burn itself out in a matter of days. The most likely reason was that the most energetic revolutionaries took off for Germany on their own.[29] Elsewhere, the front-line councils used appeals of revolutionary solidarity to overcome the confusion in the rear areas. When the soldiers' council of Antwerp seized the gasoline supply point for the Fourth Army, the army's quartermaster asked the army's own *Soldatenrat* to intervene to restore the army's fuel supply. Lewinsohn and other Fourth Army council members traveled to Antwerp, where they appealed to the unruly local soldiery to consider the need of their "proletarian brothers" from the trenches.[30] In Brussels, a government appeal for order served to quiet the chaotic situation.[31]

Another threat that failed to materialize was widespread violence from hostile civilians. During the initial unrest in the *Etappe*, German troops sold weapons and supplies to Belgian civilians,[32] while Belgian mobs took advantage of the situation to plunder supply trains in Liège.[33] Yet, other than some sniping, major violent incidents between French or Belgians and German troops did not break out.[34] Lewinsohn believed the soldiers' councils were the reason. His Fourth Army council distributed multi-lingual appeals to the Belgian populace announcing the council's authority and distancing themselves from the old regime's aggression against Belgium, while calling on brotherhood between peoples. The gratifying response, he wrote, was to find Belgians greeting German troops with *"Vive la République!"*[35] Another council leader, Wilhelm Kaisen, observed a message from a Belgian mayor painted in large letters on a wall, appealing to his constituents to avoid excesses against the retreating Germans. Kaisen wrote that the Belgians who lined the roads were relatively uninterested in the passing Germans. Their eyes were turned to the West, where the Allies and, especially, their own army were approaching.[36] In other instances, the Belgians

[29] *The US Army in the World War*, XI, 28. Major General Rhodes, the American representative to the Armistice Commission, came to a similar conclusion in a message to General Pershing on November 24, but thought the rear-area troops had been "sent" home ahead of the combat formations, an unlikely point, *ibid.*, X, 152.

[30] Lewinsohn, *Revolution an der Westfront*, 14–17.

[31] *The US Army in the World War*, X, 157.

[32] Volkmann, *Revolution über Deutschland*, 75.

[33] Wilhelm Ritter von Leeb, *Tagebuchaufzeichnungen und Lagebeurteilungen aus zwei Weltkriegen*, ed. Georg Meyer (Stuttgart: Deutsche Verlags-Anstalt, 1976), 155.

[34] The writer Alfred Döblin described an incident in which German troops detonated the contents of fifty ammunition wagons as they evacuated Charleroi. The resulting explosion killed several Belgian civilians and inspired local Belgian attacks on German troops, in *Sieger und Besiegte: Eine wahre Geschichte* (New York: Aurora Verlag, 1946), 7–8.

[35] Lewinsohn, *Revolution an der Westfront*, 21–2.

[36] Kaisen, *Meine Arbeit*, 70.

approached the front-line units hoping the German soldiers would sell weapons and supplies as their comrades in the *Etappe* had done.[37] Nevertheless, the Germans felt the hostility of the Belgian people and this may have served to keep units closed up in good order.[38]

The German forces faced more than enough difficulties without civilian interference. At the northern end of the old front, the geography of road networks, terrain, and international borders posed a special problem for the retreating armies of Army Group A (formerly Crown Prince Rupprecht). Because the section of the Netherlands known as the "Maastricht Appendix" (Limburg province) jutted south near the German frontier and the Ardennes stretched north nearby, the available roads into Germany narrowed to just those few that passed in and around the old Belgian fortress of Liège. In the time available, they were not sufficient to carry the endless, retreating columns of Rupprecht's old army group.

This was the dilemma of the Schlieffen Plan in reverse. In the original conception of his infamous plan, Schlieffen had been willing to violate Dutch neutrality in order to gain deployment room for his flanking maneuver around the French armies. In 1914, Moltke the Younger was more cautious and, instead of crossing the Dutch frontier, chose to squeeze his right-wing armies through the narrow gap of open terrain around Liège. Moltke's modification nearly compromised the German offensive before it started. Had the Belgians not withdrawn the bulk of their forces from around the fortress, and had an opportunistic officer named Ludendorff not led a *coup de main* into the city, the timetable of the German plan might have been fatally delayed.

In November 1918, the retreating Germans were again marching to a demanding timetable, this time eastwards. Even before the armistice, the OHL recognized the potential bottleneck around Liège and asked the new government to seek transit permission from the Dutch. The German request put the Dutch government on the horns of a genuine dilemma. Throughout the war, the Dutch had maintained their neutrality by means of a perilous balancing act between the belligerents.[39] As the war turned against the Kaiser's armies, the Dutch had anticipated a

---

[37] Volkmann, *Revolution über Deutschland*, 75.

[38] All too often, the German sentries detailed to stay behind with the equipment to be turned over to the Allies abandoned it at the first opportunity. German General Staff, *Rückführung des Westheeres*, 10–11.

[39] Hubert van Serooskerken, *The Netherlands and World War I: Espionage, Diplomacy, and Survival* (Boston: Brill, 2001), 245–54. In order to deter invasion by either side, they had kept their army mobilized all four years of the war. In early 1918, in particular, they had genuinely feared a German invasion. The immediate cause of the mutiny was the cancellation of all leaves in anticipation of the German approach.

German request to march across the Maastricht Appendix with considerable dread. If they allowed the German passage, it would antagonize the Allies, yet the Dutch doubted whether they possessed the military means to stop a German incursion. Ironically, however, in November 1918, the unsettled political situation in the Netherlands shaped the Dutch response: units of the Dutch Army were in mutiny, and the radical socialists in the Dutch parliament had proclaimed revolution. Uncertain of their ability to resist a German incursion, the Dutch government agreed to German passage on the condition that German troops leave their weapons at the border. By the end of the German retreat, some 70,000 Germans marched through Dutch territory on their way home. The Allies were predictably furious.[40]

Along with the opening of additional routes through the Netherlands, the restoration of order in the rear area, and the prevalence of general calm among the civilian populace, the march was initially blessed by favorable weather.[41] Heavy rain or snowfall would have had a catastrophic effect on the rate of progress. As Georg Bucher wrote, "Those November days were sunny and beautiful, as though undying nature were rejoicing that the orgy of slaughter had come to an end."[42] However, good weather by itself did not guarantee that the Germans would be able to evacuate the occupied areas ahead of the Allied vanguards. The Allies, for their part, added a layer of difficulty after the march had begun by establishing intermediate phase lines that the Germans had to reach every day. The Allies also moved the target for the final evacuation from December 13 to 6.00 a.m., December 12, 1918. To reinforce their demands, the Allies announced that the separation between retreating Germans and advancing Allied troops was to be a mere 10 kilometers.[43]

The new conditions increased the enormous demands on the German troops marching east. What was needed above all was for the army staffs to prepare precisely calculated plans, and then to allow the subordinate formations the independence to adapt these plans as circumstances dictated. There could be no requests for new instructions up and down the

---

[40] Later, during the negotiations at Versailles, the Dutch had to defend themselves against efforts by the resentful Belgians to annex the Maastricht Appendix and other parts of the Netherlands. *Ibid.*, 266–322.

[41] Volkmann, *Revolution über Deutschland*, 76.

[42] Georg Bucher, *In the Line, 1914–1918*, trans. Norman Gullick (London: Jonathan Cape, 1932), 320.

[43] German General Staff, *Rückführung des Westheeres*, 12–13. As a result of lack of transportation, the Germans were forced to leave behind millions of marks' worth of equipment and several hospitals, with their patients and doctors. *Vossische Zeitung*, "An den Rheinbrücken," edition of November 28, 1918.

chain of command if something went wrong, because, for an army on the move, the telephonic and telegraphic links to handle such requests simply did not exist.[44]

The march required a flexible organization as well. Commanders redistributed their most capable leaders within the *Frontheer* in order to provide leadership where the army needed it most. Preparing for the worst, they put the most reliable divisions at the head of the long marching columns in order to secure the way against resistance from the local populace or revolutionary forces. Understrength regiments were reorganized into three or four company organizations and smaller support units were amalgamated with larger march formation to enhance control.[45] Thus, on the day of the armistice, the 236th Infantry Division had to take under its wing two additional field artillery regiments, an anti-aircraft detachment, a machine-gun sharpshooter unit, a road construction company, a veterinary hospital, a field slaughterhouse company, a munitions transport formation, and a variety of other small units.[46] Such amalgamation made good sense from an organizational and leadership perspective, but it became a headache for the combat units required to look after a veritable menagerie of support units.[47]

March planning forced more adaptation. In order to make maximum use of available time and road space, the plan put the marching soldiers on the roads during the day, and allowed headquarters and transport vehicles on the roads only at night.[48] March unit commanders maintained discipline within the moving formations, while other officers manned checkpoints at bridges and other choke points. Finally, in order to prevent straggling and desertion, army orders permitted no soldier to march alone.[49]

If prodigies of staff planning and organization were necessary to bring the soldiers home, it was the *Frontschweine* themselves who would have to do the marching. For the most part, they achieved the difficult objectives set for them. Their motivation was the thought of home and

[44] *Ibid.*, 6.   [45] *Ibid.*, 7.
[46] Second Division Historical Section, *War Diaries of German Units*, vol. IX, *Intelligence Reports*, 236th Infantry Division War Diary and Annexes, Report of December 31. In modern US Army parlance, combat units refer to such small, odd formations derisively as the "ash and trash."
[47] Thus, on November 20, the 213th Division complained to its chain of command that it had yet to link up with a company of *Landsturm*, an artillery park, two flak batteries, two searchlight units, several supply formations, three road construction units, a POW labor company, a veterinary hospital, and a unit of ethnic Italians from the Austrian army[!]. BA-MA, PH 8 I/511, 213th Inf. Div. Special Instructions, Ia/Ib #50, dated November 20, 1918.
[48] German General Staff, *Rückführung des Westheeres*, 7.
[49] BA-MA, PH 8 I/511, 213th Inf. Div. Order # 52/XI, dated November 21, 1918.

loved ones, but, even more, at this early stage of the march, the fear of falling into Allied hands. The fear was real. In a report dated November 20, the American Expeditionary Forces Headquarters recorded that the French had captured an entire German battalion after it had failed to move beyond the prescribed phase line.[50] Georg Bucher recalled one evening that his unit was moving into billets for the night when they heard the sounds of a military band.

> The wind carried the music and gathered it up so distinctly that we could recognize the tune: *Sambre et Meuse*. The French were following us. We gazed at each other silently, looked with weary and uncertain eyes at the billets which had been assigned to us. An order was shouted. A stream of curses and abuse broke loose. Then we set our teeth and marched on past the scornfully grinning civilians, on into the night. March on or be taken prisoner – there was no other alternative.[51]

Though pressed by demanding marching schedules, the German infantry and artillery units still managed to present an orderly appearance to the Allied officers assigned to observe the march. The G2 staff of the AEF's First Division learned from interviews with Luxembourgers that the first German troops to cross the frontier were men from the *Etappe* who "lacked discipline altogether." However, by November 17, the first front-line formations appeared. "All these troops showed good discipline. The officers spoke but little, seemed depressed. The men seemed much in ignorance of the armistice conditions and of the general situation."[52] A subsequent report observed, "German troops have displayed good discipline and order … The troops are giving the impression of being unbeaten and ready to fight again, under command of their officers, who are in full control. The soldiers are not throwing away their arms."[53] The American representative with the Armistice Commission, Major General C.D. Rhodes, was so disturbed by the appearance of the German units passing through Spa that he recommended the Allies be ready for "active mobile operations."[54] To this American officer, at least, the old Imperial Army was still capable of putting on an impressive parade.[55]

---

[50] *The US Army in the World War*, XI, 124–5.

[51] Bucher, *In the Line*, 321.

[52] World War Records. First Division, AEF (Regular), *Summaries of Intelligence, First Division*, vol. IV, "Report on the Retirement of the German troops through Gravenmacher," Reports of Nov. 12–22. An earlier report, on November 19, made the interesting observation that the Prussian units seemed to be marching in perfect order while the Bavarians appeared "very unmilitary and poorly disciplined."

[53] *Ibid.*, Nov. 28.

[54] Rhodes to Pershing, *The US Army in the World War*, X (i), 148.

[55] A French observer noted, "The entire German front-line army has withdrawn in orderly fashion with the precision of a machine. This marching mass has preserved

As the *Westheer* approached the German frontier, the chain of command did its best to reinforce discipline and morale with a barrage of "command messages." One division commander told his men to be proud of what they had accomplished in their "defensive war" and that only "the premature collapse of our coalition partners" forced a cease-fire on Germany. Maintain the old-fashioned discipline and trust the leaders who had taken them through so many battles, he said. "Thus shall our Field Marshal Hindenburg bring us home in good fashion."[56] On November 16, a letter of instructions for the officers of the V Reserve Corps suggested the unique responsibility the front-line troops might have for the morale of the homeland (while indicating that the idea that the German Army was "undefeated in the field" was already being fostered):

We are nearing the border.
Unfortunately, we must reckon with the possibility of increased demoralizing influences on the morale of the troops. On the other hand, the appearance that the troops present may be of decisive influence for the morale of the homeland.
I request that leaders of all ranks impress the following factors on the troops. We have been unable to win the war because of the overwhelming superiority of our enemies; we have every justification to be proud that for over 4 years we have defended against a world of enemies and prevented the entry of the enemy into our Fatherland.
The dignified and earnest bearing of the troops should banish the despondency of the homeland; the farmers and middle class at home should see that an undefeated army returns in proud and unbowed bearing.[57]

There were other, more ominous messages. One army headquarters warned:

Reports have been submitted that a large number of Spartacists (anarchistic groups who desire to inflame civil war in Germany) have been sent to the Field Army for the purposes of spreading propaganda. It is urgently important the effects of these people be kept away from the army. The instructions issued to date from the Reich leadership and the OHL on the preservation of discipline and order in the army are to be followed to the letter. Individuals that act

its order, discipline, and obedience towards its superiors, as if they had won new strength." P. Gentizon, quoted in Gytis Gudaitis, "Armeen Russlands und Deutschlands im 1. Weltkrieg und in den Revolutionen von 1917 und 1918. Ein Vergleich," unpublished dissertation, Katholische Universität Eichstätt-Ingolstadt, 2004, 502.

56 BA-MA, PH 8 I/511, 213th Inf. Div., Ia #43/X, message from the division commander (General Hammerstein), dated November 16, 1918.
57 BA-MA, PH 8 I/511, Gruppe Soden (VR Corps) Instructions #39097, dated November 16, 1918.

against that [discipline and order] are, where necessary, to be resisted with armed force.

The order indicated that some units arriving in the homeland had allowed themselves to be disarmed. "It is dishonorable behavior to give up one's weapons without resistance."[58]

Every drama needs a villain, and the characterization of the Spartacists as inflammatory anarchists represented a blatant attempt by the chain of command to build prejudices among front-line troops before they made their first contact with the revolutionaries of the homeland.[59] Spartacus would be the bogeyman.

In part, the sense of urgency in these messages reflected the indications that the bonds that held the army together were starting to loosen. Revolution was not the only threat to the army's cohesion. Lewinsohn remembered the days of late November as ones of frantic activity as his soldiers' council performed a balancing act between encouraging revolutionary fervor and emphasizing the need for discipline and order. He found himself traveling from one unit to another, in one place encouraging soldiers not to overthrow their officers, in another clearing a supply dump of plunderers. He was forced to intervene between, on one hand, soldiers wearing red ribbons that mimicked the Iron Cross decorations and, on the other, veterans who felt the symbols of their sacrifice and bravery were being mocked. This last crisis caused the Fourth Army council to ban the wearing of red decorations and issue a proclamation designed to please both factions. "If you want to carry a red flag as a symbol of the freedom we have won, let it flutter happily in the breeze. If you want to carry the black-white-red flag, the banner under which you successfully resisted a world of enemies, let it continue to wave in honor."[60]

Such Solomonic solutions helped keep the army together, but Lewinsohn conceded that the conditions of the retreat brought out "the worst elements" in the army. His soldiers' council cooperated with the officer chain of command to post guards at key train stations and supply depots, and supported threats of court martial and summary execution for those who threatened the army's food supply.[61] The chain of command reminded their units that those *Drückeberger* who commandeered "wild

---

[58] BA MA, PH 8 I/511, 213th Div. Order Ia #54/XI, dated November 22, 1918 ("Armeebefehle").

[59] To a certain extent, it may also represent the political naïveté of officers unable to distinguish between different types of socialists.

[60] Lewinsohn, *Revolution an der Westfront*, 31.

[61] *Ibid.*, 25.

Figure 5.2 German medical column on the Dutch border, November 1918. Over 70,000 German troops crossed through the Netherlands on their way home.

transport" on their own endangered all of their comrades.[62] General Hans von Winterfeldt, the German representative to the Armistice Commission, was unable to contradict Allied reports that some German troops were guilty of pillage on their way through Belgium. This lawless behavior, he explained, was due to the unreasonable pace imposed on the German Army by Allied armistice conditions.[63] Winterfeldt was making excuses, but his rationalizations had more than a little basis in fact. The harried troops that crossed the German frontier in late November still looked and acted like an army, but for how much longer?

The Rhineland

Not surprisingly, German soldiers expressed an overwhelming relief and joy as they crossed the frontier into Germany in late November.

---

[62] BA-MA, PH 8 I/511, 213th Inf. Div. Order Ia #66/XI, dated November 27, 1918 ("Abschriften aus Armee- und Gruppebefehlen").
[63] Rhodes to Pershing, December 6, *The US Army in the World War*, X (i), 238.

They had reached the Fatherland, and, instead of resentful glares from a hostile populace, the front-line soldiers received the welcome of their countrymen. Nevertheless, those responsible for bringing the army home, the front-line soldiers' councils and unit commanders, soon found that they had traded one set of problems for another. The supply situation remained bleak, and the head of the new Demobilization Office in Berlin, Lieutenant Colonel Joseph Koeth, asked the OHL to remind the homecoming troops that severe shortages existed inside Germany. As the troops were quartered in towns and villages on their way east, they should not expect that the locals would be able to provide much in the way of food and fuel. The *Westheer* would have to rely on its own resources.[64] The number of available roads grew smaller as the army drew closer to the very limited number of crossing sites over the Rhine. Moreover, as the army moved east it encountered workers' and soldiers' councils with a political agenda that could be far more militant than the ephemeral councils of the *Etappe*. In the Rhineland and the Rhine crossing sites, the army first met the Spartacus League and its allies. In places like Düsseldorf, Cologne, and Aachen, the army confronted councils that feared and despised the army's chain of command and were dedicated to undermining it. In the Rhineland, the army also found that the call of home and kin trumped duty and camaraderie. Soldiers with homes on the west bank of the Rhine began to abandon the army. Nor did the Allies cease their pursuit. Those who fell behind still risked capture and an indefinite period of imprisonment by the Allies.

The High Command sought relief from the Allies' timetable as exhaustion and overcrowding on the roads made it increasingly difficult for the army to meet the schedule for withdrawal. On November 18, General Winterfeldt protested to General Nudant, the French representative, that, since the German Army was clearly unable to resume hostilities, there was no reason to continue the killing pace imposed on the German troops marching east. The Armistice Commission referred the request to Foch, who denied it. Winterfeldt tried again on November 21 and was again denied.[65]

To meet the Allied demands, the troops with the furthest to go averaged up to 30 kilometers a day, even after rest days were cut from the schedule, and even though they left dead horses and abandoned equipment in their wake. The pace of the march bore especially heavy on the

[64] BA-R, R1501/112400, telegram from the demobilization office to the OHL, dated November 21, 1918.
[65] Volkmann, *Revolution über Deutschland*, 77.

men of the *Landsturm* and *Landwehr* battalions, many of whom were over forty years old. The soldiers' councils asked for rail transport to get the older men home, but the transport was just not available. The older men would have to march with the rest of the army.[66] The result was a prodigious performance made possible by fear of capture, but also, more and more, the excitement of reaching home. Increasingly, the men were inspired by the prospect of being with loved ones for Christmas.[67]

Their spirits were also buoyed by the welcome of their countrymen. According to one account, every little village in the Rhineland was decorated with flags and patriotic garlands, as local authorities offered speeches and farmers offered food.[68] Herbert Sulzbach wrote, "as we marched through [Münstereifel] they pelted us with flowers and decorated our horses. This is what you would imagine the victorious march through the Brandenburg Gate to have been like, but these good people gave us fresh courage and confidence. We've got another 28 kilometers to Bonn!"[69]

However, Lewinsohn's account suggests that not every place was prepared for such a welcome. The route of his Fourth Army took it through Aachen, and Lewinsohn traveled ahead of the main column to secure the army's supply sources in the city. In Aachen, he found a disturbing apathy among the citizenry along with a very hostile workers' and soldiers' council. The Fourth Army soldiers' council sent the following press release to the Aachen newspapers, "[I]t is your principal duty to greet the combatants who are undefeated in four years of fighting. The German soldier will be deeply hurt if, during their entry into Germany, you show you are alienated from them in your hearts."[70] Lewinsohn reported that the message roused the citizens from their lethargy and inspired them to give the Fourth Army a gracious welcome.[71]

---

[66] Lewinsohn, *Revolution an der Westfront*, 56. Lewinsohn recorded that his council made a special effort to put the blame for the difficulty of the march on the Allies. *Ibid.*, 57.

[67] German General Staff, *Rückführung des Westheeres*, 16.

[68] *Ibid.*, 16–17.

[69] Sulzbach, *With the German Guns*, 253. One imagines that part of the joyous response from the inhabitants of the Rhineland was prompted by relief to find the Field Army was not in the same condition as the first wave of returnees from the front who had been deserters and unruly support troops making their way home on their own. See, for example, "Die Demobilisierung der Westfront," *BT*, November 19, 1918.

[70] Lewinsohn, *Revolution an der Westfront*, 33. One notes that, here again, a Social Democrat used the idea of the army being "undefeated in the field," unintentionally feeding the idea of a "stab in the back."

[71] *Ibid.*, 34. One of the reasons that Aachen may have been less enthusiastic in its welcome to the Field Army was privation. The effects of the blockade had fallen much

More often, the celebrations were spontaneous. Years later, the same conservative critics who argued the stab-in-the-back legend would accuse the German people of treating the returning soldiers in a shameful manner. This view does not square with contemporary accounts from either Right or Left. Local authorities across Germany made enormous efforts to make the homecoming of the front-line soldier a festive one.[72]

As the army crossed the frontier into Germany, such a greeting would have been especially gratifying to the soldiers who lived in the Rhineland. They were truly home, but their situation presented a special problem to the army chain of command, which was willing to release them as soon as possible.[73] The terms of the armistice had made no provision for men discharged on the west bank of the Rhine (despite the assurances Captain Römpler had offered the men of the 115th Division); Germans found in uniform were to be captured. The Armistice Commission decided to allow German soldiers to remain in the Rhineland if they discarded their uniforms and could prove they had been properly discharged. Yet that, too, presented a problem. General Winterfeldt protested that a shortage of clothing meant that a soldier might have only his uniform to wear. Beyond that, a proper discharge was likely to be impossible because (1) the muster rolls were packed in the army's heavy baggage and thus, unavailable, (2) the hasty nature of the withdrawal made normal administrative procedures impossible, and (3) local soldiers' councils were already intervening to discharge individuals and, occasionally, whole units, on their own authority.[74] Winterfeldt's last point highlighted the new challenge the army faced as it marched into the homeland. While the officers and front-line councils believed order and discipline were essential to the success of the return march, many of the local workers' and soldiers' councils believed the goals of the revolution would be best served by dismantling the old army as rapidly as possible.[75] Though the OHL relayed an order

heavier on the cities than the countryside. Laurence Moyer, *Victory Must Be Ours: Germany in the Great War, 1914–1918* (New York: Hippocrene Books, 1995), 214.

[72] See the discussion in Richard Bessel, "Die Heimkehr der Soldaten: Das Bild der Frontsoldaten in der Öffentlichkeit der Weimarer Republik," in Hirschfeld *et al.*, eds., *Keiner fühlt sich hier mehr als Mensch*, 221–3.

[73] BA-MA, PH 8 I/511, Gruppe Soden (V Res. Corps), Ia, Ib #3919, "Annex to the OHL order regarding the discharge of military personnel with homes in the areas to be evacuated," dated November 19, 1918.

[74] Winterfeldt to General Nudant, *The US Army in the World War*, X (i), 226–7.

[75] See, for example: BA-R, 43/2485, report from Dep. IX Corps, #281/12, dated November 23, 1918. A major in this homeland garrison headquarters warned the government that Spartacist sailors in his district threatened orderly demobilization and support of the returning front-line troops.

from the cabinet that stipulated that at the local level the Field Army would be cooperating with prerevolutionary authorities, the more revolutionary homeland councils were determined to assert their role in the new order.[76] Collisions were inevitable.

Senior officers felt the special enmity of the revolutionary councils. On November 20, General von Schulenberg moved the headquarters of Army Group B to Königswinter, a picturesque town on the east bank of the Rhine near Bonn. As he traveled through the Rhineland, the general found an atmosphere of calm and order until he reached Bonn. On entering the city, he encountered a representative of a local soldiers' council, a uniformed "sixteen-year old hooligan" who leveled a rifle at him. Schulenberg recalled the feelings he had experienced when he had crossed the Rhine four and a half years earlier as the war began. To be greeted in such a fashion when returning, he wrote, was "unimaginable."[77]

In the units where officers still were a dominant force, the collision took the forms of spontaneous acts of violence against local revolutionaries. An army doctor later recalled watching "the soldiers of an artillery unit tear down a banner bearing the proclamation, 'Welcome to the German Socialist Republic.' Workers who threatened the unit commander were driven away at gunpoint."[78] Lewinsohn wrote that the units who were last to be pulled out of the line were most likely to be hostile to the appearance of lawlessness in the homeland.[79] In a message to the war ministry on November 25, the OHL explained that such attacks on revolutionary symbols were due to the demands of the return march and the difficulty of communication between headquarters and units. There had been insufficient time to "educate" the frontline troops on the new conditions in the Fatherland. The *Fronttruppen* needed to have it explained to them that a red armband did not mean Bolshevism, but rather "the success of the two socialist parties in the life of the state" and was the symbol of local security forces.[80]

The tension increased as the army closed on the Rhine, and unit headquarters began to bombard the OHL with reports complaining of

---

[76] BA-MA, PH 8 I/511, Fifth Army order, Ia #899, dated November 18, 1918. Certainly, many, perhaps most, of the homeland soldiers' and workers' councils sought to assist the passage of the Field Army. See for example, BA-BA, poster #002–001–018, "Verfügung des Arbeiter- u. Soldatenrats Mannheim" and poster #002–006–073, "Soldatenrathilfe," (Commandant and Soldiers' Councils of Berlin).

[77] BA-MA, N58/1, Nachlass Schulenberg, "Erlebnisse," 244–5.

[78] Westman, *Surgeon with the Kaiser's Army*, 179.

[79] Lewinsohn, *Revolution an der Westfront*, 30.

[80] BA-R, R43/2500/5, transcript of message to the war ministry, telephoned from the OHL, #If 107249, dated November 25, 1918. On the other hand, the OHL said, the Field Army would avoid such symbols since they had too often been used as the cover for plunder.

the depredations of the local councils. On November 19, Army Group A complained that a large numbers of trucks intended for transfer to the Allies had, instead, been confiscated by soldiers' councils from the Home Army. Elsewhere, hostile garrison troops offered the Field Army's truck drivers immediate discharge papers if they would leave their trucks behind.[81] Army Group C complained that it had lost trucks, fuel, and radios to the local *Soldatenräte*.[82] In some cases, members of the local councils may have used the symbols of revolution to mask extortion and petty thievery, but in others it was clear that some of the workers' and soldiers' councils along the Rhine and beyond were conducting a low-key, decentralized insurgency against the Field Army.[83]

Together with their officers and front-line troops they represented, the Field Army's soldiers' councils also found themselves in conflict with these more revolutionary councils inside Germany. On November 21, in a message addressed to the "workers' and soldiers' councils of the homeland," the OHL council made an early appeal to the homeland councils to, "Show our comrades that the new Fatherland knows how to honor their deeds and recognize their great suffering." They reassured the councils of the homeland garrisons that the troops of the Field Army stood solidly behind the new Ebert–Haase coalition government. The message also used compliments to placate the anxiety felt by the homeland garrisons: "Comrades and Workers! We of the Field Army thank you from the bottom of our hearts for your liberating acts in the homeland." The OHL council moreover pointedly stated that the Field Army wanted a voice in the creation of the new Fatherland and that those who would undermine democracy would be resisted.[84] Despite this appeal to solidarity, when the headquarters of the Fourth Army displaced to Krefeld, Lewinsohn and his comrades were forced to negotiate with a sailors' council that demanded the army disarm itself and turn its weapons over to the sailors.[85] In Aachen, a Spartacist council accused the Fourth Army soldiers' council of being monarchist agents of counter-revolution. The story was picked up by

---

[81] BA-R, R43/2500/5, transcript of Giebel's telephone call from the OHL, dated November 29, 1918.

[82] BA-MA, PH 8 I/511, Fifth Army order, Ia #5170, dated November 17, 1918.

[83] In Berlin, *Die Rote Fahne* demanded that Hindenburg and all counter-revolutionary officers be arrested, that the Supreme Headquarters be moved to Berlin, and the government stop the movement into Germany of any front-line troops led by their officers. *Die Rote Fahne*, "Aufputschung der Frontsoldaten," edition of December 4, 1918.

[84] BA-MA, PH 3/19, flyer, issued by the soldiers' council of the OHL; "To the Workers' and Soldiers' Councils of the Homeland," dated November 21, 1918.

[85] Lewinsohn, *Revolution an der Westfront*, 43.

a national newspaper, *Vorwärts*, which carried an article stating that the army commander, Sixt von Arnim, had reasserted control over the army and the council with the aim of crushing the revolution.[86] The front-line council was compelled to defend itself from this attack from the Left. It sent a message to the capital that protested, "In Berlin, the rumor is being circulated that the Fourth Army is taking up the battle against the revolution. If one understands revolution to mean the dictatorship of the minority [a code name for Bolshevism], this rumor is aligned with the facts." The message continued by restating the army's support for the Ebert government.[87] The OHL council had to respond to similar attacks by denouncing rumors that it was a mere tool of the High Command. It launched a printed counterattack against the leftist-oriented Executive Committee of the Berlin Workers' and Soldiers' Councils, denying that it had any authority over the councils of the army.[88]

By late November, the front-line soldiers' councils found themselves squeezed between the radicalized councils of the homeland and a renewed effort by the army's officers to assert control over both their own units and the dissident garrisons within Germany. As his troops crossed the border, the First Army commander, General Eberhard, declared the area between the frontier and the Rhine to be an "operational area." "I order all civil and military authorities to support me in the establishment of calm and order." He went on to demand the subordination of the local workers and soldiers' councils and the suppression of red flags and insignias.[89] The chain of command promulgated similar orders in the Seventh and Seventeenth Armies.[90]

In councils at every level, and particularly in the OHL council, a storm of protest rose up against these orders. Pressure from the government prompted the OHL to relieve Eberhard and a number of other officers of their command. During the same period, tensions began to grow between OHL staff and the OHL soldiers' council.[91]

---

[86] *Ibid.*, 40.   [87] *Ibid.*, 41.

[88] "Das Heer gegen den Berliner A- und S-Rat," *BT*, November 27, 1918.

[89] "Das Kommandeur der Ersten Armee gegen die Arbeiter und Soldatenräte," *BT*, 25 November, 1918.

[90] Report of US Military Attaché in the Hague to the Intelligence Section of the AEF, December 8, 1918, *The US Army in the World War*, X (i), 257–8.

[91] On November 18, an "officers only" message went out from Army Group C. It referred to a proclamation made by the OHL soldiers' council and told officers that such messages accomplished little and should be suppressed. It would only confuse the troops as to who was really in charge. Within the army group, the trustees' councils should not serve as a "parallel government" (*Nebenregierung*) as the OHL council was attempting to do. Instead, the trustees should concern themselves with

On November 22, the council demanded the right to elect officers, and intense negotiations were needed before this demand was withdrawn. By November 28, the High Command, in turn, banned the flying of red flags in the *Frontheer*. The council and the government protested, though a few days later the cabinet declared that if front-line councils chose to ban red flags in their units, in the interest of "freedom of belief" they were free to do so.[92] The battle over symbols continued as the amicable working relationship between staff and council began to go sour.

"Drang nach Hause"

In late November and the first days of December, 1918, the *Westheer*'s long columns crossed the Rhine on bridges at Düsseldorf, Cologne, Coblenz, and a handful of other sites. Of all phases of the army's return, the Rhine crossing required the most intricate planning. Some of the army's columns were close to 100 miles long, and a traffic snarl in a major city like Cologne could hold up military and civilian movement for days. Units had to adhere strictly to the crossing schedule, because there was little opportunity to send adjustments and corrections up and down the overcrowded roads. At control points near the crossing sites, general staff officers monitored the passage of units in order to ensure the steady flow of military columns and to arrange opportunities for civilian traffic to interject itself into gaps in the endless *feldgrau* columns. At other locations, engineer units set up temporary pontoon bridges to supplement the fixed bridge sites.[93]

Those who observed the Rhine crossing were impressed by the high morale of the returning front-line units. The motto of the troops was *"Parole Heimat"* (watchword "home"), and a reporter from the *Berliner Tageblatt* wrote that a real "Christmas spirit" was palpable among the troops. Wagons and trucks were so heavily decorated with greenery that the army appeared to be a forest on the move. The reporter reassured his readers that the front-line army was not a bunch of desperadoes bent on robbery and plunder. Instead, soldiers seem to offer obedience to officers gladly, seeing it as a necessity for reaching their goal, home. However, the reporter wrote, no one should be deluded into thinking the army was ready to take up the fight against the Allies again. The

raising troop morale. BA-MA, PH 8 I/511, Ia #954, transcript from Army Group Gallwitz/"C" (for officers only), dated November 18, 1918.

[92] BA-R, 43/2500/4, telegram from the cabinet to the OHL, dated November 30, 1918, and follow-up telegram dated December 9, 1918.

[93] *Ibid.*, 17–20.

Figure 5.3 Marching under the old imperial flag, a German column crosses the Rhine at Cologne, November 1918.

soldiers he interviewed were unified in their resentment of Prussian militarism. "Underneath the joy of homecoming, the men were bitter about giving their best efforts in a losing cause."[94]

Others studied the mood of the troops, as well. The Allies were clearly worried that the Germans might take up arms again and sent observers to keep a close watch on the retreating army. To this end, they interrogated members of the local population on what they had seen of troop conduct and morale. Often, such interviews suggested the sharp division between front and rear. The intelligence officer of the AEF's Third Corps recorded this statement from a Peter Knopp of Freilingen:

Most of the German troops that marched through this village during their retirement observed good order. Few orders were given by the officers, and these were respected by the men. I noticed however, that the officers appeared to be more intimate with the enlisted men than had previously been the habit. There were no demonstrations of a revolutionary character. I saw no red flags.[95]

[94] "Die Heimkehrenden," *BT*, December 1, 1918.
[95] NARA, RG 120, Box 5895, Third Army Corps G2 Report #29, dated December 14–15, 1918.

Another statement read:

> Mr. Holgkämper served as Feldwebel with the Clothing Depot at COBLENZ.
> During the withdrawal of the S.O.S. troops numerous uniforms were forcibly
> taken from the depot. He claims that none of the real soldiers, meaning the
> active line troops, were mutinous. He attributes the splendid execution of the
> withdrawal of the German armies in some measure to the influence which
> these soldiers had over the younger and less experienced men.

The former supply sergeant added that he believed that the returning
front-line troops were Germany's best guarantee for future peace and
order.[96]

Still another interview with a local villager suggested that not all
Rhinelanders were glad to see the retreating troops:

> Mr. Grimm stated that German officers who had been quartered at POLCH
> [on the west bank of the Rhine near Coblenz] complained about their cool
> reception while there. Instead of being received with admiration, they were
> looked upon as part of a beaten army, partially to be blamed for the occupa-
> tion of German soil by the enemy. These officers did not consider themselves
> beaten and were surprised and annoyed at the attitude of the people.[97]

Along with interviews, the Allied monitoring teams also took careful
notes on the order of battle and strengths of the retreating units.[98] On
November 27 and 28, for example, at Montabaur, 12 miles northwest of
the Rhine crossing site at Coblenz, AEF officers recorded the passage
of the following formations:

Unit	Officers	Men	Horses
Telephone Det. 16th Corps	1	38	26
Town Major Det., 8th Res. Corps		7	8
Balloon Plt. 2	5	60	28
Balloon Plt. 93	6	89	24
Zeppelin Staff 44	3	40	12
A.A. [Anti-Aircraft] Bty 581	3	100	41

[96] *Ibid.*, Report #30, dated December 15–16, 1918.
[97] *Ibid.*
[98] The Allies were anxious that the Germans observe the conditions of the Armistice
and had posted observers along the march routes to monitor the progress of the
Frontheer's return to Germany. The observers from the US Third Army, detailed for
occupation duty within the Reich, were interested in the composition, morale, and
destination of the units crossing the river, as well as plans for demobilization. To this
end they attempted to record the designation and strength of every unit that crossed
in the area that was to become the American sector. Their reports are especially useful, since they are not biased by Germany's internal political discord.

Unit	Officers	Men	Horses
A.A. Bty 757	4	72	75
Anti Tank Grp, "Wild Group"		23	
A.A. Grp. 12	4	30	8
A.A. Searchlight Sect. 743		17	17
Entlade Cmd. "Hempel" [?]	10	105	–
Field Artillery Battery 13	2	40	–
127th Inf. Regt. Staff and 3rd Bn.	20	470	95
Trench Mtr. [Mortar] Co., 127th I.R.	4	140	35
Part of the 476. Inf. Regt.	10	137	58
Field Hospital 208	6	60	40
3rd Bn. 476 Inf.Regt.	15	500	90
Trench Mortar Co., 476th Inf. Regt.	4	137	40
503rd Field Hospital	8	63	–
General Staff, 16th Corps	35	200	160
Column No. 1387, 406 F.A.R.[99].	–	60	50
Trains of the 1st Bav. Inf. Div.	6	250	–
Telephone Sta. 1165	1	13	6
Telephone Det.	1	18	–
1st Sqdn, 2nd Regt., Guards Dragoons	6	78	100
Quartermaster Dept., 242nd Inf. Div.	2	19	–
Army Corps Signal Command 616	1	25	–
Kolonne [Transport] 5/406	–	60	–
" 6/406	12	230	–
" 4/406	–	80	–
Tradesmen's Co. 145	2	74	–
" 146	2	111	–
" 147	4	67	–
Listening Sect. (16th Corps)	2	13	–.[100]

Examining this and similar reports from late November and early December allows some interesting observations about the condition of the army. Not surprisingly, the infantry units were badly under strength. Typically, US observers saw infantry battalions marching by with 400 to 500 men, and sometimes far fewer.[101] Second, the bulk of the support units on the road were the kind found at division level and below (anti-aircraft batteries, signal units, field hospitals, etc.). However, the presence of transport columns, town major detachments, tradesmen's companies, and army-level school troops indicate that not all of the

[99] Field Artillery Regiment.
[100] NARA, RG 120, Box 5895, US First Inf. Div. Report #104, dated December 16, 1918.
[101] The 2nd Battalion of the 9th Grenadiers, for example, counted 17 officers and 100 men; the entire 17th Infantry Regiment marched by with 19 officers and 500 men.

army's rear-area units evaporated in the aftermath of the revolution.[102] Officer memoirs and official histories may be exaggerating in their description of the vanishing *Etappe*. The large number of support formations also helps to explain how the *Westheer* numbered over 3 million when the strength at the front was something like 1.5 million. Third, the presence of Bavarian troops moving northwest from Coblenz, on the middle Rhine, at the end of November, suggests what a circuitous route some units had to take before arriving at their ultimate destination. Units moved east from wherever the armistice found them and had to continue east within their assigned sectors until they reached the east bank of the Rhine, which allowed them to move directly homeward. Finally, one is struck by the vast number of horses needed to move a First World War army.[103]

The variety of units listed in such reports also demonstrated the complexity of the army's movement and the necessity for careful organization. Once across the Rhine, the movement plan called for units to continue on to assembly areas in the interior of the country, well beyond the designated Allied occupation areas on the east bank. The Field Army's destination was the *Einladezone*, the "embarkation area," where units would be marshaled for rail and foot movement to home bases and demobilization sites.[104] Units stationed east of the Elbe would have priority on the available rail transport, while units less than 200 miles from their point of demobilization would be authorized to continue on foot.[105]

For the most part, both the general staff and the Ebert government were gratified by the orderly conduct exhibited during the Rhine crossing. Neither party, however, could be pleased about the growing hostility of the Spartacists and the revolutionary councils. In places like Cologne, the OHL was forced to intervene to prevent open combat between front-line units and the city's workers' and soldiers' council.[106] Lewinsohn accused the Spartacists from the Home Army councils

---

[102] Other reports include veterinary hospitals, labor battalions, slaughterhouse units, *Landsturm* garrisons, salvage detachments, field bakery columns, and other units typically associated with service support functions.

[103] NARA, RG 120, Box 5895, Third US Army Intelligence Summaries (incl. III Corps, 1st Inf. Div., 89th Inf. Div.).

[104] The plan called for the bulk of the 180 divisions of the Western Army to wait in the *Einladezone* for rail transport east while thirty-seven divisions hailing from the western regions of Germany marched themselves home. German General Staff, *Rückführung des Westheeres*, 19–21.

[105] BA-MA, PH 8 I/511, 213th Inf. Div. Order, Ia/Demob. #2/XI, regarding troop transport, dated 22 November, 1918.

[106] "Die rote Fahne und die Offiziere," *BT*, November 29, 1918. Leeb reports a dangerous confrontation in Düsseldorf, as well, *Tagebuchaufzeichnungen*, 158.

of seeking to hasten the dissolution of the army by spreading rumors that the OHL was withholding trains from the mission of bringing soldiers home. They were also planting false reports that the Allies had marched into Westphalia and were taking as prisoners those soldiers who were too slow to move out of their path.[107] In another instance, the 5th Bavarian Division reported that, as it marched through the Ruhr, local councils sought to undermine the unit by offering the troops free railway tickets home.[108]

In another instance, the Spartacists used intimidation to achieve their objectives. As Fritz Nagel prepared to take his anti-aircraft battery over the Rhine, "Dirty and sloppy-looking revolutionary soldiers wearing red arm bands stopped us and refused to let us across the bridge. They feared our cannons as well as the thought that our whole outfit would join the counter-revolutionary army rumored to be forming beyond the Rhine." Nagel was indifferent to the fate of the guns, since they would have to be turned over to the Allies anyway, so he receipted them over to the revolutionaries at the bridge. The front-line troops parked the battery's vehicles on the west end of the bridge and the battery proceeded on foot. "I shook hands with every man and dismissed them with instructions to get home the best way they could. That was the end of the war for me."[109]

Other incidents ended less amicably. As Colonel Reinhard rode across the Rhine as the head of his 4th Foot Guards, he was insulted by a group of sailors in the back of a truck. Angered, Reinhard rode up to the truck and tried to pull the red sash from one of the most belligerent sailors, who fell off. The other sailors backed away, except the one who had fallen off the truck and another who came after the colonel with a knife. The company of guardsmen following Reinhard overwhelmed the two sailors, beat them, and left them for the next

---

[107] Lewinsohn, *Revolution an der Westfront*, 61–3.

[108] Lipp, *Meinungslenkung*, 169. The OHL received a report that the *Arbeiter- und Soldatenrat* of Darmstadt had held up two soldiers from a support unit of the IX Corps and extorted 6,500 marks from one of the men before they would release the two.

[109] Nagel, *Fritz*, 161. Another officer recalled, "Severe violations of discipline [during the march] were entirely isolated and could regularly be explained by some alcoholic excess. Nevertheless, it was characteristic enough that here, for the first time, I witnessed a soldier trying to strip an officer of his shoulder straps. A resounding slap in the face, accompanied by a jovial remark, brought the intoxicated man back to reason and produced great hilarity among the soldiers who stood about. With this the incident was closed." Account in the *Deutsche Kriegszeitung* quoted in Fried, *Guilt*, 54.

company, which threw them into the Rhine. Reinhard's account does not say whether the sailors drowned.[110]

As the incidents cited above show, *alienation* remained a feature of the soldiers' outlook. The combat troops continued to resent the troops in the rear area and the homeland who had avoided service in the trenches. If anything, that resentment increased, for many of the *Fronttruppen* came into closer contact with the *Etappenschweine* and those in the homeland who had avoided front-line service.[111] Between them, Nagel's and Reinhard's experiences suggest the wide range of responses – surprise, resignation, disgust, anger, and, sometimes, violence – as the front encountered the revolution.

Across the Rhine

In an effort to strengthen their hand against revolutionary influences and discontent within the army and the nation, the OHL began to use selective discharge policies. As a first priority, the army offered early release to Alsatians and others who lived close to the Western frontier. The army also gave early release to national and local civil service officers and policemen.[112] In addition, Groener sent handpicked officers out to units to act as "inoculation agents" (*Serumspritzer*). Their job was to "immunize" the troops against revolutionary influences by denouncing the Spartacists and speaking in support of the Ebert government.[113]

Groener also hoped to steer the soldiers' councils in a direction that would lessen their influence on the army, while using them to bolster the Ebert government. With this end in mind, he supported the summoning of the First Congress of Front-line Soldiers' Councils on December 1 and 2 at the resort town of Bad Ems. Groener hoped the congress would call for the disarming of all the civil population, the dissolution of the soldiers' councils, and the immediate summoning of

[110] Reinhard, *Wehen der Republik*, 34–5. Reinhard recalled that when he encountered the raw recruits from the homeland garrisons they would initially fail to salute him. He began to initiate the salutes. At first, the embarrassed recruits pretended not to see him. "Eventually," he wrote, "they understood what was required of them." *Ibid.*, 54.
[111] On the other hand, any feelings of hostility toward the civilian population must certainly have been ameliorated by the hearty welcome the front-line troops received as they marched into Germany.
[112] Dreetz, "Rückführung des Westheeres," 586.
[113] Groener, *Lebenserinnerung*, 472–3. Groener conceded the *Serumspritzer* had little influence on the soldiers' desire to get home.

a National Assembly. He also wanted the front-line council to denounce the troublesome *Vollzugsrat* in Berlin.

Groener would have been encouraged by the dominance of the Majority Socialists among those who attended the congress.[114]

Yet, despite the party affiliations of those in attendance, Groener's plan misfired. Although the membership of the 326-member congress voted its support of the Ebert government, it also asserted the councils' authority over issues of rations, quarters, leave, punishments, and soldier grievances. Emil Barth, the most radical member of the cabinet, attended, leading the USPD delegation to the congress. He took on a major role at the congress, convincing the members of its executive committee to assert that discipline within the army must be based on comradely friendship. Barth also encouraged the attendees to demand more power for their own Field Army councils though, in doing so, Barth undercut the guidelines his own cabinet had set for council authority in the Field on November 12.[115]

For the moderate soldiers' councils of the Field Army, the congress had a mixed result. On the positive side, the congress reaffirmed the power of the councils. However, according to Lewinsohn, it was at Bad Ems that the front-line councils first became aware of the deep split in the government. It was evident, he wrote later, that the danger was now exclusively on the Left. The monarchist threat had passed.[116]

Bad Ems was a clear setback for Groener and a demonstration of the failure of the old elites at *managing* the attitudes of the front-line veterans. If he had hoped to turn the councils against the radical wing of the government, he had failed. Yet Groener was not moving only on the political front. As the army moved across the Rhine, he gave permission to selected officers of proven discernment to make personal visits to the units on the march. The purpose of the visits was to determine which divisions were "the best, the most reliable, and most usable."[117] The ultimate goal was to select up to ten divisions and move them by rail to

[114] Grau, "Zur Rolle der Soldatenräte," 552. The *Vossische Zeitung* reported that few red ornaments were seen; the overwhelming choice for decorations were the Reich's colors – black, white, and red – and the *Landesfarben*, the colors of the individual states. "Die Tagung der Frontsoldaten," *VZ*, December 2, 1918.

[115] Description of Bad Ems from Groener, *Lebenserinnerungen*, 470; Grau, "Zur Rolle der Soldatenräte," 556; Volkmann, *Revolution über Deutschland*, 81; Lewinsohn, *Revolution an der Westfront*, 37–8; and BA-R, R43/2500/5, transcript of Giebel's call to Ebert, dated December 9, 1918, 50.

[116] Lewinsohn, *Revolution an der Westfront*, 38.

[117] Thaer, *Generalstabdienst an der Front*, 472–3. Von Thaer was one of the most aggressively monarchist officers on the OHL staff and one of the officers (along with Groener's adjutant and Major von Schleicher) charged with finding the most reliable units.

Figure 5.4 Civilians greet a bicycle unit on the outskirts of Cologne, November 1918.

assembly areas encircling Berlin, where they would come under a special new command designated to execute a secret "Berlin Operation." Once again, in their *selection* of units, the chain of command had assumed that political reliability correlated to combat effectiveness. The result, by the first week of December, was that nine "reliable" divisions were en route to the area around Berlin.

However, these were not the only divisions the OHL had earmarked for special duty. The High Command had selected twenty divisions to serve as a *Grenzschutz*, a border security force for the west bank of the Rhine. The mission of the security forces would be to block further unauthorized advances by Allied forces while cooperating with authorized agents of the armistice. However, morale in the chosen units plummeted as the men felt they had been unfairly asked to be placed at the tail end of the demobilization queue. The soldiers felt their comrades who reached home ahead of them would snatch the remaining employment, leaving nothing for the men of the *Grenzschutz*. The commander of the 15th Bavarian Division, assigned to border duty, received this warning on December 3:

The Soldiers' Council of the 15th Bavarian Infantry Division which has the trust of the overwhelming majority of the soldiers of the division, protests the assumption of the border security mission for even the shortest period of time. Should the efforts of the division command to lead the division home as swiftly and expeditiously as possible continue to be unsuccessful; the division's Soldiers' Council will decline further work and leave to the commander the responsibility for the disorder and mass desertion that would follow as a direct result.[118]

The division commander was compelled to inform his corps headquarters that his unit could not accept the mission without the risk that the men would leave *en masse*, taking their junior officers with them. Incidents like this forced Groener to concede that the idea of a border force composed of former elements of the *Westheer* was "an illusion."[119] The army would have to rely on small, highly paid volunteer units to take over the mission intended for the twenty front-line divisions.[120]

The difficulty the OHL faced in creating a *Grenzschutz* indicated the problem the rest of the Field Army was beginning to experience as it crossed the Rhine – disintegration. Lewinsohn confessed that all through the march, a swarm of stragglers and deserters had accompanied the disciplined formations. Their number had grown daily as the army approached the homeland. The soldiers' councils set up control points at the border in order to gather up these wayward soldiers, and reinforced the struggle against dissolution by ensuring rations went to units, not individuals.[121] This system had an initial, positive effective in keeping men with their units, but once the army had crossed the Rhine, such control measures had less and less impact. Up to that point, the demands of the march meant that physical *exhaustion* continued to play a role in the limited interest soldiers could generate for political matters. However, the emotional exhaustion, the dull apathy that characterized front-line soldiers exposed too long to danger and privation clearly began to lift as the army approached the Fatherland. Officers could no longer expect their men to obey out of inertia, especially if there seemed to be a delay in moving toward home. Nor could the chain of command take advantage of the Field Army's *isolation* from events in the homeland.

In some respects, the army accelerated the disintegration through its own demobilization policies. The demobilization plan called for men from the classes of 1896–9 to remain with the colors in order to form the nucleus of a peacetime army. The army planned to give rail priority

---

[118] Lipp, *Meinungslenkung*, 168.   [119] Groener, *Lebenserinnerungen*, 472.
[120] Discussion of the *Grenzschutz* problem in German General Staff, *Rückführung des Westheeres*, 21.
[121] Lewinsohn, *Revolution an der Westfront*, 18.

to the older men of the classes of 1895 and earlier who would go home for immediate discharge, while the younger men waited to move with other divisions with later departure dates. Naturally, splitting up a unit along age lines undermined what little cohesion remained among the front-line formations.[122] In this instance, an official *selection* process worked against the chain of command.

Yet the most powerful force pulling the army apart was not its own policies, or even the activities of the Spartacists. Trumping all was the individual soldier's urgent desire to get home. On the east bank of the Rhine, beyond the threat of Allied capture or Belgian *francs-tireurs*, the old cohesion gave way to overwhelming homesickness. In one instance, a battalion of infantry marching homeward decided the commander had taken a wrong turn and might be intentionally leading them away from their home province. They broke ranks, smashed their rifles against trees, and headed homeward, taking only their blankets and their rations.[123] Groener wrote that he knew of regiments in which the men had resolved together, as they came out of the trenches, to deal a deathblow to the revolution. However, when these same men approached their home station, they had forgotten all their previous militancy as the influence of the officers was lost. The driving impulse for virtually every individual was to be discharged as soon as possible.[124] By early December, the *Westheer* estimated that as many as 1 million of its 3.2 million remaining troops had left their units to head home on their own.[125] On December 18, Colonel Walter Reinhardt, the army's representative at the Demobilization Office, reported, "the breakdown of discipline which resulted from the domestic upheaval meant that the desire to return home could no longer be contained ... upon reaching the Reich they are too influenced by the raw urge to return home."[126]

On December 5, Groener sent the cabinet an update on the progress of the *Frontheer*'s return to the homeland. The news was both good and bad. On the positive side of the ledger, thirty divisions had already reached their destinations. In the north, fifty-eight divisions had closed on assembly areas in the north, a further fifty-nine were assembling around Paderborn, Kassel, and Wetzlar, thirty more had proceeded

[122] Dreetz, "Rückführung des Westheeres," 588.
[123] *The US Army in the World War*, XI, 29.
[124] Groener, *Lebenserinnerungen*, 472–3.
[125] Report to the Reich demobilization office. Bessel, *Germany after the First World War*, 74.
[126] *Ibid.*, 75.

past Frankfurt am Main, and another thirty-one were further south. He indicated that the units in the south might be home for Christmas; those in the north would take longer. In this respect, a key issue was the state of the German railway system, which was deteriorating. Still, the marching performance of the troops had been outstanding, with the thoughts of the men being "ruled by a single thought, we should be home by Christmas." With that in mind, Groener asked the government to expedite the distribution of newspapers that included the message that it was not so important to be home by Christmas when the available railway assets were either being turned over to the Allies or were urgently needed to bring food and coal to German cities. For the units that would be last to reach their home stations, the general asked the government to reassure the men that there would still be jobs waiting. Finally, the general asked the government to impose controls on the vast numbers of men making unauthorized use of the rail system.[127]

The first three phases of the army's return – the evacuation of the occupied territories, traversing the Rhineland, and the crossing of the Rhine river barrier – had gone better, perhaps, than the government and the High Command could have expected. However, the last phase, the army's movement to its home stations, saw the plan start to unravel. As Groener's nine handpicked divisions gathered around Berlin, the rest of the Field Army was beginning to disappear.

The behavior of German front-line troops during the return from the Western Front seems to offer a validation of Leonard Smith's ideas about soldier behavior. Smith found that, in the last years of the Great War, veteran French troops offered obedience to an order only to the extent that they believed the risk they incurred was proportionate to the importance of the order and the chances that what was being ordered [an attack, a patrol, a defense of an exposed position, etc.] would succeed. The same "negotiated balance-of-power equation" can be seen (though under significantly different circumstances) among the German veterans who remained with their units after the armistice. They offered obedience to the chain of command as long that obedience served the purpose of bringing them home.[128] The farther the army moved east, the more it encountered that most powerful solvent of the bonds of *cohesion*: home and family.

From the armistice to their arrival in assembly areas on the eastern side of the Rhine, the behavior of the *Fronttruppen* remained distinctly

---

[127] BA-R, R43/2500/4, telephone call from Groener to Ebert, transcript dated December 5, 1918.

[128] Smith, *Between Mutiny and Obedience*, 11–17.

different from that of the rest of the German Army. The six response factors that made the decisions of the front-line troops distinct were dynamic in their relative importance and their interrelationship. Thus, for example, *isolation* was a fundamental aspect of the soldier's outlook when he began the march to the east. By the time he had crossed the Rhine, he encountered both political agitation and the irresistible pull of home. Isolation was no longer a major factor.

Professional skill, unusual cooperation, and individual and group motivation had made possible the *Westheer*'s long, difficult march from the Western Front. The army's planning staffs provided the professional skill, carrying on the standard of technical proficiency established by the nineteenth-century *Kriegsakademie* and the Elder Moltke. The unusual cooperation was offered at the highest level by the mutual understanding achieved by the soldier, Groener, and the party leader, Ebert. It was taken up at every subordinate level by the unit commanders of the army and the soldiers' councils established within their units. Though most officer memoirs and official histories tend to downplay the role of the front-line councils as intermediaries between the chain of command and the rank and file, accounts like Lewinsohn's convince one that the councils played a key role in getting the army over the Rhine. Finally, the success occurred because the hard-marching combat veterans were motivated, at first, by the fear of Allied capture and, then, by the irresistible desire to go home.

To describe the return march as an orderly operation runs against the grain of some interpretations of the last days of the Imperial Army. Wilhelm Deist, justifiably respected as one of the foremost historians of the period, argued that, at the end of the war, the German High Command had little influence over the troops.[129] He wrote that as a result of desertion, passive resistance, and mutiny, "[T]he military command had therefore lost control of its irreplaceable instrument."[130] Richard Bessel has picked up Deist's argument and extends it to the postwar period by arguing that the army's advanced stage of disintegration had the happy, but unanticipated, effect of easing the army's demobilization.[131] If one follows the arguments made by Deist and Bessel, the conclusion might be that there was no massive, organized return of units back to Germany. As a result, one might miss the political significance of the fact that most of the *Feldheer* returned as

---

[129] One major problem with this argument is that it ignores the heavy casualties the Allied armies suffered up through the last days of the war. Armies "on strike" do not inflict heavy losses on their enemies.
[130] Deist, "Verdeckter Militarstreik im Kriegsjahr 1918?," 205.
[131] Bessel, *Germany after the First World War*, 90.

units, not individuals. While Deist and Bessel capture important truths about the condition of the German Army of late 1918, the character of the Field Army's return to Germany suggests that the two historians have overstated the army's state of dissolution prior to crossing the Rhine.

For Ebert and his Majority Socialist allies, the army's return from the Western Front was a welcome victory. By bringing its sons and fathers home, the new republic had fulfilled its first obligation to the German nation. Those who criticized Ebert's alliance with the OHL overlooked this obligation. The march across the Rhine had been a victory for the old officer corps as well. They had done an admirable job in accomplishing a difficult mission. As the army crossed the Rhine, Groener and the army's senior leaders could nourish, for a brief time, the hope that there remained a core of reliable units from which a bulwark might be built against the radical revolutionaries.

The Spartacists observed what happened at the Rhine bridges and feared that the *Westheer*'s appearance in the German interior meant mortal danger to the revolution. On December 2, *Die Rote Fahne* warned its readers: "At the head of a powerful army under the black-white-red flag, with exemplary discipline and an artificially created hatred of 'Bolshevism' come generals, warmongers, and those devoted to the Hohenzollerns, from the West into the interior of Germany ... Above all, their hope is the solid cadres of the returning front-line troops." The report went on to say that this counter-revolutionary host was destroying revolutionary symbols, shooting down those who distributed revolutionary literature, disarming revolutionary militias, and firing on revolutionary elements in the populace.[132] The revolutionary Left was well aware that it had no military force that could challenge such "cadres."

Though the parades through the Rhine cities gave the OHL hope and the radical Left nightmares, it was all an illusion. On the west bank of the Rhine, the Field Army began to dissolve. The chain of command could no longer manage the perceptions of the *Fronttruppen*. It was clear that the "command message" had little persuasive power when it came to convincing the troops there were other priorities besides getting home.

Nevertheless, had the army arrived at the German frontier as an armed mob, losing thousands of stragglers to Allied captivity as it marched, militarism's apologists would have had a far more difficult

---

[132] *Die Rote Fahne* (Berlin), "Rustung der Revolution," December 2, 1918.

Figure 5.5 German troops at a rest area, November 1918. The sign
on the Speisehalle (dining hall) reads: "The grateful thanks of the
homeland to you who have fought and suffered for us."

job in arguing the stab-in-the-back theory. By marching in good order
across the Rhine in late November, and then sending nine complete
divisions through the Brandenburg Gate in mid December, the *Westheer*
helped to foster the illusion that the army was "undefeated in the field."
This was, perhaps, the unhappiest legacy of the return march. Wilhelm
Deist was correct in suggesting an advanced state of disintegration in
the army at the war's end, and Richard Bessel accurately depicts the last
stages of the demobilization as a free-for-all. However, their descriptions ignore an important period of around three or four weeks in which
the army held itself together for one final march.

    In early December, Germany waited the return of the front-line
troops with different emotions: anticipation, joy, and dread. Years
later, the writer Ernst von Salomon recalled his feelings as he watched
the first returning front-line unit, the 213th Infantry Division, pass
through a German town. A young cadet at the time, he was stunned by
what he saw:

Oh, God how they looked, how these men looked! What was it that approached?
These emaciated, unmoving faces under the steel helmet, these thin ranks,

these tattered, dusty uniforms! They marched, step by step, and around them a seemingly endless emptiness. It was if they carried a spell of dangerous force, as if a secret power, invisible to those outside, drove them. They still carried, bundled in a dancing wisp of visions, the chaos of thundering battles in their brain, just as they carried the mud and dust of the rutted fields on their uniforms. Indeed, they marched as if they were the emissaries of death, of horror, the deadliest, loneliest, iciest cold.

In that moment, he realized that he had no idea who these men were or what they had endured. They were not of the same world as the crowd that watched them. "And you thought after all that, that the Front would be one with you, you citizens? You thought after all, the Front would be as liberal as you, so reasonable, so full of a forgiving, understanding *Bonhomie*?!"[133]

Germany waited for the return of these men, expectant, hopeful, and anxious.

[133] Ernst von Salomon, *Die Geächteten* (Hamburg: Rohwolt, 1962), 25. The book is an autobiographical novel of von Salomon's experience as a *Freikorps* fighter and his subsequent involvement in the murder of Walter Rathenau.

6   Dissolution and conspiracy: the Army's homecoming and demobilization, December 1918

Homeland

On November 23, 1918, cheering crowds greeted the elite German *Jäger* Division as it marched through the streets of Cologne in step with the music of its regimental bands.[1] The impression the *Jägers* left with observers markedly differed from the one von Salomon had recorded with the passage of the 213th Infantry Division. With scarcely controlled enthusiasm, the *Kölnische Zeitung* described the arrival of the *Jägers* as "Unbroken, undefeated, protectors of the homeland from without and protectors of the homeland within. The steadiness and order and strict discipline that live in us, that is what one sees in these soldiers again ... In parade step, as if on the drill field, that is the way the battalions went by." The article went on to report that the units carried the black-white-red imperial flag, the Prussian flag, and their own green *Jäger* banner, each decorated with flowers and wreaths. The writer concluded that the homecoming of the soldiers was reminiscent of the glory days of 1914.[2] The *Kölnische Zeitung* wrote for an audience shaken by Germany's defeat and the revolutionary upheaval that accompanied it. Dismayed by the collapse of the old regime, many Germans cast about for something strong, familiar, and reassuring. The arrival of the *Westheer*, marching in good order, often displaying the symbols of the old order, brought hope to those most shaken by the events of November 1918. To them, the front-line troops represented the old German Army, the "real" German Army.

The report of the *Jäger* parade in Cologne would also be especially gratifying to the Berliners who read the *Vossische Zeitung*, which reprinted the description of the parade in its November 27 edition. The *Vossische Zeitung* was a prominent, liberal newspaper published in the

---

[1] The division included a number of guards' regiments to include the Guards Rifles, the Guards *Jägers*, and Guards Dragoons.
[2] Quoted in the *Vossische Zeitung*, November 27, 1918, "Der deutsche Rückmarsch: Der Einzug der Jägerdivision in Köln."

capital and, because the *Jäger* Division included units raised in the area around Berlin, many of the newspaper's readers were friends and family of the units marching through Cologne. These Berliners would have been grateful for the Rhineland's generous reception of the *Jägers* and might have looked forward to matching that celebration with their own when the division reached Berlin.

When the *Jägers* did reach Berlin, two and a half weeks later, they were part of a small army made up of the most celebrated units from the old *Kaiserheer*. Their entry into the capital was the occasion for carefully prepared ceremonial greeting that featured crowds, flags, garlands, and speeches from leaders of the old army as well as the new republic. No one could fault the Berliners for the warmth of their welcome. However, the entry of veteran combat troops into the German capital, December 10–21, had the potential to be much more than a festive event. As planned by the *Oberste Heeresleitung*, the OHL, the arrival of the veterans of the Western Front would mean an end to revolutionary unrest in Germany and a decisive suppression of "Bolshevik" extremism. That the parades did not evolve into such a political *coup de main* is, on one hand, a story of high-level political maneuvering, intrigue, and manipulation of popular opinion. On the other, however, the Berlin operation is the story of how the *Frontschweine* once again confounded the expectations of both those who led them on the Right and those that feared them on the Left.

If the footsore *Jägers* crossing the Rhine in late November were grateful for the reception they received, the joy of homecoming was tempered with a certain level of anxious uncertainty. They found themselves returning to a nation hungry, impoverished, and divided. The old imperial regime was gone but no one was certain what would finally take its place. The end of the war had brought peace and momentous political change, but it had left Germans with more questions about the future than answers. Would Germany remain a single Reich or would it spin off into its component states? Kurt Eisner's government in Munich, for example, already styled itself the "Free State of Bavaria." If Germany remained a unitary state, would it include the ethnic Germans of the old Austrian empire? Where would the boundaries of the new Germany be drawn? On the eastern frontier, the Poles and Czechs seemed to have designs on chunks of the old Reich, as did the Danes in the north, and the Belgians and French to the west. What would the Allies demand of Germany in terms of a peace settlement? It did not bode well that the Allies had imposed strict conditions for the armistice and continued the "hunger blockade" afterwards. Finally, assuming Germany remained one state, what kind of state would it be? Would it be a parliamentary democracy, a Soviet republic, or something else?

These were the question faced by Germany's new leaders, many of them unknown to the soldiers of the front-line army. Most likely, the *Fronttruppen* had heard of Friedrich Ebert, the chancellor of the new government, but they were unlikely to be familiar with some the other members of the coalition cabinet, Otto Landsberg or Emil Barth, for example. They would have been even less familiar with the leaders of the Executive Council (*Vollzugsrat*) of the Berlin Workers' and Soldiers' Councils, even though it claimed the authority to speak for all the councils in post-revolutionary Germany. If they were aware of this Executive Council, they would have been perplexed by its power-sharing relationship with Ebert's cabinet, a relationship superficially similar to the two-headed arrangement existing after the February Revolution in Russia, where Kerensky's Provisional Government had shared power with the Petrograd Soviet. Once again, though dominated in membership by Majority Socialists, the *Vollzugsrat* was more stridently revolutionary in its platform than the cabinet.[3] The tense and ill-defined relationship developed in mid November became even less comfortable in the first weeks of December.[4] At the same time, much of the real power across Germany remained diffused among the many local workers' and soldiers' councils.

On the far left of the political spectrum, outside the centers of governmental power, was the *Spartakusbund* (Spartacus League). Formed from members of the left wing of the Independent Socialists, the Spartacists believed the revolution was unfinished and openly sympathized with the Bolsheviks of Soviet Russia.[5] In the weeks that followed the downfall of the old regime, the Spartacists' most conspicuous leaders, Karl Liebknecht and Rosa Luxemburg, accused the Ebert government of compromising the revolution by leaving the old elites in positions of power in industry, the government ministries, and, especially, the army.

[3] The *Vollzugsrat*'s chairman, Richard Müller, and his confederate Brutus Molkenbuhr were considered especially radical in their views.
[4] See, for example, Herbert Michaelis, Ernst Schraepler, and Gunter Scheel, eds., *Ursachen und Folgen vom deutschen Zusammenbruch 1918 und 1945 bis zur staatlichen Neuordnung Deutschlands in der Gegenwart*, 2 vols. (Berlin: Herbert Wendler, 1958), Document 544: Vereinbarung zwischen dem Rat der Volksbeauftragten und dem Vollzugsrat des Berliner Arbeiter- und Soldatenräte vom 22. November 1918, 18–19, and Document 553: "Bekanntmachung des Rates der Volksbeauftragten und des Vollzugsrates der Arbeiter- und Soldatenräte vom 9. Dezember 1918," 33.
[5] The Spartacists would not constitute a separate political party until December 30, 1918, when they joined the left wing of the Independent Socialist to found the German Communist Party.

In late 1918, the number of Liebknecht's and Luxemburg's followers was small but growing in both numbers and militancy, especially in Germany's major cities. Historians would later judge that Liebknecht and Luxemburg were neither as cunning nor ruthless as Lenin, but in the weeks after November 9, the fiery rhetoric of the two Spartacist leaders terrified the German middle class and the army leadership, who feared that Liebknecht and his followers were plotting a Bolshevik-style Red terror.[6]

By the beginning of December, the differences between Ebert's government and the Spartacists were so irreconcilable that, to many Germans, an armed showdown seemed inevitable. While various militias and security forces were arming themselves across Germany, the key battleground would almost certainly be the capital of the Reich. In Berlin, the Ebert government looked to the city commandant, Otto Wels, a former paperhanger, to organize a *republikanische Soldatenwehr* (Republican Soldiers' Force) of several thousand volunteers.[7] Ostensibly augmenting the *Soldatenwehr* in the mission of protecting the provisional government was the *Volksmarinedivision*, the People's Naval Division. In the first days of the revolution, this curious formation had originally been formed from sailors who volunteered to serve as a guard detail around the key government buildings of the capital. By mid December, as more sailors from the fleet bases on the North Sea made their way to Berlin, its numbers grew to between 1,500 and 2,000 sailors. Elsewhere, the *Ersatz* battalions of the Berlin garrison could be counted on for large numbers, but offered very questionable cohesion and military effectiveness.[8] The police commissioner, Emil Eichorn, had his own armed group, the *Sicherheitswehr* (Security Force), whose members reflected his Independent Socialist views. Arrayed on the side of the Spartacists were a variety of workers' militias formed on the

---

[6] For such an assessment of Liebknecht, see Haffner, *Failure of a Revolution*, 141–4. Or, more recently, Detlev Peukert, *The Weimar Republic: The Crisis of Classical Modernity*, trans. Richard Deveson (New York: Hill and Wang, 1997), 32. Peukert suggested that, after their murder in January 1919, "Karl and Rosa" became much more significant as martyrs than they had been as leaders when they were alive.

[7] Colonel van den Bergh of the war ministry judged this formation to be of questionable value. It was led by men elected by the rank and file, and many of its approximately 10,000 members had signed on because of the high daily salary. Ernest van den Bergh, *Aus den Geburtsstunden der Weimarer Republik: Das Tagebuch des Obersten Ernst van den Bergh*, ed. Wolfram Wette (Dusseldorf: Droste Verlag, 1991), entry for 9 December. See also *Quellen*, II/2, Document 8: "Brief des Oberleutnant Knoerzer über die Bildung von Sicherheitsverbänden und die Haltung der Regierung, Dezember 6 1918," 23–4; and Böhm, *Adjutant*, diary entry of November 28, 91.

[8] Van den Bergh called them "nervous, suspicious, cowardly, more desirous of talking than shooting," *Aus den Geburtsstunden*, 56.

Figure 6.1 Homecoming German troops prepare to enter an
unidentified German town, December 7, 1918. The appearance of
such troops understandably encouraged the Right and frightened
the Left.

model of the Soviet Red Guards, and the *Rote Soldatenbund*, the Red
Soldiers' League. Their military value was uncertain, but, when the
Berlin garrison collapsed in the first days of the revolution, large stocks
of weapons and ammunition fell into their hands.[9]

Across the Reich

Just as the revolutionary days of early and mid November had given
way to new and uneasy power relationships in Berlin, similar adapta-
tions were being made in the other towns and cities of Germany. In
some areas, the new workers' and soldiers' councils were aggressive in
asserting their new power. In other places, the councils worked out relatively amicable working relationships with the representatives of the old

[9] The OHL estimated that up to 30,000 weapons had fallen into the hands of the "leftist elements of the population." Kriegsgeschichtlichen Forschungsanstalt des Heeres,
Die Wirren in der Reichshauptstadt und im nördlichen Deutschland, 1918–1920, from the
series, *Darstellungen aus den Nachkriegskämpfen deutscher Truppen und Freikorps* (Berlin:
Mittler und Sohn, 1940), 21.

regime. No matter what the local balance of power between old and new authorities in a given area of the homeland, that balance would be altered in late November and through December with the return of the front-line troops.

This was certainly the case with the elite Bavarian *Leib* Regiment, which returned to the homeland after a difficult retreat from the Balkan front. When it arrived in the homeland, it found the former Wittelsbach kingdom transformed into the "People's State of Bavaria," headed by the Independent Socialist Kurt Eisner. The First Battalion of the regiment marched into Munich on November 26 to a reception that mixed cheers, catcalls, and a welcome speech from the chairman of Munich's soldiers' council. The Third Battalion arrived two days later, marching in perfect order, led by the regimental commander, Colonel Ritter von Epp, who rejected a welcoming speech by any council members and, instead, ordered his troops to pass before him in review as they arrived at their barracks in the Türken caserne. The local soldiers' councils attempted to block the review but not until the bulk of the regiment had completed its march. The next day, the Second Battalion followed the first two battalions into the city. A few days later, the middle class of the city sponsored a greeting ceremony for the regiment at the Hoftheater. Eisner's government had promised not to disturb the festivities; however, during the ceremony, the USPD leader, Gustav Landauer, demanded an opportunity to speak to the troops. He proceeded to orate with what an eyewitness called a "fervent fanaticism," and, to the dismay of the burghers who sponsored the event, many of the troops were visibly moved by Landauer's revolutionary rhetoric. When he left, the eyewitness noted, "they were no longer the same troops." Yet, despite Landauer's impressive performance, the Left remained anxious about the activities of the regiment, to the point that, in order to quell rumors of a right-wing *putsch*, von Epp was compelled to create a tentative pact with the city commandant to uphold peace and order.[10]

In Munster, a garrison town in Westphalia, the soldiers' council held less power. There, the return of the 13th Infantry Regiment on December 8 received a more unalloyed reception. The citizens of Munster gave the "Thirteeners" ["*Dreizehner*"] a heroes' welcome as they marched through the city. As the regiment arrived at the *Prinzipalmarkt* in the center of the city, they found it decorated with the black-white-red flags of the old empire. The reception seemed proof

---

[10] Account of Leib Regiment's return from Schmolze, ed., *Revolution und Räterepublik in München*, 153–4; and Zorn, *Bayerns Geschichte*, 154–7. Von Epp would later become a famous *Freikorps* leader and the first *Statthalter* of Bavaria's National Socialist government.

that the populace put more faith in the front-line troops than the lightly regarded *Sicherheitsdienst* (Security Service), or the VII Corps general soldiers' council which exercised revolutionary authority for the district. With the agreement of Munster's mayor and the approval of much of the citizenry, the 13th Infantry Regiment took over security duties inside the city. The balance of power had shifted, and, later in December and January, the general soldiers' council watched almost helplessly as the citizens and the corps commander began recruiting *Freikorps* units in and around Munster.[11]

In Bremen, a large port city with a strong labor movement and a naval garrison, the revolution had taken a more radical turn. The local councils rejected the Ebert government's plans for a National Assembly, and would later, in January 1919, declare the establishment of the "Socialist Republic of Bremen." The first major front-line unit to return to the city was the 213th Reserve Infantry Regiment. Though the local workers' and soldiers' council anticipated its arrival with considerable anxiety, the unit's entry into the city on December 11 went initially without incident. The chairman of the local *Räte*, Bernhard Ecks, greeted the troops by praising the new republic, *Bürgermeister* Hildebrand led a cheer for the Fatherland, and the regimental commander, Major Kuttner, expressed the wish for a happy future. All seemed well as the unit moved to its caserne. However, the day after, fearing a counter-revolutionary conspiracy, the local revolutionaries arrested several officers and bourgeois leaders and held them until the following day.

The situation became far more earnest with the arrival of the 75th Infantry Regiment (1st Hanseatic), otherwise known as the "Bremen" Regiment. The 75th was late returning to Bremen as a result of an assignment guarding stores in the vicinity of Bonn and did not arrive on the outskirts of the city until December 28 and 29. Having discharged many of its oldest members, the regiment was down to 600 men, many of whom had the same proletarian background as the Bremen revolutionaries. Nevertheless, the unit's arrival put a sort of panic into the Independents and Spartacists of Bremen, who called for the creation of a Red Guard several thousand strong to serve as an armed counterweight to the *Fronttruppen*. As arms were distributed among the garrison troops, sailors, and workers, the officers of the 75th met with members of the city's middle class and, with them, demanded the restoration of the old city government and the authority to return to casernes within the city. Though tensions ran high, the two sides

[11] Franz-Josef Jacobi (with Thomas Küster), *Geschichte der Stadt Munster*, vol. II, *Das 19. und 20. Jahrhundert (bis 1945)* (Münster: Aschendorff, 1993), 223–7.

were able to craft a temporary arrangement that allowed the 75th to take up some of the security duties within the city and to send representatives to the Bremen workers' and soldiers' council. It appeared that violence had been avoided, and, on New Year's Day, the commander of the "Bremen" Regiment, Lieutenant Colonel Hagedorn, led his troops into a city where they were greeted by a crowd numbering tens of thousands.

Yet the city's soldiers' council had decided it could not allow an armed force of front-line troops inside the city. After the parade, as the 75th approached its barracks, it was confronted by workers and soldiers manning machine guns in windows and on trucks, led by the head of the soldiers' council, Bernhard Ecks. Ecks refused to speak with the officers and, instead, stood by a machine gun and told the men of the 75th that they were the victims of their officers' counter-revolutionary chicanery. They should lay down their weapons, he said, declare their support for the revolution, and go home. Both the officers of the regiment and the representatives of the regiment's soldiers' council protested the violation of the agreement that had allowed the unit to march into the city. After tense negotiations, the two sides reached a compromise. The 75th would give up its weapons to be stored under a guard maintained by its own troops as well as representatives of the revolutionary councils. Later, Ecks would justify breaking the agreement on the somewhat frivolous pretext that the reception of the front-line troops had featured the singing of the old *Deutschlandslied*. Armed conflict had been temporarily avoided, but, as the city's historian, Herbert Schwarzwalder observed, "All of these events, bringing Bremen to the brink of civil war, increased the hate and mistrust on both sides."[12]

Armed conflict was not avoided in the East Prussian town of Allenstein. In part, this may have been because some front-line troops did not arrive from the Western Front until late in December, when the Christmas crisis and the impending national election had exacerbated tension between the revolutionary councils and provisional government. The *Frankfurter Zeitung* reported:

On the morning of the 30th, the Artillery Regiment stationed in Allenstein was to march into the town with banners flying, accompanied by representatives of the Workmen's and Soldiers' Council. The troops refused to do this and tore up and burned the red banners. The Workmen's and Soldiers' Council then called out other troops and after repeating their order to march into the town with red banners flying, opened fire with machine guns and rifles on the

---

[12] Quotation and description of events in Bremen from Herbert Schwartzwalder, *Geschichte der Freien Hansestadt Bremen*, vol. III, *Bremen in der Weimarer Republik (1918–1933)* (Hamburg: Hans Christians Verlag, 1983), 39–50.

Figure 6.2 The OHL staff at Kassel after moving from Spa, Belgium, November, 1918. Hindenburg (1) stands in the center; Groener (3) to his right. Other officers mentioned in the text include Schleicher, extreme right, last row; Thaer stands two to the left of Hindenburg; Faupel (8) stands to his left. Franz von Papen (22) stands behind Thaer.

artillery regiment. Two officers were killed and a large number of officers and men wounded.[13]

Allenstein was an extreme case. Violence between the homeland councils and the troops returning home from the front was not the norm during December 1918, and by January most of the front-line units had dissolved. Yet there was a sequel. In the months that followed, both Bremen and Munich would be the scene of bloody fighting between the *Freikorps* and the Left, while incidents like the one in Allenstein served to inspire the vengeful ruthlessness of the front-line volunteers who fought for the government during the ensuing civil war.

Demobilization

The course of events in Munich, Munster, Bremen, and Allenstein served as examples of the troubled political situation that greeted the

[13] *Frankfurter Zeitung* quoted First Division, AEF G2, Report No. 123, January 4, 1919.

field-gray masses making their way back to the interior of the homeland. Overwhelmingly, the MSPD-dominated soldiers' councils within
the Field Army had declared themselves in favor of the Ebert government.[14] However, the complexities of the issues being debated in
Berlin – socialization of industry, the scheduling of a national assembly, and the organization of a federal state – held relatively little interest
for the front-line soldiers. They were interested primarily in schedules,
schedules for trains heading east and schedules for the discharge of
personnel.

The creation of these schedules was the business of the OHL, headed
by Field Marshal Paul von Hindenburg and Lieutenant General Wilhelm
Groener, and the war ministry under General Heinrich Scheuch.[15]
However, in a curious analogy to the bifurcated civilian government,
both the OHL and the war ministry claimed authority over the troop
units returning to Germany. According to the Siege Law of 1851,
mobilization gave the Prussian war ministry national-level authority
over forces in the homeland. Curiously, however, it did not exercise
direct authority over the deputy corps commanders,[16] who controlled
the twenty-four military districts within the Reich after the corps commander took his troops to war. Therefore, for example, in 1914, when
the commander of the III Corps, recruited in the area around Berlin
(Brandenburg), deployed his troops to his mobilization assembly areas,
his deputy assumed control over the garrisons and replacement units
in the III Corps Military District. The deputy corps commander also
received sweeping powers over civil affairs within the district, often
to the great exasperation of the civilian bureaucracy. Since the deputy
corps commanders did not report to the war ministry, each was free
to interpret his responsibility for "public safety" as he saw fit. It was a
genuinely dysfunctional system.[17]

On November 15, the *Vollzugsrat* of the Berlin workers' and soldiers'
councils had proclaimed that the Prussian war ministry under Scheuch
would be a single military authority to control the military and its demobilization. He would have authority over the OHL, the deputy corps

[14] *Vossische Zeitung* on Bad Ems, "Schluß der Frontsoldaten-Tagung," December 3,
    1918.
[15] The Prussian war ministry, to be precise. The other federal states had their own
    war ministries, but the Prussian ministry had national authority. Scheuch (1864–
    1946) had served as war minister since October 9, 1918. Van den Bergh, *Aus den
    Geburtsstunden*, 32, fn. 21.
[16] Except in Bavaria, where the deputy corps commanders reported to the Bavarian war
    ministry.
[17] Description of the Siege Law system from Gerald Feldman, *Army Industry and Labor
    in Germany, 1914–1918* (Princeton University Press, 1966), 31–3.

commanders, and all other army headquarters.[18] For the revolutionary government this move served two useful purposes: (1) it rationalized the glaring inefficiencies of the decentralized wartime system, and (2), perhaps more importantly, put the military's single senior authority in Berlin, where it could be closely monitored and controlled. On the face of it, this was a sensible move.

However, Groener and the officers of the Field Army had performed a minor miracle in bringing the *Westheer* home, and they saw no reason to disrupt a chain of command that seemed to be reasserting the army's order and discipline. Even more importantly, at their head was the powerfully symbolic figure of Hindenburg.[19] Thus, to the dismay of the war ministry, after displacing the headquarters from Spa to the Wilhelmshöhe castle outside Kassel in mid November,[20] the OHL continued to give orders to the units of the Field Army both in the East and West, even while these units moved deep into Germany. As a result, in the first months after the armistice, the relationship between the OHL and the *Kriegsministerium* was, like the relationship of *Vollzugsrat* and Ebert's cabinet, tense and ill defined.

The strained relationship was illustrated by a meeting between Colonel van den Bergh of the war ministry and Colonel Heye, chief of the operations section of the OHL.[21] Van den Bergh's diary entry does not indicate the date of the meeting but does recall the topic: what courses of action were available for maintaining internal order? Heye said the OHL's favored alternative was the employment of "reliable" troops taken from the units returning from the front. Van den Bergh denounced the proposal and warned, "The troops will melt like butter in the sun once they have spent any time in the homeland, and they would fail when they are exposed to the influence of the big city." Instead, van den Bergh recommended the deactivation of the old army's active and *Ersatz* battalions to be replaced as rapidly as possible by a well-paid, republican people's force (*Volkswehr*). Such an organization, he argued, would be based on legal grounds and could serve as the transition to a future *Reichswehr*.[22]

The two men's views could not be reconciled. Van den Bergh had experienced what the revolution looked like on the streets of Berlin, and

---

[18] BA-R, R43/2482, f.1, Executive Council Proclamation of November 15, 1918, 15.
[19] Wolfgang Elben, *Das Problem der Kontinuität in der deutschen Revolution, 1918–1919* (Düsseldorf, Droste Verlag, 1965), 142.
[20] Thaer's diary describes the move of 13–14 November as "fairly dramatic." In a number of instances, revolutionary roadblocks seemed ready to open fire on the OHL staff as it moved east into Germany. *Generalstabdienst an der Front*, 273.
[21] Recall that Heye had been the director of the *Armeeparlament* of November 9.
[22] Van den Bergh, *Aus den Geburtsstunden*, diary entry for December 25, 1918, 65.

he had worked in a war ministry that often seemed besieged by hostile elements. In his view, Heye's proposals reflected hopeless naïveté. In contrast, for Heye, the *Westheer* was the best hope of restoring order in Germany. As a representative of the front-line troops, Heye was confident that he knew what the veterans of the Western Front could do. What is more, he and the other members of the *Westheer* believed that the weakness of the army's leadership in the homeland had contributed to the debacle of November 9. The front-line troops would have to make things right.[23]

Heye's outlook also reflected the fact that the march across the Rhine had relieved much of the depression that had settled on the OHL staff in the immediate aftermath of the revolution. Groener and his subordinates believed the conduct of the troops gave reason for guarded optimism about the army's future. Yet, if their achievement in bringing the army back to Germany had restored some of their confidence, the OHL staff had little opportunity for celebration. In the first days of December, the headquarters of the Field Army faced a number of urgent and daunting missions. They included planning and executing the demobilization of the *Frontheer*, bringing troops home from the East, establishing frontier defense in the East and West, building a cadre and administrative framework for a future army, and restoring peace and order in the homeland.

Demobilization, in particular, demanded the army's immediate attention. When the war ended, there were some 6 million men waiting to be released into a resource-starved economy in fraught transition from a war footing to peacetime production. The German government had been considering the problems of demobilization since 1917, but planning had been predicated on the assumption of German victory.[24] The relatively sudden collapse of the Wilhelmine regime meant the war ministry needed a new plan in a hurry, and the Field Army needed to use every available device to hold soldiers within their units until a plan was in place.

To that end, the one soldier with the greatest remaining moral authority in the army, Field Marshal von Hindenburg, had made this appeal to the front-line troops near the end of November:

Soldiers, you that have held out loyally more than four years in the land of the enemy, think of this, how infinitely important it is for the army and the homeland that the return of the armies and the discharge of its units be carried out in full peace and order. The numerous difficulties that accompany the

---

[23] Van den Bergh complained of the OHL's attitude of "infallibility." *Ibid.*, 64–5.
[24] Bessel, *Germany after the First World War*, 76–7.

homecoming of such a massive force can only be overcome if every individual among you remains faithfully at his post until the hour of discharge from the ranks of the army comes. You, that in battle so often subordinated yourself to the well-being of others, do not forget now, that the homeland needs your sacrifice in these last hours.[25]

Hindenburg went on to promise the men that, except for the year groups 1896–9, men would be released as rapidly as possible. He cautioned them to be patient with the shortage of rail transportation and warned them not to be "seduced" into leaving their units ahead of schedule.[26]

As so often happened in the weeks after November, the proclamations of Hindenburg and the OHL reflected the view that the front-line soldiers were a body set apart from the rest of the army. The front-line soldiers, through their sacrifice, had demonstrated soldierly virtues that the government and the generals could not expect from the rest of the army. To the German officer corps represented by Hindenburg, these virtues were the basis for a successful demobilization.

What did such a demobilization look like? By November 1918, the broad goals of the army's planned demobilization had become (1) a reduction in strength to approximately prewar levels, with the rank and file drawn from the 1896–9 year groups; (2) the discharge of older men in a phased program controlled by their units from their peacetime casernes, the oldest year groups being released first;[27] (3) the designation of selected units for duty on the Eastern and Western frontiers, (4) rapid conduct of all aspects of the demobilization.[28]

On the surface the plan was sensible, but it was fatally flawed. As it turned out, the army achieved only the last objective.[29] The youngest

---

[25] "Hindenburg an das Feldheer," *Vossiche Zeitung*, 29 November 1918.

[26] *Ibid.*

[27] Priority was also to be given to railway workers, miners, social services workers, and those employed in food processing. Döblin, *Sieger und Besiegte*, 15.

[28] Description of the demobilization plan from Bessel, *Germany after the First World War*, 77. For officers the plan was different. Active (prewar) officers would remain on duty; if their unit was inactivated they would be assigned other, temporary duties. Wartime officers, if not in key positions, were to be discharged immediately. Berthold and Neef, *Militarismus und Opportunismus*, Document 61: "Verfügung des Kriegsministeriums vom 19. November 1918," 200.

[29] Some of the success of the demobilization was due to serendipitous circumstance. Instead of returning to Germany at the same time, geography, command and control, and politics caused the different elements of the Field Army to return over an extended period of time. Thus, the *Westheer* had largely closed into the homeland by December 1918, the forces in Poland, northern Russian, and the Balkans by January 1919, the forces in the Kiev Army Group by February and March, 1919. Some unfortunate German detachments in the Caucusus did not reach Germany until July 1919. *Die Schlachten und Gefechten des Grossen Krieges, 1914: Quellenwerk nach den amtliches*

year groups had been called to the colors during the last months of a lost war; they had no desire to serve the discredited army and no desire to be the last ones searching for a job in an uncertain labor market.[30] The older men were impatient to get home and tended to believe that waiting for a discharge order in an overcrowded caserne, perhaps a considerable distance from home and family (and, possibly, work), was a fool's errand. Thus, young and old soldiers left on their own initiative by the hundreds of thousands, not waiting for the discharge papers, 50-mark stipend, and a free suit of clothes offered to men who left on schedule.[31] In other cases, the OHL bowed to the pressures from army group and army headquarters, and some divisions scheduled for rail movement were allowed instead to continue their foot march east. In other cases, if a unit's march route took it near the home of one of the older soldiers, he was discharged on the spot instead of continuing on to the designated demobilization area (*Demobort*). The pressure to let the men go was enormous. Groener wrote later, "To be discharged as soon as possible was the desire of every individual. The pull of hearth and home overcame patriotic feelings. Many divisions could scarcely wait until they were loaded on to trains."[32] When a courier from the OHL visited the headquarters of Army Group D, a staff officer there told him that the enlisted staff had announced, "If you don't let us go before Christmas, then we'll walk away from the telephone and let the officers operate it themselves."[33] Concessions by the OHL only seemed to confuse the situation as (to paraphrase the Elder Moltke) counter-order followed order, which was followed, in turn, by disorder.[34]

Bezeichnungen. Collected by the Great General Staff (Berlin: Verlag von Hermann Sack, 1919), 412–19.

[30] This was a special worry of the troops on the Eastern Front, where disorder, political wrangling, and transport difficulties delayed the return of the *Ostheer*. The OHL asked the government to reassure the men in the East that they would not be disadvantaged in the hunt for work. BA-R, R43/2500/5, transcript of Giebel's call to Ebert, dated December 3, 1918, 37. Groener suggested that the government set up committees in every town and city with the sole purpose of ensuring that returning soldiers get a fair opportunity for work. This issue was a great source of concern to the front-line troops. BA-R, R43/2500/5, transcript of call from Groener to Ebert, dated December 5, 1918, 42.

[31] BA-R, R43/2482, demobilization instructions from the Executive Council, dated November 23, 1918, 33.

[32] Groener, *Lebenserrinerungen*, 473. Groener, who had made a name for himself before the war as the General Staff's railroad expert, observed that the rail situation was especially difficult due to the vast quantities of rolling stock turned over to the Allies as a result of the Armistice agreement.

[33] BA-MA, N46/130, Nachlass Groener, letter of General Staff Officer Queis, Ia, document 117751, dated August 4, 1919

[34] Allied observers were also befuddled. One AEF Intelligence summary reported, "Conflicting reports are being received regarding the number of men to be retained.

Given these circumstances, by the end of 1918, the army found it had neither enough men to reach prewar strength nor enough complete units to perform border security missions. What remained of unit *cohesion* was powerless to staunch the loss of manpower once the *Frontheer* had reached the Fatherland: it stood little chance when matched against the *Drang nach Hause*. Appeals to a unit's glorious fighting record, the brotherhood of the trenches, or the affection inspired by a highly regarded leader could do relatively little to brake the army's dissolution. Indeed, front-line soldiers were likely to exhibit the highest degree of solidarity when confronted with an impediment to the earliest possible return to home and family.[35]

The numbers tell the story. On December 17, the demobilization office of the war ministry reported that 300,000–400,000 men had already been discharged.[36] Two weeks later, the same office indicated that, of the approximately 3 million men of the *Westheer*, only 300,000 remained, along with 200,000 ill-used horses. By the end of January 1919, the 6-million-man army of November 1918 was down to 1 million. Of just over 3 million troops in the *Westheer*, an estimated 1 million departed the army without an official discharge.[37] Within six weeks of the armistice, the once-powerful army of the German Reich was melting away faster than the various staffs could update their strength reports.[38] On the last day of 1918, an order by the government announcing that the army and navy would be in a state of "demobilization" (*Demobil*) effective January 10, 1919, merely recognized an existing condition.[39]

In some places, the local authorities had been able to conduct mass discharges in fairly orderly fashion, in others they lost control, and, in still others, the activities of the local councils undermined efforts to

A discharged railroad employee says that he knows positively that only the classes of 1918 and 1919 are to be retained. The original intention of the higher authorities had been to retain the classes of 1916–1917 / 1918–1919, but this had been changed." NARA, RG 120, Box 5895, Third Army G2 Summary of Intelligence, no. 25, dated December 11, 1918.

[35] Recall the example of the 15th Bavarian Division, which threatened mass desertion when tasked with border security duty. Lipp, *Meinungslenkung*, 168.

[36] This does not include the estimated 1 million men of the *Etappe* who abandoned their units to return home during the first days of the revolution.

[37] German Historical Museum, Exhibit Item Do2/72/1054, "Maueranschlag mit einem Telegramm der Regierung an die OHL zur Aufrecherhaltung der Disziplin."

[38] Bessel, *Germany after the First World War*, 79. Richard Bessel, an American historian living in Britain, has done the most extensive modern research on Germany's military and economic demobilization. He concludes: "the German Army in late 1918 [was] capable only of doing precisely what the overwhelming mass of soldiers wanted it to do."

[39] BA-R, R43/2485/f, "Demobilization and *Landsturm* Dissolution Order," dated December 31, 1918, 153.

bring order to the process. The district commander in the X Corps District (Braunschweig), for example, complained that the local council had ignored all of the orders from the government and the war ministry, had arbitrarily dissolved all units, and discharged all officers. There was no chance for an orderly demobilization, and the corps headquarters had ended up sending soldiers from Braunschweig to process their discharges.[40]

Afterwards, Groener would have to defend himself against charges from the Right that the OHL had been responsible for allowing the old army to disintegrate. To these charges, Groener responded that, for the bulk of the army, the pressure from below gave the Supreme Headquarters no options. Some units had troops disperse on their own. In other cases, the south German states demanded the return of their soldiers even when this created north–south traffic that disrupted the generally east to west movement of the Field Army.

With a heavy heart and *under the pressure of the Front* [original underlined], because of the general urge to get home [*Drang nach Hause*], the OHL authorized part of the divisions to go to their demobilization stations by foot march, and, with agreement with the K.M. [*Kriegsministerium*], to expedite the return of the oldest year groups. However, these measures made little improvement. The urge to get home was always general.[41]

In other words, "the front" had forced Groener and his staff to give in. Here, once again, the front-line troops imposed their will on events and confounded the expectations of the army's senior leadership and the government.

For the OHL, the army's disintegration made accomplishment of its other missions problematic. Groener wrote, "In the first days after 9/10 November, we in the OHL had considered the dream that we would have enough reliable troops to build a Border Defense Force on the Rhine. This hope proved false." In frustration, he resorted to uncharacteristic hyperbole, writing that troops that had marched home in perfect order remained under the control of their officers unit the precise moment they reached the Rhine and encountered the "revolutionary atmosphere."[42]

The chain of command's *management* of soldier perceptions, like the power of cohesion, operated with limited effectiveness as the Field

[40] BA-R, R43/2485/f, "Telegram from Hanover," from *Generalkommando* X to the war ministry, dated December 1, 1918, 133.
[41] BA-MA, N 46/130, Nachlass Groener, Groener memorandum on demobilization, Ia, document 117757, dated May 30, 1919.
[42] Groener, *Lebenserinnerungen*, 472.

Army penetrated into the interior of Germany. When the chain of command cited the depredations of *Drückeberger* and homeland councils in attacking the army's supply line, this could serve to build hostility to the revolution among soldiers marching through Belgium or the Rhineland. These claims made far less impact in Brandenburg or Bavaria. Similarly, west of the Rhine, the army staffs could distribute flyers warning of the danger of Bolshevism and convince the front-line soldiers that the nation was in danger. However, when units reached their home districts where cheering citizens greeted them, such propaganda seemed irrelevant. The government might assure soldiers that there would be work waiting for every returning veteran, but, for a man cooling his heels in a caserne, waiting for the processing of his discharge papers, trusting such promises must certainly have seemed a risky proposition.

Even as it was losing control of demobilization, the German Army had to deal with the other problems pressing on and outside the frontier of the Reich. Bringing the soldiers home from the Eastern Front was, in particular, an operation that presented a myriad of complex and politically sensitive issues. On the Baltic coast German troops were organizing themselves into volunteer units to fight the Bolsheviks.[43] In the Ukraine, German units were finding it difficult to extricate themselves from the fighting between the Reds, Whites, and the Ukrainian nationalists. Field Marshal von Mackensen, meanwhile, was making a difficult retreat through Hungary with the German detachments from the Macedonian front. On the Silesian frontier, the new Polish state was fomenting insurrection among the ethnic Poles around Posen while making common cause with the most revolutionary local councils among the ethnic Germans.

Finding troops for the eastern frontier put the OHL in a special quandary. It had deployed a number of units from the *Westheer* to the Silesian border, but these, too, suffered the dissolution experienced by the remainder of the army.[44] Nor could the High Command call on units returning to Germany from inside Poland. The German garrisons of Warsaw, Lodz, and other Polish cities had largely overthrown their officer chains of command and, in many cases, turned their weapons

---

[43] This inspired enormous outrage on the Left.
[44] In a message to the troops of the 234th Division, slated for assignment on the eastern border, the chain of command warned: "Since the 234th Division has been assigned to garrison the border and must remain there for approximately half the year, I hope the cohesion that has existed among the front-line troops up to now will remain in the future. We are now coming into an area where the workers' and soldiers' councils hold power." Michaelis *et al.*, eds., *Ursachen und Folgen*, Document 747, 500.

and equipment over to Marshal Pilsudski's Polish forces as the price for transport back to Germany.[45]

Lacking reliable troops to handle the security missions along the eastern frontier, the army would eventually turn to a new expedient, formations made up of volunteers, otherwise known as *Freikorps*. German government leaders began to plan for such units even before the revolution, but the rapidly decaying condition of the army in the weeks after the armistice added immediacy to such considerations.[46] In the event, however, it was the initiative of men like General Maercker, commander of the 214th Division, which led to the more or less spontaneous creation of the earliest such volunteer units.[47] With relatively little oversight from the OHL, these new formations began to form along the Polish border, outside Berlin, and elsewhere.[48]

"Peace and order"

To Groener and his staff, however, the importance of maintaining order within the Reich trumped these problems on the frontier. The danger that weighed on every officer's mind was the frightening example of what had happened to Russia, where frightening political extremists, the Bolsheviks, had overturned a moderate revolutionary government. The Russian example, no doubt, served to inspire the pact between Groener and Ebert on November 10.[49] The secret agreement between the First Quartermaster General and the chancellor had been solidified by Hindenburg's public declaration of support for the Majority Socialist government on November 10: "It may be disseminated, that the OHL, with Reich Chancellor Ebert, until now the leader of the moderate Social Democratic Party, desire to proceed together to prevent the spread of terroristic Bolshevism in Germany."[50] Germany's military leaders still saw Ebert's government as the best hope for "saving what could be saved" of the army and the nation.[51]

---

[45] Volkmann, *Marxismus und das deutsche Heer*, 263–4. See also, Kluge, *Soldatenräte und Revolution*, 97–101.
[46] Schüddekopf, *Das Heer und die Republik*, Document 15, 48.
[47] See the bitter denunciation of the OHL's failure by a "front-line" general in General von Maercker's personal account, *Vom Kaiserheer zur Reichswehr: Ein Beitrag zur Geschichte der deutschen Revolution* (Leipzig: Verlag v. K.F. Koehler, 1921), 40–1.
[48] Schüddekopf, *Das Heer und die Republik*, 42.
[49] For a discussion of how the Russian example shaped the views of Ebert and his government, see Walter Mühlhausen, *Friedrich Ebert 1871–1925: Reichspräsident der Weimarer Republik* (Bonn: J.H.W. Dietz Verlag, 2006), 160–2.
[50] Berthold and Neef, *Militarismus und Opportunismus*, Document 21: "Befehl Hindenburgs an das deutsche Feldheer vom 10. November 1918," 150–1.
[51] On November 17, Groener wrote his wife: "What the future will bring, who knows? The Field Marshal and I want to support Ebert, who I view as a straightforward,

As well as backing Ebert, the army leadership also chose to support the key goal of the Majority Socialists, the convention of a National Assembly. To this end, on November 19, the OHL called on the chain of command of the *Westheer* to promulgate a pro-government message from the soldiers' council of the OHL. It began:

To all soldiers' councils of the Field Army!

Comrades!

Through negotiations we have had with the representatives of the soldiers' councils of the Field Army, a total agreement on goals has resulted. All want to strengthen the current revolutionary government of Ebert–Haase and greet with joy the early convention of a National Assembly, summoned with the cooperation of the members of the Field Army, which will allow the further construction of our new Reich. We refuse to have our victory over the former dictators misused to create a new dictatorship, which would lead to Russian conditions.[52]

In this regard, the senior officers of the old army found themselves in harmony with the political positions expressed by the soldiers' councils within the front-line units. As the conference at Bad Ems had shown, Majority Socialists dominated these councils. However, support of a National Assembly hardly signaled the transformation of the old army's senior leaders into advocates of social equality and representative democracy. Instead, men like Groener viewed a National Assembly as the best way to supplant the power of the soldiers' and workers' councils as well as the best means for allowing the conservative elements of German society to reassert themselves in national politics.[53]

Supporting Ebert and his policies required the officers to overcome considerable cognitive dissonance. The old Prussian, Hindenburg, would be a unrepentant monarchist until he died; Groener, the more pragmatic Württemburger, had been a monarchist as well, at least until the events of November 9 forced him to choose between his warlord and the army. The OHL staff and virtually all of the army's senior leaders were profoundly conservative and hostile to socialism as a political force. Yet, in the days after the Kaiser's abdication, they had chosen to

honorable and upstanding character, as long as the cart doesn't slide too far to the left." Quoted in Dorothea Groener-Geyer, *General Groener: Soldat und Staatsmann* (Frankfurt am Main: Societäts Verlag, 1955), 117.

[52] Berthold and Neef, *Militarismus und Opportunismus*, Document 60: "Aufruf des Soldatenrates bei der OHL an die Soldatenräte des Feldheeres vom 19. November 1918," 198.

[53] Groener's November 17 letter to his wife, Groener-Geyer, *General Groener*, 117. See also Thaer, *Generalstabdienst an der Front*, diary entry for 15 November. Thaer wrote that once peace and order were restored, a conservatively oriented republic was possible and that it was Groener's hope that the middle-class parties would unite to restore the necessary counterweight to the socialists. *Ibid.*, 269.

work in support of Ebert's government. Marxist historians have long insisted that these men were dead set on strangling the young revolution in its cradle, but this seems to overlook the fact that Groener, with Hindenburg standing behind him, probably played the decisive role in persuading Wilhelm II to abdicate. Beyond that, the German Army's leaders knew, with a final peace treaty still unsigned, that the Entente would not tolerate a Hohenzollern restoration or a military dictatorship. What the officers did want was a strong government acceptable to the populace but led decisively by a man who would protect the nation from extremism and assure the army of an "appropriate" role in the new Germany of the postwar era. Hindenburg, Groener, and their subordinates seemed to believe that Ebert fit this description as well as any man could. The army's senior officers held a simplistic understanding of the political struggles going on inside the homeland; they tended to see the Independent Socialists in Ebert's cabinet as a dangerous obstacle to vigorous action and the *Vollzugsrat* as close partner to the dangerous Spartacists.[54] Motivated by such views, the officer corps was willing to put the front-line troops, the only forces they still controlled, at the service of the former saddle-maker and union leader, Ebert.

Still, if the army's bayonets were needed to strengthen the Ebert government, they would need to be collected and deployed at the decisive political point, Berlin. And, though the army seemed to be melting away, the OHL was not as ready to abandon the hope that some part of the old army might still be employed for that purpose. Given the condition of the *Heimatheer* and the troops in the East, that part would necessarily have to come from among the *Fronttruppen* arriving in Germany from the Western Front. In a confidential message of November 16, entitled "Guidelines for Influence on the Troops," Groener wrote, "The government depends on the authorities within the federal states, which, however, have almost exclusively surrendered their power to more or less radical *A- and S- Räte*. These councils are, for most part, incapable of performing their duties." Groener went on to say that the army had told the Ebert government that they would recognize only the established authorities and would allow the local workers' and soldiers' councils an advisory role. "Whether the government is in the position to restore the old authorities is doubtful. They have, above all, no power source (*Machtfaktor*) behind them," he affirmed. Thus, the orderly return of the front-line units had an importance for Germany's future that went beyond the care and recognition of the troops.

---

[54] Rakenius offers a persuasive analysis of the OHL's political "estimate of the situation." *Wilhelm Groener als erster Generalquartiermeister*, 125–6 and 139.

The new government needs a power source on which it can support itself and provide the necessary prestige to resist all pressures. Only a cohesive, well-ordered, returning Field Army can give the present government the power and prestige to be secure against the putsches of terrorists.

Thus, the cohesive return of the Field Army has taken on a meaning far beyond military affairs; it preserves us from dangerous upheavals [to the nation].[55]

Such a message appealed to subordinate leaders to view the combat veterans under their command as the single best remaining hope for Germany's future.

However, the forces of dissolution threatened the "cohesive, well-ordered" force that Groener believed so critical. The question for the OHL was whether they could assemble sufficient "reliable" troops for a show of force that would either cow the Spartacists, or, if necessary, conduct a combat operation to suppress the government's enemies. It appeared to be a race between the army's impending dissolution and the inevitable showdown between the "Bolsheviks" and the Ebert government.[56]

The showdown might come sooner rather than later. A National Congress of Workers' and Soldiers' Councils was scheduled in Berlin for December 16–21, and the army leadership feared the congress would strengthen the council movement at the expense of the government. The OHL had already had an unhappy experience with the assembly of front-line councils at Bad Ems and feared extremists would hijack the National Congress to their own ends. Thus, the opening date of the congress gave the Berlin operation an extra urgency and new deadline: December 16.[57]

---

[55] Berthold and Neef, *Militarismus und Opportunismus*, Document 54: "Richtlinien fur die Einwirkung auf die Truppe," 187–90.

[56] In an important but mysterious letter from either Groener or Schleicher to an unknown confidant ("Lieber Freund"), the author wrote that, at that moment (December 1), the morale and discipline of the troops were good. "They will do all that the government orders. Only one danger exists: the troops are diverted to go home to see parents, wife, and child. The greater, on one hand, the authority of the officers is maintained – those now at the *front* retain their full status – and the faster, on the other hand, the troops employed [for operations in Berlin] may be relieved by national security troops formed from good elements of the Field Army, the less is this danger ... In my opinion, it all comes down to this, that the government decisively and cleverly uses the days of the entry [of the troops into the capital] to strengthen its position and create order." BA-MA, N 42/11, Nachlass Schleicher, "Lieber Freund" letter, dated December 1, 1918.

[57] Erwin Könnemann, "Der Truppeneinmarsch am 10. Dezember in Berlin. Neue Dokumente zur Novemberrevolution." *Zeitschrift für Geschichtswissenschaft*, 16 (12) (1968), 1593.

Figure 6.3 The city commandant and the Berlin soldiers' councils call for aid to homecoming front-line soldiers.

The OHL makes a plan

Good staff officers pride themselves on anticipating requirements, and the army began planning for an operation in support of the Provisional Government shortly after the army started on its return march to the homeland. In fact, two plans were developed. In Berlin, a

Colonel Hans von Haeften, the OHL's liaison to the government, and a Dr. Walter Simons, a minister in the Reich chancellery, together conceived an ambitious plan to restore peace and order.[58] They proposed to Ebert, the war ministry, and the OHL that the military be used to enact the total overthrow of the workers' and soldiers' councils and the establishment of Ebert as a provisional Reich president invested with dictatorial power. Ebert gave the idea mixed reviews. The war minister, Scheuch, thought the project had interesting prospects but refused to direct the action. For its part, the OHL, represented by Colonel Heye, believed the war ministry was the key to such an ambitious and politically charged operation, and when Scheuch opted out, so did Heye and the OHL.[59]

The OHL had a plan of its own. As originally conceived within the staff, the High Command would assemble some ten handpicked divisions around Berlin and, when the appropriate signal was given, these divisions would march into the capital and disarm the enemies of the government, if necessary by armed force. Groener may or may not have been an enthusiastic participant in the conception of the plan,[60] but already by mid November, he was ready to dispatch three of his most trusted subordinates, his own adjutant, Colonel Hans Tieschowitz, his political advisor, Major Kurt von Schleicher, and Colonel Albrecht von Thaer, to pick the units best suited for the mission.[61] As the *Westheer* streamed across the Rhine, these three officers moved from command post to command post, in and around the endless field-gray columns, to find commanders willing to certify their men were ready for what the OHL staff eventually called the "Berlin Operation."

As a result of their travels, Groener's agents identified nine divisions for the special mission. Not surprisingly, almost all were Guard units originally stationed and headquartered in the III Corps area around Berlin.[62] The choice had an additional benefit: along with their presumed steadfastness, the deployment of Guard units near their home

---

[58] Until the revolution, von Haeften had been the military liaison to the foreign ministry. After November 21, he served as a liaison between the OHL and the cabinet, Rakenius, *Wilhelm Groener als erster Generalquartiermeister*, 135.

[59] Description of the "Haeften Option" from *ibid.*, 134–5. Berthold and Neef, *Militarismus und Opportunismus*, Document 120: "Oberst von Haeften uber Vorbereitung der Konterrevolution anlasslich des Truppeneinzugs in Berlin in Dezember 1918 (Auszug)," 293–6.

[60] Rakenius believes he was initially skeptical: *Wilhelm Groener als erster Generalquartiermeister*, 134.

[61] Description of the original concept from Thaer, *Generalstabdienst an der Front*, 273.

[62] Later, the soldiers' council of the OHL would complain to the government that the officers had chosen the troops to enter Berlin without consultation with the council. It was clear, the council asserted, that the officers had picked regiments where the

station was unlikely to raise as much suspicion as would be the case with units from other parts of Germany.[63]

If the chosen units might be initially uncertain of their intended role, the nature of their mission was spelled out by a secret order issued by Army Group B on November 16. The order instructed subordinate armies that units chosen should be staffed by as many active officers as possible, should be supplied with plentiful ammunition and "close-combat weapons," and should have their machine-gun companies fully manned. Unreliable elements, the order stated, should be separated "inconspicuously" and exchanged for more reliable men during the deployment. The cover story would be that the army intended to maintain certain active divisions, and these units required weapons and ammunition to guard against plunderers and other dangerous elements cast up by the uncertain political situation.[64]

Before planning could go too far, the operation needed a commander. Since the war minister, Scheuch had shown no enthusiasm for such a *coup de main*, the OHL was an obvious choice to direct the operation. According to time-honored military principles of command and control, the logical move would have been to transfer the headquarters to Berlin, where it could maintain a close liaison with the unit commanders, the war ministry, and Ebert. However, Groener felt uneasy about the project's chances for success. The course of the demobilization had given him ample cause for worry about the steadiness of the troops. Ebert, he feared, might lack the "ruthless will and extreme boldness" required to move decisively against his enemies. Moreover, if the operation miscarried, Liebknecht and his followers might be emboldened to launch their own coup. In such a contingency, the OHL would need freedom of action that a headquarters in the capital would not offer. Finally, Hindenburg's name still carried enormous weight with the

councils were weak and the officers strong. BA-R, R43/2500/4, Eduard Weckerle, "Fur eine republikanische Volkswehr," dated January 4, 1919, 69.

[63] The deputy corps commander for the guards was headquartered in Berlin and many of the largest guards casernes were located in or near Berlin. As an additional consideration, because the guards were recruited from across Prussia, many of the guardsmen would not have homes nearby and might be less susceptible to family pressures to come home. There is some indication that the OHL sought to reinforce the first nine divisions with others. See for example, BA-R, 43/2485, telegram from the OHL to the Reich leadership, dated December 13, 1918, #5815. In this message, Groener asked permission to bring the 4th Infantry Division, on its way home to Pomerania, through Berlin. The message suggested that a route through Berlin would not take the unit too far off its path to its demobilization area.

[64] Berthold and Neef, *Militarismus und Opportunismus*, Document 53: "Befehl – streng geheim – des Oberkommandos der 11. Armee auf Weisung der Heeresgruppe B vom 16. November 1918," 186.

German people and it would be foolish to associate the field marshal with a failure.[65]

Weighing these considerations, Groener decided that it would be best to separate the OHL from the operation both in physical distance and in function.[66] His solution to the command problem was the creation of a special, corps-level headquarters. He chose as its commander an experienced and trustworthy commander, Major General Arnold Lequis, and assigned a trusted officer from his own headquarters, Major Bodo von Harbou, to serve as Lequis' chief of staff. As the divisions arrived at their initial assembly areas north, south, and west of Berlin, *Generalkommando* (General Command) Lequis would assume command of them and direct their subsequent entry into the capital.[67]

On December 1, Groener and his staff met with Lequis to establish the objectives and time-line for execution of the new command's mission. The goals they set were ambitious:

December 10: The Guards Cavalry Rifle Division would be the first unit to enter the city. Pro-government forces would occupy key government buildings and the Ebert government would issue an announcement of welcome. The *Jäger* Division and the 1st Guard Division would remain in reserve outside the city.

December 11: The German *Jäger* Division would enter the city; the 1st Guards Division would march into Potsdam. The populace would surrender all weapons and the government would issue a proclamation stating that those found in possession of weapons without the proper authorization (*Waffenschein*) would be shot (as would those who had assumed official positions without legal basis). Deserters and sailors would be given ten days to report to the appropriate unit headquarters. Reliable forces would begin sweeps through certain areas of the capital.[68]

December 12: The 4th Guards Division arrives. The government would begin certification of those claiming to be unemployed or need of special relief.

---

[65] Rakenius, *Wilhelm Groener als erster Generalquartiermeister*, 136.
[66] Groener's decision-making process and quotation from Erwin Könnemann, "Der Truppeneinmarsch am 10. Dezember in Berlin: Neue Dokumente zur Novemberrevolution." *Zeitschrift fur Militargeschichte* (GDR), 16 (1968), 1597. See also, Ekkehart Guth, *Die Loyalitätskonflikt des deutschen Offizierskorps in der Revolution, 1918–1920* (Frankfurt: Peter Lang, 1985), 64–5.
[67] Rakenius, *Wilhelm Groener als erster Generalquartiermeister*, 136.
[68] One assumes here that this meant the working-class districts like Wedding, Prenzlauer Berg, and Lichtenberg.

December 13: The 5th Guards Division arrives. The government promulgates an order throughout the entire Reich directing that the authority and symbols (rank insignia, decorations, side arms, required salutes, etc.) of the old officer corps would be restored. The legal civil authorities and troops would reassert control over their regular functions. The army would announce that all replacement (*Ersatz*) units of the Home Army would be immediately disbanded.[69]

December 14: Elements of the 1st Guards Division would march into the city.

December 15 and after: Forces in the city would be reinforced by the 3rd Guard Division followed on subsequent days by the 5th and 37th Infantry Divisions;[70] the 4th Guards Division would redeploy to Spandau. All military installations would be seized and the units that were not part of the Berlin garrison would begin evacuation of the city. Once the army had restored order, the final phase or "exit strategy" envisioned the eventual relief of Lequis' troops by a newly formed "National Guard."[71]

The plan clearly reflected the army's view of what was required to restore order. At the same time, it also suggested the officer corps' resentment of those who had avoided service at the front: cowardly deserters, rebellious young replacements, malingering workers, and the "storm birds" of the revolution, the mutinous sailors. Within days of the arrival of the first guards' battalion, the only people carrying weapons in the capital would be front-line veterans and a limited number of trusted allies. With a single, swift blow the "Berlin Operation" would restore the army's monopoly on armed power within the Reich.

The plan was clearly provocative, and Groener understood that, unless sanctioned by Ebert, the populace would almost certainly view it as a counter-revolutionary *putsch*. Therefore, on November 26, and again on December 2, Major von Harbou traveled to Berlin with the mission of briefing Ebert and gaining his support.[72] Ebert's reaction was

---

[69] The staggered issuance of the various proclamations corresponds to the ideas in the "Lieber Freund" letter (see fn. 56) in which the author wrote: "It would be a mistake for the government to issue all its demands and orders on the first few days." BA-MA, N 42/11, Nachlass Schleicher, "Lieber Freund" letter, dated December 1, 1918, 3.

[70] BA-R, 43/2385, telegram from Groener to the Reich leadership, #5055/18, dated December 10, 1918. Groener asked for the 5th and the 37th in this message. The OHL justified their march through Berlin on the basis that it would allow more troops to enjoy the welcome of the capital.

[71] Details of the plan taken from Berthold and Neef, *Militarismus und Opportunismus*, Document 113: "Aktionsprogramm der Generalkommandos Lequis für den Einmarsch der Felddivisionen in Berlin," 282–3.

[72] Harbou had made an earlier liaison visit to Berlin in late November that may have been Ebert's first exposure to the idea of such an operation. Rakenius, *Wilhelm Groener*

less than enthusiastic.[73] He and his Majority Socialist colleagues were already besieged by accusations from the Independents and Spartacists that they had failed to secure the achievements of the revolution.[74] The operation envisioned by the OHL was likely to appear a proof positive that Ebert had sold out the revolution to the militarists and monopoly capitalists.

Ebert's position was a difficult one. While he did not veto the plan, its obvious dangers led him to shy away from responsibility for it. He wanted assurances that there would be no bloodshed, something the army leadership was loath to provide.[75] Harbou, in turn, cautioned Ebert that there was little time for indecision. The major warned that the guardsmen and other soldiers who would march into the city, for all their elite status, could remain there for only a brief period. "The desire of people to return home is great, and with that in mind, one expects that, despite all [our] strenuous exhortations, the Field Army will succumb to the influence of radical elements."[76] He told Ebert the units selected for the mission were, "the last element of power available to the High Command. If they are not used decisively, the inevitable battle with the radicals will be much more difficult."[77]

The warning to Ebert was an admission by the army leadership that their confidence in the steadiness of the front-line soldiers was fading; the men who had fought so doggedly in France and Belgium were now a very thin reed upon which to base military operations inside the Fatherland. The officer corps might prepare the rank and file with "strenuous exhortations,"[78] but increasingly they feared van den Bergh's

als erster Generalquartiermeister, 136–7. Könnemann, on the other hand, believes the concept had been part of the original Ebert-Groener Pact: "Der Truppeneinmarsch," 1593. This seems unlikely and no evidence is presented.
[73] At the 1925 "stab-in-the-back" trial, Groener testified that Ebert was in full agreement. Berthold and Neef, *Militarismus und Opportunismus*, Document 191: "Kreuzverhör W. Groeners im Dolstochprozeß (Auszug)," 434–40.
[74] On November 20, for example, the Independent Socialist on the Council of Peoples' Delegates had called for Hindenburg's removal. Ebert had fended off this demand by asserting that Hindenburg had given his word of honor in support of the government and that the demobilization depended on maintaining continuity in key positions. Berthold and Neef, *Militarismus und Opportunismus*, Document 62: "Aufzeichnungen Friedrich Eberts über die Sitzung des Rates der Volksbeauftragten am 20. November 1918 (Auszug)," 201.
[75] Volkmann suggested that Ebert would have preferred the military hand him a *fait accompli* rather than to have been made an accomplice: *Revolution über Deutschland*, 125
[76] Harbou's notes quoted in Rakenius, *Wilhelm Groener als erster Generalquartiermeister*, 140.
[77] Harbou quoted in Volkmann, *Revolution über Deutschland*, 125.
[78] The OHL soldiers' council accused the officer of disseminating a flyer under Hindenburg's name at the end of November, which, if authentic, made a brazen appeal to the alienation of the front-line troops: "The Independents and Spartacus

prediction would come true and that the men of Guard Corps would –
like the rest of the army – melt like "butter in the sun."[79]

Preparation, crisis, and controversy

With the OHL holding the affair at arm's length and in the absence
of Ebert and Scheuch's wholehearted support, the "Berlin Operation"
began to look more and more like an ill-favored stepchild. To make
matters worse, two events conspired to shake the unsteady founda-
tions of the plan. The first was an abortive *putsch* attempt by pro-Ebert
forces on December 6, the second was the Left's sudden discovery
of Lequis' deployment in the days just prior to the army's march on
Berlin. Together, the two events threw the Independent Socialists and
Spartacists into a panic, and their reaction led to a series of events that
served to change the nature of the operation in a fundamental way.

The *putsch* attempt of December 6 caught both the army and Ebert
by surprise. Mass Spartacist demonstrations, Liebknecht's threats of
armed revolutionary action, along with the *Vollzugsrat*'s bitter denunciation of the Council of Peoples' Delegates, had aroused fears among
pro-government elements in the capital and prodded them to action.
Believing a showdown inevitable, two conservative officials in the
Foreign Office had conspired with moderate Socialist soldiers in the
Berlin garrison to solidify the government's position. They planned to
arrest the *Vollzugsrat* and call on Ebert to assume a presidency that
assumed dictatorial powers.

The results of their plot were both ludicrous and tragic. On the afternoon of the 6th, during a meeting of the *Vollzugsrat*, a crowd of soldiers
led by a Sergeant Fischer broke into the *Abgeordnetenhaus* (House of
Delegates) with the intention of arresting the members of the council. As fortune would have it, the most radical member of Ebert's cabinet, Emil Barth, was present. Using some well-chosen words, Barth
rebuffed the intruders and turned the *putschist* soldiers against their
leaders. Thus, one arm of the plot had miscarried. Nearly simultan-
eously, another crowd of soldiers, led by a Sergeant Spiro, appeared
before the chancellery and called for Ebert to come forth and accept

---

people want their class dominance, which they achieved without the Field Army's
concurrence, to become an enduring institution, again without the concurrence of
the Field Army. To a large extent, the homeland workers' and soldiers' councils follow them, but they are composed of young fellows that earned lots of money at home,
while the Field Army, under constant mortal danger and the greatest sacrifices of
body and soul, stood before the enemy." BA-R, R43/2500/4, Eduard Weckerle, "Für
eine republikanische Volkswehr," dated January 4, 1919, 71.

[79] Van den Bergh, *Aus den Geburtsstunden*, 65.

their offer of the presidency. Ebert appeared, offered some calming words and told the men that he could not accept such a position without consulting the other members of the government. Dismayed, Spiro's men dispersed: the other arm of the plot had misfired. The whole affair might have blown over except that a crowd of Spartacist supporters, many from the "League of Former Deserters," had marched on the government quarter the same afternoon. They were blocked by a detail from the Berlin garrison's Guard Fusiliers who either panicked when confronted by an angry mob or were fired on by provocateurs. At any event, the *Ersatz* guardsmen responded with a volley of machine-gun fire that left fourteen dead.[80]

The radical Left exploded with predictable fury. The next morning, *Die Rote Fahne* announced that counter-revolution was on the march and called on the proletarians of Berlin to respond with strikes and demonstrations. "Workers! Soldiers! Comrades! 14 corpses lie on the pavement of Berlin. Unarmed, peaceful soldiers were shot down in a cowardly act of assassination!" The paper described the incident as the result of agitation among the Berlin garrison by Ebert and Wels, the city commandant. Their aim, declared the Spartacist paper, was the creation of a genuine, counter-revolutionary White Guard.[81]

In the aftermath of the affair, Ebert's position in the government came under increased attack. At a combined meeting of the Council of Delegates and the *Vollzugsrat* on December 7, the *Vollzugsrat* accused Ebert of working in league with the old elites, and, late in the tumultuous session, the combined bodies considered a demand that Ebert leave the government. This led to an interesting caution by a member of the *Vollzugsrat*, identified only as Councilman Pörschmann: "The troops believe that the *Vollzugsrat* stands against the government and is a front for the Spartacus Group." At that point an unidentified voice in the audience protested, "I lodge a protest for the Eastern Front!" Pörschmann responded, "In any case, that is the view of the Western Front." After Pörschmann's assertion had been confirmed by Chairman (Private) Brutus Molkenbuhr, Pörschmann added, "It comes as a result of press reports. We come now to the dissension [between us and the front-line soldiers], because we are all scoundrels

---

[80] Summary of the December 6 *putsch* from the *Vossische Zeitung*, December 7, 1918, and Volkmann, *Revolution über Deutschland*, 123–4. According to Captain Gustav Böhm, an adjutant in the War Ministry, the responsibility for the little massacre fell on the shoulders on Eichorn, the Police President, who had failed to advise the garrison forces of the Spartacist demonstration scheduled for that day. Böhm, *Adjutant*, diary entry for December 6, 1918, 94. Other accounts of the affair list the number of dead at sixteen.

[81] *Rote Fahne*, December 7, 1918.

(*Lumpen*), according to the other opinion [at the front]." After a response from co-chair Richard Müller decrying the discordant nature of the meeting, the combined session closed by voting down the proposal for Ebert's removal.[82]

Pörschmann's pronouncement may or may not have had a sobering effect on the conclusion of the meeting. From the existing accounts, it is difficult to tell. What his comments do show is that those to the left of Ebert's government knew the troops marching toward Berlin held them in low esteem. If the Left acted rashly, there might yet be a reckoning. The "Western Front," as the council member called it, was already casting a long shadow over the political scene in Berlin.[83]

The OHL was already moving the "Western Front" closer to the capital; on the day of the *putsch*, Lequis' headquarters arrived in Berlin. Though both Lequis' and Groener's staff had been caught by surprise by the events of December 6,[84] the next crisis was more predictable. In the week prior to December 10, the scheduled date of the first unit's entry into Berlin, the Spartacists and Independent Socialists became aware of the deployment of large numbers of front-line combat units around Berlin. Lequis' headquarters had tried to be discreet. Instead of billeting the units in garrison installations where their presence would be conspicuous, the arriving troops were quartered in private dwellings and villages away from the larger towns. However, the sudden appearance of tens of thousands of well-armed guardsmen in the environs of the capital could not be hidden for long,[85] even had every unit been circumspect about its arrival. Some were not. The workers' and soldiers' councils around the capital bombarded the war ministry with anxious questions about arriving guard units and complaints that, in places, the guardsmen had pulled down red flags and overthrown local soldiers' councils and replaced them with "front representatives."[86] A month after the end of the war, the old resentments, front versus rear, were being played out in the towns and casernes around Berlin.

---

[82] Berthold and Neef, *Militarismus und Opportunismus*, Document 103: "Gemeinsame Sitzung des Rates des Volkbeauftraten und des Vollzugsrates der Berliner Arbeiter- und Soldatenräte am 7. Dezember 1918 (Auszug)," 264–5.

[83] This meeting also included a brief reference to "three divisions" ready to move into the capital. *Ibid.*, 262.

[84] Rakenius, *Wilhelm Groener als erster Generalquartiermeister*, 141.

[85] Von Thaer's diary entry of December 9 describes a regiment, the Pasewalk Cuirassiers, being misrouted to their home station instead of their assigned assembly area near Potsdam due to a misunderstanding by the local railroad commandant. The army found it difficult to correct the mistake because, to do so would have revealed the nature of the deployment: *Generalstabdienst an der Front*, 280.

[86] Böhm, *Adjutant*, diary entry for December 8, 1918.

Perhaps sensing that Ebert was wavering in the face of the Left's pressure, Hindenburg dispatched a note to him on December 8. It was a remarkable document. The proud old field marshal opened his letter to the former saddle-maker in courteous and flattering tones. "If I address these following lines to you, I do this because it has been reported to me that you are also a loyal German who loves your Fatherland above all, without regard to your personal opinions and desires, as I have also had to do in order to rise to the need of the Fatherland." The letter went on to remind Ebert of the new government's promise to restore order and Hindenburg's own commitment to bringing the army home successfully. The field marshal complained that, while the officer corps had faithfully discharged their duties during and after the war, they had been subjected to endless abuse from revolutionary councils. Hindenburg deplored the way the workers' and soldiers' councils had hijacked supply convoys, confiscated rations, and used monetary incentives to lure men away from their units before proper discharge. And then:

It is obvious that we can only emerge from our current circumstances if the government has at its disposal an agency that has the ability to give unfailing validity to its orders and the existing laws. Given the current situation, this agency can only be the army, and, indeed, an army in which the sharpest discipline reigns. Discipline stands and falls on the authority of the leader and the separation of the army from politics.

Hindenburg went on to ask Ebert to make public proclamation that the existing command authority remained in place in the army. The soldiers' councils must "disappear": only trustees' councils with limited authority could be tolerated. Having stated that the army needed to be separated from politics, Hindenburg then proceeded to tell Ebert that the mood of the army (and "other circles of society") reflected an urgent desire for a National Assembly at the earliest possible moment. He admonished Ebert, "In your hands lies the destiny of the German people." The field marshal concluded by pledging the continued support of the "entire army."[87]

In retrospect, the note appears to be an effort by the army leadership to steel Ebert for the coming crisis, while ensuring that Ebert supported the existing chain of command. Hindenburg's reminder that the government had the support of the "entire army" seems more than a little ironic. Just a week into December, the headquarters of the Field

---

[87] BA-MA, N 42/11, Nachlass Schleicher, Supreme Headquarters Msg. #11780, Hindenburg to Ebert, dated December 8, 1918, 8.

Army had no control of the homeland garrisons, little control over the troops returning from the East, and its grip on the remaining troops of the *Westheer* was indeed becoming uncertain. What Hindenburg could promise was almost exclusively limited to the guardsmen and other troops assembling under Lequis' headquarters. For both wings of Germany's embattled political spectrum, the future of the new republic seemed to be marching under the banners of this new command.

7 The last parade: the Guards return to Berlin, December 10–22, 1918

Banners of irony

December 10, 1918, exactly a month from the day that the Kaiser fled into exile, an elite formation of his guard carried the flag of Wilhelm's vanished empire through the Brandenburg Gate. Behind them and before them was a throng of cheering Berliners. On that day, and the days that followed, the soldiers of the Western Front conducted the last parade of the Imperial Army. The old monarchy was dead. The old army, for a while, lived on.

Had an observer, unaware of the circumstances of that day, been inserted into the crowd, this ill-informed, hypothetical observer would have been hard-pressed to understand that the troops on parade were representatives of a beaten army and that they marched through the capital of a defeated nation. The gifts the onlookers pressed into the hand of the soldiers, the flowers draped on the caissons, the stirring marches played by the bands, all seemed to mark a celebration, the arrival of a conquering host. Certainly this must have been the strangest parade ever conducted in the aftermath of a lost war.

The cameramen on hand have left an extensive photographic record of the guards' return to Berlin.[1] It captures the gray, grim weather, the size and enthusiasm of the crowds, and, in many of the pictures, the expressions of the marching *Fronttruppen*. In some of the photos, the guardsmen appear jubilant. In others, they look grim almost to the point of defiance. And in a few of the pictures, the homecoming veterans appear disoriented and bewildered. The mix of expressions was understandable. These were men who were, in turn, relieved to have survived a terrible war, gratified by the reception of their countrymen, and baffled by the situation they found in their homeland.

---

[1] See, for example, Diethart Kerbs *et al.*, *Revolution und Fotografie: Berlin, 1918–1919* (Berlin: Verlag Dirk Nishen, 1990), 37, 148, 205, 221, 255.

Figure 7.1 Berlin crowd waits for the arrival of the Guards at the Pariser Platz, December 10, 1918.

Confrontation at Nikolassee[2]

According to the timetable the OHL had created for the "Berlin Operation," the Guards Cavalry Rifle Division was to be the first of Lequis' units to march into Berlin. It was an unusual formation. The division had transformed earlier in 1918 from an elite mounted formation to front-line infantry, and, in the final campaigns of the war, it had seen combat on the Western Front as part of the First Army.[3] After the armistice, it had crossed the Rhine near Coblenz (where AEF observers noted its passage), and then proceeded to an upload area to await transportation to Berlin.[4]

[2] The descriptions of the events at Nikolassee come from Pabst's papers. BA-MA, PH 620/2, "Transcript of the Memoirs of Major Waldemar Pabst and His Post War Experiences as Ia and Chief of Staff of the GKSD." Hereafter, Nachlass Pabst.

[3] Allied intelligence had rated it as "second-class." AEF G2, *251 Divisions*, 29. In his narrative of his trip to Spa on November 9, Colonel Reinhard claimed that the outer cordon of security around the Supreme Headquarters was provided by the GKSD. This seems very possible, but difficult to corroborate.

[4] See, for example, NARA, RG 120, Box 5895, III Corps Intelligence summary, dated December 16, 1918.

Though the commander of the division, General Heinrich von Hofmann, was an experienced and well-respected officer, by the end of the war, he was exhausted and suffering from a severe heart ailment. The real guiding spirit of the division was its energetic chief of staff, Captain Waldemar Pabst.[5] Pabst was a genuine enemy of the revolution in any of its manifestations. In his unpublished memoirs, he recalled that, as the unit marched back from the front and crossed the Rhine, he became more and more concerned for Germany's future. His mistrust of the army's senior leadership was increased when he encountered a lieutenant colonel from the staff of the First Army headquarters riding around with a red pennant on his automobile, and a driver wearing a red armband. With considerable disgust, Pabst observed that the lieutenant colonel, once a fancy-uniformed member of the Kaiser's entourage, was now portraying himself as an agent of the revolution (Pabst's attitude was conditioned, no doubt, by the "front's" hostile attitude toward the staff). On the other hand, as the division moved into Germany, Pabst had been heartened by Rhinelanders who had greeted the guardsmen with cries of "March to Berlin and set things right!"[6] As the unit pressed deeper into Germany, incidents between the GKSD and local soldiers' councils inspired Pabst to create a special "Division Staff Squadron" made up of the most battle-tested NCOs and the most reliable men. When the division was challenged by militant members of a local council, the appearance of Pabst's special squadron and its hardened veterans was usually enough to get the "Reds" to back down.[7] Pabst recalled with considerable satisfaction that, with the exception of a single incident, no obstruction by the local councils lasted more than half an hour.[8]

Within days of crossing the Rhine, orders summoned the GKSD to load up on trains headed east to Berlin. The division conducted the actual load-out in an atmosphere of secrecy, and the troops began to exchange rumors and anxious questions. Pabst had the chain of command tell the men not to worry. There would be no meaningful resistance in "Red Berlin," and if there was, it would come from the hordes of

---

[5] He later recalled: "We wanted, above all to march together with social democracy in order to throttle our mutual enemy, Spartacism. If that went well, then we wanted to lay before our former allies [Ebert and the Majority Socialists] a bill for November 1918 to be settled with them." Könnemann, "Der Truppeneinmarsch," 1593.

[6] Nachlass Pabst, 4–5.

[7] Von Schulenberg recorded that a number of such detachments, "reliable" volunteers under trusted officers, were formed across the army as it returned to the homeland. One cover for such units was that they were being formed for possible employment on the Polish frontier. Schulenberg suggested that they often became the nuclei for the earliest Freikorps. BA-MA, N 58/1, Nachlass Schulenberg, 245.

[8] Nachlass Pabst, 6.

contemptible *Heimkrieger* ("homeland warriors"). Meanwhile, the covert nature of the movement confused the *Reichsbahn*, which, at first, attempted to off-load the division in the center of the capital. When this error was corrected, the first train finally arrived in a drizzling rain at the railway station at Nikolassee, a suburb on Berlin's southwest frontier, not far from the famous Wannsee.

In some respects, what happened next encapsulated all the bitterest divisions within Germany's postwar military. At the *Bahnhof* at Nikolassee, Pabst and his advance party encountered a "reception committee": 800 revolutionary soldiers and sailors dressed in wet, dirty uniforms decorated with red armbands. They stood with their hands in their pockets and rifles slung muzzle-down, "in the Russian fashion." Leading them was the omnipresent Emil Barth, the same USPD cabinet member who had challenged the OHL at Bad Ems. Pabst dismounted to meet Barth, who identified himself as a member of the ruling cabinet and addressed the captain with the announcement, "The men behind me are representatives of various soldiers' and executive councils active in Berlin, such as the Soldiers' Council of Deserters. It is our intention to receive the arriving troops, to greet them, and to clarify to them the meaning and purpose of our revolution. To this end, I want a list from you of the component units of the division and their quarters so that I may meet with them tomorrow."

If Barth's objective was to inspire Pabst's indignation, he could scarcely have done a better job. Pabst told the USPD delegate that he did not recognize a member of the cabinet as his superior in military affairs, and he did not consider such a rag-tag mob as much of a reception committee. Further, he said, he knew Barth as one of the leaders of the January 1918 strike that had left the troops at the front short of ammunition. What is more, to be "greeted" by representatives of the "Deserters' Council" was a personal insult. "We completely denounce the idea of our people being greeted by such people."

Pabst told Barth that, as a representative of the government, he might visit the division headquarters the next day in order to ensure the guardsmen were being properly taken care of. He should bring no more than three people with him. With those brusque instructions, the captain broke off the discussion in order to supervise the posting of the members of his division security squadron with machine guns and hand grenades to ensure there was no fraternization between the guardsmen and the representatives of the councils. Barth and his colleagues had no choice but to return to the capital.[9]

---

[9] Curiously, Barth had a somewhat different and more unlikely recollection of his interaction with Pabst, who, Barth wrote later, provided all required information. What is

Unlike officers in other units, Pabst was not going to be satisfied to watch his unit evaporate with the approach of the Christmas holiday. He despised what he had found in the homeland and saw his division as a weapon to overturn the worst of what had happened to Germany. In short, he was going to prepare for a showdown against the revolution. With that in mind, he sealed off the division's new quarters with barbed wire and sentries. He had good reason, for shortly after the arrival of the lead elements of the GKSD, its barracks were swarmed by curious onlookers as well as "provocateurs." Against this last group, he took it upon himself to create two groups to conduct a division-level propaganda campaign. One group was made up of old veterans, men from *Stammmannschaften*, whom he detailed to combat revolutionary agitation within the division. The other group had a more offensive orientation. He enlisted the services of a Jewish lawyer to lead this group, whose mission was spreading an anti-Spartacist message among the population. Certainly, these were unusual initiatives for the chief of staff of an infantry division, but Pabst understood that, if his division was to remain intact, it would have to be *isolated* from revolutionary influences. As he wrote later, "Civil war imposed a variety of unfamiliar tasks."[10]

The captain was ready to tackle these "unfamiliar tasks." However, Pabst seems an exceptional case. While the enlisted soldiers seemed revitalized by the proximity of their homes, the accelerating dissolution of the old army suggested a sort of moral *exhaustion* within the officer corps. In mid 1918, holding a unit together required officers of extraordinary zeal, energy, and insight; Pabst was the conspicuous example, and there seemed to be few like him. Yet the OHL's plans counted on there being enough such officers to hold the guards divisions together for a few more weeks.

As the date for the GKSD's march into Berlin approached, Scheuch summoned Pabst to the war ministry. It was a meeting that would highlight, once again, the clash of sensibilities between front and rear. The captain knew enough about conditions inside the capital to realize that were he to appear alone in an officer's uniform, he risked not only a beating but also the loss of his sidearm, his shoulder straps, and his decorations. To prevent this, he drove into Berlin with an entourage that included three staff officers in his own car and an automobile full of heavily armed members of his division staff squadron in a second.

more, in a subsequent conversation, the two men spoke candidly with one another as Pabst announced his worries for the future of the officer corps and his own uncertain prospects in postwar Germany. Barth claimed that he was able to relieve some of the officer's near-suicidal anxiety and, at the end of the conversation, Pabst thanked him! Barth, *Aus der Werkstatt*, 85.
[10] Pabst's preparations described, Nachlass Pabst, 14.

Thus, when Pabst arrived at Scheuch's office, the war minister was astounded to find Pabst in full field uniform. (Scheuch and his staff had all taken to wearing civilian attire in order to avoid harassment.) In the presence of an unknown witness, Pabst told Scheuch that he had been shocked at the appearance of "government troops" as he traveled through the city. It was readily apparent, the captain said, that if even a handful of resolute soldiers had been willing to risk their lives on November 9, the revolution could have been snuffed out with relative ease. At this point, Scheuch pulled Pabst aside and asked him how he could speak in such a fashion in the presence of the head of the soldiers' council of the war ministry. Pabst recounted that, at this point, he threw discipline to the wind and told the general that he was appalled that the Prussian war minister conducted business under the scrutiny of a former underling. One imagines that such comments were deeply humiliating to Scheuch, while Pabst left the encounter with a new level of disdain for the army's leadership.[11]

Armed or unarmed?

Meanwhile, though Liebknecht's followers had no formal intelligence service, they hardly needed one to realize that guards units were closing in on Berlin. From the cities west of Berlin, the word had spread from local workers' and soldiers' councils and newspaper accounts that the elite regiments of the old *Kaiserreich* were weeks and then days away. On December 3, *Die Rote Fahne* announced the arrival of advance elements of the Guard Corps, a signal detachment, armed and led by officers on horseback. In what seemed a clear provocation, the unit had marched through the center of Berlin under the old imperial flag as its band played the marching music of the old army. A detachment of Emil Eichorn's radicalized *Sicherheitswehr* stopped the procession as it passed the Marstall building near the imperial palace. Eichorn's men ordered the guardsmen to surrender their weapons. The guards' commander snarled his refusal, and his men rallied around him, raising their weapons menacingly against the local revolutionaries. At this point, according to the *Rote Fahne*, only the restraint of the *Sicherheitswehr* prevented a bloodbath. As Eichorn's men stepped aside, the guards formation continued its little parade, cheered by a small crowd of bourgeois onlookers.

Here was something that had not been seen in the capital since November 9, troops who obeyed their officers. These soldiers of the

---

[11] *Ibid.*; meeting at *Kriegsministerium* described, 17–18.

Western Front represented a clear threat, and the paper warned its readers, "The Guards Corps is the strongest hope of the counter-revolutionaries. The guards signalers would be followed shortly by larger guards formations." The workers and proletarian soldiers needed to prepare for the arrival of the revolution's mortal enemies (*Todesfeinde*).[12]

They did not have to wait long. On December 9, three days after the aborted *putsch* in Berlin had raised tensions to a new level, *Die Rote Fahne* abandoned the use of complete sentences to announce the arrival of the main body of Lequis' forces.

Achtung! Berlin is Surrounded!

During the last hours before going to press, this paper received news of monstrous importance. It had been confirmed that troops under *Generalkommando Lequis* have concentrated around Berlin. Guard troops and [troops] from other parts of Germany, Silesians, Erfurters, Padeborners. The troops are loyal to the monarchy [*Königstreuen*], the officers refuse any statements; deny any access to their troops. They are assigned to deploy into Berlin to establish peace and order, support the Ebert–Haase government, and to suppress the Spartacists.

They are abundantly supplied with ammunition. The artillery with full limbers and ammunition columns. The machine guns with 30,000 rounds.[13]

While the Spartacists were provoking anger and alarm outside the government, Ebert and his military supporters were finding it difficult to reassure the Independents in the Council of People's Delegates and the *Vollzugsrat* that Lequis' forces did not represent imminent counter-revolution. On the morning of Sunday, December 8, a reserve lieutenant named Heine, the head of the Potsdam soldiers' council, had reported to the soldiers' council of Greater Berlin that armed units were assembling between Potsdam and the capital. None of these units, he said, had soldiers' councils, and they had removed any red flags flying in their assembly areas.[14] Later that day, Barth returned to the headquarters of the GKSD and demanded that Pabst call off

---

[12] "Arbeiter Berlins! Proletarianische Soldaten!" *Die Rote Fahne*, December 3, 1918.

[13] "Achtung! Berlin Umzingelt!" *Die Rote Fahne*, December 9, 1918.

[14] Könnemann, "Der Truppeneinmarsch," 1595. When von Harbou heard of this he ordered the lieutenant arrested (*ibid.*, 1596). Scheuch claimed authority over the matter since Heine belonged to a garrison unit; however, the war minister failed to sign an arrest order, a failure which exacerbated the ill will between the OHL and the war ministry. Harbou later wrote that he was later able to use indirect means to get Heine removed. *Ibid.*, Document 4: "Notizen Major Harbous," 1608. See also Walter Oehme, *Damals in der Reichskanzlei: Erinnerungern aus den Jahren 1918/1919* (Berlin: Kongress-Verlag, 1958), 90. Oehme reports these events as happening on December 9, but this is certainly an error. His work is a memoir rather than a diary. Böhm's diary has them on December 8.

the march into the capital; if he did march, weapons should be left behind. Predictably Pabst refused, telling Barth that such a decision was up to General Lequis or Chancellor Ebert. In his opinion, Pabst said, it would be foolish for a unit of 12,000 to 14,000 men to march unarmed inside a city of several millions who were gripped by a "revolutionary fever."[15] Later, on the afternoon of the same day, a deputation of ten members of the *Vollzugsrat* descended on Ebert and demanded clarification of the plan for the troops assembled around Berlin. Ebert responded that the troops in question were gathering for a ceremonial greeting by the populace. Their demobilization would follow immediately. Unconvinced, the delegation made a counter-proposal,[16] suggesting that the entry of the front-line units be either called off or be subject to strict limitations. They proposed (1) that the units would carry no live ammunition, (2) that their arrival be delayed by one day in order for representatives of the socialist parties to "enlighten" the troops, (3) that only units from Berlin be allowed in the city (the sole exception being a *"Bundesbataillon"* made up of men from the other federal states of the Reich), and (4) that the units be accompanied by workers' deputations and other associations.[17]

Late that evening Ebert met with the war minister, Scheuch, and Lequis' chief of staff, Harbou. The chancellor called on the army's representatives to accept the demands offered by the members of the *Vollzugsrat*. Scheuch offered no opposition. He believed the government could not refuse the council's demand. In the aftermath of the December 6 debacle, the war minister had become discouraged about the prospects of the "Berlin Operation." He was also resentful of the OHL's control of the operation and at one point had insisted that Lequis clear all political questions through him instead of talking directly to the government. He was reported as saying, "[T]he OHL just doesn't know how things are in Berlin."[18]

As a representative of both the OHL and General Lequis, Harbou was alarmed, as he saw the prospects of a successful action being wrecked by Ebert's desire for compromise and Scheuch's waffling. Under these circumstances, an armed operation to strengthen the government against its enemies was rapidly becoming impossible. After an angry exchange

---

[15] Nachlass Pabst, 22–3.   [16] Könnemann, "Der Truppeneinmarsch," 1596.

[17] *Vollzugsrat* demands from Böhm, *Adjutant*, diary entry for December 8, 100–1. In one meeting, the Independent Socialist Ledebour accused the army of inventing the name "Lequis" as a code word. "And then, this mysterious, often-spoken name Lequis. Lequis is French, a certain person. Who is this certain person?" Scheuch replied that, behind the name, there was a well-fed, completely tangible, general of engineers. *Ibid.*, 100.

[18] Scheuch quotation, Rakenius, *Wilhelm Groener als erster Generalquartiermeister*, 143.

with the war minister, the major asked for time to inform the OHL of the conditions of the compromise and to see if they wanted to proceed with the planned entry.[19]

Groener received Harbou's update shortly before midnight on December 8, and took the news, along with his own anger and dismay, to Hindenburg. For Hindenburg, Groener, and their subordinates, the news seemed confirmation that Ebert no longer had real executive authority and that Scheuch's ministry had little to say about the course of events. In the black-and-white political outlook of the Field Army's senior leaders, it seemed clear the *Vollzugsrat* now had the upper hand.[20] Officers within the OHL staff pressed Groener to go to Berlin and take over the operation himself. However, after consideration, Groener decided against such a move. Hindenburg agreed, having said that, if the OHL moved to Berlin, "it has the appearance of compelling a kind of military dictatorship. For that, it is not yet the time. Such a dictatorship must remain a last resort after all else has failed."[21]

The next day, December 9, Groener responded to what he called the "watering down"[22] of the "Berlin Operation" two ways. The first was to telephone Lequis at 10.20 a.m. with instructions to proceed: "It is the intent of the Field Marshal that Lieutenant General Lequis act on his own initiative, if need be, refusing all contradictory instructions from government agencies or military authorities, including the War Ministry." Second, Groener drafted a strongly worded telegram to Ebert, refusing the terms of the compromise.

Groener's instructions to Lequis were extraordinary. They suggested that a clean break between the OHL and the war ministry was possible, and, more remarkably, they indicated that the Field Army's senior leadership believed the front-line troops would be willing to act contrary to the instructions of the Ebert government. This would certainly baffle the troops who had read the protestations of support for the Council of Peoples' Delegates from their own unit councils as well as the OHL itself. These instructions were likely to baffle Lequis as well.

[19] *Ibid.* See also Böhm, *Adjutant*, diary entry for December 8,
[20] Rakenius, *Wilhelm Groener als erster Generalquartiermeister*, 143–4. See also Könnemann, "Der Truppeneinmarsch," 1596–7.
[21] Hindenburg quotation from Volkmann, *Revolution über Deutschland*, 128. Thaer's diary entry of December 10 reflects the frustration of the OHL staff. He wrote that he asked Groener why the OHL did not give the order to march itself. Depressed, Groener replied, "You know yourself that we have no more to say, the order would also not reach to Berlin." Thaer ended his diary entry: "If Ludendorff was in Groener's place, it would be implemented immediately." Thaer, *Generalstabdienst an der Front*, 281.
[22] Guth, *Loyalitätskonflikt*, 66–7.

Meanwhile, Groener's telegram to Ebert represented the OHL's defiant bid to steel Ebert for the kind of difficult decisions the chancellor would have to make if the "Berlin Operation" was to be a success. It was also one of the last times the army High Command would invoke the honor of the front-line troops in order to achieve the political aims of the senior military leadership. To the *Vollzugsrat*'s first proposal, withholding ammunition from the troops, Groener replied that the purpose was to make the troops "defenseless against the Spartacus people and the Liebknecht followers." To the second limitation, delaying the march by a day, to December 11, to allow the *Vollzugsrat* to "enlighten" the troops, Groener answered that the *Vollzugsrat* had revealed itself as the "tool" of the Spartacists. The march would not be delayed, and the only emissaries sent to visit the troops were ones approved by Ebert and accompanied by Harbou. The third demand limited entry into the capital to troops stationed in Berlin. Groener called this an "insult to the entire Field Army." The fourth demand called for workers' delegations to accompany the troops. Groener responded: "In the Field Army there are members of every vocational class; in a state of equality no exception can be made for workers." Besides, he said, such an escort would be an additional affront to the troops. The men who had been at the front were capable of maintaining order and discipline for themselves. The message concluded by deploring the apparent power of the *Vollzugsrat* and asking Ebert if he was ready to fight the "tyranny of the Spartacists and Liebknechtites" as he had promised. In Hindenburg's name, Groener called on Ebert to join the field marshal in leading the troops against the enemies of the state.[23]

What influence Groener's telegram had is difficult to say. What is known is that, during a cabinet meeting on December 9, the key players in the German capital reached agreement on the final shape of the Lequis operation. The army got the parade it wanted but not the coup it had planned. In a session attended by Ebert and four of the remaining five delegates,[24] along with Harbou and Scheuch,[25] the details of the next day's march were hammered out. The cabinet set aside the demands of the *Vollzugsrat* and allowed the Guards Cavalry

---

[23] Könnemann, "Der Truppeneinmarsch," Document 2: "Telegramm-Entwurf Groeners," 1603–4.

[24] Dittmann, the Independent, was not present. Böhm, *Adjutant*, diary entry for December 9, 101.

[25] A variety of sources (Volkmann, Oehme, Könnemann) suggest Schleicher was also present and did a masterful job of swaying the argument. He is reported to have said, "A soldier coming from the front without ammunition is, indeed, no soldier" (Könnemann, "Der Truppeneinmarsch," 1597). Rakenius and Kluge indicate he was not there.

Rifle Division to enter the city with its weapons and ammunition.[26] Ebert and *Oberbürgermeister* Adolf Wermuth would greet the troops and address them in the center of the city, at the Pariser Platz. Barth, the fieriest of the Independents in the cabinet, raised objections but faced a united front from the three Majority Socialist members and only limited support from Haase, the one other Independent in attendance.[27]

The meeting did lead to two material and one symbolic concession to the Left's anxieties. The guards would leave their machine guns and armored cars behind, and, in order to prove that counter-revolution was not impending, Ebert proposed that some 35,000 soldiers within the first units to enter Berlin take an oath of support to the government. Having identified Ebert as the army's best hope to support a stand against the "Bolshevists," the officers conceded to this proposal. Thus, at seven o'clock that evening inside the Steglitz *Rathaus*, before a life-size portrait of the departed Kaiser,[28] the war minister and four of the people's delegates, Scheidemann, Haase, Dittmann, and Ebert, stood behind General Lequis as he administered an oath of allegiance to representatives of the Guards Cavalry Rifle Division and the *Jäger* Division:

We swear in our own names and, at the same time, the units we represent, to employ our entire strength for the single German republic and its provisional government, the Council of People's Delegates.[29]

Captain Böhm recorded in his diary that relatively few members of the two units were present, and that, in the whole, the ceremony made "an impression of little impact."[30]

That same evening, one of his colleagues in the war ministry, Colonel van den Bergh, offered a pessimistic prediction. "Tomorrow (10.12) is the ceremonial entry of the first front-line troops and now a new phase will begin. I am convinced that these so-called 'reliable' troops will fraternize everywhere with the other troops and the population as

[26] The *Vollzugsrat* continued to demand that the number of troops allowed in Berlin be limited to those who were garrisoned there in peacetime. BA-R, R43/2485/f, "Decision of the Executive Council," dated December 10, 1918, 115.
[27] Barth had apparently been convinced by Pabst that there was no counter revolutionary intent to the upcoming arrival of Lequis' command. Könnemann, "Der Truppeneinmarsch," 1593.
[28] Steglitz lies in the southwest (and more middle-class) section of Berlin.
[29] "Im Steglitzer Rathaus," *Vossische Zeitung*, December 10. As administered, the oath left Scheuch fuming because he had arranged with the cabinet that the oath would be only "to the existing government," not to a "single German republic." Böhm, *Adjutant*, diary entry for December 9, 1918, 101.
[30] *Ibid.*

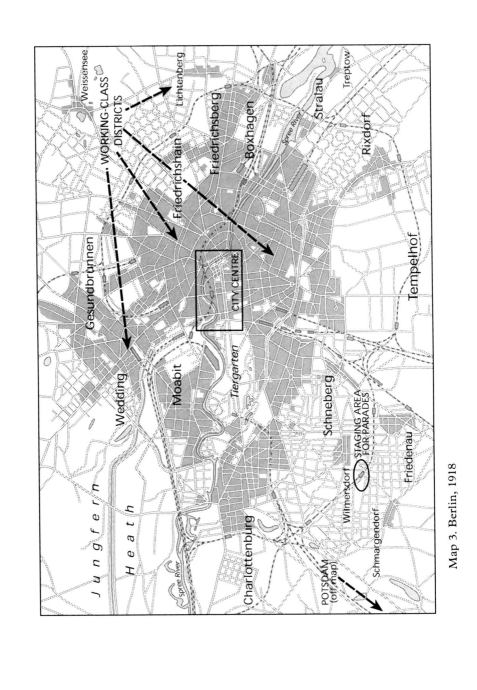

Map 3. Berlin, 1918

soon as they are exposed for some time to their influences. And that will be something else again."[31]

The guards return

By every account, December 10 was a damp, overcast, and gloomy day. Nevertheless, the morning edition of the *Vossische Zeitung* called on Berliners to give an appropriately warm welcome to the troops arriving that day. With them, the newspaper suggested, marched the honor of an unbowed army.

The troops from Berlin are coming home. They will return through the Brandenburg Gate under different circumstances from what we had antici-pated years ago. However, the welcome that the homeland offers could not be more heartfelt if Germany had emerged from the gloom of war more success-fully. They were not defeated. As upright, heroic men, they come back to a land they defended with their blood and their lives.

There was more. The paper suggested these men represented the hope for Germany's future. "Because of the blooming strength that flows back into the homeland, our eyes and senses are shown that, out of unspeakable horrors, the body of our people will emerge alive ... From these men we want to learn how to endure terrible things and then keep [one's] head up." Germany's enemies would not see her grovel. Instead, they would see quiet and forward-looking pride embodied in the front-line soldiers who would tramp down the capital's avenues that day.[32]

Early that morning, after a demanding march from the suburbs, the troops began assembling in the Heidelberger Platz in the southwestern quarter of the city.[33] Beyond the rhetoric of the *Vossische Zeitung*, the appearance of these veteran soldiers offered enormous symbolic signifi-cance. Their wagons and horses were covered with fir branches, and the flag bearers carried the black-white-red standard of the old empire as well as the flags of the empire's constituent states. They were dressed in full combat array, with steel helmets painted in camouflage colors and with full ammunition pouches. They carried 80,000 rounds of ammunition for each of their machine guns (which they carried either in defiance or ignorance of the compromise reached the day before).

[31] Van den Bergh, *Aus den Geburtsstunden*, diary entry for December 9.
[32] "Gruß an den Heimkehrenden," *Vossische Zeitung*, morning edition, December 10, 1918.
[33] Nachlass Pabst, 24.

Some of their wagons carried pictures of Hindenburg as well as other nobility. These, it must have seemed to spectators, were elite combat troops untouched by the revolution.

At 11.10 a.m., after the commander of the Guard Cuirassiers offered the men a brief address, the lead battalions stepped off from the march's start point, the Schmargendorf railway station. At the head of the procession was the division commander, General von Hofmann, and his staff, followed by Guard Machine Gun Detachment I, the Guard Cuirassier Regiment, the Life Guard Cuirassiers, and then dragoons, uhlans, and *Jäger* cavalry, all dismounted since these historic old cavalry units had fought in the last year of the war as infantry. Only the officers were on horseback. A unit band led every regiment, and they played the famous old marches, *Deutschland, Deutschland über alles*, and *Heil dir im Siegerkranz*.

Berliners lined the streets in vast crowds, and they cheered the soldiers as they passed. The trees were filled with boys, and the roofs and windows were full of spectators. On Unter den Linden alone, an estimated 80,000 to 100,000 people thronged the sidewalks. As the soldiers passed, people pressed cigars, cigarettes, and other little gifts into their hands or decorated the men and vehicles with bouquets. They heaped garlands on the wagons.

There were dissonant notes as well. Such was the crush of onlookers that authorities reported that twenty-five people required medical assistance. Amid the hurrahs, one still heard the sound of organ-grinders, some of whom were amputees or *Nervenkrank* (psychiatric cases) from the front. Reporters noticed older couples, standing silently in tears, evidently the parents of men who were not returning. Finally, if any of the spectators were familiar with military organization, they would have noticed that the marching battalions were remarkably small. The Guard Cuirassier Regiment for example, was already much depleted. It had taken heavy losses in its last battle near Reims on November 4, where it had been reduced to two officers and forty-eight men. Thus, though it was reinforced by some of the lightly wounded, it still needed augmentation from a hussar regiment in order to make a march unit of respectable size.[34]

Spartacus was present, too. Reporters noticed red flags among the forest of imperial standards. Spartacist agents walked alongside the

---

[34] In addition, some of the men from the oldest year groups had been discharged, and others who had volunteered for border defense units and other duties had also been released. Finally, the division had left security details to watch the remainder of the unit's equipment and horses. Kriegsgeschichtlichen Forschungsanstalt des Heeres, *Wirren*, 33.

Figure 7.2 The Guards Cavalry Rifle Division marches through the
Brandenburg Gate, December 10, 1918. The soldier in the soft cap
in the middle appears to be a member of the *Soldatenwehr*.

marching units handing the men flyers that called on the front-line
troops to purge the officers from their soldiers' councils.

By noon, the authorities attempted to clear a way from the
Brandenburg Gate into the Pariser Platz as the party of dignitaries
assembled and took their places on the reviewing stand. They included
the mayor and members of the cabinet as well as representatives of the
Vollzugsrat. General Lequis was present, wearing a spiked helmet and
his *Pour le Mérite*. Beside him was the war minister, Scheuch. Crowd
control was being provided by the *Soldatenwehr*, which did not seem
capable of opening a path for the troops. A senior lieutenant of the
Guards Dragoons rode through the crowd to tell Ebert that the division
commander did not want to take his unit into such confusion. Ebert
replied, "*Herr Offizier*, I must give my speech."[35] Eventually the troops
did arrive, passing through the Brandenburg Gate at about one o'clock,
as a special unit greeted them, the *Bundesbataillon* (Federal Battalion),

---

[35] Confusion noted in Reinhard, *Wehen der Republik*, 41–3. Reinhard also claimed that
part of Ebert's speech was interrupted by the arrival of a marching band.

Figure 7.3 The reviewing party at the Pariser Platz, December 10, 1918. From left to right (the postcard is mislabeled): Ebert, Lequis (commander of returning guards), Scheuch (minister of war), and Mayor Wermuth.

which included a company each of Bavarians, Saxons, Badenese, and Württemburgers.[36] Once the troops were assembled, at about 1.30 p.m., Ebert began to speak:

Comrades, welcome to the German republic, heartfelt welcome to the homeland that you have longed for, whose anxious worries hovered constantly around you. In this moment that we greet you on native soil, our first thoughts are offered to our precious dead. Oh, so many will never return.[37] Hundreds of thousands rest in quiet graves in the land of the enemy, other hundreds of thousands had to return before the end of the fight, mangled and maimed by enemy fire.

Ebert thanked the men for their sacrifices and their defense of the homeland, noting that mere words could not express the Fatherland's

[36] All details of the parade from the *Vossische Zeitung*, evening edition, December 10, 1918 and *Neue Preussische Zeitung*, December 11, 1918, except where noted.

[37] All four of Ebert's sons served in the army. Two were killed in action in 1917. A third was seriously wounded. Ebert rejected suggestions that he use his political position to have this fourth son excused from further front-line duty. Mühlhausen, *Friedrich Ebert*, 83–5.

gratitude. Then he spoke words that would haunt the Weimar Republic for the remainder of its short existence:

> Comrades, companions, citizens
> Your sacrifice and deeds are without equal.
> No enemy has conquered you.

Ebert explained this last statement by asserting that Germany had given way only after the weight of the enemy's men and *matériel* made further combat pointless. Nevertheless, he offered, it was a measure of their heroic resistance that they had kept the enemy and the effects of war away from the soil of the Fatherland. Ebert then reminded the men that they were returning to a Germany that was vastly different from the one they had left and assured the front-line soldiers of their special significance in this new Germany. "On you, above all, rests the hope of German freedom. You are the strongest bearers of the German future." Ebert suggested that, as citizens of the new republic, they should have a special appreciation for the transformation of the homeland, since they were the ones who had suffered the most under the former unjust regime. He finished by regretting that the nation had no rich rewards to offer them, but rather the hard job of building the new republic. "Now, Germany's unity lies in your hands!" There was great work, he promised, to be done in building the free "People's State of Germany."[38]

Another greeting followed Ebert's speech, this one from the *Oberbürgermeister* of Berlin. Then the troops marched away, to pass in review in front of their own division commander near the opera house, and, from there, proceeded to their respective unit casernes.

The conduct and reception of the parade of December 10 was significant on several levels. It served as a symbol of Germany's difficult transition from empire to republic. Those most unnerved by the revolution may have been reassured by the appearance of the old flags and portraits of Hindenburg, but the Brandenburg Gate had been decorated with a banner that read "Peace and Liberty" along with the black-red-orange republican flag that had first appeared in the revolution of 1848–9.[39] The entire event was a curious mix of new and old symbols.

---

[38] "Eberts Rede an die Truppen," *Vossische Zeitung*, evening edition, December 10, 1918.

[39] Manuela Achilles, "Reforming the Reich: Democratic Symbols and Rituals in Weimar Germany," unpublished doctoral dissertation, University of Michigan, 2005. The first chapter is a perceptive analysis of the clash of competing symbols on December 10, 1918.

The thanks of a grateful nation were apparent in both Ebert's words and the outpouring of welcome from the Berliners. No one doubted that the emotions of the crowd were genuine. The previous four years had been hard for all Germans, but the *Frontschweine* had certainly made the greatest sacrifices. Later, during the inter-war years, right-wing revisionists would claim that an ungrateful people had treated the returning army in shameful fashion. Certainly, the revolutionaries roughed up individual officers and ripped off their shoulder straps, but, from the borders of the Reich to the streets of Berlin, contemporary accounts describe a generous and genuine welcome to the front-line soldiers.[40]

In Ebert's words to the *Fronttruppen* one also senses a feeling of guilt and regret. Certainly the chancellor felt that Germany had asked so much of these men and had so little to give in return. Feelings of guilt also may have been mixed with anxiety. If these front-line soldiers, with their wreath-covered machine guns and *Minenwerfer*, felt the nation had cheated them, if the German people were indifferent to their achievements and their suffering, these Western Front veterans might be capable of a dangerously violent reaction.[41] Such feelings may help to explain why Ebert chose to tell them that they were "unconquered." Ebert had explained in unmistakable terms that Germany's defeat was the result of the overwhelming power of foreign enemies. Nevertheless, the apparent admission by a socialist politician that Germany had been "undefeated in the field" would later prove useful for right-wing extremists eager to support their "stab-in-the-back" claims.[42]

But Ebert's words also served as an invitation for the *Frontschweine* to integrate themselves into the new German society, one that had "shaken off the old regime that lay like a curse on our actions." At the front, the sacrifices had marked them as men of special character, devotion, and strength, virtues that would be needed in building a nation that was "sovereign of its own fate." He told them that "work is the religion of socialism," and that there would be a place for the former warriors in the noble work of creating the new Germany.[43]

[40] See Bessel, "Die Heimkehr der Soldaten."
[41] The MSPD's newspaper, *Vorwärts*, wrote, "The Brandenburg Gate, through which the troops are marching, proclaims peace and freedom; and the faces underneath steel helmets bear visages of reserved gravity ... The returning men know what they have left out there; and the misery, the hurt in the countenance of so many who quietly wave their handkerchiefs, they understand as well." Quotation from "Der Einzug der Truppen," December 11, 1918, quoted in Achilles, "Reforming the Reich," 61.
[42] *Ibid.*, 64. "Undefeated in the field" was a phrase Ebert never used. For a discussion of the way Ebert's words were twisted, see Mühlhausen, *Friedrich Ebert*, 136–7.
[43] The ideas of this paragraph are taken from Achilles, "Reforming the Reich," 65.

One may question whether the guardsmen in the parade formations were cheered by these words or any of the orations delivered at the Pariser Platz. Veteran soldiers rarely have much use for fancy speeches; they had been on the march for several hours and rations were waiting in the Moabit caserne.

As a show of force in support of the Ebert government, the parade was a resounding success.[44] Eyewitness accounts stress the appearance of heavy machine guns and artillery batteries within the marching units. The well-ordered formations of the combat-hardened veterans were a powerful contrast to the various rag-tag armed groups that had threatened the peace of the capital. Significantly, the Spartacists risked no counter-demonstrations in the presence of the well-armed guardsmen. By carrying their rifles muzzle-down and looking away as the *Fronttruppen* marched by, the revolutionary sailors in the city displayed their contempt for the guards.[45] The Spartacist press registered its dismay in print: "What was planned and prepared for was clearly stamped in the character of the entry of the bourgeoisie demonstration ... the violent crushing of the Berlin proletariat, the workers' and soldiers' councils, and their proletarian storm troops, the Spartacists."[46]

However, if the parade of December 10 was part of an operation to secure the government against its enemies, then it was only a very tentative, if successful, first step. The troops kept their weapons and ammunition, to be sure, but the government had not authorized their use except in self-defense. Most of Lequis' command was outside the city or en route, while Berlin remained an armed camp of potentially hostile forces. If the middle class had been reassured, in the working-class districts, the Spartacists were distributing weapons and denouncing the parade. In western Berlin, the crowds had been welcoming; there was

---

[44] An AEF intelligence report culled this analysis from the Berlin press: "The people of BERLIN appear to be much relieved by the return of the Guards. The performances of Liebknecht and Rosa Luxemburg and the Spartacus Group, with its irresponsible adherents of the Bolshevik type, have caused apprehension among the citizens ... the fact that on the day before the expiration of the armistice the delegates of the workers' and soldiers' councils will meet in BERLIN for their National Convention causes disquiet. This assemblage may be a signal for the Spartacus Group to start new disturbances. The Guard[s] regiments[s] are, apparently, perfectly in hand and have shown no sympathy for the red flag or for terrorizing from any quarter." NARA, RG 120, Box 5895, Third Army G2 Report no. 25, dated December 11, 1918.

[45] Döblin, *Sieger und Besiegte*, 23.

[46] "Die Gegendemonstration der Bourgeoisie," *Die Rote Fahne*, December 11, 1918. However, *Die Rote Fahne* also noted that individual soldiers seemed unsettled by the ceremony and that their contact with the revolutionary air (*Volksmilieu*) of Berlin had begun.

Figure 7.4 The parades continued for over a week. Pictured here are men of the *Jäger* Division at the Brandenburg Gate, December 11, 1918.

considerably less enthusiasm for the parade in the working-class districts in the northern and eastern sections of the city.[47]

The success of the day's parade did not seem to reduce the tension between the moderates and the extreme Left. That same day, the *Vollzugsrat* had made another demand that the newly arrived troops be disarmed. They also demanded the right to give their own welcome to the troops when the parade arrived at the Pariser Platz.[48] That night, over glasses of beer, Scheuch and his staff met with Lequis and commanders from several of the guards regiments to discuss the situation. The junior officers present, the men closest to the troops, stressed that time was running out. The rank and file, they warned, could be relied upon for only a few more days. The government needed to act immediately to limit the power of the *Vollzugsrat*. Scheuch, however,

---

[47] Kriegsgeschichtlichen Forschungsanstalt des Heeres, *Wirren*, 32
[48] On the 13th, as Brutus Molkenbuhr of the *Vollzugsrat* mounted the stage to address the 5th Guards Division, Lequis had the band strike up a loud march which drowned out Molkenbuhr's speech. Böhm, *Adjutant*, diary entry for December 13, 1918, 105–6.

was pessimistic about the government's willingness to strike, and that night, in frustration, he resolved to submit his resignation.[49]

The parades continued over the succeeding days, with the last unit, the First Guards Reserve Division, entering the city on December 22. The weather remained dreary and the crowds grew thinner after the initial procession, but the Berliners still offered each successive unit a hearty welcome. The leaders of the government took turns addressing the men at the Pariser Platz – Scheidemann spoke on the 11th, Haase on the 12th, for example – while Lequis attended each ceremony. The battle of symbols continued. On December 12, the 1st Guards Division reported to Lequis' headquarters that they had come to an understanding with local soldiers' councils on the display of red flags during the division's march into the city. On one hand, the division prohibited its soldiers from tearing down red flags outside their own casernes. On the other, they asked the councils to take down the flags flying on the bridges along the unit's parade route. Recent events had shown that, in the presence of such symbols, the chain of command might lose control of "hotheads" among the guardsmen. "In the interest of peace and order, it is not practicable, on the day of the entry march, that red flags be hoisted on the long bridges. They are too easily taken the wrong way."[50]

There were less amicable incidents. At one point, the *Vollzugsrat* forcibly detained an officer from the staff of the German *Jäger* Division for several hours after he refused to allow his troops to carry red cockades and flags. On December 15, the 4th Foot Guards returned to their barracks at the Moabit caserne, they were greeted by a jeering crowd of sailors, prisoners released from the Moabit prison, and young conscripts from their own replacement battalion. Under the leadership of the fiery Colonel Reinhard, the guardsmen overthrew the soldiers' council of their replacement battalion and evicted all of the *Ersatz* battalion's personnel from the Moabit caserne. Open warfare between the front-line troops and the garrison seemed imminent, and Lequis alerted other guards units for possible intervention.[51] Another crisis threatened on December 20 when the successor to the *Vollzugsrat*, the Central Council (*Zentralrat*) of the Workers' and Soldiers' Councils, attempted unsuccessfully to disarm one of the Life Guard Cuirassier regiments.[52]

---

[49] *Ibid.*, diary entry for December 10, 1918, 102.
[50] BA-R, R43/2486, "Report of the 1st Guard Infantry Division to *Generalkommando* Lequis," dated December 12, 1918.
[51] Incident described in Reinhard, *4. Garde-Regiment*, 398, and Kluge, *Soldatenräte und Revolution*, 241
[52] Incidents from Kriegsgeschichtlichen Forschungsanstalt des Heeres, *Wirren*, 32–3.

Through these tense days, many of the veterans of the trenches persisted in seeing the various garrison troops and sailors as cowardly shirkers. However, such attitudes would dissipate with time. The famous author Alfred Döblin observed that in many instances, when the front-line troops arrived at their home station, they would thrash the members of the homeland council.[53] Within days, however, these same soldiers were wearing red armbands and disobeying their officers. Nevertheless, one imagines that it was fairly simple for the Left to interpret the resentments of the front-line troops as an indication of reactionary manipulation by the officer corps.

The Left had reason to worry. As additional divisions moved into the capital, the OHL did not abandon the hope of achieving the operation's original objectives. Meanwhile Scheuch, even though awaiting a replacement, played a central role in thwarting their intentions. As war minister, he retained command authority over the *Ersatz* battalions that still occupied the casernes within the city, and he refused to disband or disarm these units, to dissolve their soldiers' councils, or to incorporate the *Ersatz* units into Lequis' field formations. Moreover, he gave no support to the OHL's desire to round up the deserters in the city or to "clean the undesirable elements" out of the barracks by evicting recently discharged men who remained in the casernes.[54] Instead, on December 13, Scheuch had gone so far as to order that the divisions parading through Berlin would "without exception" be demobilized in the same way as the remainder of the army. The order required Lequis to make regular reports to the war ministry on the progress of his units' demobilization.[55]

The antipathy between Scheuch and the OHL certainly had elements of a classic bureaucratic turf battle. Yet one can read more into it. Groener's headquarters and the other leaders of the front-line divisions

[53] Döblin, *Sieger und Besiegte*, 14.
[54] Scheuch's resistance described in Kluge, *Soldatenräte und Revolution*, 238; Scheuch had more than two strikes against him. In addition to the OHL's strong criticism of his policies, he faced constant attacks from the *Vollzugsrat*, who harassed and arrested members of his staff (See Berthold and Neef, *Militarismus und Opportunismus*, Document 118: "Brief des Kriegsministers von Scheuch an den Rat der Volkbeauftragten vom Dezember 10. 1918," 290–2, and BA-R, R43/2485/f, exchange of notes between the executive council and the war ministry on measures to disarm Lequis' command, dated December 10, 1918, 117.) He faced a rebellious cabal of key subordinates within his own ministry. Finally, he was a Catholic Alsatian who had been denounced throughout the army for his failure to defend the capital on November 9. Liberal historians, like Kluge, see him as one of the few senior army officers truly willing to work within the republican framework. See, especially, *Soldatenräte und Revolution*, 443–4, fn. 173 and 177.
[55] The order was countersigned by Ebert's assistant, Curt Baake: BA-R, R43/2485, war ministry proclamation dated December 13, 1918, 126.

continued to represent themselves as the leaders of the "true" soldiers. In their eyes, Scheuch was responsible for the mutinous riff-raff that had made such a mess of the homeland. The war minister, for his part, had to resent the haughty and politically naïve attitudes of the Field Army and must have seen himself as protecting the units of the Home Army (*Heimatheer*) from the arrogant, bullying tactics of the *Fronttruppen*. The resentments that existed between front and *Etappe* throughout the war were finding their way back into the homeland during the first weeks of the peace.

On December 12, Ebert met with Scheuch, Lequis, and several of the regimental commanders, again over beers. As recounted by Colonel William Reinhard, commander of the Fourth Regiment of Foot Guards, the members of the gathering exchanged some very harsh words. Reinhard had protested to Ebert that the demobilization was leaving the country defenseless; the release of the older year groups had to stop. Ebert and his trusted assistant, Undersecretary Curt Baake, replied that once the government had issued the discharge order, it could not be rescinded. Angered, Reinhard answered that the army could accomplish nothing with the younger year groups in the *Ersatz* battalions; they had been poisoned by the revolution. Baake angrily scolded the regimental commander for using such a tone of voice with the cabinet, adding, "The officer corps belongs in Golgotha; then everything will be better." Reinhard (again, according to his own account) was undismayed, saying that the Social Democrats wanted to "destroy us." Ebert attempted to calm the situation, until Reinhard demanded that the government issue an immediate deadline of forty-eight hours, after which anyone found with a weapon would be summarily shot. With that remark, both Ebert and Baake became agitated. The meeting concluded with the proposal that the cabinet vote to impose a fine on those carrying unauthorized weapons. Ebert rejected Reinhard's warning that Liebknecht would launch an uprising as soon as the older year groups were discharged.[56]

The views of the officers and the politicians seemed irreconcilable. Frustrated by Scheuch's opposition and Ebert's vacillation, Groener

---

[56] Berthold and Neef, *Militarismus und Opportunismus*, Document 117: "Besprechung zwischen Ebert und Oberst Reinhard am 10. Dezember 1918," 288–91. Berthold and Neef show this meeting on December 10, but again, Böhm's diary suggests a flawed chronology, and places this heated exchange on December 12. On the 14th, the government issued its order on prohibiting the possession of weapons by unauthorized personnel. Instead of a "shoot on sight" policy as the OHL had hoped, the order prescribed a 100,000-mark fine or up to five years' imprisonment for unauthorized possession of weapons. BA-R, R43/2485/f, Decree on the Return of Weapons and War Materials in the Possession of the Reich, dated December 14, 1918, 119.

Figure 7.5 The First Congress of Workers' and Soldiers' Councils, 16–20 December, 1918. Seated center with the white goatee is Scheidemann. To his right are Landsberg, Ebert, and Barth.

and his staff watched their narrow window of opportunity closing. On December 16, less than a week after the arrival of the first units, the National Congress of Workers' and Soldiers' Councils would open in Berlin, and the army leaders believed this event had the potential to push the country's direction well to the Left. What was worse, just over a week after that came Christmas. Those of Lequis' guardsmen eligible for discharge, and, probably, many who were not eligible, would be clamoring for their immediate release. Thus, several days after the beginning of the *Einzug* (entry), Groener sent his political advisor, Major von Schleicher, to Berlin in order to press Ebert to decisive action.[57]

Lewinsohn's ordeal

The mission was a failure. Despite Schleicher's best efforts, Ebert did not budge, and the National Congress of Workers' and Soldiers' Councils opened as scheduled. History was to record that the deliberations of this body were relatively conservative. The Majority Socialists held

[57] Thaer, *Generalstabdienst an der Front*, diary entries for December 16 and 18, 1918, 281–2.

an overwhelming majority,[58] and neither Liebknecht nor Luxemburg had been voted a seat in the congress. Among the key outcomes of the congress was support for the election of a National Assembly on January 19, 1919, and the creation of a national-level Central Council of Workers' and Soldiers' Councils (*Zentralrat*) for the "parliamentary supervision" of the Council of People's Delegates. In this role, it would replace the *Vollzugsrat*. To Ebert's satisfaction, MSPD men dominated the new council.

Despite its domination by "moderate" socialists, the congress served to emphasize the lingering suspicion and *alienation* between the home-land councils, on one hand, and the *Fronttruppen* and their representa-tives, on the other. This was reflected in the reception the congress gave Ludwig Lewinsohn during its fifth session on December 18. Lewinsohn, as a former MSPD party official and the head of the Fourth Army's soldiers' council, proposed to address the representatives on the political views of the front-line troops. Previous chapters noted that Lewinsohn had worked closely with the officer chain of command to ensure the successful return of the troops of the Fourth Army. As an NCO on an army staff, Lewinsohn was hardly a true *Frontschwein*, yet, at the congress, he stepped forward to speak for the men who were returning from the trenches. Those present were unwilling to hear what he had to say. According to the transcript kept for that day, the audi-ence met virtually every significant assertion made by Lewinsohn with catcalls, ridicule, and condemnation. He had opened defensively:

Lewinsohn: Comrades and colleagues, I speak in the name of the comrades of the Western Front. We are soldiers' councils that are frequently slandered because you do not know what we have done, because you have heard only rumors, and because you have received flyers you do not understand.

He continued by reporting that at the time of the armistice, conditions behind the front were chaotic, with widespread plunder and disorder. It was the job of "true revolutionary elements" to protect the honor of the revolution by bringing things under control. They had left in place the officers who were technical experts, because no one in the councils pretended to have the expertise gained from years of training in staff schools. He attempted to justify this cooperation with Fourth Army officers by asking the audience, "Does anyone here feel himself capable

---

[58] Along with civilian party members present, the representatives from the *Westheer* and units from the East were overwhelmingly MSPD in sympathy. Jörg Berlin, *Die deut-schen Revolution, 1918/1919: Quellen und Dokumente* (Cologne: Pahl-Rugenstein Verlag, 1979), Document 168: "Bericht des Delegierten Thomas über den Rätekongress in der Sitzung des 21er Rates Wilhelmshaven vom 3. 1. 1919 (Auszüge)," 222–5.

of undertaking the demobilization of a division or a corps? If he does, he can come to me with his address; tomorrow I'll put him at the head of a corps."

Response: Do you have that power?

Lewinsohn: Yes, we at the front have this power.

Response: But you don't!

Lewinsohn reminded the audience that the Allies had made it clear that they would not negotiate with soldiers' councils. If the congress sought a complete overthrow of the highest level of the army's leadership, they would put the continuing conduct of the armistice negotiations in jeopardy.

Response: Then we'll still have you! [Laughter]

Lewinsohn asked the audience to tone down their language and allow him to speak.

Lewinsohn: [seeking to verify his revolutionary *bona fides*]: We have expressed ourselves in terms of supporting a socialist republic, and our flyers have been available for your review.

Response: We have seen from your flyers what kind of fellow you are!

Lewinsohn: You have to remember that Berlin is not alone in the world. The front-line troops and the troop units waiting to be demobilized do not think exactly like you do. That's because they know there exists the danger that the demobilization will not go smoothly should their leaders suddenly be deposed. [Then he went on the counterattack:] For four weeks you have called out to us: counter-revolution. You constantly say, "counter-revolution." Where is it then?

Response: There it stands! [Great laughter]

Lewinsohn: If a counter-revolution was possible, it would have happened long ago.

Response: [Objections]

Lewinsohn repeated that he wanted to work with the homeland councils and that he agreed with most of their proposals. However, the councils had misrepresented the situation in the Field Army by constantly painting the officers in the darkest terms. "We had to work with these officers day and night, because we could not accomplish this work [the army's return] ourselves" [shouts]. At this point, Lewinsohn felt pressed to resort to his nominal status as a *Frontsoldat*. "We have lain [together] in the trenches." He continued, "Today, the Supreme Headquarters has [informed us] through its liaison officer with the soldiers' council of the Supreme Headquarters, that the Central Council of Soldiers of the Front has declared that not a single officer is thinking of counter-revolutionary things" [laughter]. "That is because they know that not a single unit would operate to this end."[59]

Had Lewinsohn hoped that the congress would be an expression of solidarity among the councils, front and rear, he had been rudely disabused of that idea. It appeared that the councils of the homeland were too suspicious of the soldiers of the Western Front to accept them as revolutionary allies.

Lewinsohn was not the only speaker to receive rough treatment. Dittmann, the USPD cabinet member, also spoke that day and was challenged to defend the government against accusations that it had not done enough to prevent counter-revolution. The cabinet was aware, he said, that the old reactionary spirit was still alive within the officer corps, and that there were units in the Field Army that remained "unenlightened" by the necessary revolutionary instruction. However, events had shown that the troops would almost never be manipulated into acting in a counter-revolutionary fashion. Nevertheless, he said, the government remained vigilant. Dittmann offered that, in cases in which an officer in the *Westheer* had promulgated a policy that forbade red flags or acted in a similar counter-revolutionary fashion, the cabinet had intervened and, in some cases, had an officer relieved. (Catcall: "But von Mudra is still there!")[60] Furthermore, Dittmann explained, complaints about Lequis should take into account the fact that the government was aware of his command and had summoned the general to the chancellery in order to have him offer assurances that his command contemplated no counter-revolutionary activities.[61]

The congress concluded its business on December 21. The attacks on Lewinsohn and Dittmann indicated how deeply the Left feared that the front-line units were a force ready to turn against the revolution. However, for the army's senior leaders, the most significant outcome of the congress was the passage of the so-called "Hamburg Points"[62] on December 18. These were measures designed to secure the revolution

[59] Lewinsohn's address from BA-R, R43/2487 f.1, Record of the 5th and 6th Sessions, the General Congress of Workers' and Soldiers' Councils, December 18, 1918, 43–7.
[60] Bruno von Mudra was an army commander who had been aggressively hostile to the homeland councils. He was eventually relieved for his "counter-revolutionary activities" (along with von der Marwitz, von Eberhardt, and Friedrich Sixt von Arnim). Wilhelm Dittmann, *Erinnerungen,* ed. Jurgen Rojahn (Frankfurt: Campus Verlag), 1995, 245.
[61] BA-R, R43/2487, transcript of Dittmann's remarks, dated December 18, 1918, 95–101.
[62] So-called after an MSPD delegate, Lamp'l, from Hamburg. Guth, *Loyalitätskonflikt,* 82.

by democratizing authority relationships within the military. The seven points included: the elimination of all badges of rank, decorations, or badges of nobility; assumption by the soldiers' councils of all responsibility for discipline; the election of officers; the abolition of the standing military forces; and the accelerated creation of a people's army (*Volkswehr*).[63] Ebert knew that Groener would see this measure as a betrayal of their "pact," and attempted to have it held in abeyance by adding an "eighth point," which kept the first seven from going into effect until all details had been worked out. In this, he failed.[64]

As Ebert anticipated, Groener and the rest of the officer corps did, indeed, feel betrayed.[65] In Groener's view, the adoption of the Hamburg Points would turn the remaining elements of the army into a rabble. More importantly, it meant the end of what remained of the old officer corps. The First Quartermaster General decided to attack the dangerous measure head on. On December 19, a telegram went out to subordinate commands under Hindenburg's name which began, "I do not recognize the resolution regarding military affairs adopted by the Central Committee of the Workers' and Soldiers' Councils on 12.18.18, in particular the status of officers and NCOs." The message asserted that such a drastic revision of the existing military structure could only be accomplished through the actions of a National Assembly representing the entire German people. The army, it stated, remained loyal to the Ebert government but would await further instructions.[66]

Groener himself sent the cabinet a letter of protest warning the government that adoption of the Hamburg Points would destroy the necessary relations between officers and men, jeopardize the execution of demobilization, threaten the execution of the measures required by the armistice, undermine the convention of the National Assembly, and risk anarchy across Germany. Groener had the entire staff at Wilhelmshöhe sign the letter and then boarded a train for Berlin.[67] On the afternoon

[63] Points summarized from Jörg Berlin: Document 171: "Der Kongress der AuSR Deutschlands entscheidet am 18.12, 1918 über die Kommandogewalt (die sog. 7 "Hamburger Punkte")," 229–30.
[64] Ebert's efforts and the debate within the congress described in Guth, *Loyalitätskonflikt*, 79–92.
[65] See, for example, Thaer, *Generalstabdienst an der Front*, diary entry for December 19, 1918, 283.
[66] BA-MA, N 46/130, telegram transcript, "The Position of the Army Supreme Command," dated December 19, 1918. According to Volkmann, Groener told Ebert that same day that he was coming to Berlin, but that it was his fixed opinion as well as that of the field marshal that the "entire OHL stand or falls on this question." Volkmann, *Revolution über Deutschland*, 147.
[67] In the case of the Hamburg Points, at least, Groener and Scheuch were of one mind. BA-R, R43/2482, Scheuch note to Ebert, dated December 19, 1918.

of the next day, he and Admiral von Mann of the *Kriegsmarine* went
before a combined meeting of the cabinet and *Zentralrat* to contest the
Hamburg Points.[68] In the stormy debate that followed, Groener threatened the collective resignation of the entire officer corps and the collapse of order and discipline in the army. The Hamburg Points, he said,
had been inspired by the abuses of authority by junior officers in recruit
depots in the homeland. The entire officer corps need not be punished
for the mistakes of a few (left unsaid, but, evidently, a reference to a
handful of bad apples in the rear). Meanwhile, implementation of the
resolutions would be disastrous. But not so much for the *Westfront*, he
said. Relations between officers and men were so sound that, "For the
Fronttruppen [the Hamburg Points] would make no great impression."
He implied that it was the riff-raff of the Home Army that needed to
recognize the symbols of officer authority. Badges of rank and decorations were not just a relic of the old regime. Instead, they were symbols
of the power of the new republic.[69]

This was the old army playing its last card, and the anti-militarists
blinked. At first, the Independents cried treason.[70] Barth told Groener
that if he was unable to obey the orders of the government he would be
dismissed. If the general attempted to sabotage the reforms, he would
face charges of "high treason."[71] Yet amidst this rancor, Ebert was
able to reintroduce the "eighth point" which delayed the implementation of the new policies until detailed instructions could be drafted.
In addition, he secured agreement that, in their final form, the policies
would not apply to the Field Army. For one of the last times in postwar
Germany, the front-line troops were set apart from the rest of the army
(though Groener wanted the delay to apply to the entire army) and
used as pawns in the chess match between the army and its critics. The
socialists envisioned that the armed forces of the new Germany would

---

[68] A number of accounts emphasize that Groener and Schleicher walked down
Leipzigerstrasse to the Reich chancellery in full uniform, complete with decorations
and side arms, in what appeared to be an open provocation to the anti-militarists in
the capital. As they approached the chancellery building a small crowd gathered to
harass them, but when a soldier tried to block the officers' path, he was arrested by
plainclothes policemen. Volkmann, *Revolution über Deutschland*, 149.

[69] Berthold and Neef, *Militarismus und Opportunismus*, Document 139: "Gemeinsame
Sitzung des Rates der Volksbeauftragten mit dem Zentralrat am 20. Dezember 1918,"
324–31.

[70] See Schüddekopf, *Das Heer und die Republik*, Document 10: "Besprechung in
Berlin zwischen Groener-Schleicher, Rat der Volksbeauftragten und Zentralrat am
20.12.1918," 38.

[71] Barth, *Aus der Werkstatt*, 94. The Congress of Councils, he said, had not met to offer
the generals pleasant resolutions, "but instead to decide what is necessary in the interest of the revolution."

be based on democratic principles and enlightened bonds between soldier and leader, free of the trappings of the *ancien régime*. However for the time being, the old traditions and authority relationships would remain in place for the units returning from the front.[72]

If the front-line officers retained their traditional authority, as Christmas approached they were running out of men over whom they might exercise that power. With this in mind, on December 18, Lequis and Schleicher had made a final appeal to Ebert to allow Lequis' troops to enact the key element of the OHL's plan for securing the government and the capital, the disarming (*Entwaffnung*) of the populace. Ebert was unwilling to take this bold step. In the highly charged political atmosphere of the German capital, he would settle only for a less inflammatory move. The cabinet would give the authority for disarming the Berlin populace to Scheuch's war ministry. This variation to the plan would make the city commandant, Otto Wels, and his less-than-formidable *Soldatenwehr* responsible for implementing the measure. The penalty for unauthorized possession of weapons would not be, as the army wanted, immediate execution, but rather a fine.[73] Ebert's compromise inspired an angry Lequis to comment to Colonel Reinhard, "[Now] the Social Democrats will eat the filth [*Dreck*] that they have made."[74]

Ebert's halfway measure was the final nail in the coffin of the "Berlin Operation." The war ministry had neither the will nor the means to disarm the various militias and security forces around the city. Nor did Ebert have any desire to press the issue. Finally, neither the OHL nor Lequis was willing to act without the sponsorship of the new republic's civilian leaders. Thus, a week before Christmas, the OHL's cherished coup was a dead letter. The guards regiments remained in their barracks and continued to discharge the men eligible for release.

From coup to parade

On December 10, Colonel von Thaer had written in his diary, "Now, in a great circle surrounding Berlin, stand nine good divisions, fully equipped and battle ready, in any event, only 150,000 men, [but] with

---

[72] Marxist and more liberal accounts insist that Groener's threat of mass resignation was a bluff. The *Große Hauptquartier* was not likely to take itself out of business at this critical juncture. (See, for example, Könnemann, "Der Truppeneinmarsch," 1598 and Kluge, *Soldatenräte und Revolution*, 253–60.) However, how far could Ebert risk the withdrawal of the OHL's support of his government?

[73] Thaer wrote that the Spartacists would laugh at this. Thaer, *Generalstabdienst an der Front*, diary entry for December 18, 1918, 282.

[74] Lequis' reaction from Könnemann, "Der Truppeneinmarsch," 1599.

the will to shoot in order to restore order in the land."[75] Less than two weeks later, *Generalkommando Lequis* would be unable to muster a full-strength brigade to march to the support of the Ebert government.[76] As van den Bergh had predicted, the front-line divisions had, indeed, melted "like butter in the sun." What began as a decisive military strike to solidify the Ebert government evolved, in the first ten days of December, into a parade and, in the ten days following, the disintegration of the Guards Corps.

In his memoirs, Groener attributed the failure of the "Berlin Operation" to a lack of will. Ebert and Scheuch had not done their part, which was to provide the political "top cover" for the operation as well as the necessary command and control of all the pro-government elements in the capital. Ebert had not "risen to the occasion" and had not seen the urgency for acting before Lequis' command evaporated. In the process, Groener wrote, the cabinet leader had shown a dismaying lack of insight into soldier behavior.[77] Finally, even as he prepared to depart his key position, Scheuch proved pessimistic toward the operation's prospects, jealous of the authority of those who planned it, and obstructive of the essential political measures that were the preconditions for success.

Certainly, the competing goals of Ebert, Scheuch, Groener, and Lequis were decisive in the operation's failure. However, Spartacus deserved some credit as well. On one hand, the Spartacists had not met the entry of the Guards Corps with overt violence. As the front-line soldiers approached Berlin, the chain of command had told them that the government was in grave peril, but this was not apparent as the troops marched among cheering crowds. There seemed to be no Bolshevik "Red Terror" lurking on every street corner, as the guardsmen had been led to believe. On the other hand, Liebknecht's followers continued to agitate among the troops, and, in the homesick and war-weary soldiers so close to home, Spartacist encouragements to leave the ranks must have found a receptive audience.[78]

In the final analysis, however, the operation failed because the *Frontschweine* wanted to go home. The entire OHL scheme was based

[75] Thaer, *Generalstabdienst an der Front*, diary entry for December 10, 1918, 280.
[76] Groener estimated between 1,800 and 2,000 men were available on December 23. Groener's testimony in the *Dolstochprozess* paraphrased in Groener-Geyer, *General Groener*, 197.
[77] Groener, *Lebenserinnerungen*, 474.
[78] Könnemann, "Der Truppeneinmarsch," 1599. In a report to Lequis' headquarters, the 1st Guards Division had reported that the persistence of Spartacist agitation was such that, "When they are removed from one place, shortly thereafter, they begin again somewhere else." BA-R, R43/2494/11, Ia Msg. #20, *Generalkommando* Lequis to the Reich leadership on report from the 1st Guards Division, dated December 11, 1918, 28.

on the very risky assumption that the leadership of the Guards Corps, at regiment, battalion, and company level, could hold their units together for a period of days once they had brought those units so close to home. This, in turn, assumed that the junior leaders in the combat units had both the will and the courage to resist the *"Drang nach Hause."* These all proved very poor assumptions indeed, and were, perhaps, the general staff's last demonstration of *Frontfremdheit.* For most of the men returning from the Western Front, neither clever leadership, persuasive propaganda, nor the centripetal pull of comradeship was going to keep them in crowded casernes while their families were celebrating Christmas nearby. The officers responsible for planning and directing the operation were not completely unaware of their soldiers' desires, but they underestimated how strong the wish to go home would be. Groener again: "The pull of being home for Christmas proved itself stronger than military discipline."[79]

Selection had played a conspicuous role in both the accelerated dissolution of the army in December 1918 and the course of the "Berlin Operation." On one hand, by attempting to demobilize the older year groups ahead of the restive younger classes, the army removed the steadying influence of the *Stammmannschaften* and ensured that, when the younger troops clamored for immediate discharge, there were no "old sweats" on hand to steady them. At the same time, the OHL's secret *selection* process determined which units deployed around Berlin in early December. Lequis' divisions were among the best fighting division in the old *Kaiserheer.* They were also capable of putting on an impressive show when called on to march in ordered ranks through the streets of the capital. Yet, because they were divisions recruited from Prussia, many of the guardsmen had home and family nearby. The OHL's cleverness in hiding the "Berlin Operation" by choosing troops with demobilization stations near Berlin would return to undermine that operation. Even Pabst conceded that, in the days that followed their parade through Berlin, the troops of the GKSD began to ask, "Why should we lie about here in Berlin. Our families need us at home!"[80]

Had Groener's operation succeeded, the army might have proven itself the mainstay of the Ebert government. However, this assumes that the front-line units that marched into Berlin would be willing to use armed force against the anti-government forces. In light of the events to follow, the "Bloody Christmas" crisis of December 23–24,

---

[79] Groener, *Lebenserinnerungen*, 474–5. Könnemann, an East German historian, made the notable concession that Christmas probably had a greater solvent effect on Lequis' divisions than did appeals to proletarian solidarity: "Der Truppeneinmarsch," 1599.
[80] Nachlass Pabst, 34.

this also seems a poor assumption. Throughout the first three weeks of December, the OHL had resisted efforts to liquidate the old military authority in favor of more democratic military system. The general staff officers at Wilhelmshöhe had used the technical demands of redeployment and demobilization of the "Western Front" to assert their irreplaceable status. They had used the prospect of a military operation against the government's enemies in Berlin to maintain the influence they had regained after the shock of November 9. However, as Christmas approached, their hole card, the "Western Front," had largely merged with the "Home Front." The army leaders had lost their last and strongest weapon and the Ebert government, apparently, its strongest military support. In their newly weakened condition, both the OHL and the cabinet would face the coming Christmas holiday with considerable foreboding. It promised to be a season of anxiety.

8   The last battle: "Bloody Christmas," December 23–24, 1918

> So it came to pass, that right on the day the Savior of Mankind was heralded by the words "Peace on Earth," the war of citizen against citizen of the same nation began.
>
> Captain Waldemar Pabst, Ia, GKSD[1]

Ignorant armies (Berlin: December, 1918)

As the last of the front-line divisions returned to their casernes, Germany's threadbare capital looked forward to its first peacetime Christmas in four years. For many families this was an occasion for rejoicing, as sons, fathers, and husbands came home. However, their jubilation offered only limited relief from the uncertainty that weighed on the minds of Berliners. Six weeks after revolution had swept the old regime away, a series of unsettling events reminded the citizens of the capital that Germany's political future remained uncertain. The end of the Congress of Workers' and Soldiers' Councils on December 20 had left the ruling coalition in turmoil. Bitter over their political defeat, the Independent Socialist members of the government and the radical Berlin soldiers' and workers' councils threatened to abandon their role in the governing coalition. On the 21st, crowds of Berlin workers responded to Spartacist agitation and took to the streets to commemorate the burial of those killed in the violence of December 6. Their numbers and their slogans were an ominous rebuke to the government. Then, on the 22nd, the last of Lequis' divisions marched through the streets of Berlin. An eyewitness, Count Harry Kessler, recorded the event in his diary:

[A]nother home-coming division, steel-helmeted and flower-bedecked ... was marching down Unter den Linden. But at the corner of Wilhelmstrasse, it was awaited by a crowd of war-wounded, shaking their crutches in the air or

---

[1] BA-MA, PH 620/2; Nachlass Pabst, "Niederschrift der Erinnerungen von Major Waldemar Pabst und seine Nachkriegserlebnisse als Ia and Stabschef der Garde-Kav-(Schü) Division," 41.

258

carrying placards: "Not Charity, but Justice" and "Throw out the Guilty who have reduced us to Misery and Poverty." The procession, obviously mounted by Liebknecht, moved forward in the path of the division, jostled the troops, got in their way, broke in among the ranks. It was a distressing incident which visibly affected the soldiers. Their faces were taut and the atmosphere tense. The onlookers were just as upset, but remained quiet.[2]

If the Spartacists had organized the demonstration, they deserved credit for a shrewd act of political theater. The presence of crippled men ruined the celebration of heroic units and imperial symbols. It reminded the crowd what monarchy and militarism had cost the German people. Indeed, the returning troops had received welcome speeches by Ebert and others suggesting that the front-line soldiers, because of their ordeal in the trenches, had a unique moral authority in the new Germany. Only the dead, the oratory claimed, had made a greater sacrifice. Unfortunately, there was the messy business of the war-wounded. These crippled men would not be so readily integrated into the noble ranks of the German working class. Their missing limbs and sightless eyes testified to a level of sacrifice between the honored dead and the returning guardsmen on parade.

The enemies of the Ebert government were not restricting themselves to political theater. Spartacist supporters spent the latter days of December distributing weapons among the most radicalized factory workers in the capital. Berlin was full of rumors of Soviet agents, Soviet money, and Soviet agitation.[3] Tension was building in the capital. If a showdown seemed likely, average Berliners could only hope that it might be deferred until after the holiday season. In this hope, they were to be disappointed. The long-anticipated outbreak of violence came on Christmas Eve, 1918. The German Left remembered it as "*Blutweihnachten*," Bloody Christmas.

The battle of December 24, 1918, was one of the most curious in German military history. The causes of the fighting on Christmas Eve reflected the uneasy compromises and complex political arrangements of revolutionary Germany. By the same token, the opposing sides in the battle highlighted the uncertain allegiances of the new republic's various armed groups. On one side of the fighting was a coalition socialist government divided against itself (Moderates versus Independents). As

---

[2] Harry Kessler, *Berlin in Lights: The Diaries of Count Harry Kessler (1918–1937)*, trans. and ed. Charles Kessler (New York: Grove Press, 2000), diary entry for December 22, 1918, 39.

[3] BA-R, R43/2494/k. This entire series of documents shows that through December, the government operated under the fear of a Spartacist uprising supported by Soviet money and arms.

another incongruity, the city commandant, MSPD veteran Otto Wels, had little or no control over the "military" formations in the capital. The army defending the new government, an army once the most powerful in the world, was wasting away. What remained of that army was also divided against itself (officer corps versus soldiers' councils; Field Army versus homeland garrisons), and its senior leaders, in the OHL and *Kriegsministerium*, held the political ideals of their civilian masters in contempt. In particular, the colonels and generals despised the government's unwillingness to move decisively against its opponents.

On Christmas Eve, the sworn enemy of the government was, paradoxically, one of the first units called upon to defend the revolutionary regime. There were more incongruities. The unit in question, the *Volksmarinedivision*, was led by a sailor and an army deserter who based their authority on personality and appeals to revolutionary solidarity. Between them, they had only marginal control over their own subordinates. These subordinates, in turn, held political allegiances ranging from indifference to solid Majority Socialist to pure Spartacist. It was a unit originally formed to provide security and order in the capital. Over time, it had become, in the eyes of many Berliners, the city's chief source of insecurity and disorder.

The causes and course of the fighting were unusual, as well. The actual combat on December 24 resulted from an operation approved and launched by one part of the coalition government – the Majority Socialists – without the knowledge or consent of its partners, the Independent Socialists. To make matters worse, the operation was executed by a chain of military headquarters – the OHL, Lequis' command, and an elite guard division – that were not inclined to obey either side of the ruling coalition. Thus, the battle that took place on Christmas Eve around the imperial palace and the former imperial stables embodied all the contradictions and confusion of the postwar Reich. "Bloody Christmas" revealed to the world the inability of the government to protect itself against its enemies as well as its powerlessness to control its own armed protectors. It also demonstrated the dilemmas faced by every returning front-line soldier. In the power struggles taking place across his homeland, how should he respond and where did his own allegiance lie?

The battle was far from inevitable. The Christmas Eve fighting resulted from a series of unlikely errors, oversights, and misunderstandings. It would have been a comedy of errors, if not for the corpses lying in the courtyard of the Marstall building at the end of the day. The proximate cause was trivial; the showdown started with an argument about door keys on the day before Christmas Eve.

On paper, the Ebert–Haase government and the Council of Peoples' Delegates was far from defenseless. Pledged to defend the government was the commandant's *Republikanische Soldatenwehr* (Republican Soldier Security Force), perhaps 10,000 strong, the police president's *Sicherheitwehr* (Security Force) of uncertain strength, numerous replacement battalions of the Berlin garrison, the *Studentenwehr* (Student Security Force), Suppe's force of active duty guard NCOs, a number of local vigilante groups, and finally the battle-tested veterans of the Guards Corps itself. However, as we have seen, none of these groups truly offered the hope of reliable military efficiency and loyalty. The *Soldatenwehr* was made up of ill-led volunteers, many of whom served only for the generous pay.[4] The *Sicherheitswehr*, led by the Independent police president, Emil Eichhorn, was increasingly pro-Spartacist. Other formations were relatively new, ad hoc, and untested. The guards units recently arrived from the front were wasting away so rapidly that no one could predict their strength by Christmas. Meanwhile, the chief characteristics of the garrison replacement battalions were the youth of their members and their appalling lack of discipline;[5] many had declared allegiance to the Ebert government, some not.[6]

Then there was the *Volksmarinedivision* (VMD; the People's Naval Division), conspicuous for its politically and militarily critical role of securing the main government buildings in the heart of Berlin. Because the VMD played such a central role in the turmoil and bloodshed of late December 1918, and because it fought the last remnants of the old Field Army, the division's origins, composition, and allegiances are worthy of examination. Similarly, the events that put it in conflict with the front-line soldiers of General von Lequis deserve attention, even though such a review is complicated by the controversies that surround the VMD's history.[7]

---

[4] Van den Bergh, *Aus den Geburtsstunden*. The author describes the *Soldatenwehr* troops as mercenaries without officers: "no leadership and no heroes." Diary entry for December 25, 1918, 64–5. They were organized into twelve, and later, fifteen "depots," each of four companies and approximately 1,000 men. See Kriegsgeschichtlichen Forschungsanstalt des Heeres, *Wirren*, 15–16.

[5] Van den Bergh, *Aus den Geburtsstunden*, diary entry for December 25, 1918. Van den Bergh's contemptuous assessment was that the best men had gone home and what remained were "adventurers" who enjoyed agitation and sought to avoid demobilization. Their chain of command ran through the headquarters of the III Corps and the Guard Corps to the war ministry.

[6] Though heavily biased against the Left, the most comprehensive review of the various armed groups in Berlin in December 1918 is found in Kriegsgeschichtlichen Forschungsanstalt des Heeres, *Wirren*, 11–20.

[7] In East German historiography, for example, the VMD were heroes of the November Revolution, consistently and devoutly dedicated to combating the forces of reaction.

The *Volksmarinedivision* (Berlin: November 10–mid December, 1918)

Among the units pledged to support the revolution, the VMD had a certain pride of place. It had been the first unit within Berlin specifically created to secure the new revolutionary government. On November 10, the day after the collapse of the imperial regime, sniping, looting, incendiary agitation, and various other manifestations of lawlessness left the center of the capital anxious and unsettled. Such lawlessness had made the functioning of the newly formed Ebert–Haase cabinet as well as the government ministries nearly impossible. At this point, a petty officer named Paul Wieczorek appeared at the Reich chancellery and offered the services of his comrades in a naval aviation unit stationed nearby. Impressed by the man's earnest sincerity, the war minister, General Scheuch, teamed Wieczorek with his own deputy, Colonel Walther Reinhardt, and, together, the two men cooperated to build a 200-man guard force for the key government facilities[8] near the Reich chancellery. The new unit installed itself in the Marstall building, the former imperial stables. Over the next several days, its orderly behavior and appearance served to calm things in the center of the capital.[9]

The division was formed to defend against the forces of counter-revolution. See, for example, Kurt Wrobel, *Die Volksmarinedivision* (Berlin [East]: Verlag des Ministeriums für Nationale Verteidigung, 1957), and Paul Freyer, *Sturmvogel: Rote Matrosen 1918/1919* (Berlin [East]: Militärverlag der Deutschen Demokratischen Republik, 1975). They became the "useable past" of the German socialist state and, in their honor, the East German navy was named the *Volksmarine* and a number of vessels were named after the division's leaders. (See Douglas Peifer, "Commemoration of Mutiny, Rebellion, and Resistance in Postwar Germany: Public Memory and the Formation of 'Memory Beacons'." *Journal of Military History*, 65, 4 (Oct. 2001), 1013–52.) In the accounts of those who opposed them, they were shiftless vandals who had fallen under the influence of genuinely dangerous radicals (See Wels' statement in BA-R, R43/2508/e, 5, Berlin commandant's report to the cabinet, dated December 17, 1918.) One of the division's first leaders, Graf von Metternich, described his men as an "organized band of robbers" (Volkmann, *Revolution über Deutschland*, 133). The National Socialist account in Kriegsgeschichtlichen Forschungsanstalt des Heeres, *Wirren*, 18–19, suggests the unit evolved into a uniformed protection racket. As to origins, Reinhardt's diary contradicts the East German account by claiming the unit's original function was to avoid a coup from the Left. (Fritz Ernst, "Aus dem Nachlass des Generals Walther Reinhardt." *Welt als Geschichte*, 18, 1 (1958), 46–7.)

[8] Over time these would include the Reichsbank, key rail stations, museums, cafés and hotels known for political activity, newspaper offices, as well as the Austro-Hungarian Embassy. BA-R, R43/2408/f, *Volksmarinedivision* strength report submitted to the city commandant, December 18, 1918.

[9] Description of the original guard force from Reinhardt's account is found in Ernst, "Aus dem Nachlass," 46–7. See also, Kriegsgeschichtlichen Forschungsanstalt des Heeres, *Wirren*, 17. By housing them in the Marstall instead of a local caserne, the government hoped to insulate them from the poisonous influence of the army replacement battalions.

Encouraged by this, the government sought to expand the formation, and the city commandant, Otto Wels, asked the Kiel soldiers' council for an additional 2,000 "reliable" sailors. At the time, a railway strike impeded traffic from Kiel to Berlin. Thus, on November 13, 600 sailors from Cuxhaven, rather than Kiel, reinforced the original members of the naval guard force.[10] Together with the original guard unit, these men became the nucleus of what would be called the "People's Naval Division."[11] As other sailors joined the unit, its numbers swelled, and, by November 13, 1918, the division numbered 1,500, many of them stokers and machinists from Berlin and its environs.[12] It organized itself into three detachments, each quartered in different areas of the city center.[13]

Over the next several weeks, the division continued to grow. Enlistment in the *Volksmarinedivision* entitled one to lodging, rations, regular pay, the right to bear arms, and an identity card that read: "Employed on the missions of the Ebert and Haase government."[14] Not surprisingly for a city crowded with unemployed men, these privileges drew new recruits to the division in large numbers, so that, by the end of November, it numbered 3,200.[15] With the enlarged membership, the character of the division changed. Many of the new men were not sailors, most were politically unsophisticated or even hostile to the government, and more than a few were, as even Marxist sources have conceded, "undesirable elements."[16]

The character of the leadership changed as well. Wieczorek was a murder victim just a few days after the division formed.[17] Otto Tost, a

---

[10] Gustav Noske, *Von Kiel bis Kapp. Zur Geschichte der deutsche Revolution* (Berlin: Verlag fur Politik und Wirtschaft, 1920), 48.

[11] Creation of the original guard force from Reinhardt's account found in Ernst "Aus dem Nachlass," 46–7.

[12] Wrobel, *Volksmarinedivision*, 37–8, and Bogdan Krieger, *Das Berliner Schloß in den Revolutiontagen 1918: Erinnerungen und Eindrücke* (Leipzig: Konkordia Verlag, 1922), 17.

[13] Detachment I was the largest and along with the division headquarters was in the Marstall. It took responsibility for the chancellery, the Reichsbank, and other buildings nearby. The smaller Detachment II was quartered in the Representative House, where the *Vollzugsrat* held its meetings. Detachment III, also smaller than I, was billeted in the exposition hall of the *Lehrter Bahnhof* where it served as a sort of reserve for the rest of the division. Freyer, *Sturmvogel*, 177.

[14] German Historical Museum, Berlin. Exhibit Item Do 81/58, "Ausweis eines Angehörigen des Volksmarinedivision, Berlin 1918," *Volksmarinedivision* Identification Card #154 (Seaman Heinger).

[15] Noske, *Von Kiel bis Kapp*, 65. When Noske visited the Marstall after Christmas he found that most of the sailors he talked to were men who had not been able to find work.

[16] Wrobel, *Volksmarinedivision*, 37–9.

[17] Marxist sources claim that a reactionary naval officer named Brettschneider shot Wieczorek while trying to wrest control of the division from its revolutionary

sailor with an Independent seat in the *Vollzugsrat*, succeeded him. Tost was succeeded, in turn, by a nobleman with ostensible socialist sympathies, Graf von Metternich.[18] Metternich did not last long. Implicated in the December 6 *putsch*, he fled Berlin, and the division's leadership changed again.[19] By the middle of December, Wieczorek's sailor friend Fritz Radtke served as commander and head of the division's soldiers' council. A demoted former army lieutenant and deserter, Heinrich Dorrenbach, acted as the chief of agitation and press relations.[20] Dorrenbach, in particular, was deeply committed to pulling the division farther to the Left.[21] He made common cause with the radicalized supreme sailors' council of Berlin (*Obermarinerat*[22]) and Eichhorn's *Sicherheitswehr*. In addition, his association with Spartacist leader Karl Liebknecht indicated an increasing hostility to the moderate elements of the government.[23] It would be incorrect to characterize all of the members of the *Volksmarinedivision* as Spartacists. Nevertheless, the MSPD members in the government began to view the unit as a hostile force and a potential enemy in any future trial of strength between the government and its opponents on the Left.[24] The Moderates began to look for ways to move the division out of Berlin.

The VMD's leaders were well aware of the government's growing hostility, and sailors knew that identifying with the leftist opposition had its risks. When Lequis' troops began arriving on the outskirts of Berlin in early December, a shudder of anxiety went through the ranks of the VMD. If the guardsmen truly represented the counter-revolution, as the sailors feared, the unit that prided itself as being the vanguard

---

leadership (see, for example, Wrobel, *Volksmarinedivision*, 33). Colonel Reinhardt, on the other hand, wrote that it was Wieczorek's efforts to prevent the "radicalization" of the division that cost him his life. Ernst, Aus dem Nachlass," 47.

[18] Metternich had been an official in the Foreign Office, and Marxist historiography considered him a government mole inserted into the division to monitor its political reliability. Kurt Wrobel, *Der Sieg der Arbeiter und Matrosen im Dezember 1918: Berliner Arbeiterveteranen berichten über ihren Kampf in der Novemberrevolution* (Berlin: Bezirksleitung der SED Groß-Berlin, Abteilung Agitation/Propaganda, 1958), 31. See also, Kriegsgeschichtlichen Forschungsanstalt des Heeres, *Wirren*, 18. The National Socialist account of his activities found nothing to reproach.

[19] Before he fled, Metternich warned Ebert that the VMD was becoming increasingly unreliable and should be disbanded. Hansjoachim Koch, *Der deutsche Bürgerkrieg: Eine Geschichte der deutschen und österreichischen Freikorps, 1918–1923* (Frankfurt: Ullstein, 1978), 44–5.

[20] Freyer, *Sturmvogel*, 183.

[21] *Ibid.*, 162–3.

[22] It was also known as the Council of 53 (*53er Ausschuss*).

[23] Volkmann, *Revolution über Deutschland*, 134.

[24] Holger Herwig, "The First German Congress of Workers' and Soldiers' Councils and the Problem of Military Reforms." *Central European History*, 1, 2 (1963), 158.

of the revolution was their obvious adversary.[25] Though well armed
and numerous, the seamen could have had few illusions about their
ability to stand against veterans of the Western Front. Nevertheless,
Dorrenbach and the other leaders of the division considered armed
resistance to Lequis' forces as the first guards formations moved into
the city on December 10. In the event, good judgment prevailed, and
the sailors contented themselves with a heightened status of alert and a
sullen indifference to the parades that followed.[26]

The guardsmen returned the disdain, starting with the first guards
unit to arrive, the *Garde-Kavallerie-Schützen-Division* (GKSD), the
Guards Cavalry Rifle Division. The political instruction organized
by their chief of staff, Captain Pabst, was reflected in a note sent by
the division trustees' council to the national Congress of Workers' and
Soldiers' Councils on December 18. Along with rejecting the Hamburg
Points and calling for a greater voice for the front-line troops in the
ongoing congress, the guards made a direct attack on the sailors' role
as the "lay-about darlings" of the revolution:

The service of the *Volksmarinedivision* for the revolution is recognized. However,
it cannot be accepted that it is constituted as a special organization for the
public safety of Berlin. We demand that it be demobilized and in-activated
in the same way as the Field Army's troop units. As those in the army, those
in the navy should get on with their [civilian] work. The troops of Berlin will
view the further employment of the sailors in Berlin with suspicion.[27]

Thus, the GKSD's first salvo against the VMD appeared in print. The
next one would be provided by artillery and machine guns.

The growing crisis (December 13–21, 1918)

Perhaps inevitably, the activities of the VMD brought it into conflict
with the city commandant, the Majority Socialist, Otto Wels, who was
the man responsible for public order within the capital. In the first

---

[25] Because of their role in the events of November, 1918, Rosa Luxemburg called the
sailors the "storm birds of the revolution."

[26] Krieger, *Das Berliner Schloß*, 31. At least one source suggests that Lequis considered
acting on his own initiative to suppress the *Volksmarinedivision* but reconsidered when
his subordinate commanders advised him that their troops would be unwilling to go
into action against such an enemy unless the order came from Ebert. See Volkmann,
Revolution über Deutschland, 134. The sailors' reaction to the parades taken from
Döblin, *Sieger und Besiegte*, 23.

[27] Berthold and Neef, *Militarismus und Opportunismus*, Document 134: "Stellungnahme
der Vertrauensräte der Garde-Kavallerie-Schutzen-Division vom. 18. Dezember
1918," 318–19.

Figure 8.1 Members of the *Volksmarinedivision* in front of the
imperial palace, November, 1918.

place, Wels had to consider political provocations. On December 18,
Dorrenbach led a deputation of soldiers and sailors to the national
Congress of Workers' and Soldiers' Council. After interrupting the
proceedings, he demanded that real soldiers' councils be created within
Lequis' command, that all command authority in the army be turned
over to the councils, and that a halt be made to all efforts to get the VMD
to evacuate the city.[28] This was disturbing enough, but, along with the
ideological differences Wels had with the unit's leaders, the commandant could not ignore reports that criminal elements within the division
were involved in armed robbery and extortion in the train stations in
the city center.[29] Neither could he overlook the inflated strength reports
submitted by the sailors that seemed to exaggerate their numbers in
order to draw excess pay.[30] To make matters worse, army officials
complained the sailors had extorted 300,000 marks and thousands

---

[28] Wrobel, *Der Sieg*, 39–40.
[29] BA-R, R43/2508/f, Berlin commandant's report to the cabinet 231/12, dated
December 21, 1918.
[30] BA-R, R43/2508/f, strength report of the *Volksmarinedivision*, dated December 15,
1918. The report claimed that the division had a strength of 3,250 men, of whom only
1,450 were immediately available, because of shortages of provisions and pay.

of uniform items from the commissariat of the Guards Corps. Most alarming were the reports that the sailors, having driven plunderers from the imperial palace in mid November,[31] were now either allowing or directly participating in plunder themselves. The finance ministry sent Wels a memorandum claiming that the occupants of the palace had pilfered 1 million marks of public treasure and that another 20 million was at risk if the sailors were allowed to remain in the palace.[32]

In these circumstances, Wels decided that the continued presence of a hostile and unreliable unit like the *Volksmarinedivision* in the center of the capital was intolerable.[33] In order to bring the sailors under control he developed a plan that included (1) a dramatic reduction in the size of the *Volksmarinedivision*, down to 600 men (preferably "reliable Social Democrats"), (2) the sailors' evacuation of the palace, and (3) incorporation of the unit into Wels' own *Soldatenwehr*. On December 13, after gaining Ebert's approval, Wels met to discuss the plan with the division's representatives as well as members of the Berlin sailors' central council. The sailors were predictably outraged by the accusations of larceny and were loath to abandon their own plans to increase the size of the *Volksmarinedivision* to a 5,000-man force independent of the navy. Nevertheless, by the end of the negotiations, they had agreed that, after receiving 125,000 marks,[34] they would leave the palace by December 15 and then trim their numbers to 600 hand-picked men who would be incorporated into the *Soldatenwehr*.[35] However, after Wels paid the 125,000 marks, the sailors did not fulfill their side of the agreement. The VMD failed to leave the palace by the original deadline or a subsequent one set by Wels for December 17. Predictably, hostility between the sailors and the commandant mounted. An angry Wels asked the cabinet to intervene, and, on December 21, the six delegates signed an order that they hoped would mollify both sides. The order called for the city commandant to pay an additional 80,000 marks to the VMD after they had given Wels the keys to the palace.[36]

---

[31] Krieger, *Das Berliner Schloß*, 17.

[32] BA-R, R43/2508/f, Berlin commandant's report to the cabinet, dated December 17, 1918.

[33] *Ibid.*, 5: "The current situation is untenable, threatens the national property, the security of Berlin, and damages the reputation of the government in the worst way."

[34] Some accounts see this money and the 80,000-mark "Christmas bonus" as little more than a bribe to get the unruly sailors to cooperate. See Richard Watt, *The Kings Depart. The Tragedy of Germany: Versailles and the German Revolution* (New York: Simon & Schuster, 1968), 231.

[35] BA-R, R43/2508/f, Berlin commandant's report to the cabinet, dated December 17, 1918, 5, 6.

[36] BA-R, R43/2508/f, cabinet resolution, dated December 21, 1918, 14.

That same day, December 21, Wels authorized routine pay for every unit in the Berlin garrison except for the *Volksmarinedivision*.[37] For many sailors, given their ongoing feud with the city commandant, the accusations leveled against the seamen by the conservative press, the lingering threat of Lequis' guardsmen, and the approach of Christmas at a time of hunger and need, this was a final provocation.

The government held hostage (Berlin: Monday, December 23, 1918)

The ill will between Wels and the *Volksmarinedivision* added to the volatile situation in Berlin. On the morning of December 23, the Council of People's Delegates met to consider, among other things, a proposal to move the government to a new location, preferably one that offered a calmer atmosphere and fewer interruptions. Ebert opened with the warning: "Colleagues, it can go on no more. Even the strongest nerves can hold out no longer." Ebert proposed Weimar or Rudolstadt; Barth, representing the Left, challenged the idea. Then, around midday, as if to underline Ebert's point, a chancellery official announced that a delegation of sailors led by Otto Tost[38] had entered the chancellery and demanded a hearing by the cabinet.[39] The delegates agreed to speak with Tost and his comrades, and a period of negotiation followed in which the members of the cabinet reminded the sailors of the protocol of December 13. The sailors hotly disputed the terms of the protocol, claiming that Wels had misrepresented the agreement. Eventually, the two sides reached a new agreement that stipulated, once more, that the sailors were to evacuate the palace, turn over the keys, and receive their 80,000 marks. The government would allow them to continue to guard the building. As a further concession, the delegates promised that any sailors discharged from the division might be given an opportunity to join the *Soldatenwehr*.[40]

The sailors came back two hours later, at about four o'clock in the afternoon. This time, Heinrich Dorrenbach, their most militant leader,

---

[37] Wrobel, *Der Sieg*, 44. The troops of the garrison received their pay in cash in ten-day increments. Also, on December 21, the two ministers of finance, Hugo Simon (USPD) and Albert Sudekum (MSPD), sent the government another memorandum deploring the plundering of the palace. (*Quellen*, 6/II, 18, fn. 2).

[38] Tost was a member of the *Obermarinerat*, the Supreme Naval Council, which, nominally at least, exerted command authority over the VMD.

[39] Meeting described in *Quellen*, 6/II, Document 63: "Emil Barth über die Kabinettsitzung am Samstag, 21.12.1918, vorm.," 15.

[40] Agreement described in *Quellen*, 6/II, Document 65: "Emil Barth über die Auseinandersetzung zwischen den Matrosenvertretern und dem Rat der Volksbeauftragten am Montag, 23.12.1918, mittags," 18–20.

was in charge. He brought with him a big box which contained, he said, the palace keys. The cabinet meeting had broken up, so the sailors sought out the delegate most likely to give them a favorable hearing, the outspoken left-wing Independent, Emil Barth.[41] Dorrenbach produced the keys and demanded the money due them. As the sailors stood by, Barth called Wels, reported the delivery of the keys, and told Wels to pay the VMD the money they were due. Wels refused. Ebert, not Barth, he said, had jurisdiction over military matters. Lacking an order from Ebert, Wels would only accept the delivery of the keys to his own office in the *Kommandantur* building. Frustrated, Barth offered to take responsibility for releasing the funds. Wels again declined, and Barth, in exasperation, dismissed the sailors, telling them they needed to find Ebert. Taking the keys with him, Dorrenbach and his followers stormed out of their audience with Barth to seek the chancellor.[42]

Unfortunately, the sailors did not find Ebert in his office. This was the last straw for Dorrenbach, who was convinced he was being played for a fool. As it turned out, Ebert and his colleague, Landsberg, were close by, just fifty steps away, taking a late lunch in Landsberg's personal quarters in the chancellery.[43] However, Dorrenbach was in no mood to hunt for Ebert.[44] After he left the chancellery, Dorrenbach sent word to the sailors at the guard posts around the building to close the gates, deny entry and egress, and to seize the telephone control station in order to block telephone traffic. It was obviously a desperate act, and its object was unclear. Dorrenbach might have been seeking to paralyze any government reaction while he marched on the *Kommandantur* or he might just have been acting out of pique. Either way, the *Volksmarinedivision* was going to shut down the government until they got their money.

While Ebert was at lunch, a porter informed him that sailors had blocked the entrances to the chancellery. Before long, Ebert realized that he and the other delegates present, Landsberg and Barth, were being held captive in the chancellery by their own guard force, the detail of sailors provided by the VMD. Though denied access to regular telephone service, Ebert still had use of his secret line to the OHL. This

---

[41] The sailors sought out Barth through an arrangement made after a telephone consultation with another Independent delegate, Haase (*Quellen*, 6/II, Document 77, 84–6).

[42] *Quellen*, 6/II, Document 66: "Emil Barth über seine Intervention bei Otto Wels am Montag, 23.12.1918, nachm.," 20–1. See also a defense of Wels' behavior in Eduard Bernstein, *Die deutsche Revolution, 1918/1919. Geschichte der Enstehung und ersten Arbeitsperiode der deutschen Republik* (Berlin: Verlag Gesellschaft und Erziehung, 1921), 153–4.

[43] Bernstein, *Die deutsche Revolution*, 155.

[44] *Ibid.*

was the same line he had used to make the famous call of November 10, the call that had initiated the famously controversial Ebert–Groener Pact. Now, a month and a half later, Ebert used the line to make another call, this time requesting that the OHL prepare a rescue operation.

In doing so, the chancellor set a tragic sequence of events in motion. On the other end of the line, Major Schleicher answered, reassured Ebert that the army would act promptly, informed Groener of the emergency, and alerted Lequis' headquarters to prepare for action.[45] This was the call the OHL had long been waiting for. Though Ebert wanted to avoid bloodshed, the army leadership saw the new crisis as an opportunity to strike a decisive blow against the government's enemies.[46]

Meanwhile, Dorrenbach had gone to settle affairs with Wels. Dorrenbach took with him a strong force of sailors reinforced by elements of *Sicherheitswehr*. He had also posted sailors to checkpoints around the government quarter. Wels was waiting, for he had received word of Dorrenbach's little coup from a message smuggled out of the chancellery.[47] He had alerted his own *Soldatenwehr*, but that had produced limited immediate results.[48] Thus, when Dorrenbach arrived to demand his money, Wels had little room to negotiate.

At this point, another one in a series of mishaps occurred that served to propel the crisis to its unhappy conclusion. The various accounts are contradictory, but it appears that a truck from the city garrison, unaware of the unfolding events, had driven by a sailor checkpoint on Unter den Linden. The sailors had attempted to gain the driver's attention by firing shots in the air. Hearing the shots and believing that an attack on the *Kommandantur* was under way, an armored car crewed by the *Soldatenwehr* responded with a burst of machine-gun fire. The fusillade killed a sailor and a man from the *Sicherheitswehr* and wounded several others.[49]

---

[45] Lequis had apparently received first notification from the war ministry, which also had a secret direct line to the Reich chancellery. Walter Oehme, *Damals in der Reichskanzei: Erinnerungen aus den Jahren 1918/1919* (Berlin [East]: Kongress Verlag, 1958), 193.

[46] Volkmann, *Revolution über Deutschland*, 155.

[47] Bernstein refers to passageways between the various government buildings, *Die deutsche Revolution*, 157. Oehme, an eyewitness, wrote that the sailors were not aware that one could go from the chancellery to the foreign office without going through the chancellery gates. Oehme, *Damals in der Reichskanzei*, 193.

[48] BA-R, R43/2508/f. An anonymous report in the "*Volksmarine*" file suggests that the sailors may have cut some kind of deal with their counterparts in the *Soldatenwehr*. This might help to explain the lackluster performance of the *Soldatenwehr* the next day. However, Bernstein's account suggests a fairly energetic response by the *Soldatenwehr* and the Berlin garrison. *Die deutsche Revolution*, 157–8.

[49] Bernstein, *Die deutsche Revolution*, 159. Wrobel, *Der Sieg*, 45. In Wrobel's version, the sailor who was killed, a popular man named Perlewitz, had approached the armored

Now the sailors were truly enraged. They blamed Wels for the death of their comrades and descended on the commandant's headquarters. Wels, justifiably alarmed, made a quick call for help to Lequis' headquarters and then attempted to defuse the situation by offering to pay them the 80,000 marks. Dorrenbach and his men were not appeased. They made prisoners of Wels, his adjutant, Lieutenant Anton Fischer, and the superintendent of the *Kommandantur*, Dr. Brongard, and hauled them away to the division headquarters in the Marstall.[50] The sailors roughed up Wels and told him and the other two prisoners they would be given summary judgment and then put before a firing squad.[51]

The decision to attack (Monday night and Tuesday morning, December 23–24, 1918)

The approach of nightfall found Chancellor Ebert in an unenviable situation. His own guard force was holding him captive in his chancellery. To add to his troubles, at about 7.00 p.m. the chancellor had learned the VMD had taken his city commandant and staff prisoner and threatened them with execution.[52] Elsewhere, the rebellious sailors held key positions throughout the government buildings in the center of the city. Dorrenbach and Eichhorn's men seemed to be masters of the situation. Any remedy to the crisis, short of surrender, would seem to demand bloodshed between countrymen, something, to this point, Ebert had desperately sought to avoid.

The army believed it had a solution to Ebert's dilemma and was moving to the government's assistance from a variety of directions. Shortly after receiving the alert message from the OHL, Lequis had ordered the small elements of the Guards Cavalry Rifle Division manning guard posts within the capital to reinforce the guard force at the university.

car for the purpose of discerning which faction it belonged to. The crew took him and his comrades under fire at a range of 10 meters. BA-R, R43/2508/f, transcript of telephone call from *Kommandantur*, dated December 23, 1918. In this description of the incident, the sailors said the shots came from the small force of guard troops stationed at the university building nearby. The soldiers denied this, claiming that the wild firing had also wounded one of their own men.

[50] Fischer was allegedly a lieutenant in the reserve. A former monk and theology instructor, his military credentials were suspect. What makes him one of the most curious of the characters in the events described is that he was considered treacherous and contemptible by both Right (Reinhard, *Wehen der Republik*, 56) and Left (Wrobel, *Der Sieg*, 37). Dr. Brongard was a civil service employee charged with the administration of the commandant's office (*Quellen*, 6/I, Document 14, 68, fn. 23).

[51] BA-R, R43/2508/f, transcript of Fischer's oral report of the events of December 23–24, undated; and Bernstein, *Die deutsche Revolution*, 160.

[52] *Quellen*, 6/II, Document 77: Ebert's statement in "Gemeinsame Sitzung von Kabinett und Zentralrat," 28 December 1918, 80.

They should prepare to "clean out" the chancellery.[53] The rest of Lequis' command was on the move, as well. Along with the GKSD, the 1st Guards Reserve Division, newly arrived in the capital, would move with all speed to secure the *Kommandantur* and the chancellery. These two divisions, along with additional elements of the 5th and 37th Infantry Divisions, would report their available strength and prepare for action. Nor was that the only action taken. That evening, without telling the cabinet, Scheuch put the Berlin garrison, the *Soldatenwehr*,[54] and other available forces around Berlin under Lequis' command.[55] From that point on, the Field Army would be fully in charge of any operations organized against the VMD.

For Ebert, Lequis' relief forces posed a problem. The appearance of armed front-line veterans in the middle of the capital had the potential to exacerbate the situation. To many Berliners, the guardsmen returned from the Western Front represented the potential for counter-revolution; their parades had been the living symbol of all that the revolution was supposed to have overthrown. To make matters worse, the guards were coming from Potsdam, the spiritual home of Hohenzollern militarism. There may have been an alternative to calling on the front-line units. At one point in the afternoon or evening, the soldiers' council of Potsdam called Ebert and offered him the service of 3,000 garrison troops. The chancellor declined the help. Garrison troops led by a solders' council might have had a favorable political effect on the tense situation, but their military effectiveness and ability to respond in a timely manner was certainly suspect.[56] Along with offering assistance, the leader of the Potsdam council had also warned Barth that the Guards Corps was on

---

[53] Kriegsgeschichtlichen Forschungsanstalt des Heeres, *Wirren*, 34–5. On the morning of the 23rd, a force of 700 guardsmen, eight heavy machine guns, and four artillery pieces was available at the university. However, at midday, without verifying the order with Lequis' headquarters, the commandant's staff ordered this force to return to Potsdam. The authors suspected a conspiracy with the sailors.

[54] Around 7.00 p.m. a representative of the *Soldatenwehr* reported to Ebert that they had watched Wels' arrest but, lacking orders, they had taken no action. They sought guidance from Ebert, who told them to stand by because he hoped for a peaceful solution to the crisis. *Quellen*, 6/II, Document 77, 80.

[55] BA-R, R43/2508/f, transcript of telephone call from the war ministry, dated 10.20 p.m., December 23, 1918. Lequis' guidance from Scheuch: "It must be asked constantly, what orders has General Lequis given and is Mr. Ebert informed of what Mr. von Lequis has ordered." In the same order, Lequis appointed a Colonel Schwerk to replace Wels as the acting city commandant.

[56] Kluge, *Soldatenräte und Revolution*, 263. Kluge claims that Ebert could not accept this help for fear it would undermine his alibi of the government's "defenselessness" as the basis for calling out the Guard Corps. Perhaps, but one wonders if the Potsdam soldiers' council could have assembled and moved 3,000 garrison soldiers on short notice on the day before Christmas Eve.

the move, and Ebert had to mollify the Independent Socialist delegates with the promise that the *Fronttruppen* would be withdrawn.[57] This was a promise that Ebert would not, and probably could not, keep.

Still, the chancellor tried to avoid a fight. When the first small group of guardsmen arrived at the chancellery, the sailors closed the chancellery gates and announced that they did not intend to withdraw, and Ebert personally intervened.[58] During the early evening, he also attempted to negotiate Wels' release with a three-man deputation of sailors, though he found the sailors agitated and difficult to deal with. When Ebert told them that they had no right to put conditions on the release of their hostage, one of the sailors told him, "Might makes right." After Ebert finally convinced them they would get their money, the sailors indicated a willingness to evacuate the palace and release Wels; however, this understanding led to no immediate results.[59]

At about 8.00 p.m., more pro-government forces arrived and appeared ready to strike. They were 200 well-armed and determined-looking Guards Uhlans under the command of a Colonel Tschirschky.[60] Armed with fixed bayonets, several pieces of artillery, and a strong complement of machine guns, the Guards Uhlans seemed ready to make short work of the sailors around the chancellery.[61] Harry Kessler described the scene:

As I passed down the Unter den Linden, I met a unit in steel helmets. Big, handsome fellows, it was some moments before I recognized the Third Battalion of Uhlan Guards, my own regiment. Some young officers explained that Ebert had just now sent for them. While we were speaking other soldiers in half-tattered uniforms and civilians surged around the troops and pestered them. Our men ignored the newcomers.

Kessler had served with the same unit earlier in the war, and he hoped the government planned to use his old comrades to remedy the situation in the capital. "If the Government possesses any vigor of mind, it will take advantage of the situation to evacuate, by force if need be, the marine division which has gone completely extremist."[62] His description of the encounter suggests two important insights: (1) the front-line troops marching into Berlin were aware they were marching to the aid

---

[57] Volkmann, *Revolution über Deutschland*, 156.
[58] BA-R, R43/2508/f, Chancellery report of December 23, 1918, 25–6.
[59] *Quellen*, 6/II, Document 77, 81.
[60] They were reinforced by several dozen men from the 1st Guard Reserve Division. Kriegsgeschichtlichen Forschungsanstalt des Heeres, *Wirren*, 35–7.
[61] Description of the guards from "Die Garde rückt an!" *Vossische Zeitung*, late edition, December 24, 1918.
[62] Kessler, *Berlin in Lights*, diary entry for December 23, 1918, 40.

of the provisional government, and (2) the appearance of guardsmen, even at night, was likely to attract a crowd ready to harangue them.

The army's senior leaders shared Kessler's desires for decisive action. Ebert insisted, however, that the soldiers at the scene allow the *Volksmarinedivision* a chance to withdraw, and Tschirschky and his staff went into the chancellery to negotiate. Dorrenbach had also arrived at the chancellery, this time to protest the deployment of the guards troops. An hour-long negotiation ensued. At the end of the session, Emil Barth came out from the chancellery with the intention of addressing the soldiers and sailors waiting nervously outside. He began by demanding the guardsmen unfix their bayonets. A major replied that only the officer who had given the order could countermand it. Rebuffed, Barth began an address designed to "enlighten" the combatants and help them understand their revolutionary responsibilities. Some of the soldiers jeered and others called Ebert to come forth. Barth reminded them that Ebert was just one of six delegates in the cabinet, but the soldiers persisted and Ebert once again came forth.[63] The chancellor told the soldiers that the government had been held captive by its own guard force, that the sailors had finally agreed to withdraw, and that both sides should pull back and leave the area. Ebert then offered them a message that, he hoped, would defuse the situation:

I ask you to do everything you can to avoid bloodshed. We have spilled so much blood in this war that it would simply be madness to bring about still more bloodshed; for that certainly no one would want to take the responsibility. Withdraw to your quarters; I guarantee the sailors will pull back.[64]

Given his family's loss during the war, Ebert's intervention must have been heartfelt. His brief address seemed clearly intended to appeal to the feelings of front-line veterans. It seemed to work. With some grumbling on both sides, the sailors and soldiers withdrew in opposite directions, leaving the chancellery devoid of protection.[65] For the time being, bloodshed had been averted.

At this point, a harried and tired Ebert turned his attention to the even larger units on their way to the scene, the main body of guardsmen from Potsdam. At 10.30 p.m., the chancellery prepared this message: "The Reich government issues the order to all troops of the Potsdam garrison

[63] Description of the incident taken from *VZ*, "Die Garde rückt an!" Barth later claimed he feared he was going to be beaten by the angry soldiers (*Quellen*, 6/II, Document 77, 92).
[64] BA-R, R43/2508/f, "Ebert's Speech to the Soldiers, 23.12.1918," 36.
[65] Böhm recorded that a guard detail from the 5th Infantry Division appeared shortly after midnight. Böhm, *Adjutant*, diary entry for December 23, 1918, 115.

marching en route to Berlin to stop their approach and to return to their quarters in Potsdam."[66] This prompted an immediate telephone call from Major von Harbou. The tone and substance of his message indicates that Lequis' headquarters had already received word that the first formation sent to rescue the cabinet, the Guards Uhlans, had been sent home. Instead of receiving the thanks of a grateful government, Lequis' troops were being told they were not needed. Even worse, Ebert's intervention had deflected the decisive blow the officer corps believed was so urgently needed to neutralize the government's enemies. To Harbou and his officer comrades, it seemed another such opportunity might not present itself before the last homesick *Frontschwein* abandoned the ranks. Thus, without realizing it, Ebert had crossed a final line in terms of the patience of the officers. The chancellery transcript of Harbou's call reads:

Major von Harbou advises that the Potsdam regiments cannot be turned back because one cannot expect that they will turn around at night. The troops would be completely ruined through such a march.

There are 500 men underway from Steglitz with a battery for the protection of the Reich Chancellery and the War Ministry. Harbou requests that, in any eventuality, these troops be allowed to remain at the Chancellery and the War Ministry. A new march would utterly ruin them. The troops currently withdrawn [the Guards Uhlans] are angry with the government and can no longer be used to protect the government. The government can expect nothing more from these troops because the government has refused [their] protection.[67]

Harbou's message was significant in several respects. In the first paragraph, the chief of staff of *Generalkommando Lequis* declined to obey an order from the government. For a major, even a general staff major, to rebuff an order from a chancellor marks a notable milestone in the storied road of German militarism. In the second paragraph, Harbou offered Ebert a thinly veiled rebuke for bringing about the "ruin" of the Guards Uhlans, an elite unit and one of the few remaining useful formations. However, the chief significance of the message is Harbou's use of front-line morale to coerce his civilian masters. His warning to Ebert: turn the Potsdam regiments around tonight and they will not be there for you when you need them. Soldier morale was too fragile for games of "cry wolf."

---

[66] BA-R, R43/2508/f, "Reich Government Order, dated December 23, 1918, 10:30," 37.
[67] BA-R, R43/2508/f, telephone message from Major von Harbou 12.23, 10.30, 38. Barth claimed that, earlier in the day, he had spoken with Harbou, who, most likely attempting to deceive Barth, had expressed disgust at the idea of fratricidal bloodshed. "It is madness when one must shoot at his own brother," *Quellen*, 6/II, Document 77, 93.

In that moment, Harbou was reprising a theme that Groener, Hindenburg, and other senior officers had been using since even before the Kaiser's abdication. Unable to call on the authority of the monarchy, the officers had chosen to play at the level of the socialists by invoking the moral authority of the common soldier, the proletarian in the trenches. The recurring message: let us, the army leadership, do what we need to do or you will anger, disappoint, and betray the front-line soldiers.

Harbou was not the only officer to remonstrate with Ebert during that long night. Groener also took his turn to remind the chancellor that he risked losing the support of the troops (as well as the OHL). The general's diary entry for the 23rd reads:

Ebert asks the OHL for help. Troops force way into Reichs Chancellery; Ebert forbids them to shoot and wants the Reichs Chancellery to be cleared of sailors as well as soldiers. Telephonically I advised Ebert that such actions will cause our troops to be demoralized and demanded of him that he must allow us to protect him. Otherwise we could no longer go along with him ... Major v. Harbou was directed to proceed against the sailors.[68]

Seven years later, Groener recalled the conversation.

I talked with Mr. Ebert and said that we must make use of our limited strength. If you are captured and then freed, the troops who freed you must have the chance to deal with their opponents according to wartime or martial law. If it [Ebert's caution in the face of anti-government action] happens like this again, I can stand by you no longer, because your actions serve to ruin the troops.[69]

Thus was the chancellor of the German Reich told, first by a major, then again by a general, that the government's orders could not be obeyed and that Ebert's desire to avoid bloodshed was having an adverse effect on the steadiness of the government's troops. Having narrowly avoided a *Schiesserei* (shooting incident) that same evening, Ebert had the military telling him he must accept the army's aggressive intervention. Groener had concluded with a not-too-veiled threat to abandon the "union" he and Ebert had enjoyed since November 10.

Given time to reflect during that anxious and interminable night, the chancellor might have found some bitter irony in his situation. Less than a week before, as the Congress of Workers' and Soldiers' Councils had closed, Ebert had defended the prerogatives of the officer corps and especially their command authority (*Kommandogewalt*). Now they were challenging *his* command authority. Nevertheless, according to Groener's testimony in the *Dolchstoss* ("stab-in-the-back") trial of

---

[68] BA-MA, Nachlass Groener, 46/25; Groener diary entry for December 23.
[69] Groener's testimony in the 1925 *Dolchstossprozess* quoted in Wrobel, *Der Sieg*, 46–7.

1925, Ebert gave his approval to an operation to suppress the VMD. Groener recalled, "Then I asked for his consent that, on December 24, the sailors in the palace and the Marstall should be attacked by our troops. Ebert gave this consent."[70]

The harried chancellor had little time to consider his troubled relationship with the army leadership. A more immediate issue demanded Ebert's attention, the fate of his personal friend, Otto Wels.[71] Wels was spending the night of December 23–24, bruised and fearing for his life, in a coal storage cellar in the basement of the Marstall. Through the late evening and into the early morning, Ebert, Landsberg, and Scheidemann, the three Majority Socialist delegates, along with Scheuch, the war minister, kept vigil as chancellery officials made a series of telephone calls to the Marstall to check on Wels' condition and the prospect of his release. There was a heartening report at about midnight, when the sailors released their other two captives, Fischer and Brongard, but Wels remained a prisoner. Then, at two in the morning, Radtke, the commander of the VMD, called the chancellery with chilling news, news that showed that command authority was as uncertain among the sailors as it was in the provisional government. Radtke reported that he was no longer the master of the situation and he could not vouch for Wels' safety. In fact, he said, his own life was in jeopardy because he had attempted to intercede on Wels' behalf.[72] Any deal to rescue Wels was off.[73]

For Ebert, exhausted from a day of crisis and negotiation, there seemed to be no more options. Together with the other two MSPD delegates, he gave Scheuch the authority to do whatever was necessary to rescue Wels.[74] Then, at 2.30 a.m., Ebert, Landsberg, and Scheidemann went to bed.

As it turned out, the order Ebert gave the war minister was relatively meaningless. In the first place, during the previous evening the

---

[70] Rakenius, *Wilhelm Groener als erster Generalquartiermeister*, 150. Quotation from Wrobel, *Der Sieg*, 47.

[71] Wels was a friend of all three of the MSPD cabinet delegates. Böhm, *Adjutant*, diary entry for December 23, 1918, 114.

[72] According to Fischer, Radtke claimed that, at that point, the danger to Wels came not from the sailors but from Eichhorn's *Sicherheitswehr*. Meanwhile, the militant Dorrenbach had been rendered *hors de combat* by a rifle butt to the head delivered during a scuffle with an undisclosed adversary. Anton Fischer, *Die Revolutionskommandantur Berlin* (Berlin: Selbstverlag der Verfasser, 1922), 44–5.

[73] *Quellen*, 6/II, Ebert's statement in Document 77, 82.

[74] *Ibid.* In the days after the crisis, Ebert was harried by the Independents in the coalition and the leftist press for not consulting with the three Independent delegates and not placing limits on Scheuch's action. In the truest spirit of Monday morning quarterbacking, they maintained that Ebert should have forbidden the use of artillery in any rescue operation.

minister had transferred authority over all troops in Berlin to Lequis. Though Scheuch passed Ebert's order to Lequis,[75] this did not change the preparations already under way. In the second, before Scheuch could take any action, the VMD had released Wels. During the course of the night, the sailors grew increasingly anxious about reports of guards units deploying into the city. As the most militant members of the Marstall's garrison went home for the evening, other, more prudent sailors saw an opportunity to find an intermediary, ideally one with appropriate revolutionary credentials. To this end, they sent a car to the Steglitz home of Georg Ledebour, the well-known Independent leader and member of the Berlin *Vollzugsrat*. Ledebour agreed to act as a mediator and, at about 3.00 a.m., he had secured Wels' release,[76] though Wels, exhausted by his ordeal (and, perhaps, uncertain of his captor's intentions), asked to remain at the Marstall until daylight.[77]

With the chancellery cleared of sailors, Wels and his colleagues released, and the VMD ready to evacuate the palace, it seemed that all that remained to defuse the crisis was for the government to call off its troops. Before going to negotiate with the sailors, Ledebour had gone to the chancellery to announce Wels' anticipated release. Unfortunately, he could not find Ebert.[78] It was one more mishap in a series of unhappy occurrences.

Yet, even had Ledebour found Ebert, there was no guarantee that the chancellor could stave off the events that followed. Backed by the OHL and presented with the provocation the army had long desired, Lequis was determined to act. The general's analysis of the situation and the instructions he had received had led him to identify five related missions that his troops must accomplish. First, they must ensure the government was not held captive again. This meant securing the

---

[75] Böhm, *Adjutant*, diary entry of December 23, 1918, 115.
[76] BA-MA, N23/1, Nachlass Scheuch; Walter Oehme, "Hinter den Kulissen," *Freiheit* (USPD newspaper), morning edition December 27, 1919.
[77] Fischer, *Revolutionskommandantur*, 46–7. According to Barth, Wels, exhausted and shaken, found the prospect of release into the unlighted streets around the Marstall even worse than that of remaining with his former captors. He was painfully aware of his unpopularity with the ill-disciplined sailors, and their leaders could give him no guarantees of safety. Moreover, he was exhausted, and his home was a considerable distance away in Friedrichshagen. Waiting for daylight seemed to him the preferable option. Barth, *Werkstatt*, 115 and Dittmann, *Errinerungen*, 613.
[78] BA-MA, N23/1, Nachlass Scheuch; Oehme, "Hinter den Kulissen." Oehme, who was present at the chancellery, claims that Ebert deliberately avoided Ledebour, telling his secretary to relay to Ledebour that he, the chancellor, had left for the evening when Ebert was actually in his chancellery apartment. In Oehme's account, Ebert was clearing the way for Lequis to take action, but this interpretation hardly squares with Ebert's peacemaking efforts to that point. Oehme, *Damals in der Reichskanzlei*, 57.

chancellery, the *Kommandantur*, the Reichstag, the war ministry, and other major government buildings in the city center. Second, they must liberate "Comrade" Wels. Third, they needed to capture the palace and the Marstall. Fourth, they must disarm the *Volksmarinedivision*, and fifth, they must arrange to get the sailors out of the city.[79] It was a daunting array of tasks.

In Lequis' view, if they were to be accomplished, there was little time to waste. He feared that if he did not act quickly the VMD might be reinforced by thousands of armed workers and even, perhaps, by their naval comrades from outside the capital. Thus, having been alerted for action in the afternoon of December 23, Lequis resolved to attack the sailors' stronghold early the next morning. Such an attack might have the advantage of surprise and would limit any attempts by anti-government forces to send aid to the sailors.[80] Perhaps more important, an attack conducted at the earliest possible moment gave the cabinet little opportunity to reconsider or arrange a peaceful settlement. Yet to attack on Christmas Eve morning involved considerable risk. There would be little time to gather troops and heavy weapons for the operation. The haste involved also ensured that the command and control arrangements would be makeshift at best.[81]

Given the time constraints and the depleted condition of Lequis' divisions, the attackers could not count on an overwhelming weight of numbers in the upcoming battle. Lequis and his staff estimated that 1,200 front-line fighters would be available, which meant that government troops might be outnumbered by the VMD, which had, according to some estimates, as many as 2,000 sailors in the palace and Marstall. Moreover, to reach a total of 1,200 men, Lequis would have to call on a variety of different units including, along with the Guards Cavalry Rifle Division, elements of the 1st Guards Reserve Division as well as the 5th and 37th Infantry Divisions. Added to his meager manpower total, Lequis relied upon four and a half batteries of medium and light artillery (105 millimeter and 77 millimeter). These, if used effectively, would give the attackers a decisive firepower advantage. In his estimation, this advantage along with veteran fighting prowess of the available infantry might be enough to carry out the mission successfully.[82]

[79] Nachlass Pabst, 38.
[80] Kriegsgeschichtlichen Forschungsanstalt des Heeres, *Wirren*, 37–8. The army believed the Spartacists had the capability to muster thousands of armed workers.
[81] *Ibid.*, 38, See also *ibid.*, 37–8.
[82] Order of battle information taken from *ibid.*, 38–9.

Lequis assigned tactical command of the attack on the VMD to the GKSD with its well-respected commander, General Hofmann, and fiery chief of staff, Captain Pabst. It was a logical choice. Alone of the guards divisions that had marched into Berlin during the previous weeks, the GKSD had combated the agitation of the Left with its own indoctrination campaign and, alone of the guards divisions, it had held a considerable number of its troops to their posts as Christmas approached. Moreover, the division had engaged its troops in a training program that included street fighting and house-to-house searches.[83] Even though it was the first of the guards divisions to march into the capital, it remained, on Christmas Eve, the unit best prepared to carry out the missions originally envisioned in Groener's "Berlin Operation."[84]

Yet even the GKSD was able to collect only a fraction of its combat power for a strike against the rebellious sailors. Despite the division's best efforts to maintain its strength, many guardsmen had accepted their discharges and gone home. The unit had granted Christmas leave to many more. Lack of transportation meant that the division would be unable to assemble the entire division by the time of the anticipated attack, and many of the troops would have to make a foot march from the outskirts to the center of Berlin.[85] Thus, for the main effort of the operation, Lequis' order put elements of the other three divisions under the command of Hofmann's cavalry division. It was a hastily gathered "pick-up team," and this fact was certain to make control of the operation more difficult. Even more unsettling to Hofmann and Pabst was the operation's reliance on the *Soldatenwehr.* Because of the limited number of front-line soldiers available for the attack, the *Soldatenwehr* received the critical task of sealing off the battle area from outside forces. However, the guards officers had little faith in the reliability of part-time soldiers. Adding to their worries was the fact that Wels' men were a late addition to the operation, and the front-line commanders had little time to integrate them into the tactical planning.[86]

After receiving a warning order to prepare for the mission, Pabst recommended a delay. After weighing the difficulties involved, he told

[83] Nachlass Pabst, 28.
[84] This was the judgment not only of Pabst, but also General von Lüttwitz, who later replaced Lequis (Wilhelm von Lüttwitz, *Im Kampf gegen die November-Revolution* [Berlin: Verlag Otto Schlegel, 1934], 18), General von Maercker, the famous *Freikorps* commander (Maercker, *Vom Kaiserheer zur Reichswehr,* 63), as well as the General Staff's official historian (Kriegsgeschichtlichen Forschungsanstalt des Heeres, *Wirren,* 36).
[85] According to Pabst, most of the division's motor transport had either been left on the west side of the Rhine to satisfy the armistice conditions or had been confiscated by homeland soldiers' councils. Nachlass Pabst, 38–9.
[86] *Ibid.,* 39.

Lequis that the proposed attack should be delayed by two or three days. The additional time, he suggested, could be used for more thorough preparation and also to bring in the heavier guns needed to storm the massive buildings held by the sailors. Lequis refused. It was clear, Pabst later recalled, that political considerations outweighed military planning factors.[87] After Lequis' staff had completed the operations order, Pabst repeated his reservations; Lequis again refused to consider a delay.

Pabst was not the only staff officer with reservations. At about three in the morning, Scheuch's adjutant, Captain Böhm, called Lequis' headquarters from the war ministry. He spoke with Major von Harbou:

I advised him once again of the difficulties of street fighting in Berlin. One must have stronger forces for a street fight in Berlin because one must secure the rear in all directions. *Generalkommando Lequis* indeed could not have enough units for tomorrow's battle. Major v. Harbou closed his discussion with me with the words: "You can rely on it, the show will go well."[88] [*"Sie können sich darauf verlassen, der Film klappt."*]

Despite Harbou's confidence, events would show that Böhm's concerns showed remarkable prescience.

Through the early morning hours of Christmas Eve, elements of the GKSD and the units assigned to support it arrived by train and on foot in the center of Berlin. Under darkness of early morning, they took up positions around the palace and the Marstall. Others moved to secure key buildings. Some arrived very late; a battery of the 1st Guards Reserve Field Artillery Regiment, for example, did not reach its assigned station at the general staff building until 7.00 a.m. Other units suffered misadventures. A half-battery size unit of the 5th Infantry Division on the way to the ministry of war encountered a group of sailors. The sailors disarmed the artillerymen, released them, and took the captured artillery pieces back to the palace.[89] Incidents like this served notice that there would be little chance to surprise the sailors in the morning.

Such incidents must also have been unsettling to Lequis' men. Official histories rarely comment on the mood of the troops going into an operation, especially when morale is less than perfect. Nevertheless, the general staff historian of the postwar fighting in Berlin felt compelled to note that, on the eve of the operation, the men were resolute. However, because it was Christmas Eve, and because of the disturbing events of the previous day (Ebert's efforts to make peace between the soldiers and sailors), the limited number of troops available, and the

---

[87] *Ibid.*, 40.   [88] Böhm, *Adjutant*, diary entry for December 23, 1918, 116.
[89] *VZ*, late edition of December 24, 1918, "Spartakus greift an."

Figure 8.2 Guards wait in reserve position on the Werdescher Markt for the assault on the Marstall. The Marstall itself can be seen through the morning haze. The mixture of uniforms and equipment suggests the ad hoc nature of the operation.

prospect of fighting with their countrymen, their mood was "reserved" (*zurückhaltend*).[90]

The GKSD staff had set up their command post in a university building just a few blocks from the palace, and worked through the night to gather the units assigned to the operation. As daybreak approached, Hofmann and Pabst issued final instructions[91] and took stock of the units available. The results were distressing. Instead of the 1,200 men they had planned for, only 800 had arrived. Instead of four-and-a-half batteries of artillery, only one-and-a-half were on hand, six guns in total.[92] The original planning estimates of men and guns available suggested the operation would be difficult. With the totals available at

---

[90] Kriegsgeschichtlichen Forschungsanstalt des Heeres, *Wirren*, 40.
[91] Pabst attempted to find keys for the massive doors of the palace and the Marstall. The Marstall keys, normally kept at the *Kommandantur*, were missing. The guardsmen found keys to the palace but discovered, under fire, they did not fit. *Ibid.*
[92] *Ibid.*

dawn, perhaps it was impossible. The weakness of the GKSD's little task force prompted Pabst to make one final appeal for delay to Lequis' staff. With the appeal, he added a request that his concerns be passed on to the OHL.[93]

Pabst's efforts were in vain. For Lequis and his superiors in Wilhelmshöhe, the time for reservations had passed. The operation was "on." As the sun came up on an icy Christmas Eve, a newspaper reporter found Unter den Linden looking like "a major army encampment," full of soldiers "armed for storm operations" (*sturmmässig ausgerüstet*) with steel helmets, fixed bayonets, and grenades hanging from their belts.[94] The dawn also illuminated the fields of fire for the guns of the 3rd Guards Field Artillery Regiment. Their shells would announce the last operation of the old army and the first battle of the German Civil War.

The assault (Berlin: Tuesday morning, December 24, 1918)

For the *Volksmarine* sentinels on duty at the palace and the Marstall, sunrise showed their worst fears had been realized. The "Potsdamers" had surrounded the two buildings, and the front-line veterans were clearly preparing for combat. The sailors would have to do their best to prepare a defense. At that point, it is difficult to say how many men the VMD had available to defend their stronghold. According to the division's strength returns, Detachment I, billeted in the Marstall, had 1,100 men.[95] However, many and probably most of these men spent the night at their homes around Berlin. Others had been granted Christmas leave. The usual VMD guard force was thirty men in the palace and eighty in the Marstall, where, a week before, the sailors had decided to concentrate their forces.[96] Added to this guard force, then, were any additional men who had spent the night at the palace and Marstall.[97] Thus, the sailors probably could not match the GKSD's numbers. Neither could they match their opponent's artillery,[98] though the defenders were well equipped with machine guns.[99]

[93] Nachlass Pabst, 43.
[94] *VZ*, "Die Straße Unter den Linden," late edition of December 24, 1918.
[95] BA-R, R43/2508/f, *Volksmarine* strength report of December 12, 1918.
[96] Wrobel, *Der Sieg*, 43.
[97] *Ibid.*, 47. Wrobel claims that many sailors felt it was safe to leave their posts because Ebert had promised that the events of December 23 would be followed by further negotiations.
[98] Some accounts indicate the sailors were able to put a single artillery piece into action.
[99] According to Gustav Noske, the MSPD politician who represented the government at Kiel, the VMD had sent a call for reinforcements to the ports in the north. Noske

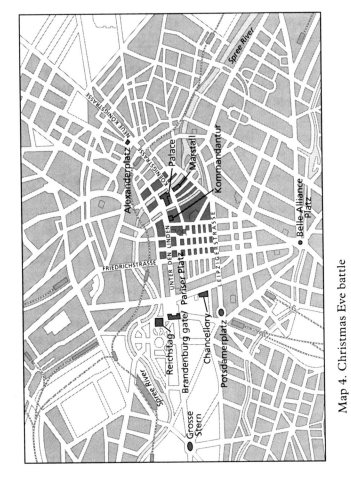

Map 4. Christmas Eve battle

Before fighting began, the guardsmen offered the sailors an ultimatum. At approximately 7.50 a.m., a delegation of five soldiers led by a lieutenant left the *Kronprinzenpalais* (Crown Prince Palace)[100] and walked the several blocks to the Marstall, which they approached under a white flag of truce. *Volksmarinedivision* sentries met them and escorted them to representatives of the division's soldiers' council. The lieutenant gave this message to the council:

We demand the complete surrender of the sailors, whose justified demands will be [then] directly fulfilled. Within ten minutes, all sailors within in the Marstall and the Palace should assemble unarmed in the *Schlossplatz* [between the Marstall and Palace]. We will allow ten minutes for consideration. If, after this period, the white flag is not shown, we will take the Palace and Marstall under fire from artillery.[101]

The soldier's delegation departed under escort. They and the rest of the GKSD waited ten minutes, watching for a white flag from the Marstall.

It never appeared. Whether or not the sailors were even able to respond to an ultimatum, especially with so little time to consider the terms, is a point open to debate.[102] Some accounts suggest that none of the VMD's leaders were available that morning, that they had spent the night elsewhere. Thus, the watch force on duty may have felt they lacked the authority to make a decision for surrender or resistance.[103] Whether defiant or indecisive, the sailors gave no sign of being ready to capitulate. Just after 8.00 a.m., the army's guns opened fire on the VMD's

wrote that, thanks to his efforts, the sailors at Kiel and other naval bases remained supporters of the government. Noske, *Von Kiel bis Kapp*, 54. Wilhelm Reinhard, the commander of the 4th Foot Guards, wrote that sailors showed up outside his unit's caserne in Moabit. They sought to incite the younger soldiers to march to the aid of the VMD. He drove them away at gunpoint. Reinhard, *Wehen der Republik*, 53–4.

[100] The *Kronprinzenpalais* was also being used as a command center.

[101] *VZ*, "Die Straße Unter den Linden."

[102] Lequis later justified the limited time given to the sailors by asserting that the ultimatum was merely the extension of talks with the government that had been going on for hours: "the 10 minutes was merely the last deadline at the end of the entire night" (*Quellen*, 6/II, 133, fn. 9).

[103] Fischer, *Revolutionskommandantur*, 46. This contradicts Wrobel's account, which claims that Dorrenbach was present to receive the ultimatum and, later, was the soul of the division's defense. However, Wrobel's version contradicts Fischer's assertion that Dorrenbach was temporarily out of action. Oehme records that Captain Pabst, resplendent in shiny, knee-high boots, had arrived at the chancellery before dawn to inform the cabinet that the GKSD would give the sailors an interval of only ten minutes to consider the guards' ultimatums, a visit that made the MSPD delegates complicit in the harsh terms of the ultimatum. Oehme, *Damals in der Reichskanzlei*, 207–8.

positions in the two buildings. The artillerymen initially directed the heaviest weight of fire against the palace, the attacker's first objective. According to an eyewitness, the first round hit between windows on the first floor and knocked out a machine-gun position. Subsequent rounds did considerable damage to the columns and façade of the building and the balcony of the building where the Kaiser had announced war in 1914.[104] The small garrison of sailors in the palace returned fire with at least five machine guns, but, after ten minutes of artillery preparation, the guards judged that they could launch their assault party, 200 men from the 1st and 3rd Guards Uhlans. Their initial assault was so successful that, by 8.10 a.m., the palace had been cleared. Those sailors who were not casualties or taken prisoner escaped through an underground passage to the Marstall.[105]

At this point, it appeared that the VMD would be a short morning's work for the soldiers, most of whom had seen far more intense combat on the Western Front. However, unfortunately for the attackers, seizing the sturdy Marstall, with a larger garrison, proved a much more difficult assignment than the palace. Attempts to rush the building met heavy machine-gun fire. Artillery fire directed at the different sides of the building had only a limited effect and could not penetrate its massive doors. A storming party armed with axes also failed to clear a way. Finally, the guardsmen decided to rely on a time-tested siege technique: they repositioned their artillery so that they might concentrate all their fire on a single point. This, they hoped, would create a breach adequate to allow the passage of an assault force.[106]

Against this prolonged bombardment, the resistance of the sailors began to flag. Despite the superficial damage to the building's exterior, inside the defenders were taking casualties. By 10.00 a.m., the sailors in the Marstall apparently had had enough.[107] The guardsmen outside saw a white flag appear in one of the windows. At first, the attackers

[104] *VZ*, "Die Straße Unter den Linden." Fischer later took the guardsmen to task for shelling the northern end of the palace, where there were clear fields of fire, instead of the less accessible south side where the VMD had its offices and guard post (Fischer, *Revolutionskommandantur*, 46). It is often the case that soldiers do what they can rather than what they should.

[105] Description of the battle for the palace from Kriegsgeschichtlichen Forschungsanstalt des Heeres, *Wirren*, 40, and *VZ*, "Die Straße Unter den Linden."

[106] Kriegsgeschichtlichen Forschungsanstalt des Heeres, *Wirren*, 41.

[107] In Wrobel's version, a courier in a small boat had come down the Spree River on the east side of the Marstall, braving the fire of the attackers, in order to deliver the news that forces were on the way to relieve the sailors. A temporary cease-fire was necessary in order to prevent machine-gun fire from the Marstall from striking their allies outside. Thus the apparent surrender was actually a clever ploy by the sailors (Wrobel, *Der Sieg*, 54). The general staff history gave the time of the appearance of the white flag as 9.10 a.m., but this conflicts with every other contemporary account and seems a mistake.

suspected a ruse designed to draw them closer into range. However, when a small party of sailors appeared at one of the doors, the soldiers ceased firing. The GKSD then sent its own negotiating party to meet the sailors, a soldier with a white flag on the end of his bayonet followed by a vehicle carrying Colonel Tschirschky and his adjutant.[108] The vehicle stopped outside the building, and the officers went inside, reappearing, after a brief interval, with a group of sailors.[109]

The battle seemed all but over. The defenders had asked for terms, and the two sides agreed to a twenty-minute cease-fire. Tschirschky took the sailors' representatives with him to the university, where they could negotiate the final terms of the surrender. Unarmed sailors began coming out of the Marstall, first as individuals, then in groups. Otto Wels emerged, a free man, though somewhat worse for his night as a guest of the VMD. A detail of guardsmen entered the building to secure the weapons left behind while the artillery teams began to limber their guns. All that remained, it seemed, was to clean up the mess.[110] The GKSD liaison officer at the chancellery made this brief report: "Marstall is occupied by us, the sailors have accepted all of our demands, delivered up [their] weapons; Wels is free."[111]

The debacle (Berlin: Tuesday, Christmas Eve, December 24, 1918)

Just a few minutes later, another report announced a dramatically different situation:

Report [of a] captain of the General Staff: The sailors have broken the settlement[,] refused to surrender weapons, the population is at hand in great number, taken positions against [or around] the sailors, military appears too weak to push them back, need reinforcements or Ebert should come and speak to the people.[112]

---

[108] Tchirschky, who commanded a cavalry brigade in the GKSD, was the tactical commander of the assault.

[109] Description of Marstall action from Kriegsgeschichtlichen Forschungsanstalt des Heeres, *Wirren*, 41, and *VZ*, late edition of December 24, 1918, "Die Straße Unter den Linden" and "Eine Gefechtspause."

[110] The details in this paragraph are taken from the three sources listed in note 109, above.

[111] BA-R, R43/2408/f, "Eine Meldung des Verbindungsoffizieres der Garde-Schutzen Division," dated December 24, 1918, 45, entry for 11.05 a.m. This message is missing from Wrobel's account, which claims the sailors never considered surrender. The real reason for the cease-fire, according to a sailor at the scene, was to protect the women and children who lived in the Marstall: Wrobel, *Der Sieg*, 57.

[112] BA-R R43/2408/f, "Eine Meldung des Verbindungsoffizieres der Garde-Schutzen Division," dated December 24, 1918, 45, entry for 11.10 a.m. Again, if Ebert had a taste for irony, he might have observed that, the day after the army had demanded

Figure 8.3 Artillery impact on the Marstall building during the
guards' assault on Christmas Eve, 1918.

What happened next has been described in a number of conflicting ways. What is certain is that suddenly a vast crowd approached the rear of the GKSD positions from all directions: the Spree Canal, Kaiserstrasse, Alexanderplatz, and Unter den Linden.[113] Just as the guardsmen began to relax in their machine-gun posts, artillery crews, and storm groups, the throng pressed around them, haranguing them, disarming them, and, in some instances, beating and shooting them. Among the crowd were women and children, who, according to some accounts, led the columns and challenged the soldiers to fire on them. Some in the crowd were armed, most were not. The crowd included members of the VMD who had spent the night at home. Others present included the sailors' allies, the *Sicherheitswehr*, while still others were members of the *Soldatenwehr* who had gone over to the side of the sailors.[114] Most were workers and workers' families. The general staff history estimated their total number at 100,000.[115]

Where had they come from? As soon as the guns had opened fire on the palace and Marstall, representatives of the various groups hostile to the Ebert government – conspicuously Eichhorn's *Sicherheitswehr*, along with the Spartacist League, the *Volksmarine* Division, the left wing of the USPD – began to circulate through the working-class districts, sounding the alarm. "The monarchist counter-revolution has begun!" "Come to the palace to defend the revolution!" Although Berlin's working class divided their sympathies between the MSPD, USPD, and the Spartacus League, the battle cry of counter-revolution was sufficient to mobilize them to empty neighborhoods and factories by the thousands. By 10.00 a.m., they were pressing against the barricades the *Soldatenwehr* had established to isolate the battle area. In the presence of the vast crowd that harangued and cajoled them, the *Soldatenwehr* wavered in some places and in others joined the crowd, and it appears that the only thing that prevented the great mass of people from pushing directly toward the palace and Marstall was the sound of cannon and machine-gun fire. When the firing ceased, the crowd could not

that they be allowed to rescue him, they were, that morning, asking *him* to rescue *them*.
[113] Dominique Venner, *Söldner Ohne Sold: Die Deutsche Freikorps, 1918–1923* (Berlin: Paul Neff Verlag, 1974), 43.
[114] The official history notes that only Suppe's volunteer detachment of active NCOs maintained their barrier. Kriegsgeschichtlichen Forschungsanstalt des Heeres, *Wirren*, 41.
[115] Description of the crowd taken from several sources, including Kriegsgeschichtlichen Forschungsanstalt des Heeres, *Wirren*, 41; Freyer, *Sturmvogel*, 191. Volkmann, *Revolution über Deutschland*, 160–1; and *VZ*, "Eine Gefechtspause."

be restrained any longer.[116] The GKSD committed its small reserve to reinforce the barricades, but it was no use.[117]

Once again, the ubiquitous Harry Kessler was an eyewitness, this time to the scene in the square between the palace and the Marstall:

Sailors with machine guns stood at the windows [of the Marstall], which were battered to pieces. The square was black with people. They were waiting for something, though without knowing what – whether a battle, a mass meeting, perhaps Liebknecht's appearance – just waiting and unafraid because for thousands curiosity outvied fear. At the same time these bystanders formed the best bulwark of defense for the mutinous sailors. Until these spectators were dispersed or pushed back, the Government troops would be unable to renew their attack.

As he watched, a unit of guards artillery arrived on the scene.

[It was] at once surrounded by a seething mob yelling insults, which revealed that many here were on Liebknecht's side. A sergeant, wearing a red-black-gold armband, climbed on a limber and made a speech audible right across the square. A parley is going on, he announced, and brothers should not shoot and kill each other. It worked, mainly, because of the calm way he spoke. The troop [of artillery] was let through and drove off.[118]

As Kessler's account suggested, the objective of the bewildered guardsmen had to change. Where, moments before, they had sought to finish clearing two buildings of rebellious sailors, by noon the issue became withdrawal under extreme pressure. In the presence of a vast and hostile crowd, could the GKSD extricate itself from the scene? With difficulty, the soldiers were able to withdraw their artillery pieces[119] but elsewhere the crowds seized machine guns and roughed up officers who attempted to regain control.[120] The *Sicherheitswehr* arrested several officers caught in the maelstrom. After the crowd had jostled them and pulled off their shoulder straps and ribbons, the officers were taken as captives to the police presidium.[121] The guardsmen that had entered the Marstall were in an especially vulnerable position and made their way to safety with difficulty.

---

[116] Böhm, *Adjutant*, diary entry for December 24, 1918, 116–17. Wrobel's account includes half a dozen eyewitness accounts of those summoned to the support of the *Volksmarinedivision: Der Sieg*, 54–8.

[117] Kriegsgeschichtlichen Forschungsanstalt des Heeres, *Wirren*, 41.

[118] Kessler, *Berlin in Lights*, diary entry for December 24, 1918, 41.

[119] A point the general staff history insists on: Kriegsgeschichtlichen Forschungsanstalt des Heeres, *Wirren*, 41. As a point of honor, the GKSD felt compelled to stress the recovery of the guns in the press several days later. *VZ*, December 27, 1918, "Eine Erklärung der Garde-Kavallerie."

[120] *VZ*, "Eine Gefechtspause."

[121] Kriegsgeschichtlichen Forschungsanstalt des Heeres, *Wirren*, 43.

Seeing the shifting course of events, the sailors' representatives had broken off negotiations and renounced their capitulation. The VMD withdrew the white flags and resumed their defensive positions around the Marstall. Soon it became clear that they had no more to fear from "the Potsdamers."

As events ran their course around the Marstall, the members of the cabinet responded in different ways. The three MSPD delegates, Ebert, Landsberg, and Scheidemann, monitored the action from the chancellery. Barth awoke to the sound of cannon fire. Excitable and energetic as always, he rushed first to the war ministry, where he demanded that Scheuch tell him who had ordered the guards to bombard the VMD. Scheuch replied, probably in truth, that he did not know. Barth then proceeded to the headquarters of the GKSD, where Pabst told him that the operation had been launched on the orders of the government. Outraged, Barth demanded an immediate cease-fire. Pabst declined. Barth then went to his office in the chancellery where he called Harbou and again demanded a cease-fire. Harbou explained to the angry delegate that only Ebert could issue such an order. Predictably, Barth flew out of his office to find the chancellor. By the time he had found the three delegates from the MSPD, the guardsmen were in trouble. In response to Barth's indignant demand for answers, Ebert professed that he had no idea who had given approval but that he was very willing to call the war ministry and order an end to the unhappy affair.[122] The last two delegates, the Independents Haase and Dittmann, arrived shortly thereafter to mediate between Barth's furious indignation and Ebert's dismay and embarrassment.[123]

By early afternoon, matters began to sort themselves out. The crowds around the Marstall began to thin as people went home to celebrate Christmas. The GKSD, though shaken, had withdrawn in relatively good order. Later, the general staff history claimed that at this point, the troops were ready to rejoin the fight, but this seems unlikely.[124] At two o'clock in the afternoon, the troops that remained were assembled and marched out of the city.[125] A newspaper reporter wrote that the soldiers offered a good impression, but that their position was difficult, because they would not fire on women and chil-

---

[122] Description of Barth's circuit taken from Nachlass Pabst, 46–7; Volkmann, *Revolution über Deutschland*, 160–1; *Quellen*, 6/II, Document 70: "Emil Barth und Wilhelm Dittmann über die Kabinettsitzung am Dienstag, 24.12 1918, vorm.," 30–1; and Barth, *Werkstatt*, 104–5.

[123] Volkmann, *Revolution über Deutschland*, 162.

[124] Kriegsgeschichtlichen Forschungsanstalt des Heeres, *Wirren*, 41–4.

[125] *Ibid.*, 42.

dren. As to the politics of the situation, "They don't know where they actually stand."[126]

Not so their opponents. The defenders of the Marstall, initially stunned by their unlikely victory, now celebrated and waxed belligerent. One sailor told a reporter from the *Vossische Zeitung*, "There is no question of negotiation. Ledebour was turned down by Ebert yesterday. The Potsdamers must be shot down."[127] Another reporter from the MSPD's newspaper, *Vorwärts*, described the scene in the center of Berlin.

Around 12.00 I saw approximately 200 armed civilians in march column enter the Marstall, the entire area around the Marstall including the Königstrasse up to the City Hall is occupied by the sailors' supporters armed with machine guns. The sailors and their allies demand that the Ebert-Haase government stand down immediately.[128]

To avoid further bloodshed, the two sides needed a new settlement, but the commander of the GKSD, General Hofmann, was unwilling to parley with the sailors. Representatives of the government intervened to arrange a meeting for the purposes of negotiating a settlement. Thus, General Hofmann and Captain Pabst met at the university that afternoon with members of the Central Council (*Zentralrat*) the Supreme Naval Council (*Obermarinerat*), leaders of the *Volksmarinedivision*, and the Berlin soldiers' councils. Together, they came to an agreement that salvaged far more from the situation than the government could have hoped for, given the circumstances. Its conditions were:

1. The *Volksmarinedivision* would evacuate the palace in accordance with the original agreement of December 18.
2. The *Volksmarinedivision* would be incorporated into the *Soldatenwehr* and subordinated to the city commandant. The final form of the incorporation would be worked out later.
3. The sailors promised in the future to never again take action against the government. Disagreements would always be subject to negotiations.
4. The division from *Generalkommando Lequis* [GKSD] will withdraw immediately.
5. The state of alert would be lifted for the garrison and the *Volksmarinedivision*.
6. Commandant Wels is immediately released.[129]

---

[126] *VZ*, "Spartakus greift ein," late edition of December 24, 1918.   [127] *Ibid*.
[128] *Vorwärts*, edition of December 24, 1918; quoted in Wrobel, *Der Sieg*, 59.
[129] Agreement paraphrased from BA-R, R43/2508/f, cease-fire agreement of December 25, 1918, 31.

As the representatives of the various bodies put their signatures to this document and departed, they must have wondered how long this temporary peace would last.

Meanwhile, the soldiers and sailors counted their losses. The general staff history recorded that the battle cost the GKSD two men dead, and ten wounded, versus the loss of fifty-six dead to their enemies.[130] In cabinet deliberations during the days following, the number of sailors counted as slain ranged from seven to seventy. East German historians reversed the ratio of losses given by the general staff by asserting that the sailors had lost a half dozen killed versus fifty-six killed in action among the guardsmen. Here, as in so many aspects of these events, the truth is elusive. One is inclined to believe the lower figures for both sides. Notably, for the GKSD their losses are accounted for by rank and by unit in the official history, and as for the sailors, the public funeral for the VMD's dead, attended by thousands on December 29, saw the burial of only seven of their men.[131]

In terms of the forces engaged on each side (a battalion or less), the losses incurred, and the duration of the action, the battle of December 24 was a minor affair. By Western Front standards, the scale of the fighting around the palace and the Marstall amounted, at most, to a minor trench raid, barely worth mentioning in dispatches. However, unlike the thousands of small skirmishes in France and Belgium, the battle between the guards and the sailors had the entire German nation as an audience. Thus, the events of Christmas Eve would have vast significance for the course of the Germany's political development and the collapse of civil peace.

The *Frontschwein*'s dilemma, revisited

From the end of October to late December, a series of momentous political events had left the German Army's front-line soldiers bewildered: Ludendorff's relief, the Kaiser's abdication, the revolution in Germany, the return to the homeland, demobilization, and the final homecoming parades. The previous chapters have examined the response of *Frontkämpfer* in the entire *Westheer*, or, in the case of the abdication and the "Berlin Operation," a number of carefully selected units, usually over a period of days and weeks. The crisis of Christmas Eve, 1918, however, allows one to consider what was, essentially, the experience of one unique unit – the Guards Cavalry Rifle Division – during a period

---

[130] Kriegsgeschichtlichen Forschungsanstalt des Heeres, *Wirren*, 43, fn. 1.
[131] *Die Rote Fahne*, "Der Bestattung der sieben Matrosen," December 30, 1918.

Figure 8.4 In the courtyard of the Marstall, VMD sailors inventory
weapons captured from the guards during the Christmas Eve battle.

of less than forty-eight hours. First, there is a fairly self-evident point:
on the morning of Christmas Eve, the poor front-line veteran caught
in the mêlée of hostile Berliners found himself in a uniquely perplex-
ing situation. The day before he had been one of the few remaining
soldiers in the barracks, as many of his comrades would have already
been discharged or sent on leave. Second, unexpectedly alerted, he
had marched from the fringes of a great city to its very center, where,
with little time for explanation, his officers asked him to take part in a
battle, not against Spartacists, as he might have expected, but against
the former heroes of the November revolution, the sailors from Kiel
and Cuxhaven. Then he may have found himself in a tactically untenable situation, under attack by the troops detailed to protect his back.
Alternatively, the confused guardsman was being pushed around, his
weapons torn from his hands, as civilians accused him of being a tool
of the monarchists and a traitor to the revolution. For him to rejoin the
battle meant clearing fields of fire, which might have meant shooting
into crowds that included women and children, something he would
not do. Whatever the veteran expected from the Christmas Eve action,
it did not resemble the circumstances that emerged at the end of the
battle. No men could have been more befuddled than the front-line
soldiers on the Schlossplatz that morning.

The interrelated factors that shaped the front-line soldiers' behavior are still relevant for this compressed case study. The most significant on Christmas Eve were *selection* (both by the chain of command and the soldiers themselves), *isolation* (versus fraternization), *management* of perceptions, physical *exhaustion*, and *alienation* from those who had not shared the front-line experience.

To continue with another obvious point, the OHL and the cabinet were intensely purposeful in their *selection* of front-line troops of the GKSD to suppress the *Volksmarinedivision*. Ebert had given the rescue mission to the front-line troops even though he was offered an alternative, 3,000 men from the Potsdam soldiers' councils. At that point, thanks to Pabst's energetic indoctrination, Lequis' headquarters saw the GKSD as the most reliable force available for a very difficult mission. Of the nine divisions selected for the "Berlin Operation," the GKSD was the only one in which the unit leadership had aggressively sought to keep the unit intact. How the division decided who received Christmas leave and who stayed in the barracks is not clear; whether the men were available because of devotion to duty or because they had no other place to go, it is difficult to say. The GKSD was reinforced by elements of the 1st Guards Reserve Division, while the 5th and 37th Divisions contributed troops to the mission of securing key government buildings nearby. The reason Lequis chose these units is almost certainly that they were the most recently arrived divisions. The artillery that supported the assault on the palace and the Marstall had arrived only the day before the crisis began. Thus, the 1st Guards Reserve Division would have had little time to hemorrhage strength to discharges and desertion. On the other hand, the more recent arrivals would have had practically no time to orient themselves to the puzzling political situation in the capital. The 5th and 37th were also recent arrivals and were units recruited outside of the Berlin area.[132] Their men were unlikely to have friends and relatives in the mob that swarmed over the government troops on Christmas Eve. However, they must have been puzzled and disappointed at being so far from home during the holiday.

In their barracks outside the city, the men of the GKSD had been less accessible to the kind of agitation that undermined the other units of Lequis' command. Contrast their relative *isolation* with that of

[132] BA-R, R43/2485, telegram from Groener to the RL (Reichsleitung), #5055/18, dated 10 December, 1918. The 5th was stationed in Brandenburg but recruited from elsewhere in Prussia. The 37th was drawn originally from East Prussia (though it had drawn replacements from across the empire, including Alsace-Lorraine). Allied intelligence had rated both divisions highly but both had been badly depleted in the fall of 1918 (AEF G2, *251 Divisions*: 5th, 108–11 and 37th, 425–8).

Reinhard's 4th Foot Guards quartered in Moabit caserne in the middle of downtown Berlin. In Moabit, the troops would have been unable to avoid daily contact with one of the most radicalized urban populations in Germany. Couple the advantages of the GKSD's geographical location with Pabst's active effort to limit access to his men, and it becomes easier to understand why the GKSD was intact while the other divisions of Lequis' command arriving in Berlin after them were not.

The activities of the GKSD's leadership, however, were what truly set the division apart from the other combat units around Berlin. Pabst was one of the few officers who realized that the army had to ready itself for an ideological struggle and that the perceptions of his men would need careful *management*. His creation of defensive and offensive indoctrination cells showed his awareness that the front-swine's old deference to rank, flag, and Kaiser would not hold the unit together under the new and confusing circumstances of post-revolutionary Germany. Later, the OHL would hold his efforts up to the rest of the army as an example of the kind of soldier management necessary under revolutionary circumstances. Yet Pabst knew the limitations of his troops as well, and this explains his objections to Lequis' staff regarding the over-hasty preparation of the Christmas Eve operation. One can be sure that the guardsmen had little understanding of the chain of events that had led to the falling out between the government and the *Volksmarinedivision*. Nor could they have been completely aware of what was behind the decision to use force against the sailors. In this respect, the OHL and Lequis had failed to set the conditions for success. This failure was based on their unwillingness to acknowledge what a fragile instrument the remaining front-line units had become.[133]

On the day of battle, the units were also tired. Many of the soldiers involved in the GKSD's attack on Christmas Eve had been alerted in the afternoon or evening of December 23. As Pabst related, many had to conduct a long foot march to reach the scene of the battle. Some did not arrive until just before the palace's bombardment got under way. How physical *exhaustion* affected their response to the arrival of thousands of civilians around their positions, it is impossible to determine.

[133] Over four and a half years, attrition had gnawed away at the *cohesion* of every unit in the German Army. By late 1918, no unit had very many of its original members left. However, the GKSD had been formed as a rifle division only in January of the war's last year. It had seen heavy fighting on the Western Front since then, but the limited duration of that fighting may have allowed the survival of a solid nucleus of long-service men (AEF G2, *251 Divisions*). Beyond that, the GKSD was composed of some of the most elite cavalry units in the old army. Regiments like the Guards Uhlans and the Guards *Cuirassiers* possessed the tradition and elite status that might sustain a unit in difficult times.

However, footsore and sleep-deprived, the guardsmen and their leaders were unlikely to have the mental agility to cope effectively with the unexpected: the arrival of tens of thousands of civilians.

What, then, of *alienation?* This factor played an uncertain role in the Christmas Eve battle. The note the trustees' council of the GKSD sent to the Congress of Workers' and Soldiers' Councils on December 18 suggests that the guardsmen were jealous of the sailors' special status. One imagines that the troops of the GKSD may also have been aware of the *Volksmarinedivision*'s growing reputation as a public nuisance. Anecdotal evidence suggests that the soldiers resented the sailors for their limited exposure to combat and their relatively civilized living conditions.[134] There was no love lost between front-line soldiers and revolutionary sailors[135] and this would be reflected in the *Freikorps'* treatment of sailor prisoners in the fighting of the next year.[136] Nor did those who had stayed with their units in the last months of the war sympathize with deserters; one of the best-known deserters in postwar Germany led the *Volksmarinedivision*. On the other hand, the alienation felt by combat troops towards the home front must have been significantly reduced. By late December, the guardsmen and their fellow soldiers had been in the homeland for several weeks. This meant they had a growing awareness that privation was the central feature of civilian life in late 1918. The appeals made by the Berliners who pressed around them on the morning of Christmas Eve were likely to have had a stronger effect than they might have had just after the armistice, when the homeland seemed so remote to the *Frontschweine*.

Taken together, this collection of factors shaped the behavior of the several hundred guardsmen assembled to fight the government's enemies in the center of Berlin. Cohesion, selection, and skillful management, in particular, brought them to the battlefield and sustained them through the siege that, briefly at least, produced the surrender

---

[134] An example: at two o'clock on the afternoon of the battle, front-line soldiers from the 12th Infantry Regiment and the 3rd Pioneer Battalion guarded the entrances to the chancellery. A crowd of 200 gathered outside the building, and, led by a civilian and a sailor, they began to harangue the soldiers. One of the soldiers raised an objection. The sailors in Berlin have nothing to complain about, he said. In comparison to the *Fronttruppen*, they have always had it better. *VZ,* "Nach der Schlacht," late edition of December 24, 1918.

[135] Wrobel, an East German historian, concedes that many of the sailors who attempted political agitation among the guards got a "thrashing" for their efforts. Wrobel, *Der Sieg,* 38.

[136] In March 1919, in a Berlin courtyard, a *Freikorps* officer captured a number of sailors by using the promise of back pay as bait. The officer, an *Oberleutnant* Marloh, proceeded to execute thirty of those who seemed to him most likely to be leaders. Richard Müller, *Der Bürgerkrieg in Deutschland* (Berlin: Olle und Wolter, 1974), 183.

Figure 8.5 The Marstall building in the aftermath of the Christmas
Eve battle, December 1918.

of the *Volksmarinedivision*. Then a totally unexpected situation confronted the troops of the GKSD: the arrival of tens of thousands of
civilians. The inadequate preparation of the operation had placed the
troops in an untenable situation and no advantages in *esprit*, elite status, or bold leadership could have completely rescued them from the
disruptive effect created by the onslaught of Berlin's workers. One
might describe their situation as the ultimate breakdown of *isolation*.
"Revolutionary influences" were not only present – they were actively
tugging on the soldiers' weapons. Thus, the GKSD failed, as would
any unit in the old army. What is remarkable is that the troops rescued
their guns and retreated in some semblance of order. That Major von
Schleicher was later able to describe the division's morale, two days
later, as "restored" is also remarkable and suggests the strength of the
GKSD's cohesion and the effectiveness of it key leaders. It also begins
to explain why the GKSD would reappear as a different kind of fighting force a few short weeks later. In January 1919, the Guards Cavalry
Rifle Division returned to the streets of Berlin strengthened and more
resolute. Entering the capital for the third time in less than two months,
the unit would begin to establish the GKSD's reputation as one of the
most murderous of the *Freikorps*.

9   From debacle to civil war: the aftermath of "Bloody Christmas," December 1918–January 1919

The consequences (Berlin: December 25, 1918, to January 1, 1919)

For the Ebert government, there was no way to put a cheerful interpretation on the situation. The events of Christmas Eve had been a disaster. The majority of the working population of Berlin, whatever their political persuasion, put the blame for the bloodshed on Ebert and the Majority Socialists. Through the next week, the Independents in the cabinet, Haase, Dittmann, and especially Barth, grilled Ebert and his Majority Socialist colleagues on the events of December 23–24.[1] The Independent delegates pressed their advantage by demanding that the Majority Socialist Central Council provide answers to seven pointed questions about the government's behavior, including the decision to call in the troops on December 23, the approval of the ten-minute ultimatum on December 24, and the implementation of the Hamburg Points.[2] The Spartacist leaders who, up to then, had played a relatively minor role in events, also moved to take full advantage of the government's discomfiture. With a renewed militancy, Liebknecht called for mass demonstrations to protest the attack on the VMD. Christmas Day saw crowds of up to several hundred thousand marching through falling snow to denounce Ebert, Landsberg, and Scheidemann as "bloodhounds."[3] Liebknecht told the crowd that Christmas Eve was proof that their class enemies were still far from defeated, and called for the creation of a Red Guard to protect the revolution.[4]

These political attacks were troubling, but Ebert and his colleagues feared worse. On one hand, the government's main buildings were virtually unguarded; on the other, the Spartacists and their allies were

---

[1] *Quellen*, 6/II, Document 79: "Die Fragen der USPD-Volksbeauftragten an den Zentralrat."
[2] BA-MA, Nachlass Scheuch, N23/1, 67. *Die Freiheit*, "Die Fragen unsrer Genossen," December 29, 1918.
[3] Wrobel, *Der Sieg*, 61–2.   [4] *Ibid.*

sure to be emboldened by the course of events. With this in mind, on the night of the 24th, Groener asked Ebert what he planned to do. For the moment the government no longer had reliable troops at hand. Ebert replied ruefully that he would spend the night with friends and leave the chancellery in the care of the porter. When the Spartacists showed up, he said, they would find an empty building.[5] In truth, on the evening of Christmas Eve, the government held a special train at the Anhalter train station in the event the government needed to make a hasty evacuation.[6] For much of the week immediately following Christmas, the Majority Socialist delegates kept a low profile, staying in private dwellings outside the center of the city and sometimes meeting in secret locations.[7] Meanwhile, their enemies tested their own growing strength. Several hundred Spartacist supporters had broken off from the Christmas demonstration and seized the *Vorwärts* building. The guard force at the newspaper offices, forbidden to use their weapons, offered no resistance.[8]

For the officer corps, the events of December 24 were much worse than a defeat; they were a humiliation. The Ebert government had called for help and the Field Army had sent the best of what it had left, only to see those troops dispersed by a mob of civilians. If the Spartacists finally launched their anticipated coup, the army seemed powerless to combat it. On that Christmas Eve afternoon, Major von Harbou sent the OHL a depressing assessment: "[T]he troops of *Generalkommando Lequis* are no longer capable of active operations. There exist only the remnants of combat-ready units with which to occupy the main buildings [of the government] ... With the means used thus far, I see no way to support and defend the government." An entire army, he said, would be needed to remedy the situation. Perhaps gratuitously he added, "The result of today's clash could become politically catastrophic for the government."[9] That evening Groener entered this blunt and concise assessment of the entire "Berlin Operation" in his diary, "The entry operation (*Einzug*) is finished."[10]

The bad news from Berlin stunned the officer corps, and, in the immediate aftermath of the debacle, there was a measure of despair within the OHL staff. At a meeting of department chiefs, officers spoke of dissolving the headquarters so that they could go home to defend their

[5] Groener, *Lebenserinnerungen*, 476.
[6] Böhm, *Adjutant*, diary entry for December 24, 1918, 117–18.
[7] BA-MA, Nachlass Scheuch, N23/1. Oehme, "Hinter den Kulissen."
[8] *VZ*, "Ein neuer Putsch," December 26, 1918.
[9] Volkmann, *Revolution über Deutshland*, 163.
[10] BA-MA, Nachlass Groener, 46/25, diary entry of December 24, 1918.

families against the impending anarchy.[11] Schleicher offered a strong rebuttal of this defeatism, reminding the staff that events in Berlin served to gain time for the creation of volunteer units. If the army surrendered now, they would be leaving Germany to a grim fate. Groener, though depressed himself, backed Schleicher's position.[12] The next day he and Schleicher set the example for mandatory gaiety by dancing with the female stenographers at the OHL's Christmas party. Later, when recalling those days, Groener wrote that one had to have faith that the solid nucleus of the army would endure.[13]

Because the war ministry staff was much closer to the danger its members found faith more difficult to maintain. On Christmas Day, Colonel van den Bergh wrote that the danger of a leftist *putsch* was growing: "Since yesterday, 12.24, the danger of a Liebknecht–Ledebour government has risen to an extreme. But Liebknecht will want to let the matter mature. When the Field Army is dissolved, he will move more surely."[14] The colonel condemned the OHL and Lequis' lack of political awareness for the failure that resulted. His boss, General von Scheuch, was equally distressed with the failures of the Field Army but found military incompetence to be the chief failing. When Major von Harbou appeared at the war ministry the day after the battle, Scheuch rebuked a man he already disliked, stating:

The events of yesterday present themselves as a three-part defeat, first as a defeat of the troops on the street, second as defeat of the military's relationship to the government, and, third, as a defeat for the government's relationship with the people. The trust of the government in the military has been severely shaken. The troops deployed are temporarily no longer effective. It gives the impression that *Generalkommando Lequis* busied itself too much in political matters and too little in military preparations.[15]

Harbou was not the only one to feel Scheuch's ire. When the chief of the chancellery, Curt Baake, asked the war minister why the military had failed so badly on Christmas Eve, Scheuch replied, "Because they [the government] have sawn the timbers of my house, my officer corps, to pieces."[16]

This would not be Scheuch's only grievance against the cabinet. In the aftermath of "Bloody Christmas", he found himself one of the scapegoats of the affair. The MSPD delegates protested that they had

[11] Volkmann, *Revolution über Deutschland*, 163–4.
[12] Thaer, *Generalstabdienst an der Front*, diary entry for January 2, 1919, 287.
[13] *Ibid.*, 283–4, and Groener, *Erinnerungen*, 475.
[14] Van den Bergh, *Aus den Geburtsstunden*, diary entry for December 25, 1918, 66–7.
[15] Böhm, *Adjutant*, diary entry of December 25, 1918, 118–19.
[16] *Ibid.*, 119.

never given him a "blank check" to seek Wels' rescue. Scheuch, they claimed, had organized the attack on the sailors on his own initiative. What followed was an acrimonious exchange between the war minister and his political masters in government meeting rooms and in the Berlin press.[17] As it was, Scheuch had been waiting for the government to find a successor since mid December. At the end of the year, when the cabinet settled on Colonel Reinhardt of the demobilization branch, Scheuch departed, a bitter man.[18]

Plenty of blame was dispensed in the ensuing days and much of it fell on Lequis. Lequis sought to justify himself but, although the general had been an instructor at the *Kriegsakademie*, he unfortunately had taken no courses in media relations. The day after the battle, he proceeded to throw gasoline on the fire of public outrage. The December 25 edition of the *Vossische Zeitung* carried an interview with the general that proved enormously embarrassing to both the government and the High Command. Lequis told his interviewer that he had come to Berlin with the purpose of supporting the government and maintaining peace and order at any price. Thus, by announcing that he led a full-fledged military operation, Lequis directly contradicted Ebert's assertion two weeks earlier that Lequis' command served only as an administrative headquarters charged with the sole purpose of arranging the Guards Corps' homecoming. As the interview continued, the general showed no awareness of the niceties of coalition politics, suggesting that the chancellor played an active role in the guards' deployment to Berlin. "All soldiers had but one thought, as I did, to help the government. For them, Ebert was the man who represented the government." Lequis then proceeded to recite the preconditions for Groener's secret "Berlin Operation."

When I came here, I found a situation that was immediately recognizable as difficult and demanded the most rapid action. Certain preparations for the establishment of a strong governmental power were indeed ordered here but not fully executed. For that, I understood, was the disarming of all those not authorized to carry a weapon. The necessary laws were negotiated but still not executed. [Here he refers, among other things, to the decision to have Wels instead of Lequis disarm the city and the failure to enforce the measures needed to control deserters and sailors away from their stations.] ... My soldiers were filled, as I told you, with pride and joy a week ago, with the best possible spirit.

[17] BA-MA, Nachlass Scheuch, N23/1, 67. Oehme, "Hinter den Kulissen."
[18] For his feelings on the treatment of the officer corps, see Berthold and Neef, *Militarismus und Opportunismus*, Document 128: "Abschiedsgesuch des Kriegministers Scheuch vom 15. Dezember 1918," 307–9.

Lequis complained that if his troops had moved against the enemies of the government ten days sooner, then his men would have achieved the desired outcome. By waiting, the pull of home and family along with the effect of Spartacist agitation served to weaken his force. With this assertion, Lequis put the blame for the defeat of Christmas squarely on those above him, the government and the OHL. Finally, he offered the opinion that, in order to preserve peace and order and strengthen the government, a greater deployment of troops might be necessary. Such a view was guaranteed to excite the Left.[19]

In an effort at damage control, Scheuch promptly relieved Lequis and dissolved his command, while Groener sent Harbou, a former member of the OHL staff, on four weeks' leave. Another order placed Lequis' troops, or what remained of them, under General Walther von Lüttwitz, the commander of the III Corps district around Berlin.[20] There were other casualties. Two days after Christmas, Otto Wels announced that his nerves could no longer endure the work of city commandant.[21]

Several blocks away from Wels' office the officers taken prisoner by the *Sicherheitswehr* spent Christmas making their way back to their units. In the immediate aftermath of the fighting, members of Eichhorn's unit and sympathizers had stood the officers against a wall and leveled their rifles at them. Other members of the *Sicherheitswehr* had prevailed on their comrades to spare the prisoners. Ultimately, Eichhorn arranged for the officers' release after they had promised to take no part in further fighting. The officers finally left the police presidium under the cover of darkness, dressed in civilian clothes.[22] It was hardly the proudest moment in the history of the Prussian Guards.

The remainder of the GKSD's *Frontkämpfer* spent Christmas in their barracks between Potsdam and Berlin. According to some accounts, some had left the ranks in disgust after Ebert's mediation on the night of the 23rd; others after the fiasco on Christmas Eve.[23] The cabinet sent them a message intended to encourage them after the ignominy they had experienced. "The government thanks the troops for their loyal conduct and expects that you will maintain such loyalty in the

[19] *VZ*, "Generalleutenant Lequis über die Lage," interview with Erich von Salzmann, December 25, 1918. Böhm wrote in his diary that Lequis' indiscreet remarks left the government "badly compromised." *Adjutant*, diary entry for December 25, 1918, 119–20.
[20] Kriegsgeschichtlichen Forschungsanstalt des Heeres, *Wirren*, 44.
[21] Fischer, *Revolutionskommandantur*, 48.
[22] Kriegsgeschichtlichen Forschungsanstalt des Heeres, *Wirren*, 43.
[23] Groener-Geyer, *General Groener*, 126. Kriegsgeschichtlichen Forschungsanstalt des Heeres, *Wirren*, 43–4.

Figure 9.1 On December 29, 1918, Otto Tost, leader of the
Berlin Senior Naval Council, orates at the funeral procession of
VMD sailors killed on Christmas Eve. The crisis that will lead to
Spartacus Week was building.

future."[24] The official history, reporting through the lens of National
Socialism, recorded that the rank and file of the GKSD was disdainful
of the message and disgusted with the government. Restoring the morale
of these men would require very special handling. Yet, in Waldemar
Pabst, they had a chief of staff whose insights into soldier morale and
motivation would enable the division to reincarnate itself.

Preparing the army for civil war (Wilhelmshöhe, December 26, 1918)

Nothing inspires change in a military organization like embarrassment.
The day after Christmas Groener brought his staff and a number of

---

[24] Kriegsgeschichtlichen Forschungsanstalt des Heeres, *Wirren*, 43.

trusted front-line commanders together to review recent events and decide what must be done to restore the army's ability to defend the government and preserve the officer corps. It was a sober session in which the First Quartermaster General and his subordinates worked together to see what could be rescued from the wreckage of the old army. Amid the debris, they hoped to find something that might be useful in preparing for the likelihood of civil war.

Schleicher, the political officer, opened with a review of the army's relationship with the government. He reminded the other officers that their chief adversaries in the cabinet were Haase and Barth. For the time being, he indicated, the Hamburg Points had been blocked. Ebert had played a role and the army needed to support him without giving the appearance of counter-revolutionary activity. Groener interrupted Schleicher's brief to reinforce the point. The officer corps, he said, must be very judicious in its behavior. Imprudent acts by "individual hot-heads" must cease. Circumspection must be balanced with an effort to counteract the effect of socialist propaganda on the army's politically immature rank and file.

Schleicher resumed his briefing, turning the discussion to the recent events in Berlin. Using the understatement preferred by staff officers, he described the Christmas Eve fighting as a "rebuff" to the government. The Independents and Liebknecht had been strengthened. Groener, predictably, had much to say on this topic. Some of those listening may have been surprised to hear him say that the GKSD was "well prepared for the mission." He explained: "They were instructed by a variety of speakers, including politicians in civilian attire ... a truly intensive enlightenment (*Aufklärung*)." The attentive officers realized that Groener was saying that the old methods of preparing troops for battle were no longer sufficient. Political preparation was as important to the army's future operations as military preparation. Even though the GKSD had failed to neutralize the sailors, Pabst's training methods in the GKSD were a model for the rest of the army.

Groener went on to offer his overview of the entire "Berlin Operation," including its unhappy end on Christmas Eve.

For Ebert, the overall current situation in Berlin has deteriorated. The troop deployment, which Ebert approved, did not have the desired success. Jealousy between Lequis and the war ministry played a role. Ebert would have welcomed a genuine success but is reluctant to take responsibility for the necessary instructions. So it is with most politicians. Military leaders must act on their own responsibility.

Here Groener offered his fellow officers the stern reality of civil–military relations in the post-revolutionary republic. Commanders could not wait for unambiguous guidance from the politicians. Moreover, new circumstances meant that careful planning was even more important than in conventional military operations. The Christmas Eve battle illustrated the point.

The attack on the palace and the Marstall was not sufficiently prepared. Such operations should be preceded by a warning order that allows preparation to proceed until the details have been determined. Traffic barriers are very important. Negotiations must be refused. They offered Ledebour the opportunity to assemble masses of people, including women and children.[25] The troops were unprepared for this. They did not know how to perform police functions.

Groener also commented on the performance of the local commander: "The situation has been made worse by a foolish interview by Lequis. *Generalkommando Lequis* is dissolved."

Schleicher turned the agenda to the current situation in the capital. Government troops still held the key buildings. Meanwhile, he said, volunteer formations are assembling outside Berlin in Wannsee, Döberitz, and Zossen. The GKSD was in reasonably good shape and their morale has been restored "thanks to the well-conceived instruction of the General Staff Officer Pape [*sic*: Pabst]."

Here, again, the GKSD and the captain who was its guiding force were held up to the army as the example of what was needed. Schleicher's mention of it showed how much the OHL considered it a key to the situation in Berlin. More than 180 divisions had crossed the Rhine in the previous six weeks, but now the Field Army had focused its attention on this single division on the outskirts of the capital, a unit so badly used just two days before. The focus, that is, until, the new volunteer formations were ready.

If anyone missed the point, Schleicher proceeded to describe what the army would have to look like for the trials ahead. Leaders could no longer be chosen by the old conventions; rank, class, and seniority would have to give way to leadership, energy, and political awareness. Because ideology shaped the battlefield, commanders had to be men who had the trust of their subordinates; the braid on their shoulders was no longer enough. For example, he said, a lieutenant was leading the 3rd Guards Regiment. The Guards Fusilier Regiment was being led by a sergeant-lieutenant (a wartime reserve rank) and active officers were serving under him. By the same token, trustee councils were no longer a nuisance designed to satisfy the demands of a republican regime.

---

[25] Here Groener was ill informed. Eichhorn, not Ledebour, was the key man in organizing the crowds that came to the palace on Christmas Eve.

As a conduit for improved internal communication, the councils had become an essential element in every unit, a prerequisite for preserving discipline and building trust between officers and men.[26]

By highlighting the GKSD's methods and describing the new leadership principles the army required, Schleicher had previewed many of the most conspicuous features of the formations that would carry the burden of fighting the civil war, the *Freikorps*. He also offered them the simple political goal that should guide the exercise of commanders' personal initiative in the uncertain situations that would follow: defend the National Assembly. With national elections scheduled for January 19, 1919, the High Command saw the convention of a National Assembly as the single greatest hope for reining in the Left and restoring the conservative elements of German society.

Schleicher introduced a variety of other political considerations. Almost all related to two central conclusions one could have drawn from the course of the presentation: (1) the officer corps was going to be deeply involved in political matters, and (2) in the existing period of national peril, the army was going to look very different from the old *Kaiserheer*.[27] The meeting signaled a conclusion reached by senior military leaders: the old army was gone.

New men

The last days of December were anxious ones for the chancellor and the First Quartermaster General. Yet even while they were bracing themselves for a Spartacist coup, political and military events were reshaping the balance of power in Germany. One of most important of these occurred in the cabinet itself. On December 28, 1918, the three Independent Socialist delegates, Haase, Dittmann, and Barth, left the government. In the final session, the three Independents blasted the Majority Socialists for failing to rein in the old forces of German

[26] Other necessary measures included establishing "model" units and cleaning the riffraff out of casernes. Troublesome soldiers' councils were to be shut down, and many commands had found that an investigation of misappropriation of government property was frequently useful to this end.

[27] Among other things, he discussed the propaganda campaign against Spartacus and for Ebert. On the government's initiative to create a republican *Volkswehr* (People's Guard), he said the OHL would make a show of studying the problem while stalling for time. He re-emphasized the political instruction in the GKSD as an example for the army. The meeting considered the new Officers' League, and Groener gave guidance on the nature of officers' political involvement. The description of this meeting is taken from *Quellen*, 2/II, Document 12: "Aufzeichnung uber eine Besprechung der Obersten Heeresleitung mit Chef der Stabe und Frontoffizieren," December 26, 1918, 31–8.

Figure 9.2 Defense Minister Noske inspects *Freikorps* Huelsen at Zossen training area, outside Berlin. Before the January crisis, he proclaimed: "Someone must be the bloodhound."

militarism and blamed Ebert and his two MSPD colleagues for the "bloodbath" of December 24.[28] The uneasy coalition of November 10 was dead.

The cabinet moved swiftly to replace them with two new delegates from their own party. They gave Rudolf Wissell a portfolio that included social and economic issues. The truly momentous choice, however, was the other man they selected. He was Gustav Noske, and he took over responsibility for military matters. Along with a distinguished record of party activity, Noske had a reputation for drive and competence, and he took special pride in his ability to work with not only common soldiers and sailors but also generals and admirals. Sent to the tumultuous port of Kiel during the November naval mutinies, he had earned a national reputation by re-establishing order and maintaining the naval garrisons solidly in the MSPD camp.[29] Ebert called for his advice after the

---

[28] *Quellen*, 6/II, Document 81: "Antwort der USPD-Volksbeauftragten auf die Erklarung des Zentralrats. 28/29.12.1918 nachts," 137–8. Pressure from their own party was also a key factor in driving the three USPD members out of the cabinet.

[29] On Christmas Eve, when the *Volksmarinedivision* sent a call for help to Kiel, Noske offered, instead, several thousand sailors ready to fight for the Ebert government. Noske, *Von Kiel bis Kapp*, 54.

Christmas Eve fiasco, and Noske traveled to the capital on December 27. Speaking bluntly, he told Ebert that the entire nation was disgusted with the state of affairs in Berlin. The provisional government must be ready to deal forcefully with its enemies.[30]

Noske's was not the only new face in a key position. The government appointed Wilhelm Reinhard, the dynamic commander of the 4th Foot Guards, to replace Wels as city commandant. Wels' adjutant, Lieutenant Fischer, challenged the appointment, having himself been acclaimed by the soldiers' councils of Berlin as the new commandant. Not unexpectedly, these same councils rejected Reinhard's appointment. The colonel found a pragmatic solution to the problem. Though utterly contemptuous of Fischer, he allowed the glib and ambitious former monk to act as the front man for the commandant's headquarters while he worked behind the scenes to prepare the pro-government troops in Berlin for civil war.[31] In doing so, Reinhard worked closely with General Walther von Lüttwitz, Lequis' replacement, and Colonel Walther Reinhardt, Scheuch's successor in the war ministry, both of whom proved to be capable and energetic men.[32]

Though the key people in Wilhelmshöhe had not changed, there was a clear shift in the function of the OHL as well. Throughout the period after November 9, the socialist government had endured the continued existence of the Field Army headquarters because Groener and his staff had portrayed themselves as having an essential apolitical role in administration and logistics. They provided the military-technical expertise necessary to ensure the accomplishment of several critical postwar tasks: the return of front-line forces to the homeland, execution of the terms of the armistice, demobilization, and the establishment of frontier security forces. In the wake of Christmas Eve, the OHL took on the role of senior operational headquarters for defense of the provisional government against its internal enemies.[33]

The battles around the palace and Marstall served to bring new people into key places in the government and army. Their energy dispelled some of the gloom. Nevertheless, for the OHL and its civilian masters, the unpleasant fact remained that, for the time being, they could call

[30] Ibid.   [31] Reinhard, Wehen der Republik, 55–8.
[32] William Mulligan, The Creation of the Modern German Army: General Walther Reinhardt and the Weimar Republic, 1914–1930 (New York: Berghahn Books, 2005), 44–58. Reinhardt's appointment resulted in a curious situation. Reinhardt, a Württemburger, was the chief of the Prussian ministry of war while Groener, also a Württemburger, was, under Hindenburg, the head of the Prussian-dominated general staff.
[33] The changing role of the OHL is considered in Rakenius, Wilhelm Groener als erster Generalquartiermeister, 154, and Kluge, Soldatenräte und Revolution, 265.

on barely 150 reliable troops in the capital of the Reich. Groener would remember this as the most difficult time of the postwar period.[34]

On December 31, Count Kessler recorded in his diary, "The last day of this dreadful year. 1918 is likely to remain the most frightful date in German history."[35]

Epilogue: Spartacus Week and the rise of the *Freikorps*

The new year, 1919, was less than a week old when the Spartacists finally moved against the government.[36] On January 4, hundreds of thousands of workers filled the streets of Berlin to protest the government's attempt to dismiss USPD leader Emil Eichhorn from his post as police president of Berlin. Emboldened by the size and militancy of the crowds, leaders of the left wing of the USPD, the newly established Communist Party, and the powerful revolutionary shop stewards, gathered in council to announce a general strike, the overthrow of the provisional government, and the cancellation of the national elections. Beyond these measures, the council had no plan to consolidate power, nor could it coax either the Berlin garrison or the VMD to throw their support behind the uprising. While their leaders deliberated over what to do next, Spartacist supporters seized the newspaper quarter, provisions depots, post offices, and several railway stations. By January 6, they appeared ready to storm the last remaining bastions of governmental support in the capital, the Reich chancellery and the Moabit caserne.

During the crisis days of December and early January the new commandant of Berlin, Colonel Wilhelm Reinhard, had maintained the dwindling remnants of his Fourth Foot Guards in Moabit caserne as a sort of pro-government island surrounded by the "sea" of revolutionary Berlin. Using men who remained with the regiment as well as those who answered his urgent recall order, the colonel was able to cobble together a small unit of volunteers 300 strong.[37] Together with a similar-sized battalion of guards NCOs led by Sergeant Gustav

---

[34] Groener's testimony in the "stab-in-the-back" trial cited in Wrobel, *Der Sieg*, 60.

[35] Kessler, *Berlin in Lights*, diary entry for December 31, 1918, 47.

[36] For the purposes of this summary of events, the government's enemies will be referred to as Spartacists following contemporary usage, though technically (1) the Spartacus League had been absorbed into the Communist Party and (2) the most militant leaders of the uprising were probably the revolutionary shop stewards (*Obleute*) rather than the leaders of any political party. Eberhard Kolb described the rising as "hopelessly mismanaged and to some extent half-hearted." Kolb, *Weimar Republic*, 16.

[37] In order to distinguish it from the regiment's demobilized *Ersatz* battalions, he named his little battalion the "Mobile Fourth Foot Guards."

Suppe, he had formed "Volunteer Regiment Reinhard" as a sort of proto-*Freikorps*.[38]

When the Spartacists attacked, Reinhard and his allies were prepared, though just barely. At Moabit caserne, the guardsmen used an artillery piece firing blank ammunition to stop an assault and machine-gun fire to disperse it. At the Reich chancellery, Suppe's men fired on a storming party attempting to break down the gate, leaving some sixty of the attackers killed or wounded. Despite this initial success, Reinhard's forces were too weak to do anything but hold their positions, but, in subsequent days, a variety of makeshift volunteer formations reinforced them. With a combined strength of around 2,500 men, Reinhard's command was strong enough to overcome most of the resistance of the insurrectionists and retake the key buildings within the capital.

On the same day as the first protest march, January 4, the government's new defense minister, Gustav Noske, had accompanied Ebert on a visit to Zossen, the army training area outside Berlin. At Zossen, the two politicians observed one of the new volunteer formations, General von Maercker's *Landesjägers*, march past the reviewing party in well-ordered formations.[39] Impressed by the appearance of these "real soldiers," Noske slapped Ebert on the shoulder and said, "You can relax; now it will all work out all right."[40] Noske waited a week to ensure the new volunteer units were ready, and then, on January 11, he led them into the capital. The headquarters staff for the newly arrived troops was provided by the Guards Cavalry Rifle Division, making its third entry into Berlin in just over a month. The march route took the troops from the southwest suburbs of the city into its center, where, just over three weeks before, the division had been greeted by cheering crowds. This time, the sidewalks were almost empty, and the troops moved with weapons ready (though, by that point, Reinhard's men had crushed most of the resistance in the city).[41] Noske's newly arrived units served as a show of force, an intimidating demonstration that the government had the power to defend itself against all threats from the Left.[42]

The Spartacus Week was a bloody defeat for the Left and an ominous debut for the *Freikorps*. For the volunteer units in the capital and elsewhere in Germany, the fighting in Berlin in January 1919 was just the first of a series of campaigns that eventually ranged from Latvia

---

[38] Reinhard, *4. Garde-Regiment*, 398–9.
[39] Von Maercker had been the commander of the 214th Division, and he built his *Freikorps* on the remnants of the division.
[40] Maercker, *Vom Kaiserheer zur Reichswehr*, 64.
[41] BA-MA, RM 6/471, Reinhard report to Lüttwitz, January 12, 1919.
[42] Noske, *Von Kiel bis Kapp*, 74.

312   The Final Battle

Figure 9.3 "On the roof of the Brandenburg Gate. Government
troops are armed with machine guns and hand grenades for battle
against members of the Spartacus group." Action during Spartacus
Week, January 1919.

to the Ruhr. Though the *Freikorps* movement was made up of disparate elements and campaigned against a variety of enemies, the battles
of Spartacus Week reflected two of the most significant features of
all *Freikorps* operations. One was the *Freikorps*' overwhelming tactical
superiority over its enemies; superiority based on the combat experience of its leaders and the extensive use of heavy weapons – mortars,
flamethrowers, field guns, and even tanks and aircraft – against all
types of resistance. The other feature was a vindictive ruthlessness that
resulted in a series of atrocities during the course of the German Civil
War.[43] The most famous example came on January 15, when Captain
Pabst and the Guards Cavalry Rifle Division took their revenge for

[43] A volunteer in *Freikorps* von Epp wrote in a letter, "If I were to write you everything,
you would say I was telling you lies. No pardon is given. We shoot even the wounded.
The enthusiasm is great, almost unbelievable. Our battalion has had two deaths, the
Reds 200–300. All who fall into our hands get the rifle butt and then are dispatched
with a shot ... We were much more humane against the French in the war." Fried,
Guilt, 192. An after-action review by the staff of the GKSD in March 1919 advised
officers never to negotiate with the enemy. Reflecting the lessons of the Christmas
Eve battle, it wrote that the only acceptable outcome was immediate surrender or the
final destruction of the opposing force. BA-MA, PH 8/V/28, GKSD Memo. Ia #223,
"Experiences from the Street Fighting in Berlin," dated March 31, 1919.

Blutweihnachten with the brutal murder of the two Communist leaders, Karl Liebknecht and Rosa Luxemburg.[44]

In many respects, the fighting methods and ruthless behavior of the *Freikorps* were direct legacies of the Western Front experience. Because the *Freikorps* leaders were veterans of the *Materialschlacht*, they were prepared to make the best use of the storm-troop tactics and heavy weapons employed on the Great War's battlefields. Beyond that, after experiencing combat of unprecedented violence, many had been convinced that they had been betrayed by a part of German society that deserved no quarter. Though this study is chiefly concerned with the immediate impact of front-line troops on the events of November and December, no discussion of the *Frontheer*'s legacy can ignore the role of the *Freikorps* in making the German Civil War a bitter memory for much of German society.

The memoirs of *Freikorps* fighters make much of the spirit of the volunteer formations. However, the *Freikorps* had nothing that might be described as a unified political outlook or a positive political program. What linked these men together were the things they were opposed to and resented. A far from exhaustive list might include: disorder, socialists, the Treaty of Versailles, deserters, mutinous sailors, Bolshevism, the Allied powers, democratic politics, the Poles, profiteers, and bourgeois culture. The *Freikorps* officers were men who would never reconcile themselves to the events of November 9 and November 11, 1918. In an attempt to characterize this negative worldview, the German historian Otto-Ernst Schüddekopf called this disparate grab-bag of animosities "Prussian nihilism."[45] Though, ostensibly, they fought for the republic and took an oath of allegiance to it, they almost always fought under the colors of the old *Kaiserreich*, and supplemented it by wearing symbols like oak leaves, as well as more ominous totems, such as death's heads and swastikas.

The diversity and independence of the different volunteer units helps to explain why exact figures for the number of *Freikorpskämpfer* are not available.[46] At their peak strength, they probably numbered between

---

[44] Forty-three years later, in an interview with *Der Spiegel*, "Ich Liess Rosa Luxemburg Richten" (16 [April 18, 1962], 38–44), Waldemar Pabst claimed he had received the tacit approval of Ebert and Noske for the murders.

[45] Schüddekopf, *Das Heer und Die Republik*, 45. "What do we believe in? you ask. Nothing besides action. Nothing besides the possibility of action ... Our job is to attack, not to govern." Von Salomon, quoted in Robert Waite, *Vanguard of Nazism: The Free Corps Movement in Postwar Germany* 1918–1923 (New York: W. W. Norton and Co., 1952), 269.

[46] Soldiers joined the *Freikorps* for a variety of reasons. Some were recruited to serve on the Silesian frontier, where they fought the Poles; some, like the infamous Iron

Figure 9.4 Recruiting poster for the GKSD reincarnated as a
Freikorps. "Your Fatherland is in danger. Report ..."

150,000 and 400,000 men, with many of those counted in the latter
figure coming from transitory, local security formations. How many

Division, were attracted by offers of land in the Baltic states in return for service
against the Bolsheviks; still others, like von Maercker's *Landesjägerkorps* and the
Erhardt Brigade, were involved in extended campaigns against the Communists
across the whole of Germany. At least one, the *Regiment Reichstag*, was recruited by
the MSPD and had a genuine republican character. Many others were transitory formations, *Bürgerwehr* and the like, dedicated to local security missions.

Figure 9.5 *Freikorps* troops take cover behind a captured British tank in Berlin during the March 1919 crisis.

were combat veterans is difficult to say, and a point to be kept in mind is that the vast majority of front-line soldiers went home after their discharge. Nevertheless, it seems fair to say that the front-line veterans gave the *Freikorps*, especially the early *Freikorps*, much of their essential character.

They were not the young republic's military of choice. The *Freikorps* had their legal basis in a government order of December 12, 1918, which authorized the raising of volunteer formations for the purpose of border defense and internal security.[47] Though the provisional government envisioned the eventual establishment of a republican *Volkswehr* (People's Army) with a heavy representation of proletarian volunteers, such volunteers were never recruited in significant numbers. Generally, those working-class men with army experience wanted no more of it, and those younger men who had not yet served were even less inclined to submit themselves to military service.[48] Instead, the several dozen

---

[47] Berthold and Neef, *Militarismus und Opportunismus*, Document 124: "Gesetz zur Bildung einer freiwilligen Volkswehr vom 12. Dezember 1918," 302–3.
[48] For the efforts to build the *Volkswehr*, see Kluge, *Soldatenräte und Revolution*, 325–41.

Freikorps created across Germany in 1918 and 1919 were led by front-line officers, often built on the framework of Imperial Army combat units, and manned by other elements of society, such as the lower middle class and peasantry.[49] Unemployed white collar workers as well as university students and cadets, in particular, were significantly over-represented in the ranks of the volunteer formations. However, the most important elements in the *Freikorps* ranks, in numbers and influence, were the NCOs and reserve officers with front-line experience. These were men who had gained an element of status in the old, class-conscious army, a status that transcended class origins. Most of them saw no way to retain that social promotion in postwar Germany. The wartime expansion of the army had created thousands of new officers, and there was little place for these men in the peacetime army.[50] If the *Freikorps* traced their lineage to the Western Front, it was chiefly through such men.

Moreover, if the six response factors used thus far have served to explain the unique behavior of the front-line troops in their response to defeat and revolution, they may also be constructively applied to analyzing the choice made by those combat veterans who joined the *Freikorps*. In several instances, one finds paradoxical results. Physical *exhaustion* and the moral exhaustion that accompanied war-weariness, for example, do not explain the appeal of the volunteer units to *Fronttruppen*; however, one suspects that, after several weeks of recuperation at home, many soldiers found fatigue replaced by restlessness and a desire to act. For others, a sort of inertia may have prevailed, especially for those who found it difficult to reintegrate themselves into society. As one *Freikorps* leader wrote, "War had become their trade and they did not exert themselves to find another."[51] Similarly, *isolation* no longer played the same role, because the returned soldiers could see conditions inside the homeland with their own eyes. However, the yearning for home and family was replaced, for some, by the day-to-day exposure to the poverty, hunger, political unrest, and economic uncertainty of postwar Germany. Paradoxically, because this was not the homeland they had

---

[49] Yet the class origin of the volunteers is not as significant as it might first appear, because the *Freikorps* tended to reject class as a form of identity.
[50] Social composition of the *Freikorps* from Koch, *Der deutsche Bürgerkrieg*, 52–64. A postwar survey of Bavarian reserve officers found that almost a quarter served in the *Freikorps*. Waite, *Vanguard of Nazism*, 48.
[51] Manfred von Killinger, quoted in Venner, *Söldner ohne Sold*, 57. For those soldiers who remembered the sheer physical suffering and debilitation that accompanied service in the trenches, *Freikorps* service was something quite different. There were no extended tours in the mud of the trenches or unendurable periods of enemy shell fire. Instead, the *Freikorps* fighters could expect hot food, good pay, and a roof overhead most nights.

dreamed of, immersion in society rather than isolation from it may have prodded some *Frontschweine* to action. And this point leads the analysis to the next factor, *alienation*. If *Freikorps* memoirs have a common thread it is this profound sense of estrangement from the homeland. In the eyes of many returning veterans, the *Etappenschweine* seemed to rule the "new" Germany, and the red flags of the homeland soldiers' councils seemed a taunt rather than an inspiration. The sailors who had avoided any real fighting were the heroes of the revolution, while the workers excused from front-line service had first crack at the best jobs and had lined their pockets with bloated wages. If the *Bürgerschaft* of a soldier's hometown had offered a festive greeting, others were less willing to honor the sacrifices of a Western Front veteran. For young men who had grown up in the trenches, postwar society must have often seemed a place where selfish individualism replaced the camaraderie of the front. Finally, if war had been the defining experience of one's life (as it had been for men like Adolf Hitler), the pettiness of day-to-day living in German society might seem nearly unbearable. Though the unhappy ending of the war was not a central issue to many common soldiers, it was a source of burning resentment for many young officers who wanted to revenge themselves on the "November criminals."[52] Such attitudes were reflected in the atrocities committed by the *Freikorps* and an open hostility to the republic that culminated in the Kapp *putsch* of 1920.

The alienation felt by the volunteers led, in turn, to *selection*, specifically self-selection, which was obviously the salient feature of *Freikorps* membership. Hostility to the republic and postwar society were mixed with the other motivations that led volunteers enlist. These ranged from genuine patriotism to the need for a steady wage, or even the criminal desire to exploit opportunities for violence and plunder. Self-selection and the ubiquity of alienation served to enhance *cohesion*. The *cohesion* that had characterized front-line units was strengthened by the fact that all *Freikorps* men were volunteers, many had front-line experience, and that, frequently, much of society looked upon them as outlaws. In the *Freikorps*, the disoriented front-line veteran found "comradeship, understanding, economic security, and a continuation of the military life he had learned to love."[53] Finally, when Maercker and Reinhard encouraged the establishment of trustees among the enlisted members

---

[52] In a diary entry of January 1919, a Captain Berthold, *Freikorps* officer and former fighter pilot with a *Pour le Mérite* and fifty-five victories, wrote: "I will never forget the days of outrage, lies, and barbarity ... They remain an indelible stain on the history of Germany ... How I hate the [revolutionary] rabble." Venner, *Söldner ohne Sold*, 56.
[53] Waite, *Vanguard of Nazism*, 42.

of their units, it suggested that the front-line officers had learned hard lessons about soldier *management*.[54] In the *Freikorps*, the distance between officers and men was significantly compressed. Some have attributed this to the familiar spirit within the elite storm-troop formations carried over to the volunteer formations.[55] However, throughout the army of 1918, the experience of the trenches had produced a leveling effect; officer–soldier relationships had been renegotiated both in the last years of the war and on the march back to the homeland. The old *Kadavergehorsam* would not work in the *Freikorps*. Instead, the *Freikorps* leaders motivated their men by claiming that theirs was a righteous cause. By crushing the Bolsheviks, they were saving Germany from a terrible fate.[56]

---

[54] Reinhard, *Wehen der Republik*, 61. [55] *Ibid.*, 69–71.
[56] Maercker, *Vom Kaiserheer zur Reichswehr*, 58. They also made appeal to the spirit of the *Freikorps* of the War of Liberation against Napoleon in 1813.

10 Conclusion: *Frontschweine* and revolution

Incident in Halle

For Kurt Anker, captain of the general staff, the army's demobilization in late 1918 meant a wrenching loss of both employment and status, and, like so many of his brother officers, he was suddenly a man with time on his hands.[1]

Anker was an unrepentant monarchist and saw no place for himself in the service of the new revolutionary regime. He despised every aspect of the revolution, and saw it as tragic national disaster. Given the bitter freedom that comes with unemployment, he decided to travel across Germany. His memoir indicates no plan for his journey. Perhaps it was the desire to see the postwar evolution of his homeland at first-hand. Or perhaps it was gesture of defiance. The captain had only one set of civilian clothes, and, as a result, he spent most of his time in the uniform of a Prussian general staff officer. He made a brazen, public show of his silver epaulets and saber and, later, recalled with satisfaction that his audacious display went largely unchallenged.

As fighting broke out across Germany in early 1919, Anker was staying at the Golden Ball hotel (*Goldene Kugel*) in Halle. As he prepared to check out, he heard a knock at his door. Opening it, he was confronted by two revolutionary sailors. They carried a machine gun and wore embarrassed expressions on their faces. They asked the captain's pardon but *Freikorps* troops were approaching the city. They anticipated

---

[1] During the last years of the Great War, Anker served as the OHL's intelligence liaison with Army Group Crown Prince. There, his duties allowed him to build a close relationship with both the Crown Prince and the army group chief of staff, General von Schulenberg. Thus, on November 10, Anker was present to listen to Schulenberg's tearful description of the struggle he had waged at Spa to prevent Groener from jettisoning the Kaiser. Shortly afterwards, Anker accompanied the Crown Prince in the first stages of the journey that took the Hohenzollern heir into exile with his father. After the armistice, Anker remained with the army group staff as it orchestrated the homeward march of its sixty divisions. He left the headquarters, finally, when it disbanded itself near Kassel. The vignette here and in what follows comes from Anker, *Unsere Stunde*, 88–91,

a fight and their leaders had identified Anker's balcony as a useful machine-gun position. The captain pointed to his open trunk and clothes arranged on the bed and told the sailors that he was on his way out. The balcony, he said, was at their disposal. One of the sailors replied, "By all means continue your packing, *Herr Hauptmann*. There is no hurry." With a note of pride, the sailor went on to confide that he had served as the batman for a ship's captain during the war. He knew how to store an officer's belongings and would help Anker finish packing. The job was finished in short order and the sailor offered to help the captain carry the heavy trunk down to the lobby.

As he was leaving, Anker felt compelled to ask the two courteous sailors why they were serving with the Spartacists. The other sailor said, "Oh, it's not all so bad with us. *Herr Hauptmann* should come over to our side. With us the pay is best and discipline is tight." The captain thanked them for the friendly offer, but declined.

"A shame," the sailor answered ruefully, "we have so few skilled officers."

The story has significance on several counts. Anker himself used it to support his view that Germany had not experienced a "real" revolution in 1918 at all. Instead, it had suffered a collapse which had enabled all sorts of ambitious and unprincipled opportunists to step into the resulting power vacuum. One might challenge his anachronistic interpretation, but, certainly, the incident reinforces the point that Germany's old elites continued to have a disproportionate influence in what remained, to a large degree, a deferential society.

The friendly banter between the die-hard Prussian and the two Spartacist sailors may illustrate yet another, perhaps larger, point about the German Revolution. Along with the adjectives that historians most often used – "unfinished," "unfulfilled," or betrayed," for example – it was a *strange* revolution. Consider that, after the old monarchy had been swept away, the first leader of the new "socialist republic" was a man who claimed to hate revolution "like sin." Then, that he and the other men who, a month before, proclaimed the new revolutionary order to crowds of Berliners, saluted the symbols of the fallen monarchy as its battle flags paraded through the center of that same city. Finally, at Christmas, when the "revolutionary" government needed rescue, it turned to men like Pabst and Reinhard, who loathed every aspect of the revolution, to crush the very group who had served as the revolution's vanguard in early November. Strange, indeed.

The sailors' deference to Anker suggests another point important to this study, that military institutions have the ability to make soldiers and sailors behave in ways contrary to their "class interests." Coercion is the ready explanation for such behavior, yet hardly a complete one, as Anker's story suggests. Training, leadership, socialization, camaraderie, and appeals to patriotism all had roles to play. Without them, one is at a loss to explain the dogged resistance of the German troops on the Western Front in the last days of the war or much of their behavior in the weeks that followed the war's end.

A final point to be drawn from the story may be obvious but is hardly banal. It is reflected in the parting comment the sailor made to Anker, "We have so few skilled officers." No matter what fields of fire Anker's balcony offered or how great the revolutionary zeal of the machine-gun crew, one knows, given historical hindsight, that the sailors would be crushed when the *Freikorps* arrived. For all the importance of inspirational rhetoric, a just cause, or mass organization, the victors in revolutionary combat and civil war are usually those with the most effective military forces; metaphorically, the side with the sharpest bayonets. The *Freikorps'* leaders had honed theirs in terrible places like Passchendaele and the Argonne Forest.

The early *Freikorps* were one of the front-line soldiers' most immediate legacies to the new Weimar Republic. The veterans who volunteered for these units preserved the Majority Socialist government that many of them despised, while their operations left a record of brutality that poisoned the political atmosphere of the Weimar Republic. The memory of the violence between 1919 and 1923 contributed to an irreconcilable divide between the two wings of the German Left, a divide that persisted until the Nazis crushed both the Social Democrats and the Communists ten years later.

Beyond the immediate impact of the *Freikorps*, a number of longer-term legacies were also significant and served to reinforce the multitude of factors that ultimately undermined the Weimar Republic. This study has chiefly concerned itself with the way choices made by front-line veterans affected the immediate aftermath of the revolution, the last seven or eight weeks of 1918. A consideration of after-effects that carried into the late 1920s and early 1930s – the glorification of the wartime experience by those like Ernst Jünger and the polarization of German politics by paramilitary organizations like the *Stahlhelm* are examples – lies beyond the scope of this study. These have been popular topics investigated by others at great length. A recent history of the Third Reich by Richard Evans offered a representative interpretation. While conceding that most soldiers went home to a normal life at the end of the war, he wrote: "Yet in the end, ex-soldiers and their resentments did play a crucial part in fostering a climate of violence and discontent after the war was over and the shock of adjusting to peacetime pushed many to the far right."[2] This "climate of violence and discontent" was built on deceptions like the "stab-in-the-back" legend and the perception of society's ingratitude toward the *Frontkämpfer*.[3] It was a climate in which the nascent elements of National Socialism would prosper.

Summing up

By concentrating on the behavior of German front-line soldiers during the period of the last months of 1918, this study has attempted to shed some light on a relatively neglected aspect of the famously "incomplete" German revolution. Illustrated histories of the November Revolution have typically featured pictures of triumphant-looking soldiers and sailors marching with red flags or driving through the Brandenburg Gate on commandeered vehicles. Such pictures seem to offer dramatic evidence that the revolution carried the day on the bayonets of the German military. This study argues there was another side to the story. The narrative offered here is based on the premise that the million-and-a-half front-line soldiers in the trenches in late 1918 had an important but somewhat overlooked role in determining the course of the revolution's earliest stages, in preserving the political influence of the officer corps, and creating at least one long-term myth, that of the "stab in the back." By demobilizing themselves, they had deprived the Ebert government of any support from the old army. Finally, through their role in the *Freikorps*, they had contributed to the antagonisms that seriously weakened the Weimar Republic.

The sequence of events deserves review. The final days of the First World War found the German Army on the Western Front pressed to the limits of its endurance. Though the beginning of armistice negotiations had shaken soldier morale, the *Frontheer* did not collapse before revolution on the home front had swept away the old monarchy. At the same time, the outbreak of the revolution did not assure the downfall of the old regime until the Kaiser discovered that the Field Army was not going to rally to his defense. Though the events of November 9 left the old elites dismayed and depressed, they discovered that at least one part

---

[2] Richard Evans, *The Coming of the Third Reich* (New York: Penguin Press, 2004), 69.
[3] SA leader Ernst Röhm wrote: "The goal of my politics is to obtain by fighting for the German frontline soldier the share in leadership due him and also to ensure that the ideal and spirit of the front line prevails in politics." *Geschichte eines Hochverräters*, quoted in Eleanor Hancock, "Ernst Rohm and the Experience of World War I." *Journal of Military History*, 60, 1 (Jan. 1996), 39–60.

of the army remained under the control of its officers: the troops on the Western Front. The front-line troops initially rejected revolutionary behavior in favor of obedience and cooperation with the chain of command. During the weeks that followed, these men provided Groener with his essential bargaining chip in negotiating the survival of the old officer corps. As the Field Army marched back to Germany in good order, it served to rebuild the confidence of the officer corps and terrify those who believed that counter-revolution was possible. However, when the OHL and war ministry attempted to build a new army on the framework of these hard-marching formations, the troops again confounded expectations by turning the demobilization from an orderly process into something that resembled a stampede toward home and family. For a time, *Drang nach Hause*, not discipline, became the order of the day.

The Supreme Headquarters sifted through the wreckage of the Field Army to find nine divisions that could enter the German capital, secure the Ebert government, and cow the "Bolshevists," while strengthening their own position in the post-revolutionary order. The assembly of Lequis' command and their impressive parades through the center of Berlin suggested that these might be achievable goals. However, as cabinet, OHL, and war ministry squabbled, the front-line units of Lequis' command melted away. By Christmastime, only a handful of combat troops were available to answer the government's plea for help. Manipulated by their officers and hectored by a massive crowd, these troops failed to defeat the government's enemies. As the remnant of the old army retreated from the city on Christmas Eve, 1918, Ebert's government and the OHL had no choice but to seek a new basis of military power. Their options seemed limited to only one: the *Freikorps*.

Throughout November and December 1918, the *Frontschweine* shaped the decisions of Germany's political and military leaders in significant ways. So, for example, after the army had crossed the Rhine, had the returning troops submitted themselves to the demobilization plan; had they reported for duty to guard Germany's frontiers; or volunteered in large numbers to stay with units detailed for internal security, the Ebert government would have had different options.

By this point, the front-line troops had already betrayed the expectations of one political authority, the Kaiser. Had the troops selected by the OHL during November 7–9 – units like the 2nd Guards Division, or the Naumburger *Jägers* – followed their orders, they might have given Wilhelm a thin reed to grasp and, thus, temporarily prevented his early abdication. With this, the unlikely alternative outcome might have been the early outbreak of civil war. The front-line troops' choice not to fight their countrymen made the sweeping initial success of the revolution possible.

After the abdication, one of the most important roles played by the *Frontheer* in the short term was to justify the continued authority of the officer corps. The revolution had seen German militarism at its most demoralized and inept in the hapless response of the Home Army to the November uprising. However, the subsequent weeks showed that the agents of German militarism still possessed strong survival instincts. The technical requirements involved in holding the Field Army together, bringing it home, and demobilizing it allowed the officer corps to demand a continued role in postwar Germany.[4] The officers fulfilled the first parts of the assignment by bringing the army back over the Rhine intact. By the time they had lost most of their control of demobilization, the Ebert government needed their services in the impending test of strength with the Spartacists.

Perhaps equally important was the role of front-line soldiers in establishing a minimum level of plausibility for the "stab-in-the-back" story. Had the *Westheer* collapsed before the revolution overcame the homeland; had the front-line troops overthrown their officers in the immediate aftermath of the revolution; had the units of the old army not appeared in well-ordered formations at the Rhine bridges and on the boulevards of German cities, the legend was likely to have been stillborn. There would have been no greeting from Chancellor Ebert at the Brandenburg Gate telling the front-line troops that they had returned from the field undefeated. The tragic consequence of the *Frontheer*'s response to the revolution was that it allowed the lie to take root in the German popular imagination.

Of the consequences described above, only the refusal of front-line troops to rally to the Kaiser was an outcome with positive results. Their refusal averted civil war or, at least, delayed its onset. The remaining outcomes, the failure of demobilization to produce an alternative to the *Freikorps*, the continued role of the anti-republican officer corps at the head of the army, and the impetus given the *Dolchstosslegende*, would all contribute to the sickliness of Germany's interwar political culture. Add to that, in the immediate aftermath of the war, the *Freikorps*' character as vicious, illegitimate offspring of the *Frontheer* and the consequences of what front-line soldiers chose to do between November

---

[4] Ironically, though one of the Allied war aims had been the suppression of German militarism, the harsh nature of the Entente's initial armistice conditions served to push Ebert into Groener's arms.

and December 1918 must be judged as critically important as well as tragically unfortunate.

Through the period considered, the behavior of front-line soldiers frequently perplexed both the officers who led them and the government that sought their support, as well as the revolutionaries who saw them as enemies. Along with describing the role of front-line soldiers in the revolution, this study has attempted to look past this perplexity to analyze why the soldiers made the choices they did. The interdependent reasons for the behavior of the *Frontschweine* have been placed under the categories of *exhaustion* (both physical and moral); *isolation* (from revolutionary influences); *alienation* (from those who had not shared the "front" experience); *selection* (by the chain of command and through their own choices); *cohesion* (with comrades, leaders, and unit); and *management* (of perceptions by the military hierarchy). The role of each factor was clearly dynamic during the period considered. Thus, if one wished to choose the reason why soldiers were initially indifferent to news of the revolution in the homeland, *exhaustion* and *isolation* seem the key factors. By the time the troops reached their demobilization stations, the collapse of *cohesion* and the failure of the army's attempts at *management* of the rank and file's expectations appear as the most conspicuous factors in explaining soldier behavior. Finally, by the time an unhappy veteran found himself recruited by the *Freikorps, alienation* from postwar society along with the prospect of regaining the social benefits (camaraderie, a strong leader figure, etc.) provided by *cohesion* were, arguably, the two central motivating factors.

The story of the men who returned from the Western Front suggests, perhaps, other conclusions. Along with illuminating the early history of the Weimar Republic, the role of the front-line troops in the revolution of 1918 may offer insights that go beyond the German experience. In particular, this story may allow military historians and political scientists to generalize some tentative lessons about the way military function and organization determines soldier behavior during a time of revolution. In a curious way, the experience of the German Imperial Army paralleled two other imperial armies of the First World War, the forces of the Russian tsar and the Habsburg emperor. Most accounts of the Russian Army's collapse in 1917 describe a process that worked from rear to front;[5] equally, in late 1918, the Austro-Hungarian

---

[5] For a brief discussion of the early effect of the Russian Revolution at the "front," see Allan Wildman, "The February Revolution in the Russian Army." *Soviet Studies*, 22, 1 (1970), 3–23. A more detailed account is found in his two-volume work, *The End of the Russian Imperial Army: The Old Army and the Soldiers' Revolt (March–April 1917)* (Princeton University Press, 1980).

units on the Italian front continued to hold their positions well after the empire had fragmented in national sub-elements.[6] The collapse of the Imperial German Navy offers another parallel. German naval officers testified that, for the most part, the crews of torpedo boats, destroyers, and U-boats, the vessels seeing regular combat service, did not readily join the mutiny that swept through the crews of capital ships that had remained in dock for months.[7] One imagines, for example, that the close quarters and dangerous missions of a U-boat resulted in a *cohesion* (and *insulation*) that was resistant to mutiny, while the bored battleship crews had time for obsessive resentment of the cigars and schnapps available in the officers' mess. In every one of these cases, proximity to combat seemed to condition the political behavior of First World War soldiers. Paradoxically, those with the most to gain from revolution were the least likely to foment or join it.

One might also draw conclusions about what is currently described as "conflict termination." This study had argued that the *Westheer's* dogged resistance in the last days of the war and its orderly retreat back to Germany gave credence to the "stab-in-the-back" legend. For a nation (and an officer corps) in denial about its military defeat, the parades of December seemed to justify a suspension of disbelief. What if the Allies had been more determined to stamp their victory on German consciousness? What if the Coldstream Guards had marched through the Brandenburg Gate instead of the Prussian Guards, or *poilus* and doughboys had swaggered down the boulevards of Munich instead of the *Leib* Regiment? What if the Allies had required the German Army to surrender *all* of its arms before marching home? What if the Entente had established an occupation headquarters in Berlin with oversight authority over national affairs (instead of the handful of observers who dodged machine-gun fire during Spartacus Week)? If, as Clausewitz defined it, war is an act of violence for the purpose of making the enemy submit to our will, then a successful outcome must include the clear message that submission is justified. In this respect, the Allied victory was incomplete. The war had ended with the German Army intact and, with only a small exception near the Swiss border, holding a front line

[6] See vol. VII of Rudolf Kiszling *et al.*, Bundesministerium für Landesverteidigung, *Österreich-Ungarns letzter Krieg* (Vienna: Militärwissenschaftlichen Mitteilungen, 1930–8), 571–758.

[7] BA-MA, N 46/130/2, memorandum of Admiral Adolf von Trotha, "Gedanken uber den Zusammenbruch." In an interesting parallel to the role of *selection* in the front-line force, the admiral suggested that leadership in the capital ships had been undermined by the navy's policy of sending the best officers to the U-boat force. See also Dan van der Vat, *The Grand Scuttle: The Sinking of the German Fleet at Scapa Flow in 1919* (Annapolis, MD: Naval Institute Press, 1986), 108.

well beyond the Reich's frontiers. In the immediate postwar period, only a fraction of Germans had to endure Allied occupation. The Guards Corps' impressive parades through Berlin in mid-December meant that those who were unwilling to accept Germany's defeat seemed to have their skeptical outlook confirmed.[8]

Front-line veterans and their experience as a group left a tragic inheritance for the Weimar Republic. There were tragic outcomes for individuals, too. To an extent, the fate of the political leaders of the first post-revolutionary government reflected the grim fortunes of the Weimar Republic. Of the five members of Ebert's cabinet, one, Hugo Haase, died of an assassin's bullet in 1919; three, Scheidemann, Landsberg, and Dittmann, were forced into exile when Hitler came to power. (Scheidemann died in Denmark in 1933, Landsberg died in the Netherlands in 1957, Dittmann returned from exile to die in Bonn in 1951.) Barth endured a period of captivity under the Nazis and died of natural causes in Berlin in 1941.[9] Otto Wels, the Berlin city commandant whose imprisonment had led to the Christmas Eve battle, rose to the head of the Majority Socialist Party and, in 1933, went before jeering Brownshirts in the Reichstag as the lone member to denounce the Enabling Act giving dictatorial powers to Hitler. After fleeing Germany, he died in Paris in 1939.[10]

For the military men, there were mixed outcomes. Ironically, political involvement proved lethal for the two majors who played key roles in the "Berlin Operation," Kurt von Schleicher and Bodo von Harbou. Schleicher's ambitions won him both the chancellor's job and the murderous enmity of Adolf Hitler. In 1934, Groener's former political officer was shot to death, along with his wife, in the "Night of the Long Knives." During the Second World War, Harbou served as the chief of staff of the military occupation headquarters for Belgium and Northern France. Vocal in his anti-Nazi views and eventually

---

[8] Those who argue that the US invaded Iraq in 2003 with insufficient force point to the fact that many Iraqi towns did not see US troops until weeks after Baghdad had fallen. Much of the Iraqi population did not have an immediate confrontation with defeat. Another insight may be offered by comparing the US decision to disband the Iraqi Army in 2003 with the German officers corps' instincts for self-preservation (and the Allies' failure to achieve their goal of quashing German militarism) in the aftermath of the First World War.

[9] Biographical data on the cabinet members from Erich Matthias' introductory chapter in *Quellen*, first series, vol. VI, part i, *Die Regierung der Volksbeauftragten, 1918/1919*, xv–lxxxviii.

[10] William Maehl, *The German Socialist Party: Champion of the First Republic, 1918–1933* (Philadelphia: American Philosophical Society, 1986), 206–7. Other biographical data on Wels from Robert Westrich, *Who's Who in Nazi Germany* (Routledge, 2001), 274.

implicated in the July 20 plot against Hitler, he committed suicide in prison.[11]

The men who built the first *Freikorps* out of the wreckage of the old army seemed to fare better. Captain Waldemar Pabst, the man who planned the Christmas Eve attack, would build the GKSD up to a corps-size unit of 40,000 men. In 1920, he was one of the ringleaders of the Kapp *putsch* and, when the *putsch* collapsed, he fled to Austria. There he gained prominence in right-wing politics as the founder of the *Heimwehr*. Returning to Germany, he worked as an arms dealer during the Second World War and died – unrepentant – in his homeland in 1970.[12] He was never prosecuted for his role in the murder of Liebknecht and Luxemburg.[13] Colonel Wilhelm Reinhard, who crushed the Spartacus uprising of January 1919, died in 1955 after serving as an SS *Grüppenführer* in the Third Reich and president of a popular veterans' organization, the *Kyffhäuser Bund*.[14]

Beyond these outcomes, the dilemmas and contradictions of Weimar Germany seem even more tragically epitomized by the fate of the two pragmatists united by the secret pact of November 10, 1918, Wilhelm Groener and Friedrich Ebert. Through the last weeks of 1918, the two men had worked together in an attempt to manipulate the front-line troops to their own ends, Ebert to sustain the provisional government and Groener to preserve the officer corps. Their efforts would result in accusations of treason against both. Conservatives like Schulenberg and Bauer labeled Groener a traitor to the monarchy for his support of the republic in its time of crisis, while Ebert was accused of betraying the revolution by the Left and of betraying the Kaiser by the Right. When the outcome of the "stab-in-the-back" trial of 1925 suggested that Ebert was guilty of treason for his role in the munitions strike of 1918, the verdict devastated him.[15] He died that same year, and many have argued that his efforts to defend himself caused Ebert to ignore

---

[11] Peter Hoffmann, *The History of the German Resistance, 1933–1945*, trans. Richard Barry (Cambridge, MA: MIT Press, 1977), 517. His rival from the post-revolutionary period, the *Kriegsminister* Lieutenant General Heinrich Scheuch, retired in 1919, survived the war and died in 1946. Böhm, *Adjutant*, 23, fn.2. Harbou's superior during the Berlin Operation, General Lequis, served in the *Reichswehr* until 1920 and died in 1949. Böhm, *Adjutant*, 96, fn. 424.

[12] See Pabst's interview in *Der Spiegel*, "Ich Liess Rosa Luxemburg Richten." Other biographical data from Böhm, *Adjutant*, 124, fn. 8.

[13] As recently as 2007, neo-Nazis petitioned the government to have an area in Berlin renamed Waldemar-Pabst-Platz.

[14] Gerhard Engel et al., *Groß-Berliner Arbeiter- und Soldatenräte in der Revolution 1918–1919* (Berlin: Akademie Verlag, 1997), 233, fn. 57.

[15] Kolb, *Weimar Republic*, 73. Ebert's chief objective during the strike had been to end it as soon as possible.

the peritonitis that eventually killed him. As one of the republic's last ministers of defense, Groener did what he could to limit Nazi influence within the *Reichswehr* and, in a brief term as minister of the interior, sought to ban Hitler's SA, the "Brownshirts." It was for naught. He was forced to resign in 1932, betrayed largely though the efforts of his former political officer and protégé, Kurt von Schleicher, and abandoned by the old field marshal, von Hindenburg.[16] Groener died in May 1939, while the most famous *Frontschwein*, Adolf Hitler, prepared to take Germany into a second, more terrible world war.[17]

Men set apart

The experience of the Western Front had affected millions of men (including Hitler) in a powerful way. From that experience, veterans carried away reservoirs of both massive bitterness and powerful camaraderie. Von Salomon saw an extreme version of that bitterness and camaraderie in the veterans who joined the *Freikorps*: "The front was their home, was the Fatherland, and was the nation. And no one spoke of it. No one believed in words, they believed in each other. The war compelled them, the war ruled them, the war would not let them go, they would never go home, they would never belong completely to us."[18]

The same unique camaraderie was captured in a scene from *The Road Back*, Erich Maria Remarque's sequel to *All Quiet on the Western Front*. A few days after the war's end, a platoon of front-line infantry arrives by train at their hometown. Shortly after they disembark, their wounded platoon leader is set upon by a crowd of revolutionary soldiers intent on removing the lieutenant's shoulder straps and other badges of rank. Suddenly aroused, the platoon deploys in combat formation with rifles and grenades at the ready, prepared to defend their lieutenant. The front-line soldiers have no political agenda, nor any love for officers in general, but they are ready to fight for someone who shared their experience in the trenches.

[16] *Ibid.*, 117–18.
[17] In his last testament, Groener sent greetings to Wilhelm II. By *Wehrmacht* order, active officers were forbidden to attend the general's funeral. Groener-Geyer, *General Groener*, 344–5. On September 1, 1939, Hitler announced to the Reichstag, "I have once more put on that [soldier's] coat that was most sacred and dear to me. I will not take it off until victory is secured, or I will not survive the outcome." The Führer went on to assure the German people that "November 1918 will never be repeated in the history of Germany." William Shirer, *The Rise and Fall of the Third Reich: A History of Nazi Germany* (New York: Simon & Schuster, 1960), 599.
[18] Von Salomon quoted in Koch, *Der deutsche Bürgerkrieg*, 55.

A one-armed veteran steps from among the mob and mediates. His words defuse the situation and the crowd begins to disperse. The one-armed man comes forward. "I was there too, Mate," he blurts out. "I know what is what, as well as you do. Here ...," he shows his stump excitedly. "Twentieth Infantry Division, Verdun." The platoon accepts his intervention and moves on. As they depart, the one-armed man salutes the lieutenant. Remarque observes, "He is saluting not a uniform, not the war; he is saluting his mates from the Front."[19] Together, they were men set apart.

[19] Erich Maria Remarque, *The Road Back* (sequel to *All Quiet on the Western Front*) (New York: Ballantine, 1998 [originally published, 1930], 65–7.

Bibliography

ARCHIVAL SOURCES AND RESEARCH COLLECTIONS

Bundesarchiv-Bildarchiv, Koblenz, Germany (online)
Bundesarchiv-Militärchiv, Freiburg, Germany
Bundesarchiv-Reich, Berlin-Lichterfelde, Germany
Combined Arms Research Library, Ft. Leavenworth, KS
Militärgeschichtliches Forschungsamt, Potsdam, Germany
Military History Institute, Carlisle Barracks, Pennsylvania
United States National Archives, College Park, MD

MEMOIRS, DIARIES, AND OTHER FIRST-PERSON ACCOUNTS

A German War Deserter's Experiences [no author listed]. Trans. J. Koettgen. New York: B.W. Huebsch, 1917.

Anker, Kurt. *Unsere Stunde kommt! Erinnerungen und Betrachtungen über das nachrevolutionäre Deutschland.* Leipzig: Leipziger Graphische Werke, 1923.

Barth, Emil. *Aus der Werkstatt der deutsche Revolution.* Berlin: Hoffmanns Verlag, 1919.

Bauer, Max. *Der grosse Krieg in Feld und Heimat: Erinnerungen und Betrachtungen von Oberst Max Bauer.* Tübingen: Osiander'sche Buchhandlung, 1921.

Beckmann, Ewald. *Der Dolchstossprozess in Munchen vom 19. Oktober bis 20. November 1925.* Munich: Süddeutsche Monatshefte, 1925.

Bergh, Ernst van den. *Aus den Geburtsstunden der Weimarer Republik: Das Tagebuch des Obersten Ernst van den Bergh.* Ed. Wolfram Wette. Düsseldorf: Droste Verlag, 1991.

Binding, Rudolf. *A Fatalist at War.* Trans. Ian Morrow. Boston, New York: Houghton Mifflin, 1929.

Blücher von Walhlstatt, Evelyn Mary. *An English Wife in Berlin: A Private Memoir of Events, Politics, and Daily Life in Germany Throughout the War and the Social Revolution of 1918.* New York: E.P. Dutton and Co., 1920.

Böhm, Gustav. *Adjutant in Preussichen Kriegsministerium, Juni 1918 bis Oktober 1919.* Ed. Heinz Hurten and Georg Meyer. Stuttgart: Deutsche Verlags-Anstalt, 1977.

Bucher, Georg. *In the Line, 1914–1918.* Trans. Norman Gullick. London: Jonathan Cape, 1932.

Dittmann, Wilhelm. *Erinnerungen*. Ed. Jurgen Rojahn. Frankfurt: Campus Verlag, 1995.

Ebbinghaus, Christof von. *Die Memoiren des Generals von Ebbinghaus*. Supplement: Gustav Eckerle and Dr. von Schneider. "Der Sturm auf das Wilhelmpalais." Stuttgart: Bergers Literärisches Büro, 1928.

Fischer, Anton. *Die Revolutionskommandantur Berlin*. Berlin: the author, 1922.

Groener, Wilhelm. *Lebenserinnerungen: Jugend, Generlstab, Weltkrieg*. Ed. Hilles von Gaetringen. Göttingen: Vandenhoeck und Ruprecht, 1957.

Hesse, Kurt. *Das Marne Drama des 15. Juli 1918: Wahrheiten aus der Front*. Berlin: Mittler und Sohn, 1920.

Hitler, Adolf. *Mein Kampf*. Ed. John Chamberlain, *et al*. New York: Reynal and Hitchcock, 1939 (originally published 1925).

Hohenborn, Adolf Wild von. *Briefe und Tagebuchaufzeichnungen des preussischen Generals als Kriegsminister und Truppenführer im Ersten Weltkrieg*. Ed. Helmut Reichold. Boppard am Rhein: Harald Boldt Verlag, 1986.

Hohenzollern, Wilhelm. *Erinnerungen des Kronprinzen Wilhelm*. Ed. Karl Rosner. Stuttgart, Berlin: Cotta'sche Buchhandlung, 1922.

Jünger, Ernst. *The Storm of Steel: From the Diary of a German Stormtroop Officer on the Western Front*. Trans. Basil Creighton. New York: Howard Fertig, 1996 (first published 1920).

Kaisen, Wilhelm. *Meine Arbeit, mein Leben*. Munich: List Verlag, 1967.

Kessel, Hans von. *Handgranaten und Rote Fahnen: Ein Tatsachenbericht aus das Kampf gegen das rote Berlin 1918–1920*. Berlin: Verlag für Kulturpolitik, 1933.

Kessler, Harry. *Berlin in Lights: The Diaries of Count Harry Kessler (1918–1937)*. Trans. and ed. Charles Kessler. New York: Grove Press, 2002.

Lambach, Walther. *Ursachen des Zusammenbruchs*. Hamburg: Deutschnationale Verlagsanstalt, 1920.

Leeb, Wilhelm Ritter von. *Tagebuchaufzeichnungen und Lagebeurteilungen aus zwei Weltkriegen*. Ed. Georg Meyer. Stuttgart: Deutsche Verlags-Anstalt, 1976.

Lewinsohn, Ludwig. *Die Revolution an der Westfront*. Charlottenburg: Mundus Verlagsanstalt, 1919.

Ludendorff, Erich. *Meine Kriegserrinerungen, 1914–1918*. Berlin: Mittler und Sohn, 1919.

Lüttwitz, Walter von. *Im Kampf gegen die November-Revolution*. Berlin: Verlag Otto Schlegel, 1934.

Maercker, Georg von. *Vom Kaiserheer zur Reichswehr: Ein Beitrag zur Geschichte der deutschen Revolution*. Leipzig: Verlag v. K.F. Koehler, 1921.

Müller, Georg [Admiral]. *Regierte der Kaiser? Kriegstagebücher, Aufzeichnungen und Briefe des Chefs des Marine-Kabinetts Admiral Georg Alexander von Müller, 1914–1918*. Göttingen: Musterschmidt-Verlag, 1959.

Nagel, Fritz. *Fritz: The World War I Memoirs of a German Lieutenant*. Ed. Richard Baumgartner. Huntington, WV: Der Angriff Publications, 1981.

Niemann, Alfred. *Revolution von Oben – Umsturz von Unten. Entwicklung und Verlauf der Staatsumwälzung in Deutschland, 1914–1918*. Berlin: Verlag für Kulturpolitik, 1927.

Kaiser und Revolution: Die Entscheidenden Ereignisse in Großen Hauptquartier im Herbst 1918. Berlin: Verlag für Kulturpolitik, 1928.

Noske, Gustav. *Von Kiel bis Kapp.* Berlin: Verlag für Politik und Wirtschaft, 1920.

Nowak, Karl F. *Die Aufzeichnungen des Generalmajors Max Hoffmann* (2 vols.). Berlin: Verlag für Kulturpolitik, 1929.

Oehme, Walter. *Damals in der Reichskanzlei: Erinnerungen aus den Jahren 1918/1919.* Berlin: Kongress-Verlag, 1958.

Oertzen, Friedrich. *Kamerad, reich mir die Hände: Freikorps und Grenzschutz, Baltikum und Heimat.* Berlin: Verlag Ullstein, 1933.

Payer, Friedrich. *Von Bethmann-Hollweg bis Ebert: Erinnerungen und Bilder.* Frankfurt: Frankfurts Societäts, 1923.

Reinhard, Wilhelm. *1918–1919: Die Wehen der Republik.* Berlin: Brunnen-Verlag, 1933.

Röhm, Ernst. *Die Geschicht eines Hochverräters.* Munich: Verlag Frz. Eher and Son, 1934.

Rupprecht, Crown Prince of Bavaria. *In Treue Fest. Mein Kriegstagebuch.* Ed. Eugen von Frauenholz. Berlin: Mittler und Sohn, 1929.

Salomon, Ernst von. *Die Geächteten* [autobiographical novel]. Hamburg: Rowohlt Verlag, 1962.

Scheidemann, Philip. *Memoirs of a Social Democrat.* Trans. J.E. Mitchell. Vol. II. London: Hodder and Stoughton, 1929.

Siegert, Gerhard. *Bis zum bitteren Ende: Vier Jahre Stellungskrieg.* Leipzig: Koehler Verlag, 1930.

Sulzbach, Herbert. *With the German Guns: Four Years on the Western Front, 1914–1918.* Trans. Richard Thonger. Hamden, CT: Archon Books, 1935; reprinted 1998.

Thaer, Albrecht von. *Generalstabdienst an der Front und der O.H.L.* Göttingen: Vandenhoeck und Ruprecht, 1958.

Westman, Stephen. *Surgeon with the Kaiser's Army.* London: William Kimber, 1968.

Wilhelm II. *The Kaiser's Memoirs.* Trans. Thomas R. Ybarra. New York: Harper and Brothers, 1922.

Velburg, Gerhard. *Rumänische Etappe: Der Weltkrieg, wie ich ihn sah.* Berlin: Wilhelm Köhler Verlag, 1930.

PUBLISHED DOCUMENT COLLECTIONS

Afflerbach, Holger. *Kaiser Wilhelm II. als Oberster Kriegsherr im Ersten Weltkrieg: Quellen aus der militärischen Umgebung des Kaisers, 1914–1918.* Munich: Oldenbourg Verlag, 2005.

Ahnert, Kurt. *Die Entwicklung der deutschen Revolution und das Kriegsende in der Zeit vom 1. Oktober bis 30. November 1918.* Nuremberg: Bergverlag Nürnberg, 1918.

Auermann, Detlev, ed. *Allgemeiner Kongress der Arbeiter-und-Soldatenräte Deutschlands, von 16. bis 21. Dezember 1918. Stenographische Berichte.* Glashütten in Taunus, 1919.

Auswärtigen Amt and Reichsministerium des Innern. *Amtliche Urkunden zur Vorgeschichte des Waffenstillstandes 1918: Auf Grund der Akten der Reichskanzlei des Auswärtigen Amtes und des Reichsarchivs.* In the series *Die Ursachen des Deutschen Zusammenbruchs im Jahre 1918.* Berlin: Deutsche Verlagsgesellschaft für Politik und Geschichte, 1927.

Berlin, Jörg. *Die deutschen Revolution, 1918/1919: Quellen und Dokumente.* Cologne: Pahl-Rugenstein Verlag, 1979.

Berthold, Lothar and Helmut Neef. *Militarismus und Opportunismus gegen die Novemberrevolution.* Frankfurt am Main: Verlag Marxistische Blätter, 1978.

Cordes, Gunter, ed. *Krieg Revolution Republik: Die Jahre 1918 bis 1920 in Baden und Württemburg. Eine Dokumentation.* Ulm: Vaas Verlag, 1978.

Craig, Gordon. "Reichswehr and National Socialism: The Policy of Wilhelm Groener, 1928–1932." *Political Science Quarterly,* 63, 2 (June 1948), 194–229.

Deist, Wilhelm, ed. *Militär und Innenpolitik, 1914–1918* (2 vols.). In the series *Quellen zur Geschichte des Parlamentarismus und des politischen Parteien.* Düsseldorf: Droste Verlag, 1970.

Deutschen Waffenstillstandkommision. *Der Waffenstillstand, 1918–1919, I. Der Waffenstillstandsvertrag von Compiegne und seine Verlängerungen nebst den finanzielle Bestimmungen.* Berlin: Deutsche Verlagsgesellschaft für Politik und Geschichte, 1928.

Eine Ehrenrettung des deutschen Volkes: Dolchstoss-Prozess, München, Oktober–November 1925: Zeugen und Sachverständigen-Aussagen. Eine Sammlung von Dokumenten. Munich: Druck und Verlag G. Birk and Co., 1925.

Frankfurter Zeitung. *Der grosse Krieg: Eine Chronik von Tag zu Tag. Urkunden, Depesche und Berichte der Frankfurter Zeitung,* vol. 97 (1918). Frankfurt am Main: Druck und Verlag der Frankfurter Societäts-Druckerei, 1918.

Johann, Ernst, ed. *Innenansicht eines Krieges: Bilder, Briefe, Dokument, 1914–1918.* Frankfurt: Verlag H. Scheffler, 1968.

Kastner, Albrecht. *Revolution und Heer: Dokumente aus dem Militärarchiv der DDR.* Berlin: Militarverlag der DDR, 1987.

Kolb, Eberhard and Reinhard Rurup, eds. *Der Zentralrat der Deutschen Sozialistischen Republik, 19.12.1918–8.4.1919.* Vol I of *Quellen zur Geschichte der Rätebewegung in Deutschland 1918/1919.* Leiden: E.J. Brill, 1968.

Lutz, Ralph, ed. *The Fall of the German Empire, 1914–1918.* Hoover War Library Publications. Stanford University Press, 1932.

Marx, Heinrich, ed. *Handbuch der Revolution in Deutschland 1918–1919,* vol. I, *Vorabend 9–15 November.* Berlin: Alexander Gruebel Nachf. Verlagsbuchhandlung, 1919.

Matthias, Erich and Rudolf Morsey, eds. *Die Regierung des Prinzen Max von Baden.* In the series *Quellen zur Geschichte des Parlamentarismus und der politischen Parteien,* first series, vol. II. Düsseldorf: Droste Verlag, 1962.

Michaelis, Herbert, Ernst Schraepler and Gunter Scheel. *Ursachen und Folgen vom deutschen Zusammenbruch 1918 und 1945 bis zur staatlichen Neuordnung Deutschlands in der Gegenwart* (2 vols.). Berlin: Herbert Wendler, 1958.

Miller, Susanne with Heinrich Potthoff, eds. *Die Regierung der Volksbeauftragten 1918/19.* In the series *Quellen zur Geschichte des Parlamentarismus und der politischen Parteien, first series,* vol. VI (ii/2). Düsseldorf: Droste Verlag, 1969.

Ritter, Gerhard and Susanne Miller, eds. *Die deutsche Revolution, 1918–1919.* Frankfurt: Fischer Taschenbücher, 1965.

Schüddekopf, Otto-Ernst. *Das Heer und die Republik: Quellen zur Politik der Reichswehrführung, 1918 bis 1933.* Hanover and Frankfurt: Norddeutsche Verlagsanstalt, 1955.

Troeltsch, Ernst, ed. *Spektator-Briefe: Aufsatze über die deutsche Revolution und die Weltpolitik 1918/1922.* Tübingen: 1924; reprinted Aalen: Scientia Verlag, 1966.

Ulrich, Bernd and Benjamin Ziemann, eds. *Frontalltag im Ersten Weltkrieg: Quellen und Dokumente.* Frankfurt: Fischer Taschenbuch Verlag, 1994.

Untersuchungsauschusses der deutschen Verfassunsgebenden National Versammlung und des Deutschen Reichstages, 1919–1930. Series 4, *Die Ursachen des deutschen Zusammenbruchs im Jahre 1918* (11 vols.). Berlin, Deutsche Verlagsgesellschaft für Politik und Gesellschaft, 1925–9.

Der Vetretertag der Soldatenräte des Feldheeres am 1. Dezember in Bad Ems überreicht vom Soldatenrat bei der Obersten Heeresleitung. Wilhelmshöhe bei Cassel: Soldatenrat, Heeresleitung, 1918.

Why Germany Capitulated on November 11, 1918. A Brief Study Based on Documents in the Possession of the French General Staff. London: Hodder and Stoughton, 1919.

OFFICIAL/UNIT HISTORIES

[British] General Staff. *Handbook of the German Army in War: April, 1918.* Imperial War Museum; reprinted Nashville: Battery Press, 1996.

Brosius, Hans. *Das k. p. (magdeburgisches) Jäger Bataillon Nr. 4.* Berlin: "Der Soldat" Verlagsgessellschaft, 1934.

Bundesministerium für Landesverteidigung. *Österreich-Ungarns letzter Krieg, 1914–1918.* Ed. Rudolf Kiszling et al. Vienna: Militärwissenschaftlichen Mitteilungen, 1930–8.

Castendyk, Hermann. *Das Kgl. Preuss. Infanterie-Regiment "Herzog Ferdinand von Braunschweig" (8. Westfälisches Nr. 57) im Weltkrieg 1914–1918.* Oldenburg: Druck und Verlag von Gerhard Stalling, 1936.

Center of Military History (US). *The United States in the World War, 1917–1919,* vols. X and XI, Washington, DC, 1991.

Demobilmachungs-Vorschrift für das XVII Armeekorps (Zusatzbestimmungen zum Demobilmachungsplan fur das deutsche Heer). 1918 (?).

First Division, AEF (Regular), World War Records. *Summaries of Intelligence, First Division,* vol. IV (December 25, 1917 to November 30, 1918) and vol. V (December 1, 1918 to Conclusion). Washington, DC: First Infantry Division Historical Section, 1930.

[German] General Staff. *Die Rückführung des Westheeres.* Berlin: Mittler and Son, 1919.

Groß Generalstab. *Die Schlachten und Gefechte des Großen Krieges, 1914–1918: Quellenwerk nach den amtliches Bezeichnungen.* Berlin: Verlag von Hermann Sack, 1919.

Heeres-Sanitätsinspektion des Reichswehrministerium. *Sanitätsbericht über das deutsche Heer (Deutsche Feld und Besatzungsheer im Weltkriege, 1914–1918)*, vol. III, *Die Krankenbewegung bei dem Deutschen Feld und Besatzungsheer.* Berlin: Mittler und Sohn, 1934.

Kriegsgeschichtlichen Forschungsanstalt des Heeres. *Der Weltkrieg, 1914 bis 1918*, vol. XIV, 1944. Reprinted Bonn: Bundesarchiv, 1956 [German official history].

Die Wirren in der Reichshaupstadt und im nordlichen Deutschland, 1918–1920. Berlin: E.F. Mittler und Sohn, 1940.

Infanterie-Regiment Bremen im Felde 1914–1918. Bremen: Verlag Franz Leuwer, 1919.

Ponath, Gustav. *Die Geschichte des 5. Westpreussischen Infanterie-Regiments Nr. 148.* Breslau: Buchdrückerei Diesdorf, 1929.

Records of Intelligence Section of the General Staff, AEF. *Histories of Two Hundred and Fifty-One Divisions of the German Army Which Participated in the War (1914–1918).* Washington: GPO, 1920.

Reinhard, Wilhelm. *Das 4. Garde-Regiment zu Fuss: Nach den amtlichen Kriegstagebüchern und personlichen Aufzeichnungen bearbeitet.* Berlin: Gerhard Stalling Verlag, 1924.

Schwerin, Eberhard von. *Konigl. Preuss. Sturmbataillon Nr. 5 (Rohr).* Zeulenroda: Druck und Verlag Bernhard Sporn, 1939.

Second Division Historical Section, Translations. *War Diaries of German Units Opposed to the Second Division (Regular) 1918*, vol. IX, *Meuse–Argonne.* Washington, DC: Army War College, 1935.

Seiz, G., et al. *Geschichte des 6. Badischen Infanterie Regiments Kaiser Friedrich III. Nr. 114 im Weltkrieg 1914 bis 1918.* Zeulenroda: Druck und Verlag Bernhard Sporn, n.d.

Staff of the 26th Reserve Division. *Die 26. Res. Division: 1914–1918.* Stuttgart: Verlag von Staehle und Friedel, 1920.

Stephan, Karl. *Der Todeskampf der Ostmark, 1918/19: Die Geschichte eines Grenzschutzbataillons.* Schneidemühl: Comenius Buchhandlung, 1935.

Taischik, Eugen. *Das Kgl. Preuss. 2. Feldart. Regt. Nr. 23. in Weltkrieg.* Altenburg: Verband ehemaliger Angehöriger des 2. Rheinischen Feldartillerie Regiments Nr. 23, n.d.

War Office [United Kingdom]. *Statistics of the Military Effort of the British Empire during the Great War: 1914–1920.* London: His Majesty's Stationery Office, 1922.

zu Wied, Wilhelm. *Das 3. Garde-Ulanen-Regiment in dem Weltkriege, 1914–1918.* Berlin: Verlag Tradition Wilhelm Kock, 1929.

CONTEMPORARY NEWSPAPERS (NOVEMBER 1918 TO JANUARY 1919)

Berliner Tageszeitung
Berliner Volkszeitung
Neue Preussiche Zeitung (Berlin)

Die Rote Fahne
Vorwärts (Berlin)
Vossische Zeitung (Berlin)

ARTICLES AND ESSAYS

Bessel, Richard. "Die Heimkehr der Soldaten: Das Bild der Frontsoldaten in der Öffentlichkeit der Weimarer Republik," in *Keiner fühlt sich hier mehr als Mensch: Erlebnis und Wirkung des Ersten Weltkriegs*. Ed. Gerhard Hirschfeld, Gerd Krumeich, and Irina Renz. Essen: Schriften der Bibliothek für Zeitgeschichte, 1993.
"The Great War in German Memory: The Soldiers of the First World War, Demobilisation and Weimar Political Culture." *German History*, 6, 1 (1988), 20–34.
"The 'Front Generation' and the Politics of Weimar Germany," in *Generations in Conflict: Youth Revolt and Generation Formation in Germany, 1770–1960*. Ed. Mark Roseman. New York: Cambridge University Press, 1995.
Bessel, Richard and David Englander. "Up from the Trenches: Some Recent Writing on the Soldiers of the Great War." *European Studies Review*, 11 (July 1981), 387–95.
Bruntz, George. "Allied Propaganda and the Collapse of German Morale in 1918." *Public Opinion Quarterly*, 2, 1 (January 1938), 61–76.
Deist, Wilhelm. "The Military Collapse of the German Empire: The Reality Behind the Stab-in-the-Back Myth." Trans. E.J. Feuchtwanger. *War in History*, 3, 2 (April 1996), 186–207.
"Verdeckter Militärstreik im Kriegsjahr 1918," in *Der Krieg des Kleinen Mannes: Eine Militärgeschichte von unten*. Ed. Wolfram Wette. Munich: Piper GmbH, 1992.
Dreetz, Dieter. "Rückführung des Westheeres und Novemberrevolution." *Zeitschrift für Militärgeschichte* (GDR), 7 (1968), 578–89.
"Versuche des deutschen militärischen Führung zur Verhinderung oder sofortigen Niederschlagung der Novemberrevolution 1918." *Zeitschrift für Militärgeschichte* (GDR), 17, 5 (1978), 524–33.
Epkenhans, Michael, ed. "'Wir als deutsches Volk sind doch nicht klein zu kriegen ...' Aus den Tagebüchern des Fregattenkapitäns Bogislav von Selchow 1918/1919." *Militärgeschichtliches Mitteilungen*, 55, 1 (1996), 165–224.
Ernst, Fritz. "Aus dem Nachlass des Generals Walther Reinhardt." *Welt als Geschichte*, 18, 1, 39–65.
Feldman, Gerald. "Economic and Social Problems of the German Demobilization, 1918–19." *Journal of Modern History*, 47, 1 (March 1975), 1–47.
Foerster, Jürgen. "Ludendorff and Hitler in Perspective: The Battle for the German Soldier's Mind, 1917–1944." *War in History*, 10, 3 (2003), 321–44.

Ganz, A. Harding. "The German Expedition to Finland, 1918." *Military Affairs*, 44, 2 (April, 1980), 84–91.

Geyer, Michael. "Catastrophic Nationalism." *Relevance*, 10, 2 (Spring 2001), 3–6.

"Insurrectionary Warfare: The German Debate about a Levée en Masse in October 1918." *Journal of Modern History*, 73 (2001), 459–527.

Grau, Roland. "Zur Rolle der Soldatenräte der Fronttruppen in der Novemberrevolution." *Zeitschrift für Militärgeschichte* (GDR), 5 (1968), 550–64.

Griebel, Alexander. "Das Jahr 1918 im Lichte Neuer Publikation." *Vierteljahrshefte für Zeitgeschichte*, 6, 4 (1958), 361–79.

Hancock, Eleanor. "Ernst Röhm and the Experience of World War I." *Journal of Military History*, 60, 1, 39–60.

Hayes, Peter. "'A Question Mark with Epaulettes'? Kurt von Schleicher and Weimar Politics." *Journal of Modern History*, 52, 1 (March 1980), 35–65.

Herwig, Holger. "The First German Congress of Workers' and Soldiers' Councils and the Problem of Military Reforms." *Central European History*, 1, 2 (1963), 150–65.

Hull, Isabel. "Military Culture, Wilhelm II, and the End of the Monarchy in the First World War," in *The Kaiser: New Research on Wilhelm II's Role in Imperial Germany*. Ed. Annika Mombauer and Wilhelm Deist. New York: Cambridge University Press, 2003, 235–58.

Hussey, J. "The Movement of German Divisions to the Western Front, Winter, 1917–1918." *War in History*, 4, 2 (1 April, 1997), 213–20.

Kaehler, Siegfried. "Vier quellenkritische Untersuchungen zum Kriegsende 1918." *Nachrichten der Akademie der Wissenschaften in Göttingen*, Philologisch-Historische Klasse, 8 (1960), 434–53.

Könnemann, Erwin. "Der Truppeneinmarsch am 10. Dezember in Berlin: Neue Dokumente zur Novemberrevolution." *Zeitschrift für Geschichtswissenschaft* (GDR), 16, 12, 1592–609.

Kruse, Wolfgang. "Krieg und Klassenheer: Zur Revolutionierung der deutschen Armee im Ersten Weltkrieg." *Geschichte und Gesellschaft*, 22 (1996), 530–61.

Küster, Heinz. "Zur Militärpolitik des Spartakusbundes in der Novemberrevolution." *Zeitschrift für Militärgeschichte*, 5, 1 (1966), 84–91.

Lerch, Theodor von. "Critical Views Concerning the Final Battles on the German West Front Based on Personal Impressions" (lecture delivered at the Science Club, Vienna, January 23, 1919). Translation published Washington, DC: US Army War College, 1922.

Lipp, Anne. "Heimatwarhnehmung und soldatsches 'Kriegserlebnis'," in *Kriegserfahrungen. Studien zur Sozial- und Mentalitätsgeschichte des Ersten Weltkriegs*. Ed. Gerhard Hirschfeld, Gerd Krumeich, Dieter Langewiesche, and Hans-Peter Ullmann. Essen: Schriften der Bibliothek für Zeitgeschichte, 1997, 225–42.

McRandle, James and James Quirk. "The Blood Test Revisited: A New Look at German Casualty Counts in World War I." *Journal of Military History*, 70, 3 (July 2006), 667–702.

Mulligan, William. "Civil–Military Relations in the Early Weimar Republic." *Historical Journal*, 45 (2002), 819–41.

Peifer, Douglas. "Commemoration of Mutiny, Rebellion, and Resistance in Postwar Germany: Public Memory, History, and the Formation of 'Memory Beacons'." *Journal of Military History*, 65, 4 (2001), 1013–52.

Ruge, Wolfgang. "Neue Dokumente über den Soldatenrat bei der Obersten Heereleitung." *Zeitschrift für Geschichtswissenschaft* (GDR) 16, 11 (1968), 1402–21.

Rurup, Reinhard. "Problems of the German Revolution." *Journal of Contemporary History*, 3, 4 (October 1968), 109–35.

"Demokratische Revolution und 'dritter Weg.' Die deutsche Revolution von 1918/1919 in der neueren wissenschaftlichen Diskussion." *Geschichte und Gesellschaft*, 9 (1983), 278–301.

Schmelz, Hans and Martin Virchow, eds. "Ich Liess Rosa Luxemburg Richten." *Spiegel* Gespräch mit dem Putsch-Hauptmann Waldemar Pabst. *Der Spiegel*, 16 (April 18, 1962), 38–44.

Schmidt-Rechberg, Wigand. "Von der Entlassung Bismarcks bis zum Ende des Ersten Weltkrieges," in *Handbuch für deutschen Militärgeschichte, 1648–1939*. Freiburg: Militärgeschichtlichen Forschungsamt, 1982.

Showalter, Dennis. "Army and Society in Imperial Germany: The Pains of Modernization." *Journal of Contemporary History*, 18, 4 (October 1983), 583–618.

"The German Soldier of World War I: Myths and Realities," in *A Weekend with the Great War: Proceedings of the Fourth Annual Great War Interconference Seminar*. Ed. Steven Weingartner. Shippensburg, PA: White Mane Publishing, 1995, 63–86.

"The Homesick Revolutionaries: Soldiers' Councils and Newspaper Propaganda in German-occupied Eastern Europe, 1918–1919." *Canadian Journal of History*, 9 (April 1976), 69–86.

Strachan, Hew. "The Morale of the German Army 1917–1918," in *Facing Armageddon: The First World War Experienced*. Ed. Hugh Cecil and Peter Liddle. London: Leo Cooper, 1996.

"The Break-up of the German Armies on the Russian Front in November, 1918." *The Army Quarterly* (UK), 34 (April–July 1937), 33–42.

Watson, Alex. "Fear in Combat and Combating Fear: British and German Troops in Endurance Warfare, 1914–1918." Unpublished paper delivered to 2002 conference, "War, Virtual War, and Challenges to Communities," Oxford, UK.

"'For Kaiser and Reich': The Identity and Fate of German Volunteers, 1914–1918." *War in History*, 12, 1 (January 2005), 44–74.

"Junior Officership in the German Army during the Great War, 1914–1918." *War in History*, 14, 4 (November 2007), 429–53.

Weinberg, Gerhard. "Abschriften deutscher Heeresakten aus dem Ersten Weltkrieg im National Archiv in Washington." Special edition of *Jahresbibliographie Bibliothek für Zeitgeschichte*, 35 (1963), 499–509.

Ziemann, Benjamin. "Fahnenflucht im deutschen Heer 1914–1918." *Militärgeschichtlichen Mitteilungen*, 55, 1 (1996), 93–130.

OTHER SECONDARY SOURCES

Achilles, Manuela. "Reforming the Reich: Democratic Symbols and Rituals in Weimar Germany." Unpublished dissertation, University of Michigan, 2003.

Altrichter, Friedrich. *Die seelischen Kräfte des Deutschen Heeres im Frieden und im Weltkriege.* Berlin: Mittler und Sohn, 1933.

Autorenkollektiv. Institut für Marximus-Leninismus. *Illustrierte Geschichte der Novemberrevolution in Deutschland.* Berlin (GDR): Dietz Verlag, 1968.

Baumont, Maurice. *The Fall of the Kaiser.* Trans. E. Ibbetson James. New York: Alfred Knopf, 1931.

Benoist-Mechin, J. *Der Kaiserreich zerbricht.* Oldenburg and Hamburg: Gerhard Stalling, 1965.

Berndorff, Hans. *General zwischen Ost und West: Aus den Geheimnissen der deutschen Republik.* Hamburg: Hoffmann und Campe Verlag, 1955.

Bernstein, Eduard. *Die deutsche Revolution. Geschichte der Enstehung und ersten Arbeitsperiode der deutschen Republik.* Berlin: 1921.

Bessel, Richard. *Germany after the First World War.* Oxford: Clarendon Press, 1993.

Bidwell, Shelford and Dominick Graham. *Firepower: The British Army Weapons and Theories of War, 1904–1945.* Barnsley: Pen and Sword Books, 1982.

Bouton, Miles. *And the Kaiser Abdicates: The German Revolution, November 1918–August 1919.* New Haven: Yale University Press, 1921.

Breit, Gotthard. *Das Staats- und Gesellschaftsbild deutscher Generale beider Weltkriege im Spiegel ihrer Memoiren.* Boppard am Rhein: Boldt Verlag, 1973.

Butenschön, Rainer. *Wozu muss Einer der Bluthund Sein? Der Mehrheitssozialdemokrat Gustav Noske und der deutsche Militarismus des 20. Jahrhunderts.* Heilbronn: Distel Verlag, 1997.

Chickering, Roger. *Imperial Germany and the Great War, 1914–1918.* New York: Cambridge University Press, 1998.

Chorley, Katherine. *Armies and the Art of Revolution.* 1943; reprinted Oxford University Press, 1975.

Cron, Hermann. *Die Organisation des deutschen Heeres im Weltkrieg.* Berlin: Mittler and Son, 1923.

Delbrück, Hans. *Delbrück's Modern Military History.* Trans. Arden Bucholz. Lincoln: University of Nebraska Press, 1997.

Dickhuth-Harrach, Gustav von, ed. *Im Felde unbesiegt.* Munich: Lehmanns Verlag, 1920.

Diehl, James. *Paramilitary Politics in Weimar Germany.* Bloomington: Indiana University Press, 1977.

Dietz, Otto. *Der Todesgang der deutschen Armee: Militärische Ursachen.* Berlin: Karl Curtius, 1919.

Döblin, Alfred. *Sieger und Besiegte: Eine wahre Geschichte.* New York: Aurora Verlag, 1946.

Dreetz, Dieter, Klaus Gessner, and Heinz Sperling. *Bewaffnete Kämpfe in Deutschland, 1918–1923.* Berlin: Militärverlag der Deutschen Demokratischen Republik, 1988.

Duppler, Jörg and Gerhard Gross, eds. *Kriegsende 1918: Ereignis, Wirkung, Nachwirkung.* Munich: Oldenbourg Verlag, 1999.

Elben, Wolfgang. *Das Problem der Kontinuität in der deutschen Revolution: Die Politik der Staatssekretäre und der militarischen Führung vom November 1918 bis Februar 1919.* Düsseldorf: Droste Verlag, 1965.

Ellis, John and Michael Cox. *The World War I Databook: The Essential Facts and Figures for All the Combatants.* London: Aurum Press, 1993.

Engel, Gerhard, *et al. Groß-Berliner Arbeiter- und Soldatenräte in der Revolution 1918–1919.* Berlin: Akademie Verlag, 1997.

Evans, Richard. *The Coming of the Third Reich.* New York: Penguin Press, 2004.

Ferguson, Niall. *The Pity of War.* New York: Basic Books, 1999.

Feuchtwanger, E.J. *From Weimar to Hitler: Germany, 1918–1933.* New York: St. Martin's Press, 1993.

Fischer, Kurt. *Deutsche Truppen und Entente-Intervention in Südrussland, 1918/1919.* Boppard am Rhein: Boldt Verlag, 1973.

Freyer, Paul. *Sturmvogel: Rote Matrosen, 1918/19.* Berlin: Militärverlag der Deutschen Demokratischen Republik, 1975.

Fried, Hans. *The Guilt of the German Army.* New York: MacMillan, 1943.

Goerlitz, Walter. *November 1918: Bericht über die deutsche Revolution.* Hamburg: Gerhard Stalling Verlag, 1968.

Gordon, Harold. *The Reichswehr and the German Republic.* Princeton University Press, 1957.

Grossman, Dave. *On Killing: The Psychological Cost of Learning to Kill in War and Society.* New York: Little, Brown, and Co., 1995.

Gudaitis, Gytis. "Armeen Russlands und Deutschlands im 1. Weltkrieg und in den Revolutionen von 1917 und 1918. Ein Vergleich." Unpublished dissertation, Katholische Universität Eichstatt-Ingolstadt, 2004.

Guth, Ekkehart. *Der Loyalitätskonflikt des deutschen Offizierkorps in der Revolution 1918–20.* Frankfurt am Main: Peter Lang, 1983.

Haffner, Sebastian. *Failure of a Revolution: Germany 1918–19.* Trans. Georg Kapp. New York: Library Press, 1972.

Hallen, Andreas, Diethard Kerbs, and Ingo Materna, eds. *Revolution und Fotografie, Berlin 1918/1919.* Berlin (GDR, FRG): Verlag Dirk Nishen, 1990.

Harris, J.P. *Amiens to the Armistice: The BEF in the Hundred Days' Campaign.* London: Batsford, 1998.

Herbst, W., Ingo Materna, and H. Tropitz, eds. *Die Novemberrevolution in Deutschland.* Berlin: Volk und Wissen Volkseigener Verlag, 1958.

Herzfeld, Hans. *Die deutsche Sozialdemokratie und die Auflösung der nationalen Einheitsfront im Weltkriege.* Leipzig: Verlag von Quelle und Meyer, 1928.

Heuss, Theodor, ed. *Friedrich Ebert, 1871–1971.* Bonn: Inter Nationes, 1971.

Heussler, Helmut. *General Wilhelm Groener and the Imperial German Army.* Madison: University of Wisconsin Press, 1962.

Hirschfeld, Gerhard, Gerd Krumreich, Dieter Langewiesche, and Hans-Peter Ullmann, eds. *Kriegserfahrungen. Studien zur Sozial- und Mentalitätsgeschichte des Ersten Weltkriegs.* Essen: Schriften der Bibliothek für Zeitgeschichte, 1997.

Hirschfeld, Gerhard, Gerd Krumreich, and Irina Renz, eds. *Keiner fühlt sich hier mehr als Mensch ...: Erlebnis und Wirkung des Ersten Weltkriegs.* Essen: Klartext Verlag, 1993.

Hofacker, Eberhard von. *Der Weltkrieg.* Stuttgart: Verlag von W. Kohlhammer, 1928.

Hoffmann, Peter. *The History of the German Resistance, 1933–1945.* Trans. Richard Barry. Cambridge, MA: MIT Press, 1977.

Hull, Isabel. *The Entourage of Kaiser Wilhelm II, 1888–1918.* Cambridge University Press, 1982.

Jahr, Christoph. *Gewöhnliche Soldaten: Desertion und Deserteure im deutschen und britischen Heer, 1914–1918.* Göttingen: Vandenhoeck und Ruprecht, 1998.

Kellett, Anthony. *Combat Motivation: The Behavior of Soldiers in Battle.* Boston: Nyhoff Publishing, 1982.

Kluge, Ulrich. *Soldatenräte und Revolution. Studien zur Militärpolitik in Deutschland, 1918–1919.* Göttingen: Vandenhoeck und Ruprecht, 1975.

Koch, Hansjoachim. *Der deutsche Bürgerkrieg: Eine Geschichte der deutschen und österreichischen Freikorps, 1918–1923.* Frankfurt: Ullstein, 1978.

Kolb, Eberhard, ed. *Friedrich Ebert als Reichpräsident: Amtsfuhrung und Amtsverständnis.* Munich: Oldenbourg Verlag, 1997.

Konrad, Helmut and Karin Schmidlechner. *Revolutionäres Potential in Europa am Ende des Ersten Weltkrieges: Die Rollen von Strukturen, Konjukturen, und Massenbewegungen.* Vienna: Bohlau Verlag, 1991.

Knoch, Peter, ed. *Kriegsalltag: Die Rekonstruktion des Kriegsalltags als Aufgabe der historischen Forschung und der Friedenerziehung.* Stuttgart: J.B. Metzlersche Verlagsbuchhandlung, 1989.

Krieger, Bogdan. *Das Berliner Schloß in den Revolutiontagen 1918: Erinnerungen und Eindrücke.* Leipzig: Konkordia Verlag, 1922.

Küster, Thomas and Franz-Josef Jakobi. *Geschichte der Stadt Münster, vol. II, Das 19. und 20. Jahrhundert (bis 1945).* Münster: Aschendorff, 1993.

Lambach, Walter. *Ursachen des Zusammenbruchs.* Hamburg: Deutschnationale Verlagsanstalt, 1920.

Lang, Curt. *Military Institutions and the Sociology of War.* Beverly Hills and London: Sage, 1979.

Leed, Eric. *No Man's Land: Combat and Identity in World War I.* Cambridge University Press, 1979.

Lipp, Anne. *Meinungslenkung im Krieg: Kriegserfahrungen deutscher Soldaten und ihre Deutung 1914–1918.* Göttingen: Vandenhoeck und Ruprecht, 2003.

Lupfer, Timothy. *The Dynamics of Doctrine. The Changes in German Tactical Doctrine during the First World War.* Ft. Leavenworth, KS: Command and General Staff College, 1981.

Lutz, Ralph. *The German Revolution, 1918–1919.* New York: AMS Press, 1968.

Lynn, John. *The Bayonets of the Republic: Motivation and Tactics in the Army of Revolutionary France, 1791–1794.* Boulder: Westview Press, 1996.

Marx, Heinrich. *Handbuch der Revolution in Deutschland 1918–1919.* Berlin: A. Grübel, 1919.

Maehl, William. *The German Socialist Party: Champion of the First Republic, 1918–1933.* Philadelphia: American Philosophical Society, 1986.

Materna, Ingo. *Der Vollzugsrat der Berliner Arbeiter- und Soldatenräte.* Berlin (GDR): Dietz Verlag, 1978.

Mombauer, Annika and Wilhelm Deist, eds. *The Kaiser: New Research on Wilhelm II's Role in Imperial Germany.* New York: Cambridge University Press, 2003.

Moyer, Laurence. *Victory Must Be Ours: Germany in the Great War, 1914–1918.* New York: Hippocrene, 1995.

Mühlhausen, Walter. *Friedrich Ebert 1871–1925: Reichspräsident der Weimarer Republik.* Bonn: J.H.W. Dietz Verlag, 2006.

Muller, Richard. *Der Bürgerkrieg in Deutschland.* Berlin: Olle und Wolter, 1974.

Petzold, Joachim. *Der 9. November 1918 in Berlin: Berliner Arbeiterveteranen berichten über die Vorbereitung der Novemberrevolution und ihren Ausbruch am 9. November in Berlin.* Berlin: Bezirksleitung der SED Groß-Berlin, Abteilung Agitation und Propaganda, 1958.

Deutschland im Ersten Weltkrieg, vol. III, November 1917 bis November 1918. Berlin: Akademie Verlag, 1970; reprinted 2004.

Pfaelzer, Gerhard. *Von Spa nach Weimar: Die Geschichte der deutschen Zeitenwende.* Leipzig: Grethlein und Co., 1929.

Rakenius, Gerhard. *Wilhelm Groener als Erster Generalquartiermeister. Die Politik der Obersten Heeresleitung 1918/1919.* Boppard am Rhein: Boldt Verlag, 1977.

Remarque, Erich. *All Quiet on the Western Front.* New York: Ballantine, 1987 (originally published, 1928).

The Road Back [sequel to *All Quiet on the Western Front*]. New York: Ballantine, 1998 (originally published, 1930).

Schmidt, Ernst. *Heimatheer und Revolution: Die militärischen Gewalten im Heimatgebiet zwischen Oktoberreform und Novemberrevolution.* Stuttgart: Deutsche Verlags-Anstalt, 1981.

Schmolze, Gerhard, ed. *Revolution und Räterepublik in München 1918/19 in Augenzeugenberichten.* Munich: Deutscher Taschenbuch Verlag, 1978.

Schreiber, Shane. *Shock Army of the British Empire: The Canadian Corps in the Last 100 Days of the Great War.* Westport, CT: Praeger, 1997.

Schulze, Hagen. *Freikorps und Revolution.* Boppard am Rhein: Boldt Verlag, 1969.

Schumann, Dirk. *Politische Gewalt in der Weimarer Republik, 1918–1933: Kampf um die Strasse und Furcht vor der Burgerkrieg.* Essen: Klartext Verlag, 2001.

Schuster, Kurt. *Der Rote Frontkämpferbund, 1924–1929.* Düsseldorf: Droste Verlag. 1975.

Schützinger, Hermann. *Zusammenbruch: Die Tragödie des deutschen Feldheeres.* Leipzig: Ernst Oldenburg Verlag, 1924.

Schwarte, M. *Der Grosse Krieg, 1914–1918.* Leipzig: Buchhandel Barth, 1923.

Schwartzwalder, Herbert. *Geschichte der Freien Hansestadt Bremen,* vol. III, *Bremen in der Weimarer Republik (1918–1933).* Hamburg: Hans Christians Verlag, 1983.

Shirer, William. *The Rise and Fall of the Third Reich: A History of Nazi Germany.* New York: Simon & Schuster, 1960.

Sidman, Charles F. *The German Collapse in 1918.* Lawrence, KS: Coronado Books, 1972.

Smith, Leonard. *Between Mutiny and Obedience: The Case of the French Fifth Infantry Division during World War I.* Princeton University Press, 1994.

Sontheimer, Kurt. *Antidemokratisches Denken in der Weimarer Republic.* Munich: Nymphenburger Verlagshandlung, 1962.

Steely, Melvin. "Kurt von Schleicher and the Political Activities of the Reichswehr, 1919–1926." Unpublished dissertation, Vanderbilt University, 1971.

Thoß, Bruno, and Hans-Erich Volkmann. *Erster Weltkrieg, Zweiter Weltkrieg: Ein Vergleich: Krieg, Kriegserlebnis, Kriegserfahrung in Deutschland.* Paderborn: Ferdinand Schöningh, 2002.

Ulrich, Bernd. *Die Augenzeugen. Deutsche Feldpostbriefe in Kriegs- und Nachkriegszeit 1914–1933.* Essen: Klartext-Verlag, 1997.

Usadel, Georg, ed. *Deutsche Volksnot: der Nachkriegszeit.* Leipzig: B.G. Teubner, 1937.

van der Vat, Dan. *The Grand Scuttle: The Sinking of the German Fleet at Scapa Flow in 1919.* Annapolis, MD: Naval Institute Press, 1986.

van Serooskerken, Hubert. *The Netherlands and World War I: Espionage, Diplomacy, and Survival.* Boston: E.J. Brill, 2001.

Venner, Dominique. *Söldner ohne Sold: Die deutschen Freikorps: 1918–1923.* Berlin: Paul Neff Verlag, 1974.

Volkmann, Erich. *Der Grosse Krieg, 1914–1918.* Berlin: Hobling Verlag, 1922.

Der Marxismus und das deutsche Heer im Weltkriege. Berlin: Verlag von Reimar Hobbing, 1925.

Revolution über Deutschland. Oldenburg: Stalling, 1936.

Vorwerck [Captain]. *Deutschlands Zusammenbruch: Seine Ursachen und Folgen.* Oldenburg: Gerhard Stalling Verlag, 1919.

Waite, Robert. *Vanguard of Nazism: The Free Corps Movement in Postwar Germany 1918–1923.* New York: W.W. Norton and Co., 1952.

Watson, Alexander. *Enduring the Great War: Combat, Morale and Collapse in the German and British Armies, 1914–1918.* Cambridge University Press, 2008.

Watt, Richard. *The Kings Depart. The Tragedy of Germany: Versailles and the German Revolution.* New York: Simon & Schuster, 1969.

Weintraub, Stanley. *A Stillness Heard around the World: The End of the Great War, 1918.* New York: E.P. Dutton, 1985.

Westarp, Graf Kuno von. *Das Ende der Monarchie am 9. November.* Ed. Werner Conze. Berlin, 1952.

Westrich, Robert. *Who's Who in Nazi Germany.* New York: Routledge, 2001.

Wette, Wolfram, ed. *Der Krieg des Kleinen Mannes: Eine Militärgeschichte von unten.* Munich: Piper GmbH, 1992.

Militarismus und Pazifismus: Auseinandersetzung mit den Deutschen Kriegen. Bremen: Donat Verlag, 1991.

Whalen, Robert. *Bitter Wounds: German Victims of the Great War, 1914–1939.* Ithaca: Cornell University Press, 1984.

Witt, Peter-Christian. *Friedrich Ebert: Parteiführer, Reichskanzler, Volks-beauftragter, Reichspräsident.* Bonn: Verlag Neue Gesellschaft, 1987.

Wrisberg, Ernst von. *Der Weg zur Revolution, 1914–1918.* Leipzig: K.F. Koehler, 1921.

Heer und Heimat, 1914–1918. Leipzig: K.F. Koehler, 1921.

Wrobel, Kurt. *Der Sieg der Arbeiter und Matrosen im Dezember 1918: Berliner Arbeiterveteranen berichten über ihren Kampf in der Novemberrevolution.* Berlin: Bezirksleitung der SED Groß-Berlin, Abteilung Agitation/ Propaganda, 1958.

Die Volksmarinedivision. Berlin (GDR): Verlag des Ministeriums für Nationale Verteidigung, 1957.

Ziemann, Benjamin. *War Experiences in Rural Germany, 1914–1923.* Trans. Alex Skinner. Oxford and New York: Berg Publishers, 2007. (Originally published as *Front und Heimat: Ländliche Kriegserfahrungen in südlichen Bayern 1914–1918.* Essen: Klartext Verlag, 1997.)

Zorn, Wolfgang. *Bayerns Geschichte im 20. Jahrhundert: Von der Monarchie zum Bundesland.* Munich: Verlag C.H. Beck, 1986.

Index

Studies in the Social and Cultural History of Modern Warfare

Titles in the series:

Lightning Source UK Ltd.
Milton Keynes UK
UKOW05f0505120913

217071UK00010B/167/P